TEXTILES

fifth edition

TEXTILES

norma hollen *Professor Emeritus*
IOWA STATE UNIVERSITY

jane saddler *Professor Emeritus*
IOWA STATE UNIVERSITY

anna l. langford *Assistant Professor*
IOWA STATE UNIVERSITY

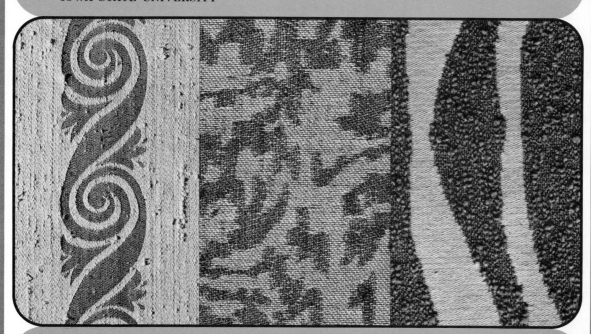

Macmillan Publishing Co., Inc.
NEW YORK

Collier Macmillan Publishing
LONDON

Earlier editions © 1955 and copyright © 1964,
1968, and 1973 by Macmillan Publishing Co., Inc.
Some material on fabrics © 1952 by Norma
Hollen and Jane Saddler in *Modern Textiles*

Macmillan Publishing Co., Inc.
866 Third Avenue, New York, New York 10022
Collier Macmillan Canada, Ltd.

Library of Congress Cataloging in Publication Data

Hollen, Norma R
  Textiles.

  Includes bibliographical references and index.
  1. Textile industry. 2. Textile fibers.
3. Textile fabrics. I. Saddler, Jane, joint author.
II. Langford, Anna L., joint author. III. Title.
TS1446.H6 1979   677   78-6081
ISBN 0-02-356130-0

Printing: 1 2 3 4 5 6 7 8   Year: 9 0 1 2 3 4 5

Preface

This text was written for use in an introductory or single college course in Textiles. It provides a broad view of the production and utilization of fabrics with the emphasis on consumer values.

The organization of the text is from fiber to finished fabric. The text contains four basic units: Fibers, Yarns, Fabric Construction, and Fabric Finishes including Dyeing and Printing. A final chapter, "Selection and Care of Textile Products" summarizes and applies facts presented in the basic units. Each unit is complete enough in itself to permit a different sequence for study if desired.

The basic units are organized initially to give a general background and then to provide specific information. The Fiber unit chapters include traditional background or historical development, production processes, aesthetics, durability, comfort and care characteristics, new developments and major end uses. The sequence of the Yarn unit chapters is designed for easy learning rather than from the historical development of yarns: Filament Yarns, Spun Yarns, Yarn Classification. The Three Basic Weaves are first discussed and this is followed by a discussion of basic Filling and Warp Knits. The other weaves and knits are discussed in chapters based on fabric appearance, for example, Pile Fabrics and Figured Fabrics. Many instructors prefer to teach all of the weaves at one time. A chart of weaves, along with their characteristics and page references is given on page 162 of the text. Fabric Construction Processes from simple to complex are outlined and accompanied by illustrations of typical fabrics in Chapter 21. The other chapters on fabric construction are in a somewhat different sequence than in most textiles texts. The Fabric Finishes Unit contains chapters on Routine Finishes, Finishes for Beauty, and Functional Finishes.

A background in science is not necessary to understand the text. Technical information in the fiber section is included to show the complexity of man-made fiber production and to give an understanding of new developments.

The economic factors in textile production greatly influence the kinds of products that are made available to consumers. Comparative costs of production are made even though they may change from year to year. Consumer values are stressed in the text, but recognition is also given to producer values and to their problems in textile production and marketing.

Terminology is a problem in these days of the Women's Liberation Movement. We have used the words *he* and *his* instead of *he* or *she* or *his* or *hers* in the traditional way; that is, *he* or *his* meaning "any one person." The term *man-made fibers* is still being used in the industry to describe those fibers that are not produced by nature. Strictly speaking, the term is still accurate today since all of the *not natural* fibers that have been produced are the result of research and experimentation done by men. In the future another name for *man-made fibers* may be used.

It is hoped that the text will help students:

- Predict fabric performance based on knowledge of fibers, yarns, fabric constructions, and finishes in conjunction with informative labeling.

- Make wise selections of textile products for specific end uses.

- Care for fabrics and garments satisfactorily.

- Use textile terminology correctly.

v

- Know current laws and labeling requirements that regulate textile distribution.

- Understand how production processes affect the characteristics and costs of fabrics.

- Appreciate past developments in textiles and recognize the need for future developments.

- Develop an interest in textiles that will motivate further study.

- Identify fibers, yarns, and fabrics by analysis and some simple household tests.

We wish to express our appreciation to the instructors at Iowa State University who have evaluated the text and have made valuable suggestions for this revision. Mrs Grace Kunz edited the chapter on knitting; Dr. Charles Kim checked the formulas and shared many of his resource materials; Mrs. Harriet Lewis, throughout the many years of our association, has given us insight into the many perplexing problems of organizing and presenting textile concepts in the various textile courses at Iowa State.

We wish also to thank Professor Renee Thackery of Brigham Young University, and the critic at Syracuse University who have reviewed the fourth edition of *Textiles,* for their corrections and their suggestions for this revision. We wish to thank Dr. Joan Laughlin at the University of Nebraska and Dr. Alvertia Quesenberry at Ball State University for reviewing and making suggestions for improvement of this revision.

We wish to express our appreciation to Scalamandra Silks, Inc., who supplied photographs for chapter headings and to members of The Textile Industry who have provided information and photographs.

Norma Hollen
Jane Saddler
Anna L. Langford

Contents

vii

Introduction

1

Food, shelter, and clothing are the basic needs of everyone. All clothing is made from textiles and shelters are made more comfortable and attractive by the use of textiles.

Everyone is surrounded by textiles from birth to death. We walk on and wear textile products; we sit on fabric-covered chairs and sofas; we sleep on and under fabrics; textiles dry us or keep us dry; they keep us warm and protect us from the sun, fire, and infection. Clothing and household textiles are aesthetically pleasing and vary in color, design, and texture. They are available in a variety of price ranges.

The industrial and medical uses of textiles are many and varied. The automotive industry, one of the largest industries in the United States uses textiles to make tire cords, upholstery, carpeting, head liners, window runners, seat belts, and shoulder harnesses.

Man has traveled to the moon in a 20-layer, $100,000 space suit that has nylon water-cooled underwear. Life is prolonged by replacing worn-out parts of the body with woven or knitted fabric such as polyester arteries and velour heart valves. Disposable garments are worn by doctors and nurses. Bulletproof vests protect hunters and soldiers, and safety belts make automobile travel less dangerous. Three-dimensional, inflatable "buildings" keep out the desert heat and Arctic cold.

This text was written for consumers—not average consumers but educated consumers who, when they purchase textile items, want to know *what* to expect in fabric performance and *why* fabrics perform as they do. Textiles are always changing. They change as fashion changes and to meet the needs of changing life-styles of people. New developments in production processes also cause changes in textiles, as do government standards for safety, environmental quality and energy conservation. These changes are discussed but the bulk of the text is devoted to basic information about apparel and household textiles with an emphasis on fibers, yarns, fabric construction, and finishes. All of these elements are interdependent and contribute to the beauty and texture, the durability and serviceability, and the comfort of fabrics. These elements also determine how fabrics and/or garments should be reconditioned.

Much of the terminology used in the text may be new to the students and many facts must be memorized. But to understand textiles in a broad aspect one must first learn the basics. The historical development, the basic concepts, and the new developments in textiles are discussed. Production processes are explained briefly. A knowledge of production should give the student a better understanding of and appreciation for the textile industry.

In the United States the textile industry is a tremendous complex. It includes the natural and man-made fiber producers; the spinners, weavers, knitters, throwsters, yarn converters, tufters, nonwoven producers and finishers, the machinery makers, and many others. More people are employed in the textile industry than in any other manufacturing industry—about $3\frac{1}{2}$ million. Textile products valued at over $20 billion are produced each year by systems that are increasingly being directed by computers. In Japan, at the push of a button, an operator supposedly can dye wool fabric in over 2,000 color combinations without flaw or error.

The textile industry has developed from an art-and-craft industry perpetuated by guilds in the early centuries, through the Industrial Revolution in the eighteenth and nineteenth centuries, when the emphasis was on mechanization and mass production, to the twentieth century with its emphasis on science and technology.

In this century, man-made fibers were developed and modified textured yarns were created. New fabric construction and increased production of knits occurred, and many finishes and sophisticated textile production and marketing systems were developed. These developments have been beneficial to consumers. The man-made fibers and durable press have made practically all clothing "easy care." The use of nylon in hosiery has virtually eliminated the need for darning. The new developments in textiles have also created some problems for consumers, particularly in the selection of apparel and household textiles. So many things look alike. Knitted fabrics look like woven fabrics and vice versa, vinyl and polyurethane films look like leather, fake furs look like real furs, acrylic and polyester fiber fabrics look like wool. The traditional cotton fabrics are usually polyester or polyester/cotton blends.

To make textile selection a bit easier for consumers, textile producers and their associations have set standards and established quality control programs for many textile products. The federal government has passed laws to protect consumers from unfair trade practices, namely, The Wool Products Labeling Act, The Fur Products Labeling Act, The Textile Fiber Products Identification Act, and The Flammable Fabrics Act. The first three laws are "truth-in-fabrics" legislation and to be beneficial knowledge on the part of the consumer about fibers and furs is required. The Flammable Fabrics Act is protective legislation that prohibits the sale of dangerously flammable apparel and household textiles. The Federal Trade Commission issued the Permanent Care Labeling Rule in 1972. Its purpose is to inform the consumer how to care for fabrics and garments.

Emphasis on energy conservation, environmental quality, noise abatement, health, and safety affect the textile industry as well as other industries. The efforts of the textile industry to meet standards set by the federal government affect the consumer indirectly—mostly by higher prices for merchandise. Energy conservation is being achieved by using solar heat and faster production methods. Nonpollution of streams and air is being achieved by reducing or eliminating the use of water in many finishing processes and by adding equipment to machines to cleanse and purify the water or air before it is emitted. The Occupational Safety and Health Administration has set standards for noise levels and dust and lint levels that make the mills healthier places in which to work. Much progress has been made in providing flame-resistant fibers and finishes in response to the Consumer Products Safety Commission's implementation of the Flammable Fabrics Act. The CPSC also has commissioned the testing of fabrics for toxicity and carcinogenicity, and can request that suspect fabrics be removed from the market.

Textile fabrics can be beautiful, durable, comfortable, and easy to care for. They can satisfy the needs of all people at all times. Knowing how fabrics are created and used will give a better basis for their selection and understanding of their limitations.

Textile Fibers and Their Properties

2

A fiber is a pliable hairlike strand that is very small in diameter in relation to its length. Fibers are the fundamental units used in the making of textile yarns and fabrics. They contribute to the hand, texture, and appearance of fabrics; they influence and contribute to the performance of fabrics; they determine to a large extent the amount and kind of service required of fabrics; and they influence the cost of fabric. Successful textile fibers must be readily available, constant in supply, and inexpensive. They must have sufficient strength, pliability, length, and cohesiveness to be spun into yarns.

Textile fibers have been used to make cloth for the last 4,000 or 5,000 years. Until 1885, when the first man-made fiber was produced commercially, fibers were obtained only from plants and animals. The fibers most commonly used were wool, flax, cotton, and silk.

Silk has always been a highly prized fiber because of the smooth, lustrous, soft fabrics made from it; it has always been expensive and comparatively scarce. It was, therefore, logical for man to try to duplicate silk. Rayon (called artificial silk until 1925) was the first man-made fiber. Rayon was produced in filament until the early 1930s when an enterprising textile worker discovered that the broken and wasted rayon filaments could be used as staple fiber. Acetate and nylon were also introduced as filaments to be used as silklike fibers.

Many man-made fibers were produced in the first half of the twentieth century and from that time onward tremendous advances have been made in the man-made fiber industry, primarily modifications of the parent fibers to provide the best combination of properties for specific end uses.

Textile processes—spinning, weaving, dyeing, and finishing of fabrics—were developed for the natural fibers. Man-made fibers were, therefore, made in the image of the natural fibers.

Classification

Of the many natural fibers, those that are most widely used are wool, cotton, flax, and silk. There are 19 families of man-made fibers—and many type modifications, variants, or second- and third-generation fibers.

Fibers are divided into *generic* families on the basis of their chemical composition. All fibers are listed in the following chart by generic name, and the man-made fibers are accompanied by the date of their original production in the United States.

Fiber Properties

Note to student: This section on fiber properties relates to all fibers. Scan the material presented here and use it as a constant reference source as you study each fiber. The tables on pages 11 to 14 make it easy to see how each fiber compares with the others.

Fiber properties contribute to the properties of a fabric. For example, strong fibers make durable fabrics that can be light in weight; absorbent fibers are good for skin-contact apparel and for towels and diapers; fibers that are self-extin-

Textile Fibers; Generic Names

Natural Fibers	Man-Made Fibers	
Asbestos	Acetate (1925) and Triacetate (1955)	
Cotton	Acrylic (1950)	Nylon (1939)
Flax	Anidex* (1969)	Nytril (1950)
Jute	Aramid (1963)	Olefin (1958)
Mohair	Azlon*	Polyester (1951)
Silk	Glass (1935)	Rayon (1911)
Wool	Lastrile*	Saran (1939)
	Metallic (1948)	Spandex (1960)
	Modacrylic (1949)	Vinal*
	Novoloid (1969)	Vinyon* (1940)

* Not produced in the U.S.

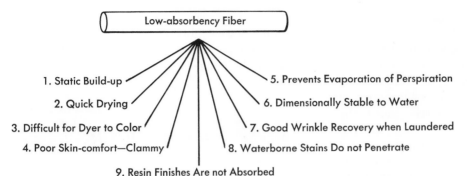

Low-absorbency Fiber

1. Static Build-up
2. Quick Drying
3. Difficult for Dyer to Color
4. Poor Skin-comfort—Clammy
5. Prevents Evaporation of Perspiration
6. Dimensionally Stable to Water
7. Good Wrinkle Recovery when Laundered
8. Waterborne Stains Do not Penetrate
9. Resin Finishes Are not Absorbed

Fig. 2-1 Properties related to low absorbency.

guishing are good for children's sleepwear and protective clothing.

To analyze a fabric to predict its performance, one usually starts with the fiber content. Knowledge of the fiber's properties will help one to anticipate the contribution that the fiber will make to the performance of a fabric and the garment made from it. Some contributions of fibers are desirable and some are not. Figure 2-1 illustrates this fact by giving some of the contributions of a low-absorbency fiber.

Fiber properties are determined by the nature of the *external structure,* the *chemical composition,* and the *internal structure.*

External Structure or Morphology

Length. Fibers are sold by the fiber producer as filament, staple, or filament tow. *Filaments* are long *continuous* fiber strands of indefinite length, measured in yards or meters. They may be either monofilament (one fiber) or multifilament (a number of filaments). Filaments may be smooth or textured (crimped in some way), as shown in Figure 2–2. *Staple fibers* are measured in inches or centimeters and range in length from $\frac{3}{4}$ of an inch to 18 inches. Staple fibers are shown in Figure 2–3. All the natural fibers except silk are staple in form. The man-made fibers are made into staple form by cutting filament tow into short lengths. *Filament tow* consists of a loose rope or strand of several thousand man-made fibers without a definite twist. Tow is usually crimped after spinning (Figure 2–4). Filaments are used in smooth silk-like fabrics; staple is used in cottonlike or wool-like fabrics.

Diameter, Size, or Denier. Fiber size plays a big part in determining the performance and hand of a fabric (how it feels). Large fibers give crispness, roughness, body, and stiffness. Large fibers also

resist crushing—a property that is important in carpets, for example. Fine fibers give softness and pliability. Fabrics made with fine fibers will drape more easily.

Natural fibers are subject to growth irregularities and are, therefore, not uniform in size or development. In natural fibers, fineness is a major factor in determining quality. Fineness is measured in microns (a micron is 1/1,000 millimeter or 1/25,400 inch).

Diameter Range (microns)	
Cotton	16–20 microns
Flax	12–16 microns
Wool	10–50 microns
Silk	11–12 microns

Fig. 2-2 (*Left*) Textured filament yarn. (*Right*) Regular filament yarn.

Fig. 2-3 Man-made staple fiber.

In *man-made fibers,* diameter is controlled by the size of the spinneret holes and by stretching during or after spinning. Man-made fibers can be made uniform in diameter or can be thick-and-thin at regular intervals throughout their length. The fineness of man-made fibers is measured in *denier. Denier is determined by weighing 9,000 meters of yarn (or fiber). It is the weight in grams of this unit length.* Staple fiber is sold by denier and fiber length; filament fiber is sold by the denier of the yarn or tow. Yarn denier can be divided by the number of filaments to give filament denier; for example,

$$\frac{40 \text{ denier yarn}}{20 \text{ filaments}} = 2 \text{ denier per filament.}$$

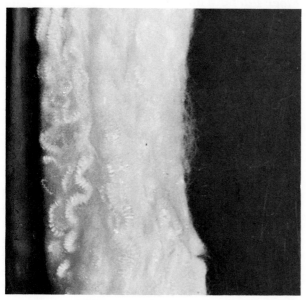

Fig. 2-4 Filament tow.

One to 3 denier corresponds to fine cotton, cashmere, or wool; 5 to 8 denier is similar to average cotton, wool, or alpaca; 15 denier corresponds to carpet wool size.

Clothing fibers range from 1 to 7 denier. Fiber of the same denier is not suitable for all uses. Clothing fibers do not make good carpets and carpet fibers do not make good clothing.

Carpet fibers range in denier from 15 to 24. One of the early mistakes made by the carpet industry was that of using clothing fibers for carpets. These fibers were too soft and pliable, and the carpets did not have good crush resistance. Rayon carpet fiber (1953) was the first fiber made especially for carpets.

Carpet wools are usually a mixture of fibers of different deniers. Except for size, carpet fibers have the same characteristics as the other fibers in the family to which they belong. For example, neither carpet wools nor clothing wools are very flammable and both have good resiliency.

Cross-Sectional Shape. Shape is important in luster, bulk, body, texture, and hand or feel of a fabric. Figure 2–5 shows typical cross-sectional shapes. These shapes may be round, dog-bone, triangular, lobal, bean-shaped, flat, or strawlike.

The natural fibers derive their shape from (1) the way the cellulose is built up during plant growth, (2) the shape of the hair follicle and the formation of protein substances in animals, and (3) the shape of the orifice through which the silk fiber is extruded.

The shape of man-made fibers is controlled by the spinneret and the spinning method. The size, shape, luster, length, and other properties of man-made fibers can be varied by changes in the production process.

Surface Contour. Surface contour is defined as the surface of the fiber along its shaft. Surface contour may be smooth, serrated, striated, or rough. It is important to the hand and texture of the fabric. Figure 2–5 shows some of the differences in the surface contours of different fibers.

Crimp. Crimp may be found in textile materials as

- Molecular crimp—flexible-molecular-chain configuration
- Fiber crimp—waves and twists along the fiber.

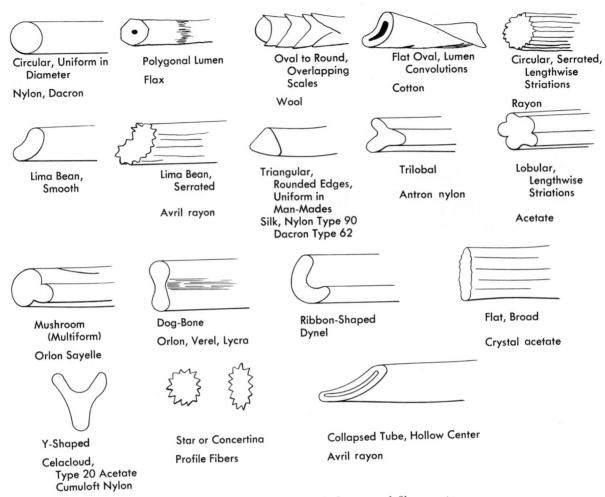

Circular, Uniform in Diameter

Nylon, Dacron

Polygonal Lumen

Flax

Oval to Round, Overlapping Scales

Wool

Flat Oval, Lumen Convolutions

Cotton

Circular, Serrated, Lengthwise Striations

Rayon

Lima Bean, Smooth

Lima Bean, Serrated

Avril rayon

Triangular, Rounded Edges, Uniform in Man-Mades Silk, Nylon Type 90 Dacron Type 62

Trilobal

Antron nylon

Lobular, Lengthwise Striations

Acetate

Mushroom (Multiform)

Orlon Sayelle

Dog-Bone

Orlon, Verel, Lycra

Ribbon-Shaped Dynel

Flat, Broad

Crystal acetate

Y-Shaped

Celacloud, Type 20 Acetate Cumuloft Nylon

Star or Concertina

Profile Fibers

Collapsed Tube, Hollow Center

Avril rayon

Fig. 2-5 Typical cross-sectional shapes and fiber contour.

• Yarn or weave crimp—bends that result from the interlacing or interlooping of yarns in a fabric.

Fiber crimp refers to the waves, bends, twists, coils, or curl along the length of the fiber. Fiber crimp increases cohesiveness, resiliency, resistance to abrasion, stretch, bulk, and warmth. Crimp increases absorbency and skin-contact comfort but reduces luster. A fiber may have one of three kinds of crimp. *Mechanical crimp* is imparted to fibers by passing them through fluted rollers, twisting them, or flattening one side (see Chapter 17). *Natural or inherent crimp* occurs in cotton and wool. *Latent or inherent crimp* exists in an undeveloped state in bicomponent man-made fibers. It is developed in the completed garment by suitable solvents or by heat treatment.

Fiber Parts. The natural fibers, except for silk, have three distinct parts: an outer covering, called a *cuticle* or skin; an inner area; and a central core that may be hollow. Figures 3-4, and 5-4 show the structural parts of wool and cotton.

The man-made fiber parts are not as complex as those of the natural fibers and there are usually just two: the skin and a solid core.

Chemical Composition

The chemical composition is the basis for the classification of the fibers into generic groups such as cellulose, protein, and acrylic. It is also the factor that makes one fiber family (generic group) different from the others. Some fibers are made from a single chemical compound, some are made from two different compounds, and some have compounds grafted to their molecular chains.

- Homopolymers—fibers composed of a single substance
- Copolymers—fibers composed of two substances
- Graft polymers—side branches are attached to the "backbone" chain of the molecule, which gives the molecular chains a more open structure and less crystallinity; dye receptivity is increased.

Some fibers have molecules with chemically reactive groups; others are chemically inert. A chemically inert molecule can be made reactive by grafting it with reactive groups.

Internal Structure or Molecular Arrangement

Fibers are composed of millions of molecule chains. The length of the chains, which varies just as the length of fibers varies, is described as *degree of polymerization*. Polymerization is the process of joining small molecules—monomers—together. Long chains indicate a high degree of polymerization and a high degree of fiber strength.

Molecule chains are sometimes described in terms of weight. The molecular weight is a factor in properties such as fiber strength, extensibility, and fabric pilling. (A bundle of longer chains is harder to pull apart than a bundle of shorter chains.) The molecular weight is expressed as intrinsic viscosity and is determined by viscosity tests; higher viscosity means higher molecular weight or longer molecular chains. Some intrinsic viscosity values are

- 0.9   higher strength and higher pilling
- 0.6   average
- 0.4   lower strength and lower pilling.

Molecular chains have different configurations in fibers. When molecular chains are nearly parallel to the lengthwise axis of the fiber, they are said to be *oriented;* when they are randomly arranged they are said to be *amorphous. Crystalline* is the term used to describe fibers that have molecular chains parallel to each other but not necessarily parallel to the lengthwise axis of the fiber (Figure 2-6). Different fibers vary in the proportion of oriented, crystalline, and amorphous areas. Molecular chains are not visible but their arrangement is theorized by X-ray analysis.

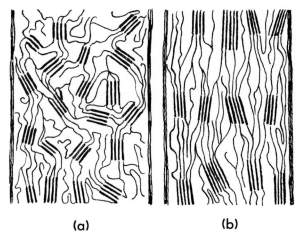

Fig. 2-6 Crystalline polymers. (a) Not oriented. (b) Oriented.

Man-made fibers are in a random, unoriented state as they are extruded from the spinneret. *Stretching* or *drawing* increases the crystallinity and orderly arrangement, reduces the diameter, and packs the molecules together (Figure 2-7). The amount of crystallinity and orientation relates to the physical properties of the fiber, such as strength, elongation, moisture absorption, and abrasion resistance, and also to the receptivity of the fiber to dyes.

Unstretched or Undrawn   Stretched or Drawn

Fig. 2-7 Before and after drawing the fiber.

Molecular chains are held to one another by *cross links* or by interchain forces called *hydrogen bonds* and *van der Waals forces.* The forces are similar to the attraction of a magnet for a piece of iron. The closer the chains are together, the stronger the bonds are. Hydrogen bonding is the attraction of positive hydrogen atoms of one chain for negative oxygen or nitrogen atoms of an adjacent chain. Van der Waals forces are similar but weaker bonds. It is in the crystalline area that hydrogen bonding and van der Waals forces occur.

Fiber Property Charts

The fibers within each generic family have individual differences. These differences are not reflected in the charts shown here except in a few specific instances. The figures are averages or medians and are intended as a general characteri-

Fiber Property	*Is Due to*	*Contributes to Fabric Property*
Abrasion resistance is the ability of a fiber to withstand the rubbing or abrasion it gets in everyday use.	Tough outer layer, scales, or skin Fiber toughness Flexible molecular chains	Durability Abrasion resistance Resistance to splitting
Absorbency or moisture regain is the percentage of moisture a bone-dry fiber will absorb from the air under standard conditions of temperature and moisture.	Hydroxyl groups Amorphous areas	Comfort, warmth, water repellency, absorbency, static buildup Dyeability, spotting Shrinkage Wrinkle resistance
Aging resistance	Chemical structure	Storing of fabrics
Chemical reactivity is the effect of acids, alkali, oxidizing agents, solvents.	Polar groups of molecules	Care required in cleaning—bleaching, ability to take acid or alkali finishes
Cohesiveness is the ability of fibers to cling together during spinning. Not important in continuous filament.	Crimp or twists	Resistance to ravel
Cover is the ability to occupy space for concealment or protection.	Crimp, curl, or twist Cross-sectional shape	Warmth in fabric Cost—less fiber needed
Creep is delayed elasticity. Recovers gradually from strain.	Lack of side chains, cross links, strong bonds; poor orientation	Streak dyeing and shiners in fabric
Density—see *Specific Gravity*		
Dyeability is the fibers' receptivity to coloration by dyes.	Amorphous areas and dye sites	Aesthetics and colorfastness
Elastic recovery is the ability of fibers to recover from strain.	Molecular structure: side chains, cross linkages, strong bonds	Processability of fabrics Resiliency Delayed elasticity or creep
Elasticity is the ability of a stretched material to return immediately to its original size.		
Electrical conductivity is the ability to transfer electrical charges.	Chemical structure: polar groups	Poor conductivity causes fabric to cling to the body, electric shocks
Elongation is the ability to be stretched, extended, or lengthened. Varies at different temperatures and when wet or dry.	Fiber crimp Molecular structure: molecular crimp orientation	Increases tear strength Reduces brittleness Provides "give" and stretchiness
Feltability refers to the ability of fibers to mat together.	Scale structure of wool	Fabrics can be made directly from fibers Special care required during washing
Flammability is the ability to ignite and burn.	Chemical composition	Fabrics burn
Hand is the way a fiber feels: silky, harsh, soft, crisp, dry.	Cross-sectional shape, crimp, diameter, length	Hand of fabric
Heat conductivity is the ability to conduct heat away from the body.	Crimp Cross-sectional shape	Warmth
Heat sensitivity is the ability to soften, melt, or shrink when subjected to heat.	Heat vibrates molecules Fewer intermolecular forces and cross links	Determine safe washing and ironing temperatures
Hydrophilic, hygroscopic—see *absorbency.*		

Fiber Property Chart (*Cont.*)

Fiber Property	Is Due to	Contributes to Fabric Property
Luster is the light reflected from a surface. More subdued than shine; light rays are broken up.	Smoothness Fiber length Flat or lobal shape	Luster
Loft or compressional resiliency is the ability to spring back to original thickness after being compressed.	Fiber crimp Stiffness	Springiness, good cover Resistance to flattening
Mildew resistance	Low absorption	Care during storage
Moth resistance	Molecule has no sulfur	Care during storage
Pilling is the balling up of fiber ends on the surface of fabrics.	Fiber strength	Pilling
	High molecular weight	Unsightly appearance
Specific gravity and density are measures of the weight of a fiber. Density is the weight in grams per cubic centimeter, and specific gravity is the ratio of the mass of the fiber to an equal volume of water at 4°C.	Molecular weight	Warmth without weight Loftiness—full and light Buoyancy to fabric
Stiffness or rigidity is the opposite of flexibility. It is the resistance to bending or creasing.	Ratio of breaking stress to breaking strain	Body of fabric Resistance to insertion of yarn twist
Strength is defined as the ability to resist stress and is expressed as tensile strength (pounds per square inch) or as tenacity (grams per denier).	Molecular structure—orientation, crystallinity, degree of polymerization	Durability, tear strength, sagging, pilling Sheerer fabrics possible with stronger fine fibers
Sunlight resistance is the ability to withstand degradation from direct sunlight.	Chemical composition	Durability of curtains and draperies, outdoor furniture, outdoor carpeting
Toughness	Outer surface or "skin" of fiber	Resists rupture from deformation, gives frictional resistance
Wicking is the ability of a fiber to transfer moisture along its surface.	Chemical and physical composition of outer surface	Makes fabrics comfortable

zation of each generic group. The figures were compiled from the following sources:

• Charts: Man-Made Fiber Chart, *Textile World* (1970)
   Properties of the Man-Made Fibers, *Textile Industries* (1971/1972)
   Man-Made Fiber Deskbook, *Modern Textiles* (March, 1977)
• Bulletins: Textile Fibers and Their Properties, AATCC Council on Technology 1977
   Technical bulletins, Du Pont, Celanese, and Monsanto
   Man-Made Fiber Fact Book, Man Made Fiber Producers Association Inc. 1974, 1977

Abrasion Resistance	
Nylon	Excellent
Olefin	
Polyester	
Spandex	
Flax	
Acrylics	to
Cotton	
Silk	
Wool*	
Rayon	
Acetate	
Glass	Poor

*Varies with coarseness of fiber.

Absorbency

Fiber	Moisture Regain*
Natural Fibers	
Cotton	7–11
Flax	12
Silk	11
Wool	13–18
Man-made Fibers	
Acetate	6.0
Arnel triacetate	3.2
Acrylic	1.3–2.5
Aramid	4.5
Flurocarbon	0
Glass	0 –0.3
Modacrylic	0.4–4.0
Novoloid	5.5
Nylon	4.0–4.5
Nylon Qiana	2.5
Olefin	0.01–0.1
Polyester	0.4–0.8
Rayon	15
Rayon HWM	11.5–13
Saran	0.1
Spandex	0.75–1.3
Vinyon	0.5

*Moisture regain is expressed as a percentage of the moisture-free weight at 70° Fahrenheit and 65% relative humidity.

Density and Specific Gravity*

Fibers	Density (g/cc)
Natural Fibers	
Cotton	1.52
Flax	1.52
Silk	1.25
Wool	1.32
Man-made Fibers	
Acetate	1.32
Acrylic	1.17–1.18
Aramid	1.38–1.44
Flurocarbon	2.2
Glass	2.49–2.73
Modacrylic	1.30–1.37
Novoloid	1.25
Nylon	1.14
Nylon Qiana	1.03
Olefin	0.91
Polyester	1.22 or 1.38
Rayon	1.50–1.52
Saran	1.70
Spandex	1.20–1.22
Vinyon	1.33–1.35

*Ratio of weight of a given volume of fiber to an equal volume of water.

Elastic Recovery

Fiber	% Recovery from 2–5% Stretch
Natural Fibers	
Cotton	75
Flax	65
Silk	92
Wool	99
Man-made Fibers	
Acetate	58
Acrylic	92
Modacrylic	88
Nylon	100
Olefin	95
Polyester	97
Rayon	54
Spandex	99

Elongation: Breaking

Fiber	% Elongation at Break	
	Standard*	Wet
Natural Fibers		
Cotton	3–7	9.5
Flax	2.0	2.2
Silk	20	30
Wool	25	35
Man-made Fibers		
Acetate	25	30
Acrylic	20	26
Aramid	2.3	4
Glass	3.1	same
Modacrylic	14	same
Nylon	23	28
Nylon HT	16	18
Olefin	15–25	same
Polyester	18	same
Polyester HT	9	same
Rayon	15	20
Rayon HWM	6.5	7.0
Rubber	500	same
Spandex	500	same

Note: A minimum of 10% is desirable for ease in textile processing.

*Standard condition: 65% relative humidity, 70°F. Lower figure of percentage range used.

Fiber Strength

Fiber	Breaking Tenacity (grams/denier)	
	Dry	Wet
Natural Fibers		
Cotton	4.0	5.0
Flax	5.5	6.5
Silk	4.5	3.9
Wool	1.5	1.0
Man-made Fibers		
Acetate	1.2 –1.5	0.8–1.2
Acrylic	2.0 –3.5	1.8–3.3
Aramid (filament)	4.3 –5.1	3.2–3.9
Aramid (staple)	3.7 –5.3	2.7–4.1
Flurocarbon	2.0	same
Glass	7.0	same
Modacrylic	2.0 –3.5	same
Novoloid	1.5 –2.5	1.3–2.3
Nylon 6 (filament)	6.0 –9.5	5.0–8.0
Nylon 6 (staple)	2.5	2.0
Nylon 66 (filament)	3.5 –7.2	3.2–6.5
Nylon 66 (staple)	3.0 –6.0	2.6–5.4
Nylon 66 HT	6.0 –9.5	5.0–8.0
Olefin	4.8	6.0
Polyester (filament)	4.0 –5.5	same
Polyester (staple)	2.5 –5.5	same
Polyester (filament HT)	6.3 –9.5	same
Rayon	0.73–2.6	0.7–1.8
Rayon HT	3.0 –6.0	1.9–4.6
Rayon HWM	2.5 –5.5	1.8–4.0
Rubber	0.34	same
Saran	1.5	same
Spandex	0.6 –0.9	same
Vinyon	0.7 –1.0	same

Sunlight Resistance

Glass	Excellent
Acrylic	
Modacrylic	
Polyester	
Flax	
Cotton	to
Rayon	
Triacetate	
Acetate	
Olefin	
Nylon	
Wool	
Silk	Poor

Effect of Acids

Natural Fibers	
Cotton	Harmed
Flax	Harmed
Silk	Harmed by mineral acids, resistant to organic acids
Wool	Resistant
Man-made Fibers	
Acetate	Weakened
Acrylic	Resistant to most
Aramid	Resistant to most
Glass	Resistant
Modacrylic	Resistant
Nylon	Harmed
Olefin	Resistant
Polyester	Resistant
Rayon	Harmed
Spandex	Resistant

Thermal Properties

Fiber	Melting Point		Softening Sticking Point		Safe Ironing Temperature*	
	°F	°C	°F	°C	°F	°C
Natural Fibers						
Cotton	Nonmelting				425	218
Flax	Nonmelting				450	232
Silk	Nonmelting				300	149
Wool	Nonmelting				300	149
Man-made Fibers						
Acetate	446	230	364	184	350	177
Arnel triacetate	575	302	482	250	464	240
Acrylic			400–490	204–254	300–350	149–176
Aramid	Does not melt—carbonizes above 800°F					
Glass			1400–3033			
Modacrylic	410	210	300	149	200–250	93–121
Novoloid	Nonmelting					
Nylon 6	414	212	340	171	300	149
Nylon 66	482	250	445	229	350	177
Olefin	275	135	260	127	150 (lowest possible)	66
Polyester PET	480	249	460	238	325	163
Polyester PCDT	550	311	490	254	350	177
Rayon	Nonmelting				375	191
Saran	350	177	300	149	Do not iron	
Spandex	446	230	347	175	300	149
Vinyon	285	140	200	93	Do not iron	

*Lowest setting on irons: 185–225°F.

Effect of Alkali	
Natural Fibers	
Cotton	Resistant
Flax	Resistant
Silk	Damaged
Wool	Harmed
Man-made Fibers	
Acetate	Little effect
Acrylic	Resistant to weak
Aramid	Resistant
Glass	Resistant
Modacrylic	Resistant
Nylon	Resistant
Olefin	Highly resistant
Polyester	Resistant
Rayon	Resistant to weak
Spandex	Resistant

Effect of Organic Solvents	
Natural Fibers	
Cotton	Resistant
Flax	Resistant
Silk	Resistant
Wool	Resistant
Man-made Fibers	
Acetate	Resistant except for acetone, phenol, and chloroform
Acrylic	Resistant
Aramid	Resistant
Modacrylic	Resistant to most
Nylon	Resistant except for phenol and formic acid
Olefin	Chlorinated hydrocarbons may degrade fibers
Polyester	Resistant
Rayon	Resistant
Spandex	Resistant

Fiber Identification

The procedure for identification of the fiber content of a fabric depends upon the nature of the sample, the experience of the analyst, and the facilities available. Since laws require the fiber content of apparel and household textiles to be indicated on the label, the consumer may only need to look for identification labels. If the consumer wishes to confirm or check the information on the label, the burning test and some simple solubility tests may be used.

Visual Inspection

Visual inspection of a fabric for appearance and hand is always the first step in fiber identification. It is no longer possible to make an identification of the fiber content by the appearance and hand alone because man-made fibers can be made to resemble the natural fibers. However, observation of the following characteristics is helpful.

1. Length of fiber. Untwist the yarn to determine length. Any fiber can be made in staple length but not all fibers can be filament. For example, cotton and wool are always staple.

2. Luster or lack of luster.

3. Body, texture, hand—soft-to-hard, rough to smooth, warm-to-cool, or stiff-to-flexible.

Burning Test

The burning test can be used to identify the chemical composition, such as cellulose, protein, mineral, or chemical, and thus identify the group to which a fiber belongs. *Blends cannot be identified by the burning test.* If visual inspection is used along with the burning test, fiber identification can be carried further. For example, if the sample is cellulose and also filament, it is rayon; but if it is staple, a positive identification cannot be made.

General directions for the burning test:

1. Ravel out and test several yarns from each side of the fabric to see if they have the same fiber content. Differences in luster, twist, and color will indicate that there might be two or more kinds of fibers in the fabric.

Fig. 2-8 Fiber identification by the burning test.

2. Hold the yarn horizontally, as shown in Figure 2–8. Use tweezers if desired. Feed the yarns slowly into the edge of the flame from the alcohol lamp and observe what happens. Repeat this several times to check results.

See the chart on page 16 for an identification of fiber groups.

Microscope Test

A knowledge of fiber structure, obtained by seeing the fibers in the microscope and observing some of the differences among fibers in each group, is of help in understanding fibers and fabric behavior.

Positive identification of most of the natural fibers can be made by using this test. The man-made fibers are more difficult to identify because some of them look alike and their appearance may be changed by variations in the manufacturing process. Positive identification of the man-made fibers by this means is rather limited. Cross-sectional appearance is helpful if more careful examination is desired.

Longitudinal and cross-sectional photomicrographs of individual fibers are included in the fiber chapters. These may be used for reference when checking unknown fibers.

Directions for using the microscope:

1. Clean the lens, slide, and cover glass.

2. Place a drop of water on the slide.

3. Untwist a yarn and place the loosened fibers on the slide. Cover with the cover glass and press down to eliminate air bubbles.

4. Place the slide on the stage of the microscope and then focus with low power first. If the fibers have not been well loosened, it will be difficult to focus on a single fiber.

5. If a fabric contains more than one kind of fiber, test each fiber. Be sure to check both the warp and filling yarns.

Solubility Tests

Solubility tests are used to identify the man-made fibers by generic class and to confirm iden-tification of natural fibers. Two household tests, the acetone test for acetate and the alkali test for wool, are described on pages 27 and 62, respectively.

In using the tests the specimen is placed in the liquid in the order listed. The specimen is stirred for 5 minutes and the effect is noted. Fiber, yarns, or small pieces of fabric may be used. The liquids are hazardous and should be handled with care. Chemical laboratory exhaust hoods, gloves, aprons, and goggles should be used.

Identification by Burning

Fibers	When Approaching Flame	When in Flame	After Removal from Flame	Ash	Odor
Cellulose Cotton Flax Rayon	Does not fuse or shrink from flame	Burns	Continues to burn, afterglow	Gray feathery smooth edge	Burning paper
Protein Silk Wool	Fuses and curls away from flame	Burns slowly	Usually self-extinguishing	Crushable black ash	Burning hair
Acetate	Fuses away from flame	Burns with melting	Continues to burn and melt	Brittle black hard bead	Acrid
Acrylic	Fuses away from flame	Burns with melting	Continues to burn and melt	Brittle black hard bead	—
Modacrylic	Fuses away from flame	Burns very slowly with melting	Self-extinguishing, white smoke	Brittle black hard bead	—
Nylon	Fuses and shrinks away from flame	Burns slowly with melting	Usually self-extinguishing	Hard gray or tan bead	Celerylike
Olefin	Fuses and shrinks away from flame	Burns with melting	Usually self-extinguishing	Hard tan bead	—
Polyester	Fuses and shrinks away from flame	Burns slowly with melting; black smoke	Usually self-extinguishing	Hard black bead	Sweetish odor
Saran	Fuses and shrinks away from flame	Burns very slowly with melting	Self-extinguishing	Hard black bead	—
Spandex	Fuses but does not shrink from flame	Burns with melting	Continues to burn with melting	Soft black ash	—

Solubility Tests

Solvent	Fiber Solubility
1. Acetic acid glacial, 75°F	Acetate, Triacetate
2. Hydrochloric acid, 20% concentration, 1.096 density, 75°F	Nylon 6, nylon 6,6
3. Sodium hypochlorite solution (pH 11), 75°F	Silk and wool (silk dissolves in hydrochloric acid at 75°F)
4. Xylene (meta), 282°F (boil)	Olefin and saran (saran dissolves in 1.4 dioxane at 200°F); olefin is not soluble.
5. Ammonium thiocyanate, 70% concentration, 266°F (boil)	Acrylic
6. Butyrolactone, 70°F	Modacrylic, acetate
7. Dimethyl formamide, 200°F	Spandex, modacrylic, acrylic, acetate
8. Sulfuric acid, 75% concentration, 1.065 density, 75°F	Cotton, flax, rayon, nylon, acetate
9. Cresol (meta), 200°F	Polyester, nylon, acetate

Protein Fibers and Wool

3

Natural protein fibers are of animal origin; wool and specialty wools are the hair and fur of animals and silk is the secretion of the silkworm. Man-made protein fibers, *azlon,* are made by dissolving and resolidifying protein substances from animal or grain sources.

Many of the natural protein fibers are prestige fibers today. Silk, vicuña, cashmere, and camel are in this category. Wool, once one of the most commonly used fibers, has been replaced in many end products by the acrylics, nylon and polyester. Man-made protein fibers are no longer made in the United States. In the 1940s and 1950s, Aralac made from milk casein and Vicara made from the zein of corn were produced, but these fibers were not successful because they were too weak to be used alone and too expensive to compete with other blending fibers, particularly rayon and acetate.

Protein fibers are composed of various amino acids that have been formed in nature into polypeptide chains with high molecular weight. They contain the elements *carbon, hydrogen, oxygen,* and *nitrogen.* Wool in addition, contains *sulfur.* Protein fibers are amphoteric, having both acidic and basic reactive groups. The protein of wool is keratin whereas that of silk is fibroin.

A simple formula for an amino acid is

amino group (basic)   carboxyl group (acidic)

Protein fibers have some properties in common because of their chemical composition. These properties are important to the consumer because they indicate the care required of the fabrics. Silk and wool have some different properties because their physical and molecular structures are different (see the following charts).

Properties Common to All Protein Fibers

Properties	Importance to Consumer
Resiliency	Resists wrinkling. Wrinkles hang out between wearings. Fabrics tend to hold their shape.
Hygroscopic	Comfortable in cool, damp climate. Moisture prevents brittleness in carpets.
Weaker when wet	Handle carefully during washing. Wool loses about 40% of its strength and silk loses about 15%.
Specific gravity	Fabrics feel lighter than cellulosics of the same thickness.
Harmed by alkali	Use neutral or slightly alkaline soap or detergent. Perspiration weakens the fiber.
Harmed by oxidizing agents	Chlorine bleaches damage fiber so should not be used. Sunlight causes white fabrics to turn yellowish.
Harmed by dry heat	Wool becomes harsh and brittle and scorches easily with dry heat. Use steam! White silk and wool turn yellow.
Flame resistance	Do not burn readily, are self-extinguishing, have odor of burning hair, and form a black crushable ash.

Differences between Silk and Wool

Silk	Wool	Importance to Consumer
CHON	CHONS	Wool is harmed by moths and beetles
Extended polypeptide chains	Folded polypeptide chains	Wool is more elastic and resilient
Highly crystalline	More amorphous areas	Silk is strong. Wool is more absorbent
Solid fiber	Four parts to fiber, scaley outer layer	Wool shrinks and felts
Smooth	Fiber crimp, molecular crimp	Wool is warmer, and more resilient. Silk is smoother, and more lustrous
Filament, usually	Staple only	Wool is fuzzy. Silk is smooth

Wool

Wool was one of the first fibers to be spun into yarns and woven into cloth. Before the Industrial Revolution, when fibers were spun by hand, wool and flax were the most widely used textile fibers. Wool was so important to England that King Edward III in 1350 decreed that the Lord Chancellor must sit on a wool sack so that he would remember the economic importance of the wool industry. In the House of Lords, today, the Lord Chancellor sits on a cloth covered seat stuffed with wool—a wool sack.

In recent years, wool's share of the market has steadily declined (see the following chart). The wool industry in the United States has been hard hit by the influx of foreign imports, by competition from man-made fibers, and by the added expense of meeting pollution standards. Wool-processing plants have been a major source of river pollution, and many plants have been forced to close. (Wool fibers are biodegradable—a plus factor when compared to synthetic fibers).

Many people now consider both wool and silk to be luxury fibers. Designers continue to use these fibers extensively in their collections and the average consumer is most likely to have a wool coat. Wool and silk products, however, are not as readily available as they once were. The high initial cost and the cost of care of wool and silk products have discouraged many potential customers.

In the 1960s when man-made fibers were used in increasing amounts in sweaters, blankets, carpeting, and in many kinds of outerwear, wool was promoted as Nature's Wonder Fiber by the Wool Bureau. This is an apt description of wool. Wool has a combination of properties that are unequaled by any man-made fiber; namely, ability to be shaped by heat and moisture, ability to absorb moisture in vapor form without feeling wet, comfortable warmth in cold weather, initial water repellency, feltability, and flame retardance.

Sheep were probably the first animals domesticated by man. The covering of primitive sheep consisted of two parts: a long, hairy outer coat that was used primarily for rugs and felt, and a light, downy undercoat that was very desirable for clothing. The fleece of present-day domesticated sheep is primarily the soft undercoat. It is thought that cross breeding of sheep to increase the amount of undercoat began about A.D. 100. By A.D. 1400 the Spanish had developed the merino sheep, whose fleece contains no hair or kemp fiber. Kemp is a coarse, brittle, dead-white fiber found in the fleece of primitive sheep and still found in the wools of all breeds of sheep except the merino.

Sheep were not known to the American Indian. The sheep of the Navajo are descendants of an unimproved long-haired breed brought over from Spain. The only carpet wool now produced in the United States comes from these sheep. The sheep are quite small, with an undercoat of fibers 3 to 4 inches long and an outer coat 4 to 6 inches long. Carpet wools are made of a mixture of fine fibers, long hairy fibers, and kemp. Most of the world's supply of coarse carpet wools come from nomadic flocks in Asia, Argentina, New Zealand, and Scotland.

Production

Merino sheep produce the most valuable wool—making up about 30 per cent of the world production. About 60 per cent of merino wool comes from Australia. Lamb's wool comes from animals less than 7 months old and is finer and softer because it is the first shearing and the fiber has only one cut end; the other end is the natural tip

Mill Consumption of Fibers in the United States (Thousand Metric Tons)*

Year	Wool		Silk		Cotton		Man-Made Fibers	
	Amt	% of Mkt	Amt	% of Mkt	Amt	% of Mkt	Amt	% of Mkt
1965	457	5.3	6.3	0.1	4452.6	52.5	3614.1	42.4
1970	273	2.9	1.8	—	3773.6	39.5	5501.3	57.6
1975	132	1.2	1.0	—	3068.7	28.9	7415.8	69.5
1976	145.9	1.3	2.5	—	3389	29.2	8081.4	69.6

*Textile Organon (June 1977).

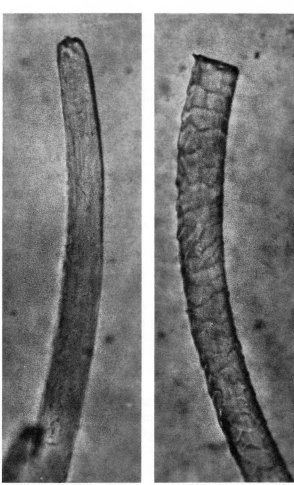

Fig. 3-1 Lamb's-wool fiber showing natural tip on left. Cut end on right.

(Figure 3-1). The term *lamb's wool* usually identifies it on a label.

Shearing contributes to the high cost of producing wool. In 1970 a study of an anticancer drug led to U.S. Department of Agriculture experiments with *chemical shearing.* Very small amounts of the drug will interrupt cell growth in the hair roots; in 6 or 7 days, when the new growth gets above the skin so that the sheep will not be left bare, the fleece can be "peeled" off. The fibers break at the weak spot. No side effects have been detected and it is hoped the process can be in use by the late 1970s.

Grading and *sorting* are two marketing operations that put wools of like character together. In *grading,* the whole fleece is judged for fineness and length. Fine combing wools measure $2\frac{1}{2}$ inches or more in length. French combing wools are $1\frac{1}{2}$ to $2\frac{1}{2}$ inches long. The coarser clothing wools are around $1\frac{1}{2}$ inches. *Sorting* breaks up the individual

Fig. 3-2 Natural crimp in wool fiber.

fleece into various qualities. The best quality wool comes from the sides and shoulders, the poorest comes from the lower legs. Figure 3-2 shows the crimp in wool fiber.

Fineness, color, crimp, strength, length, and elasticity are wool-fiber characteristics that vary with the breed of the sheep. There are about 30 breeds of improved sheep in the world.

Wool is creamy white in color. It is often used in this state because of its sensitivity to bleaches. Strong bleaches, sunlight, and heat will cause white wool to yellow.

Quality of apparel wool is based on fineness and length and does *not* necessarily imply durability since fine fibers are not as durable as coarse fibers. In 1964 the Wool Bureau adopted the Woolmark as a symbol of quality to be used on all merchandise that meets the Wool Bureau's specifications for quality. In 1970—recognizing the increasing use of blends—the Wool Bureau adopted a Woolblend mark for blends with a high percentage of wool. The Woolmark and Woolblend symbols are shown in Figure 3-3.

PURE WOOL   WOOLBLEND
MARK

Fig. 3-3 Woolmark and Woolblend symbols of quality. (*Courtesy of The Wool Bureau, Incorporated.*)

Francis Chichester, in his solo voyage around the world in 1966 used his ship as a "floating test bed for wool" and had the Woolmark painted on the bow of the ship.—*Textile Industries,* **117** (January 1967).

Legislation

True wool is the fleece of the sheep. The term *wool* legally includes hair fiber from the Angora goat, Cashmere goat, camel, alpaca, llama, and vicuña. True wool comes from several sources:

- Sheared wool—from live sheep
- Pulled wool—from the pelts of meat-type sheep
- Reused wool—from worn clothing
- Reprocessed wool—from cutters' scraps.

Wool is often blended with less expensive fibers to reduce the cost of the fabric or to extend its use. Congress passed the Wool Products Labeling Act in 1939 to protect consumers as well as producers, manufacturers, and distributors from the unrevealed presence of substitutes and mixtures and to inform the consumer of the source of the wool fiber. The law requires that the label must give the fiber content in terms of per cent and also give the source. The act does *not* state anything about the quality. The consumer must rely on feel and texture to determine quality.

The terms that appear on the label of a garment made of wool fiber are defined by the Federal Trade Commission as follows:

1. Wool—new wool or wool fibers reclaimed from knit scraps, broken thread, and noils. (Noils are the short fibers that are combed out in the making of worsted yarns)

2. Reprocessed wool—scraps of new woven or felted fabrics that have been garnetted (shredded) back to the fibrous state and used again in the manufacture of woolens.

3. Reused wool—(shoddy) from old clothing and rags that have been used or worn. The rags are cleaned and sorted and shredded into fibers. Reused wool is often blended with new wool before being respun. It is usually used in utility fabrics—interlinings and mackinaw-type fabrics that are thick and boardy.

The term *virgin wool* on a label does *not* necessarily mean good quality. The term is not de-

fined by the law but has been defined by the Federal Trade Commission as wool that has never been processed in any way. This eliminates knit clips and broken threads from being labeled as virgin wool.

Reclaimed wool is important in the textile industry. However, these fibers lose some of the desirable properties of new wool during the wool garnetting process. Some fibers are broken by the mechanical action and/or wear. The fibers are not as resilient, strong, or durable as new wool.

Physical Structure

Length. The length of wool fibers ranges from 1 to 6 inches, depending on the kind of animal and the length of time between shearings. Long, fine wool fibers, used for worsted yarns and fabrics, have an average length of $2\frac{1}{2}$ inches. The shorter fibers are used in woolen fabrics. The diameter of wool fiber varies from 10 to 50 microns. Merino lamb's wool may average 15 microns in diameter. Wool fibers have natural crimp.

Distinctive Parts. The wool fiber is made up of a cuticle, cortex, and a medulla that is usually absent in fine wools (Figure 3-4).

The cuticle is made up of an epicuticle and a horny nonfibrous layer of scales. In fine wools the scales completely encircle the shaft and each scale overlaps the bottom of the preceding scale like parts of a telescope. In medium and coarse wools the scale arrangement resembles shingles on a roof or scales on a fish (Figure 3-5). The free edges of the scales project outward and point

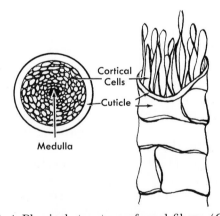

Fig. 3-4 Physical structure of wool fibers. (*Courtesy of Werner von Bergen from* Industrial and Engineering Chemistry (*September 1952*); *reprinted by permission.*)

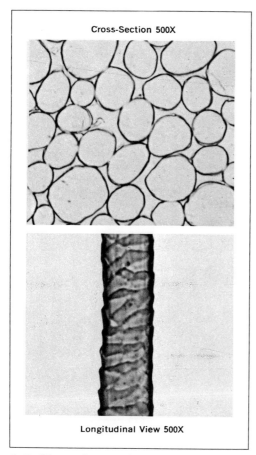

Cross-Section 500X

Longitudinal View 500X

Fig. 3-5 Photomicrographs of wool; Cross-section (*above*); Longitudinal (*below*). (*Courtesy of American Association of Textile Chemists and Colorists.*)

toward the tip of the fiber. They cause skin irritation for some people. The scale covering gives wool its abrasion resistance and felting property.

The epicuticle is a thin nonprotein membrane that covers the scales. This layer gives water repellency to the fiber; it is easily damaged by mechanical treatment.

The *medulla* is a honeycomblike core containing air spaces that increase the insulating power of the fiber. It appears as a dark area when seen through the microscope and is helpful in fiber identification but does not influence the color of the fiber.

The *cortex* is the main part of the fiber. It is made up of long flattened, cigar-shaped cells with a nucleus near the center. In natural-colored wools, the cortical cells contain melanin, a colored pigment.

Because the cortical cells on the two sides of the wool fiber have a somewhat different chemical composition and react differently to moisture,

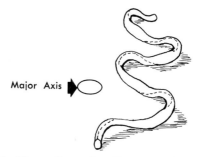

Major Axis

Fig. 3-6 Three-dimensional crimp of wool fiber. (*From G. E. Hopkins,* Wool As an Apparel Fiber. *Copyright, 1953 by Holt, Rinehart and Winston, Inc.*)

wool is a *natural bicomponent fiber.* One side of the fiber swells when the fiber gets wet, and this causes a decrease in the natural crimp of the fiber. When the fiber dries, the crimp returns. Notice in Figure 3-6 the twists and waves of wool's *three-dimensional crimp.* In the best merino wools there are as many as 30 crimps per inch whereas in poor quality wools there are as few as 5. Wool has been described as a giant molecular coil spring with outstanding resiliency. This *resiliency* is excellent when the fiber is dry and poor when it is wet. If dry fabric is crushed in the hand, it tends to spring back to its original shape when the hand is opened. The wool fiber can be stretched as much as 30 per cent of its original length. When stress is applied, the waves and bends of the fiber straighten out, and when stress is removed, the fibers recover their original length. Recovery takes place more slowly when the fabric is dry. Steam, humidity, and water hasten recovery. This is why a wool garment will lose its wrinkles more rapidly when it is hung over a bathtub of steamy water. Wool is said to have perfect elasticity in water.

Chemical Composition and Internal Structure

Raw wool contains 10 to 25 per cent grease, which is recovered during scouring and sold as *lanolin* for use in cosmetics and medicines.

Wool fiber is a protein called *keratin.* It is the same protein that is found in human hair, fingernails, horns, and hooves. Keratin is made up of carbon, hydrogen, oxygen, nitrogen, and sulfur. The individual wool molecule consists of flexible molecular chains held together by natural cross links—cystine (or sulfur) linkages and salt bridges. The cystine linkage is the most important part of the molecule (Figure 3-7). Any

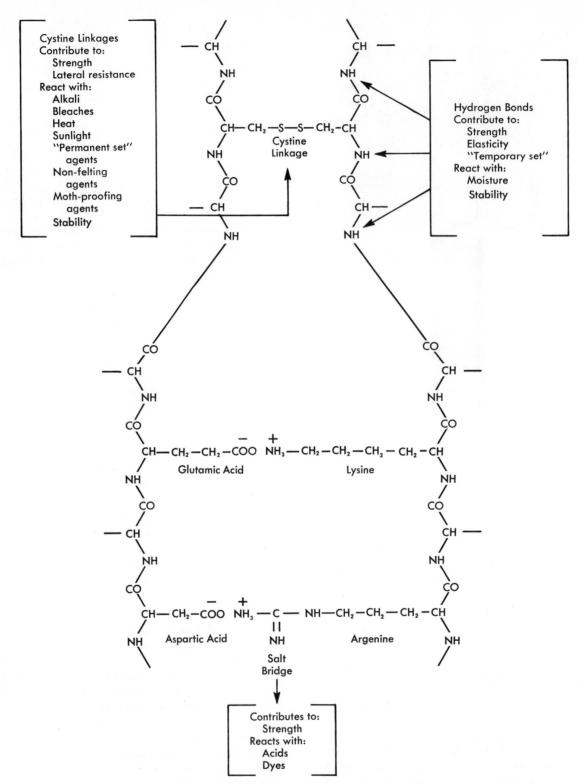

Fig. 3-7 Structural formula of the wool molecule.

chemical such as alkali that damages this linkage can destroy the entire structure. In controlled reactions, the linkage can be broken and then reformed. Minor modifications of the cystine linkage that result from ironing and steaming have a beneficial effect; those from careless washing and exposure to light have a detrimental effect.

Fiber Properties

Aesthetic Properties. Wool, because of its physical structure, contributes *loft* and *body* to fabrics. Wool outerwear fabrics (sweaters and suitings) and carpets are the standard "looks" and textures by which similar man-made fiber fabrics are measured.

Durability Properties. Wool fibers are *weak,* having a tenacity of 1.5 g/d dry and 1.0 g/d wet but wool fabrics are very durable. The durability of wool is the result of the *excellent elongation* (25 per cent) and *elastic recovery* (99 per cent) of the fibers. When stress is put on the fabric the crimped fibers elongate, then the molecular chains unfold. When stress is removed the cross links pull the fibers back almost to their original positions. The *tear strength* of wool is *poor.* Wool has *fair abrasion resistance. Flexibility* of wool is excellent. Wool fibers can be bent back on themselves 20,000 times without breaking, as compared to 3,000 times for cotton and 75 for rayon. Atmospheric moisture helps wool to retain its flexibility. Wool carpets, for example, become brittle if the air is too dry.

Comfort Properties. Absorbency. Wool is more hygroscopic than any other fiber. It has a *moisture regain* of from 13 to 18 per cent under standard conditions. All animal fibers are superior to other fibers in that they absorb moisture without surface wetting. This phenomenon has long been recognized as a major factor in avoiding sudden temperature changes at the skin. This is illustrated by the comfort associated with wool swimsuits and the difference in warmth between an all-polyester knit suit and a wool/polyester-blend knit suit. In the winter, when people go from a dry indoor atmosphere into the damp outdoor air, the heat generated by the wool fibers in absorbing moisture helps protect the wearers' bodies from the impact of the cold atmosphere.

Wool's *excellent resiliency* is important in pro-

viding *warmth.* The wool fibers can recover from crushing and the fabrics will remain porous and capable of incorporating much air. "Still" air is one of the best insulators because it keeps body heat close to the body. Wool is a poor conductor of heat so that warmth from the body is not dissipated readily.

Wool fibers are initially *water repellent.* In a light rain or snow the water will run off or remain on the fabric surface. In a heavier rain wool will absorb a lot of moisture without feeling wet. Eventually wool will absorb enough moisture so that it will feel wet and heavy.

Coarse wool fabrics are often irritating to the skin. Some people are allergic to the chemical components of wool and itch or break out in a rash or sneeze when they wear or handle wool.

Properties Related to Care. Since wool fibers are not stable, wool fabrics are *subject to shrinkage.* The somewhat amorphous molecular structure of wool permits water molecules to penetrate and when they do the wool fiber swells and the molecular chains can be easily deformed.

Felting. Felting, a unique and important property of wool, is based on the scale structure of the fiber. Under mechanical action, such as agitation, friction, and pressure in the presence of heat and moisture, the wool fiber tends to move rootward and the edges of the scales interlock, thus preventing the fiber from returning to its original position in the fabric. The result is the shrinkage or felting of the cloth.

Movement of the fibers is speeded up and felting occurs more rapidly under extreme or severe conditions. A wool garment can be shrunk down to half its original size. Lamb's wool will felt more readily than other wool. In soft, fluffy fabrics the fibers are not firmly held in position and are free to move, so these fabrics are more susceptible to felting than are the firmly woven worsteds. The felting property is an advantage in making felt fabric directly from fibers without spinning or weaving. The felting property is a disadvantage because it makes the laundering of wool more difficult. Treatments to prevent felting shrinkage (see Chapter 36) are based on the principle of smoothing off the rough edges of the scales.

Fulling, or *milling,* is a cloth-finishing process in which the cloth is washed in a thick soap solution and squeezed by wooden rollers to shrink the cloth and close up the weave by bringing the

Fig. 3-8 Wool cloth before (*left*) and after (*right*) fulling.

yarns closer together. After fulling, the cloth has more body and cover, as shown in Figure 3–8. The shrinking is dependent on the action of heat and moisture on the molecule structure and also on the scale structure. *Fulling, the process, should not be confused with felting, the property.*

Shaping of Wool Fabrics. Wool fabrics can be shaped by heat and moisture—a definite aid in tailoring. Puckers can be pressed out; and excess fabric can be eased and then pressed flat or rounded as desired. Pleats can be pressed into wool cloth with heat, steam, and pressure, but they will not last through washing.

> Hydrogen bonds are broken by moisture and heat so the wool structure can be re-shaped by the mechanical action of the iron or press. Simultaneously, the heat dries the wool and new hydrogen bonds are formed in the wool structure as the water escapes as steam. The new hydrogen bonds maintain the wool in the new shape so long as the humidity is low. In high humidity or if the wool is dampened with water, the new hydrogen bonds are broken and the molecular structure reverts to its former shape. This is why garments shaped by ironing lose their creases or flatness and show relaxation shrinkage on wetting.—"What Happens When Setting Wool," *Textile Industries,* **130** (October 1966): 344.

Permanent "set" can be achieved in much the same way and by chemicals similar to those used in the permanent waving of hair. The Si-Ro-Set finish, developed in Australia, uses the chemical ammonium thyglycollate. The fabric is sprayed or soaked with the chemical and then set as pleats or the like by steaming or steam pressing for a required period of time. During setting the cystine linkage splits between the two sulfur atoms and new linkages are formed.

Another finish that minimizes the effect of moisture in laundering is the Wurlan finish, developed by the Western Utilization Research and Development Laboratory at Albany, California. A polyamide-type solution is applied that forms a microscopic film on the surface of the scales and masks them.

Effect of Acids. Wool is generally resistant to mineral acids but will decompose in hot sulfuric acid. Acids are used in the manufacture of wool fabrics to remove cellulose impurities, such as leaves or burrs, that may still be in the fabric after weaving. This treatment is called *carbonizing* (see Chapter 34). Acids are also used to activate the salt bridges and thus make dye sites available to the dye.

Effect of Alkalis. Wool is very sensitive to the action of alkali. The alkali test can be used to

Fig. 3-9 Identifying wool fiber by the alkali test.

identify wool fiber, not only in 100 per cent wool fabrics but also in wool blends. The test is a simple one and can be done by the homemaker using lye, which can be purchased in any supermarket.

- Use a 5 per cent solution of lye.
- Heat to boiling 1 tablespoon of lye per pint of water in a glass or granite container.
- Immerse a strip of fabric or yarns (Figure 3–9).

The wool reacts to the alkali by turning yellow, then becoming slick and jellylike, and finally going into solution. If the fabric is a blend, the wool in the blend will disintegrate, leaving only the other fibers.

Mild alkalis—in warm or cool water—can be used in scouring the raw wool fibers to remove grease. Dry-cleaning solvents are also used for this purpose.

Effect of Organic Solvents. Wool has good resistance to dry-cleaning solvents.

Effect of Moths. Wool is attacked by moth larvae and other insects. The most effective way to prevent moth damage to wool is to alter the molecular structure of the fiber. The mothproofing process consists of chemically breaking the cystine linkage (—S—S—) and reforming it as —S—CH$_2$—S— (see Chapter 36).

Thermal Properties. Wool becomes weak and harsh at elevated temperatures, and it scorches

readily. Wool fabrics should always be pressed with moist heat. Wool is weakened by strong sunlight.

Flammability. Wool burns very slowly and is self-extinguishing. It is normally regarded as flame-resistant. For curtains, carpets, and upholstery to be used in trains, planes, ships, hotels, and other public buildings, wool is often given a flame-retardant finish.

When wool burns, it gives off only moderate amounts of smoke and carbon monoxide and is a minor impediment to evacuation from the site of a fire as compared to other materials that are likely to be present. The temporary resistance to burning of wool may be increased by the use of phosphates or borates. Durable fire-retardant effects can be obtained by the use of small amounts of a variety of protective compounds with little detectable change in the physical or chemical behavior of the wool fiber.

Care of Wool Fabrics

Wool does not soil readily and the removal of soil from wool is relatively simple. Grease and oils do not spot wool fabrics as readily as they do fabrics made of other fibers. (Wool in its natural state is about 25 per cent grease). *Dry cleaning is preferable* for cleaning wool.

Laundering of wool fabrics should be done with care to prevent fuzzing and shrinkage. Mild alkalis, soaps, and detergents used in home laundry cause little if any damage, if heat and agitation are kept at a minimum.

- Avoid: chlorine bleach
    agitation
    alkali
    hot water (warm or cool water can be used).

Machine-washable wools are available in sweaters, blankets, hand-knitting yarns, and fabrics for home sewing. Wool garments are labeled with permanently attached care instructions. Care instruction labels are available for wool fabrics on request.

Use a good brush on collars and the inside of cuffs after each wearing. A firm, soft brush not only removes dust but also gently lifts the fibers back to their natural springiness. Damp fabrics should be allowed to dry before brushing. Gar-

Goat Family	Camel Family	Others
Angora goat—mohair	Camel's hair	Angora rabbit—angora
Cashmere goat—cashmere	Llama	Fur fibers
	Alpaca	Musk ox—qiviut
	Vicuña	
	Guanaco	

ments should have a period of rest between wearings to recover from deformations. Baggy elbows and skirt seats will become less baggy as the garment rests. Hanging the garment over a tub of hot steamy water or spraying a fine mist of water on the cloth will speed up recovery.

If wool fabrics become shiny from pressure, sponge with a 5 per cent solution of white vinegar. Then steam, and the fibers will swell and become fluffier. If surface fibers wear off, use fine sandpaper to restore the nap. Fine sandpaper will also remove *light* scorch.

Unless *mothproofed,* wool fabrics should be stored so that they will not be accessible to moths. Moth larvae will also eat, but not digest, any fiber that is blended with wool. Wool fabrics should be cleaned before storage and should be stored with moth crystals in a closed container.

Specialty Hair Fibers

Most specialty wools are obtained from the goat, rabbit, and camel families.

Specialty wools are available in smaller quantities than sheep's wool so they are usually more expensive. Like all natural fibers, wools vary in quality. Figure 3–10 is the quality symbol used on all mohair products that meet performance standards established by the Mohair Council.

Specialty wool fibers are of two kinds: the coarse, long outer hair and the soft, fine undercoat. Coarse fibers are used for interlinings, upholstery, and some coatings; the very fine fibers are used in luxury coatings, sweaters, shawls, suits, and dress fabrics.

Mohair

Mohair, the fiber of the Angora goat, is produced in Turkey, South Africa, and the United States. Texas is the largest producer of mohair. The goats (Figure 3-11) are sheared twice a year, in the early fall and early spring. The fiber length is

- 4 to 6 inches for half a year
- 8 to 12 inches for a full year.

Mohair fibers have a circular cross section. Scales on the surface are scarcely visible and the cortical cells show through as lengthwise striations (Figure 3-12). There are some air ducts between the cells that give mohair its lightness and fluffiness. Few of the fibers have a medulla.

Mohair is one of the most resilient fibers and

Fig. 3-10 Mohair symbol of quality.

Fig. 3-11 Angora goats. (*Courtesy of the Mohair Council of America.*)

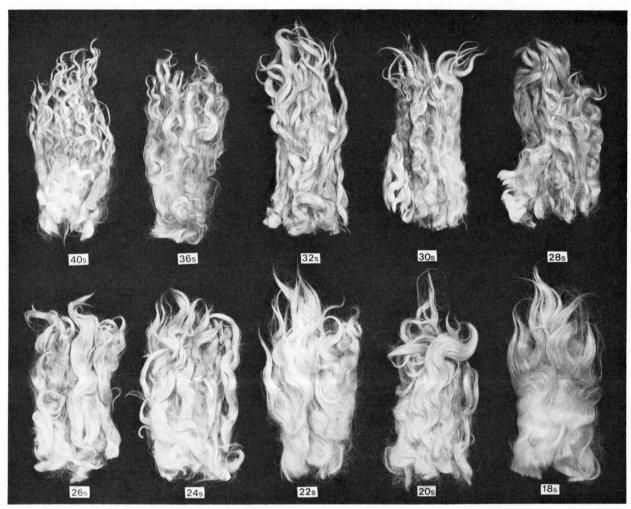

Fig. 3-12 Grades of mohair fibers used to make different size yarns. Higher numbers refer to finer yarns. (*Courtesy of the Mohair Council of America.*)

has none of the crimp found in sheep's wool, giving it a silklike luster and a smoother surface that is more resistant to dust than wool. (Figure 3-13). Mohair is very strong and has good affinity to dye. The washed fleece is a lustrous white.

Chemical properties are the same as those of wool. Mohair makes a better novelty *loop* yarn than wool or the other specialty hair fibers.

- Uses of mohair: Upholstery and draperies
  Men's suitings
  Bouclé coatings for women
  Pile fabrics; embossed and curled like fur
  Laces
  Wigs and hairpieces
  Oriental-type rugs.

Qiviut

Qiviut, a rare and luxurious fiber, is the underwool of the domesticated musk ox. Successful domestication projects have been conducted in Alaska. A large musk ox will provide 6 pounds of wool each year. The fiber can be used just as it comes from the animal, for it is protected from debris by the long guard hairs and has a low lanolin content. The fleece is not shorn but is shed naturally and is removed from the guard hairs as soon as it becomes visible. The price initially was $35 to $50 per pound.

Eskimo women have been taught the art of hand knitting with qiviut. Their first products were lacy scarves with designs taken from the Eskimo artifacts, and each pattern is identified with a particular village.

PROTEIN FIBERS AND WOOL 29

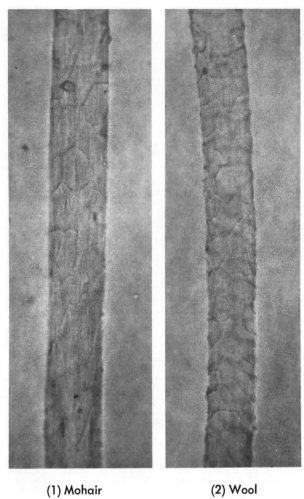

(1) Mohair   (2) Wool

Fig. 3-13 Microscopic view of mohair and wool.

Cashmere

Cashmere comes from a small goat raised in Kashmir, China, Tibet, and Mongolia. The fibers vary in color from white to gray to brownish gray. The goat has an outer coat of long coarse hair and an inner coat of down. The hair is combed by hand from the animal during the molting season, and care is taken to separate the coarse hair from the fine fibers. Only a small part of the fleece is the very fine fiber, probably not more than $\frac{1}{4}$ pound per goat. Cashmere is used in high-quality apparel. Fabrics are warm, buttery in hand, and have beautiful draping characteristics. Cashmere is more sensitive to chemicals than wool.

Camel's Hair

Camel's hair is obtained from the two-hump Bactrian camel of Mongolia and Tibet. It is said to have the best insulation of any of the wool fibers, since it keeps the camel comfortable under extreme conditions of temperature during a day's journey through the cold mountain passes and the hot valleys. The hair is collected by a "trailer" who follows the camel caravan and picks up the hair as it is shed and places it in a basket carried by the last camel. The trailer also gathers the hair in the morning, at the spot where the camels lay down for the night.

Because the camel's hair gives warmth without weight, the finer fibers are much prized for clothing fabrics. They are often used in blends with sheep's wool, which is dyed the tan color of camel's hair.

There are so many qualities of cashmere and camel's hair that care should be taken by the consumer to determine the quality of fiber he is buying. The best way to judge the quality is by the feel. Consumers should be guided by the reputation of the manufacturer or retailer.

Llama and Alpaca

Llama and Alpaca are domesticated animals of the South American branch of the camel family. The fiber is 8 to 12 inches in length and is noted for its softness, fineness, and luster. The natural colors are white, light fawn, light brown, dark brown, gray, black, and piebald.

Vicuña and Guanaco

Vicuña and guanaco are wild animals of the South American camel family. They are very rare, and the animals must be killed to obtain the fiber. Vicuña is the softest, finest, rarest, and most expensive of all textile fibers. The fiber is short, very lustrous, and a light cinnamon color.

Angora

Angora is the hair of the Angora rabbit, which is raised in France and in small amounts in the United States. Each rabbit produces only a few ounces of fiber, which is very fine, fluffy, soft, slippery, and fairly long. It is pure white in color.

Silk

4

Silk culture, according to Chinese legend, began in 2640 B.C. when a Chinese Empress Si-Ling-Chi became interested in silkworms and learned how to reel the silk and make it into fabric. It was through her efforts that China developed a silk industry that was monopolized by China for 3,000 years. Sericulture spread to Korea, to Japan, westward to India, and then finally to Spain and Italy. Silk fabrics, imported from China, were coveted by other countries; in India the fabrics were often picked out and rewoven into looser fabrics or combined with linen to provide more yardage from the same amount of silk filament. In 1975 the United States imported two thirds of its silk from the Peoples' Republic of China and one third from Brazil.

Silk is universally accepted as a luxury fiber. The International Silk Association of the United States emphasizes the uniqueness of silk by its slogan "only silk is silk." Silk has a unique combination of properties not possessed by any other fiber:

- "Dry" tactile hand
- Natural luster
- Good moisture absorption
- Lively suppleness and draping qualities
- High strength

In 1972, the cost of silk was approximately $5 per pound and silk made up only 0.2 per cent of the world consumption of fibers. See the chart on page 20 for consumption of silk in the United States.

The beauty and hand of silk and its high cost are probably responsible for the man-made fiber industry. In the early days there was no scarcity of other natural fibers and thus no need to try to duplicate them. Silk, being a solid fiber, was fairly easy to duplicate.

Production

Sericulture is the name given to the production of *cultivated* silk, which begins with the silk moth, which lays eggs on specially prepared paper. When the eggs hatch, the worms are fed on fresh, young mulberry leaves. After about 35 days the silkworms are about ten thousand times as heavy as when they were born, and they are full of liquid silk. Twigs or straw are placed on the feeding trays and the silkworms start to spin their

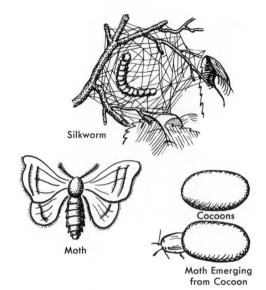

Fig. 4-1 Silkworm, moth, and cocoon.

cocoons. The silk is forced from two glands through a common orifice in the head. The two silk filaments are surrounded by a gummy substance called sericin. In 2 or 3 days the silkworm has spun out about 1 mile of filament and completely surrounded itself in a cocoon. It then begins to change into a chrysalis and then to a moth. The moth secretes a fluid that dissolves the silk at one end to permit the moth to crawl out (Figure 4–1).

To obtain filament silk, the chrysalis must be killed before it changes to a moth. The cocoon is boiled to kill the larvae and soften the sericin. After boiling, the cocoons are brushed to find the outside ends of the filaments and then several filaments are reeled to make a skein of yarn (Figure 4–2). Each cocoon yields about 1,000 yards of filament. This is *raw-silk* or *silk-in-the-gum*. Much usable silk is not reeled. Broken filaments, silk from cocoons in which the moths were al-

Fig. 4-2 Winding silk filaments on a reel.

lowed to escape, and silk from the inner portion of the cocoons are called *waste silk*. This silk is degummed and spun as any other staple fiber.

Wild silk production is not controlled; instead, wild silkworms feed on oak leaves and produce brown, orange, yellow, or green fibers. The moth cuts the filaments as it emerges from the cocoon, so that the fibers cannot be reeled but must be used as staple fibers for *spun silk*.

Tussah silk is a product of wild silkworms that are native to India and China.

Duppion silk comes from two silkworms who spin their cocoon together. The yarn is irregular in diameter and is used in linenlike silk fabrics for women's wear and men's suits.

Physical Structure

Silk is a natural continuous filament fiber. It is a solid fiber, smooth but irregular in diameter along its shaft. The filaments are triangular in cross section with rounded corners (Figure 4-3). Silk fibers are very fine—1.25 denier/filament.

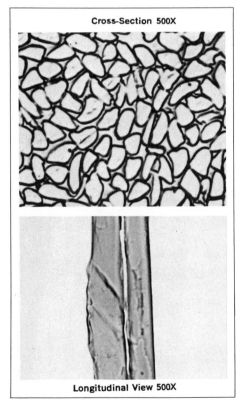

Cross-Section 500X

Longitudinal View 500X

Fig. 4-3 Photomicrograph of silk fiber: (*top*) cross-sectional view; (*bottom*) longitudinal view. (*Courtesy of American Association of Textile Chemists and Colorists.*)

Chemical Composition and Molecular Structure

Silk fibroin contains CHON in polypeptide chains. Silk has reactive amino (NH_2) and carboxyl (COOH) groups. The molecular chains are not folded as in wool, but are almost fully extended and packed closely together. As with all fibers, there are some amorphous areas between the crystalline areas.

Properties

Aesthetic Properties. Silk has a soft luster—the model for man-made filaments. Fabrics are usually smooth and have a luxurious hand.

Durability Properties. Silk is a strong fiber with a tenacity ranging from 3.5–5.0 g/d dry. It loses some strength when it is wet.

The density of silk is 1.25 g/cc. In filament form it does not have good covering power. Before the development of nylon, silk was the only strong filament and silk fabrics were often weighted to make them feel heavier. Silk will readily absorb metallic salts. Weighted silk is not as durable as regular silk and wrinkles more readily. In 1923 the Federal Trade Commission ruled that silk with more than 10 per cent weighting (15 per cent in black) could not be labeled *Pure dye silk*. It is doubtful that any silk is weighted today.

Silk has a breaking *elongation* of 20 per cent. It is not as elastic as wool, and since there are no cross-linkages to pull back the molecular chains, silk does not regain its original length.

Comfort Properties. Silk has good *absorbency* with a moisture regain of 11 per cent and like wool it is hygroscopic. This makes silk fabrics comfortable in summer in skin contact apparel. Silk, like wool, is a poor conductor of heat so that silk scarves and raw silk suitings are comfortably warm. The weight of a fabric is important in heat conductivity—sheer fabrics, possible with filament silk, will be cool whereas heavy suiting fabrics will be warm.

Silk is smooth and soft and is thus not irritating to the skin.

Care Properties. Silk fibers do not *shrink*. They swell a bit when wet but the molecular chains are not easily distorted. Crepe fabrics will shrink if washed but this is the result of yarn structure not fiber content.

Silk fabrics do not soil readily because of the smoothness of the fibers. Silk is harmed less by strong *alkalis* than is wool. Tussah silk is very resistant to alkalis. Weak alkalis do little damage to silk but concentrated alkalis destroy the luster and cause some fiber damage. Bleaches should be avoided.

Dry cleaning is usually recommended for silk garments because of the yarn structure or non-fast colors, or because the manufacturer assumes that the consumer wants to dry-clean expensive garments. Some silk garments can be laundered in mild detergent with gentle agitation. They must be pressed after washing. After washing, pure dye silks should be ironed damp under a press cloth. Wild silks should be ironed dry.

Silk is resistant to dilute acids and to organic acids. *Scroop*, a peculiar noise made by silk when it is crushed or moved, is produced by treatment with dilute organic acids, which are thought to have a surface-hardening effect. Scroop is not a sign of quality. Other effects, such as crepelike surfaces, may be created by the shrinking action of some acids.

Silk is sensitive to *sunlight*, which causes white silk to yellow and all silk to lose strength. Upholstery and drapery fabrics should be protected from direct exposure to light. White silk fabrics have a tendency to yellow with age. Weighted silks deteriorate even under good storage conditions because they break at folds.

Silk burns like other proteins (see page 16). Silk fabrics are damaged by perspiration.

Natural Cellulose Fibers and Cotton

5

All plants are fibrous. The fiber bundles of plants give strength and pliability to their stems, leaves, and roots. Textile fibers are obtained from those plants in which the fibers can be readily separated from the materials surrounding them.

Natural cellulose fibers are classified according to the portion of the plant from which they come (see chart).

Natural Cellulose Fibers

Seed Hairs	Bast Fibers	Leaf Fibers*
Cotton	Flax	Abaca (Manila hemp)
Coir (coconut)*	Hemp	Piña (pineapple)
Kapok*	Jute	Sisal
Milkweed*	Ramie	Raffia
*Not discussed in text.		

Regenerated cellulose fibers (rayon) are made by dissolving and then resolidifying natural cellulose from pine trees or cotton linters.

Fibers differ in physical structure but are alike in chemical composition. The arrangement of the molecular chains in fibers, although similar, vary in orientation and length. Fabrics made from these fibers will thus have different appearances and hand but will react to chemicals in essentially the same way and will require essentially the same care.

Cellulose Structure

The basic unit of the cellulose molecule is the *glucose unit,* which is the same for both natural and regenerated fibers. The glucose unit is made up of the chemical elements carbon, hydrogen, and oxygen.

Chemical Nature of Cellulose

The chemical reactivity of cellulose is related to the three hydroxyl groups (OH groups) of the glucose unit. These groups react readily with moisture, dyes, and special finishes. Chemicals such as bleaches that cause a breakdown of the molecular chain of the cellulose usually attack the oxygen atom and cause a rupture there.

The cellulose molecule is a long linear chain of glucose units. The length of the chain is a factor in fiber strength.

Natural and regenerated cellulose differ in the length of the molecular chain.

Cellulose Source	Length of Chain
Cotton	1000(+)
Pine tree cellulose	700–800
Regular rayon	300–450
High-wet-modulus rayon	450–600
High-wet-modulus polynosic rayon	550–750

Cellulose Fibers: Properties

Properties Common to All Cellulose Fibers

Properties	Importance to Consumer
Good absorbency	Comfortable for summer wear
	Good for towels, diapers, and handkerchiefs
Good conductor of heat	Sheer fabrics cool for summer wear
Ability to withstand high temperature	Fabrics can be boiled or autoclaved to make relatively germ free. No special precautions in ironing

Properties Common to All Cellulose Fibers (Cont.)

Properties	Importance to Consumer
Low resiliency	Fabrics wrinkle badly unless finished for recovery
Lacks loft. Packs well into compact yarns	Yarns can be creped. Tight, high-count fabrics can be made Makes wind-resistant fabrics
Good conductor of electricity	Does not build up static
High density (1.5±)	Fabrics feel heavier than comparable fabrics of other fiber content
Harmed by mineral acids, but little affected by organic acids	Fruit stains should be removed immediately from a garment to prevent setting
Resistant to moths	Storage problem is simplified
Attacked by fungi	Soiled garments should not be put away damp
Flammability	Cellulose fibers ignite quickly, burn freely, have an afterglow and gray feathery ash. Filmy or loosely constructed garments should not be worn near an open flame
Moderate resistance to sunlight	Draperies should be lined

Cotton

Cotton is the most widely used of the textile fibers. In 1976, the mill consumption of all man-made fibers was 8,081.4 thousand metric tons, whereas that of cotton alone was 3,389 thousand metric tons.

Cotton has a combination of properties—durability, low cost, easy washability, and comfort—that have made it desirable for summer clothes, work clothes, towels, and sheets. This unique combination of properties has made cotton a standard for great masses of the world's people who live in warm and subtropical climates. Even

though the man-made fibers have encroached on the markets that were once dominated by 100 per cent cotton fabrics, the cotton-look is still maintained and cotton forms up to 65 per cent of the fibers in fiber blend fabrics.

Cotton cloth was used by the people of ancient China, Egypt, India, and Peru. Fabrics of cloth from Egypt give some evidence that cotton may have been used there in 12,000 B.C., before flax was known. Cotton spinning and weaving as an industry began in India, and fabrics of good quality cotton cloth were being produced as early as 1500 B.C. The Pima Indians were growing cotton when the Spaniards came to the New World. One of the items that Columbus took back to Queen Isabella was a hank of cotton yarn.

The United States did not enter the world markets for cotton until 1800. Cotton was grown in the Southern colonies as soon as they were established, but until Eli Whitney invented the sawtooth cotton gin in 1793, cotton fibers had to be separated from the seeds by hand—a very time-consuming and laborious job.

Production

Cotton grows in any part of the world where the growing season is long. The United States, China, and Russia lead in cotton production. Cellulose will not form if the temperature is below 70°F. Cotton grows on bushes 3 to 6 feet high. The blossom appears, falls off, and the *boll* begins its growth. Inside the boll are seeds from which the fibers grow. When the boll is ripe, it splits open and the fluffy white fibers stand out like a powder puff (a boll contains seven or eight seeds) (Figure 5-1). Each cotton seed may have as many as 20,000 fibers growing from its surface.

Fig. 5-1 Opened cotton boll. (*Courtesy of Cotton, Inc.*)

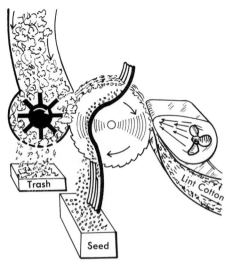

Fig. 5-2 Cotton gin.

Cotton is picked by hand or by machine. Machine-picked cotton contains many immature fibers—an inescapable result of stripping a cotton plant. However, mechanization and weed control have reduced the number of man-hours required to produce a bale of cotton. After picking, the cotton is taken to a *gin* to remove the fibers from the seed. Figure 5-2 shows a saw gin, in which the whirling saws pick up the fiber and carry it to a knifelike comb, which blocks the seeds and permits the fiber to be carried through.

The fibers, called *lint,* are pressed into bales weighing 500 pounds, ready for sale to a spinning mill. The average yield is $2\frac{1}{2}$ bales per acre. However, Arizona, the state with the largest production per acre, has produced as much as 5 bales per acre. The seeds, after ginning, look like the buds of the pussywillow. They are covered with very short fibers—$\frac{1}{8}$ inch in length—called *linters.* The linters are removed from the seeds and are used to a limited extent as raw material for the making of rayon and acetate. The seeds are crushed to obtain cottonseed oil and meal.

Physical Structure

Raw cotton is creamy white in color. The fiber is a single cell, which, during growth, pushes out of the seed as a hollow cylindrical tube over one thousand times as long as it is thick.

The *quality* of cotton depends on the staple length, the number of convolutions, and the brightness of the fiber.

Length. Cotton fibers range from $\frac{1}{2}$ to 2 inches in length, depending on the variety. There has been a decline in the use of the shorter staple; most production is now a medium-long staple, $1\frac{1}{32}$ to $1\frac{2}{32}$ inches. The more specialized long staple cottons, such as the Sea Island cottons, have disappeared completely. The finest varieties now are from the Pima strain, which was developed by cross-breeding the American cotton, grown by the Pima Indians, with Egyptian cotton.

- Long staple—over $1\frac{1}{8}$ inches
  Pima and Supima varieties
- Short staple—under $1\frac{1}{8}$ inches
  Upland varieties such as Acala and Deltapine.

Convolutions. *Convolutions* or ribbonlike twists characterize the cotton fibers (Figure 5-3). When the fibers mature, the boll opens, the fibers dry out, and the central canal collapses; reverse spirals cause the fibers to twist. The twist forms a natural crimp that enables the fibers to cohere to one another, so that despite its short length, cotton is one of the most spinnable fibers. The convolutions can be a disadvantage, since dirt collects in the twists and must be removed by vigorous washing. Long-staple cotton has about 300 convolutions per inch; short-staple cotton has less than 200.

Width. Cotton fibers vary from 16 to 20 microns in diameter. The cross-sectional shape varies with the maturity of the fiber. Immature fibers tend to be U-shaped and the cell wall is thinner; mature fibers are more nearly circular, with a very small central canal. In every cotton boll there are immature fibers. The proportion of immature to mature fibers cause problems in processing, especially in spinning and dyeing. Notice in the photomicrograph the difference in size and shape.

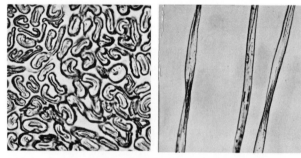

Fig. 5-3 Photomicrograph of cotton: (*left*) cross-sectional view; (*right*) longitudinal view. (*Courtesy of American Association of Textile Chemists and Colorists.*)

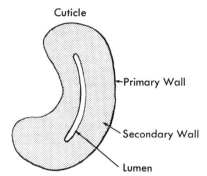

Fig. 5-4 Cross section of mature cotton fiber.

Distinctive Parts. The cotton fiber is made up of a cuticle, primary wall, secondary wall, and lumen (Figure 5-4). The fiber grows to almost full length as a hollow tube before the secondary wall begins to form.

The *cuticle* is a waxlike film covering the primary or outer wall. The *secondary wall* is made up of layers of cellulose (Figure 5-5). The layers deposited at night differ in density from those deposited during the day; this causes *growth rings,* which can be seen in the cross section. The cellulose layers are composed of *fibrils*—bundles of cellulose chains—arranged spirally. At some points the fibrils reverse direction. These *reverse spirals* (Figure 5-6) are an important factor in the twist, elastic recovery, and elongation of the fiber. They are also the weak spots, being 15 to 30 per

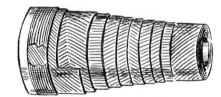

Fig. 5-5 Layers of cellulose (schematic).

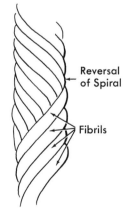

Fig. 5-6 Reverse spirals in cotton fiber.

cent weaker than the rest. It is believed that if these reversals could be strengthened, cotton would stage a comeback in 100 per cent durable-press garments. Cellulose is deposited daily for 20 to 30 days until, in the mature fiber, the fiber tube is almost filled.

The *lumen* is the central canal, through which the nourishment travels during growth. When the fiber matures, the dried nutrients in the lumen give the characteristic dark areas that can be seen with the microscope.

Chemical Composition and Molecular Arrangement

Cotton, when picked, is about 94 per cent cellulose; in finished fabrics it is 99 per cent cellulose. Like all cellulose fibers cotton contains carbon, hydrogen, and oxygen with reactive hydroxyl (OH) groups. Cotton has 2,000–12,000 glucose residues per molecule. The molecular chains are in spiral form.

Properties

Aesthetic. No fiber in itself is beautiful but the beauty of fabrics is partly the result of the physical structure of the fibers, and beauty is "in the eye of the beholder." Cotton fabrics certainly have consumer acceptance. The soft sheer batistes, the fine muslins, the sturdy denims and corduroys have influenced fashion for years.

Durability. Cotton is a *medium strength* fiber having a breaking tenacity of 3.5–4.0 g/d. It is stronger when wet. Long staple cotton makes stronger yarns because there are more points of contact between the fibers when they are twisted together. Cotton can stand rough handling during laundry. The *elongation* of cotton is low, 3 per cent, and it has low elasticity, making it a rigid fiber.

Comfort. Cotton makes very comfortable skin-contact fabrics because of its *absorbency* and its *good* heat and electrical *conductivity*. It is lacking in any surface characteristics which might be irritating to the skin. Cotton has a moisture regain of 7 per cent. When cotton becomes wet, the fibers swell and become somewhat plastic. This property makes it possible to give a smooth, flat finish to cotton fabrics when they are ironed, and makes high count woven fabrics water repellent.

Care. Cotton fibers are *stable.* They do shorten a bit when wet but on drying their original length is restored. Shrinkage of cotton fabrics is not the result of any property of the fibers but rather is a result of the finishing of the fabric.

Cotton is harmed by *acids.* It is not greatly harmed by *alkalis.* Cotton can be washed with strong detergents and under proper conditions it will withstand chlorine bleaches. Cotton is resistant to *organic solvents* so that it can be safely dry-cleaned. Cotton is attacked by *fungi* especially in starched fabrics.

Cotton oxidizes in sunlight, which causes white and pastel cottons to yellow and all cotton to degrade. Some yellow dyes are especially sensitive to sunlight and when used in curtain fabrics the dyed areas disintegrate.

Cotton is not thermoplastic. It can safely be ironed at high temperatures. Cotton burns readily.

Cotton has very low resiliency. The hydrogen bonds holding the molecular chains together are weak and when fabrics are bent or crushed, particularly in the presence of moisture, the chains move freely to new positions. When pressure is removed, there are no forces within the fibers to pull the chains back to their original positions so the fabrics stay wrinkled. Creases can be ironed in easily, and wrinkles can be pressed out easily, but wrinkling while wearing remains a problem. The use of crease resistant finishes or blending with polyester has largely overcome this disadvantage of cotton.

Mercerized Cotton

John Mercer, using a cotton cloth to filter a sodium hydroxide (NaOH) solution, noticed that the cloth was changed during the process. He demonstrated the beneficial effects of caustic soda on cotton and from that time (1844) on,

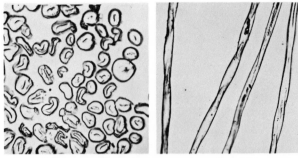

Fig. 5-7 Photomicrograph of mercerized cotton: (*left*) cross-sectional view; (*right*) longitudinal view. (*Courtesy of American Association of Textile Chemists and Colorists.*)

mercerization of cotton has been a common finish for yarns and fabrics (see Chapter 34). Mercerization (treating yarns or fabrics with NaOH) causes a physical change in the fiber. The fibers swell, becoming more rodlike and rounder in cross section, and the number of convolutions decreases (Figure 5-7).

The effects of mercerization are:

- *Increased strength* to the fibers. The molecular chains are no longer in spiral form and are more oriented in length making the fibers 30 per cent stronger.

- *Increased absorbency* because of the swelling of the fiber. This opens up the molecular structure so that more moisture can be absorbed. The moisture regain is 11 per cent. Mercerization is done primarily to improve the dyeability of cotton yarns and fabrics.

- *Increased luster* because the fibers become rounder with fewer convolutions and thus reflect more light. Mercerization for luster is done under tension and on long staple cotton yarns and fabrics.

Flax and Other Bast Fibers

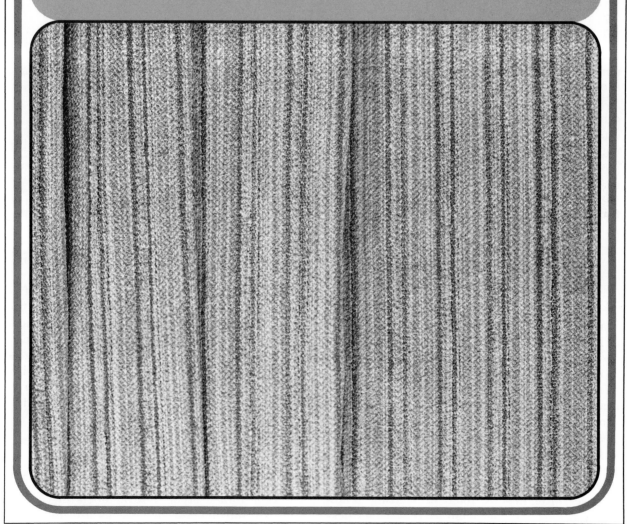

Flax and jute are the most important bast fibers; hemp and ramie are less commonly used.

Bast fibers come from the stem of the plant. Hard labor is required to process bast fibers, so that production of these fibers has flourished in countries where labor is cheap. Complete mechanization in the production of bast fibers has yet to be achieved. Harvesting is done by pulling or cutting the plants. Flax is usually pulled either by hand or by machine. After harvesting, the seeds are removed from the plants.

Bast fibers lie in bundles in the stem of the plant just under the outer covering or bark. They are sealed together by a substance composed of pectins, waxes, and gums. To loosen the fibers so that they can be removed from the stalk, the pectin must be decomposed by a process called *retting* (bacterial rotting). There are some individual fiber differences in the process, but the major steps are the same. Retting is done in the fields (dew retting), in streams, or in large retting tanks, where the temperature and bacterial count can be carefully controlled.

After the plants are dried, the woody portion is removed by *breaking or scutching*. Figure 6–1 shows flax at different stages of processing.

Most of the fibers are separated from one another and the short fibers are removed by *hackling or combing*. The processes of spinning, weaving, and finishing cause further separation of the fibers; however, some fibers still cling together, and this gives the characteristic thick-and-thin yarn that is associated with the uneven linenlike texture in some fabrics made of bast fibers.

Flax

Flax is one of the oldest textile fibers. Fragments of linen fabric were found in the prehistoric lake dwellings in Switzerland; linen mummy cloths, more than 4,500 years old, were found in Egyptian tombs. The linen industry flourished in Europe until the eighteenth century. With the invention of power spinning, cotton replaced flax as the most important and widely used fiber.

Flax is a *prestige fiber* as a result of its limited production and relatively high cost. The term *linen* refers to cloth made from flax. This term is, however, often misused today in referring to fabrics that look like linen—fabrics that have thick-

Fig. 6–1 Flax fiber at different stages of processing.

and-thin yarns and are fairly heavy or crisp. The term *Irish linen* always refers to fabrics made from flax. (The former use of flax in sheets, tablecloths, and towels has given us the term *linen* to describe textile items—for example, bed linens and table linens.)

The unique and desirable characteristics of flax are its body, strength, and thick-and-thin fiber bundles, which give texture to fabrics. The main limitations of flax are low resiliency and lack of elasticity. Most dress and suiting linens are given wrinkle-resistant finishes. In 1977, one fashion emphasis was a "return to the naturals." In the advertisements for blouses and dresses made of handkerchief linen, wrinkling was stressed as a desirable feature.

Structure

Flax is unlike other natural fibers in that the length and fineness dimensions are not clearly

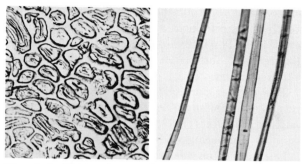

Fig. 6-2 Photomicrograph of flax: (*left*) cross-sectional view; (*right*) longitudinal view. (*Courtesy of Du Pont Company.*)

definable. The primary fibers, which average 0.5 to 2.15 inches in length and a few microns in diameter, are bound together in fiber bundles and are never completely separated into individual fibers. Flax fiber, as commonly used, is made up of many primary fibers.

Flax fibers can be identified under the microscope by crosswise markings called *nodes* or *joints* (Figure 6–2). The markings on flax have been attributed to cracks or breaks during harvesting, or to irregularity in growth. The fibers may appear slightly swollen at the nodes and resemble somewhat the joints in a stalk of corn. The fibers have a small central canal similar to the lumen in cotton. The cross section (Figure 6–2) is several-sided or polygonal with rounded edges.

Flax fibers are grayish in color when dew retted, and yellowish in color when water retted. Flax has a more highly oriented molecular structure than cotton, and is, therefore, stronger than the cotton fiber.

Short flax fibers are called *tow,* and the long, combed, better-quality fibers are called *line.* Line fibers are ready for spinning into yarn. The short *tow* fibers must be carded to prepare them for spinning into yarns that are used in less expensive fabrics. (Flax accounts for a relatively small amount of textile fiber consumption.)

Properties

Aesthetic. The thick-and-thin yarns in dress linens give an attractive appearance to fabrics. Fine handkerchief and table linens have smoothness and soft luster. Good quality linen damask tablecloths have become collector's items.

Durability. Flax is a strong fiber having a breaking tenacity of 5.5 g/d when dry and 6.5 g/d when wet. Linen thread was once used to sew shoes. Flax has low elasticity and flexibility. Linen fabrics are more likely to wear out when ironed repeatedly on the same folds. To make linens last longer, avoid pressing creases in them. For example, iron linen napkins flat, then fold into desired shape, but do not press.

Comfort. Flax has a moisture regain of 12 per cent and has no static buildup. It is a good conductor of heat.

Care. Flax is resistant to alkalis and to organic solvents. It is also resistant to high temperatures. Linen fabrics can be dry-cleaned or washed without special care and bleached with chlorine bleaches. Linen fabrics have very low resiliency and require ironing after washing. Linen fabrics are more resistant to sunlight than cotton.

Ramie

Ramie, or grasscloth, has been used for several thousand years in China. It is grown in areas that have a hot humid climate. In the United States ramie is grown in the Everglades region of Florida.

When seen under the microscope, ramie is very similar to flax fiber. It is pure white. It is one of the strongest fibers known and its strength increases when it is wet. It has silklike luster. Ramie also has a very high resistance to rotting, mildew, and other organisms.

Ramie has some disadvantages. It is stiff and brittle, owing to the high crystallinity of its molecular structure. Consequently, it lacks resiliency and is low in elasticity. Ramie breaks if folded repeatedly in the same place.

Ramie is used in fabrics resembling linen, such as suitings, shirtings, tablecloths, napkins, and handkerchiefs.

Hemp

The history of hemp is as old as that of flax. Because hemp lacks the fineness of better quality flax, it has never been able to compete with flax for clothing. Some varieties of hemp are, however, very difficult to distinguish from flax.

The high strength of hemp makes it particularly suitable for twine, cordage, and thread for stitching the soles on soldier's shoes. After World War II, the demand for hemp declined; it is now one of the less important fibers.

Jute

Jute was known as a fiber in biblical times. Jute is the cheapest textile fiber and is the second most widely used vegetable fiber, ranking next to cotton. India and Pakistan are the principal producers of jute. The individual fibers in the jute bundle are short and brittle. It is the weakest of the cellulose fibers.

The greater part of the jute production goes into bagging for sugar, coffee, or is used in carpet backing, rope, cordage, and twine. Olefin fibers are now competing with jute in these areas.

Burlap is often a fashion fabric for apparel and decorative home furnishings. Chemical finishes can be used to overcome the natural odor of jute and to make it softer. Jute has low sunlight resistance and poor color fastness. It is also brittle and subject to splitting and snagging.

Introduction to Man-Made Fibers

7

In the seventeenth century a scientist named Hooke suggested that if a proper liquid were squirted through a small aperture and allowed to congeal, a fiber like that of the silkworm might be produced. Almost 300 years later, the first successful fiber was made from a solution of cellulose by a Frenchman, Count de Chardonnet. In 1910 rayon fibers were commercially produced in the United States, and acetate was produced in 1925. By 1940 the first noncellulosic or synthetic fiber, nylon, was made. During the next 30 years, 18 more generic fibers and many modifications or variants appeared on the market. The increasing number of new fiber names appearing on labels has created a great deal of confusion for the consumer.

Man-Made Fibers			*Generic Names*
Cellulosic	*Noncellulosic or Synthetic*		*Mineral*
Acetate	Acrylic	Nytril*	Glass
(Triacetate)	Anidex*	Olefin	Metallic
Rayon	Aramid	Polyester	
	Azlon*	Rubber	
	Lastrile*	Saran	
	Modacrylic	Spandex	
	Novoloid	Vinal*	
	Nylon	Vinyon*	

*Not produced in the United States.

Legislation and Generic Names

In 1958, Congress passed legislation to regulate labeling of textiles in order to protect the consumer through the enforcement of ethical practices and to protect the producer from unfair competition resulting from the unrevealed presence of substitute materials in textile products. This law, the Textile Fiber Product Identification Law, covers *all* fibers except as already covered by the Wool Products Labeling Act and with certain other exceptions.

Although the law was passed in 1958, it did not become effective until 1960. During this interval the Federal Trade Commission held hearings in regard to inequalities or injustices that the law might cause. Then it established rules and regulations to be observed in enforcing the law. The following list of man-made fiber generic names was established by the Federal Trade Commission in cooperation with the fiber producers. A *generic name* is the name of a family of fibers all having similar chemical composition. (Definitions of these generic names are included with the discussions of each fiber.)

The following information is required on the label for most textile items.

1. The *per cent* of each natural or man-made fiber present must be listed in the order of predominance by weight. Fibers representing less than 5 per cent cannot be named unless they have some constructive value.

2. The *name* of the manufacturer or his registered identification number. (Trademarks may serve as identification, but they are *not required* information.)

3. The first time a trademark appears in the *required* information, it must appear in immediate conjunction with the generic name and in type or lettering of equal size and conspicuousness. When the trademark is used elsewhere on the label, the generic name shall accompany it in legible and conspicuous type the *first* time it appears.

4. Country of origin.

Trade Names

The experimental fiber is given a trade name (trademark), which distinguishes the fiber from other fibers of the same generic family that are made and sold by other producers. A producer may adopt a single *trademark,* a word or symbol, which may be used to cover all (or a large group) of the fibers made by that company. For example, "Orlon" is no longer used to designate a single acrylic fiber made by Du Pont but is a broad descriptive name covering a family of related Du Pont acrylic fibers each of which is sold to the manufacturer by type number. Other examples are Monsanto's Blue C nylon and polyester quality products. Trademarks are also used for quality products and are protected by a quality-control program.

The fiber producer must assume all the responsibility for promoting his fiber. He must sell not only to his customers, the manufacturers and retailers, but to his customer's customer—the consumer.

Fiber Spinning

It took many years to develop the first spinning solutions and to devise spinnerets to convert the solutions into filaments. The first solutions were made by treating cellulose so it would dissolve in certain substances. It was not until the 1920s and 1930s that man first learned how to build long-chain molecules from simple substances.

All man-made fiber spinning processes are based on these three general steps.

1. Preparing a viscous or syrupy dope.

2. Extruding the dope through a spinneret to form a fiber.

3. Solidifying the fiber by coagulation, evaporation, or cooling.

The *raw material* may be a natural product such as cellulose or protein, or it may be chemicals that are synthesized into resins. These raw materials are made into solutions by dissolving them with chemicals or by melting. The solution is referred to as the *spinning solution or dope*.

Extrusion is a very important part of the spinning process. It consists of forcing or pumping the spinning solution through the tiny holes of a spinneret.

A *spinneret* is a small thimblelike nozzle (Figure 7-1). Rayon is spun through a spinneret that is made of platinum—one of the few metals that will withstand the action of acids and alkalies. Acetate and other fibers are extruded through stainless-steel spinnerets. Spinnerets are costly—as much as $1,000 each—and new developments are closely guarded secrets. The making of the tiny holes is the critical part of the process. Fine hairlike instruments or laser beams are used. Ordinarily the holes are round, but many other shapes are used for special fiber types (see page 8).

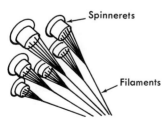

Fig. 7-1 Spinnerets. (*Courtesy of the American Viscose Division of FMC.*)

Fig. 7-2 Collecting fibers from several spinnerets to make a rope, called filament tow, which will be cut into staple fiber.

Each hole in the spinneret forms one fiber. *Filament fibers* are spun from spinnerets with 350 holes or less. Together these fibers make a filament yarn. *Filament tow* is an untwisted rope of thousands of fibers. This rope is made by putting together the fibers from 100 or more spinnerets, each of which may have as many as three thousand holes (Figure 7-2). This large rope of fibers is crimped and is then ready to be made into staple by cutting to the desired length. (See Chapter 18 for methods of breaking filament tow into staple.)

Spinning Methods. Spinning is done by three different methods. These methods are compared briefly in Figure 7-3. Details of the methods are given in later chapters.

Man-made fibers are produced to satisfy a market or to supply a special need. The first man-made fibers made it possible for the consumer to have silklike fabrics at low cost. The synthetics gave the consumer fabrics with improved properties unlike any natural fiber fabric.

The production program for a new fiber is long and expensive, and millions of dollars are invested before any profit can be realized. First, a research

Wet Spinning:
Acrylic, Rayon, Spandex

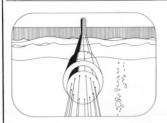

1. Raw material is dissolved by chemicals.
2. Fiber is spun into chemical bath.
3. Fiber solidifies when coagulated by bath.

Oldest process
Most complex
Weak fibers until dry
Washing, bleaching, etc., required before use

Dry Spinning:
Acetate, Acrylic, Modacrylic, Spandex,
Triacetate, Vinyon

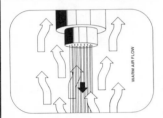

1. Resin solids are dissolved by solvent.
2. Fiber is spun into warm air.
3. Fiber solidifies by evaporation of the solvent.

Direct process
Solvent required
Solvent recovery required
No washing, etc., required

Melt Spinning:
Nylon, Olefin, Polyester, Saran

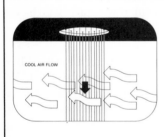

1. Resin solids are melted in autoclave.
2. Fiber is spun out into the air.
3. Fiber solidifies on cooling.

Least expensive
Direct process
High spinning speeds
No solvent, washing, etc., required
Fibers shaped like spinneret hole

Fig. 7-3. Drawings (*Courtesy of Man-Made Fiber Producers Association, Inc.*)

program is planned to develop the new fiber. Then a *pilot plant* is built to scale-up laboratory procedures to commercial production. This pilot plant may produce as much as 5 million pounds of fiber, which is used to test and evaluate the fiber and to determine and evaluate end uses. When the fiber is ready, a commercial plant is built.

A *patent* on the process gives the producer 17 years of exclusive right to the use of the process—time to recover the initial cost and make a profit. The price per pound during this time is high, but it drops later. The patent owner can license other producers to use the process. Con-

tinuing *research and developmental* programs correct any problems that arise and produce new fiber types modified for special end uses.

Common Fiber Modifications

When a man-made fiber is produced it supposedly has a combination of properties that makes it better for certain end uses than other fibers. If the fiber is successful, new end uses are sought for it. The disadvantages of the new fiber also become apparent and efforts are made to improve or modify it. Over the years the modifications of fibers become standard and although created for one fiber, these modifications are soon used by most fiber producers.

Modifications of the basic fiber are achieved by changing the spinning solution, altering the spinning conditions, or changing the processing after spinning.

Modifying the Spinning Solution

Delustering. The basic fiber is usually a *bright* fiber. It reflects light from its surface. To deluster a fiber, titanium dioxide—a white pigment—is added to the spinning solution before the fiber is extruded. In some cases, the titanium dioxide can be mixed in at an earlier stage, while the resin polymer is being formed. The degree of luster can be controlled by varying the amount of delusterant, producing dull or semidull fibers. Figure 7–4 shows three cones of yarn of different lusters.

Delustered fibers can be identified under the microscope by what appear to be peppery black spots (Figure 7–4). The particles of pigment absorb light or prevent reflection of light. Absorbed light causes degradation or "tendering" of the fiber. For this reason bright fibers that reflect

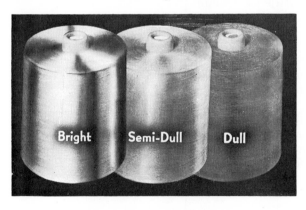

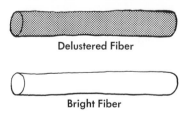

Delustered Fiber

Bright Fiber

Fig. 7-4 (*Top*) Bright, semi-dull, and dull rayon yarns. (*Courtesy of the American Viscose Division of FMC.*) (*Bottom*) A delustered fiber and bright fiber as they would look under a microscope.

light suffer less light damage and are better for use in curtains and draperies. The initial strength of a delustered fiber is less than that of a bright fiber. Rayon, for example, is 3 to 5 per cent weaker when it is delustered.

Solution Dyeing. Solution dyeing (pigmentation) was developed originally as an answer to the gas-fading of green, gray, or blue dyes used in acetate. It is the addition of colored pigments or certain dyes to the spinning solution or to the resin polymer. These fibers are referred to as solution-dyed, dope-dyed, spun-dyed, or producer-colored. Pigmentation provides color permanence that is not obtainable in any other way. The light stability and colorfastness to washing are unchanged for the life of the garment. Since the pigments are uniformly distributed throughout the fiber, crocking or change of color with wear is no problem.

Black is usually the first color to be used, and then other colors are produced as suitable fast-color pigments are developed. Solution-dyed fibers cost more per pound than uncolored fibers. This difference is offset later by the cost of dyeing yarns and fabrics. The colored fibers have been used in automotive upholstery, curtains, and in swimsuits that will be exposed to chlorine and/or salt water. One disadvantage of the fibers from the manufacturer's standpoint is that he must carry a large inventory to be able to fill orders quickly. He is also less able to adjust to fashion changes in color, because it is not possible to strip the color from these fibers and redye them.

Whiteners and Brighteners. Whiteners and brighteners are added to the spinning solution to make whiter fibers or fibers that resist yellowing. The additive used is an optical bleach or fluorescent dye that causes a whiter light to be reflected from the cloth. These whiteners are permanent to washing and dry cleaning. They are an advantage in foundation garments because they eliminate the necessity for bleaching. The fibers are used in white shirts, blouses, and the like. Blanc-de-Blanc is a trade name for whiter fibers produced by the Enka Company. Many of the fibers are sold by type number.

Other Modifications. Antistatic agents, flame retardants, and sunlight-resistant substances can be added to the spinning solution. The dye affinity of fibers also can be changed.

Modifications of Spinning Process

The size and shape of the spinneret holes can be varied to make filaments of different diameters and cross-sectional shapes. These modifications affect the hand and appearance of fabrics. In rug fibers the cross-sectional shape is changed to give the fibers improved soil-hiding properties.

Intermittent spinning (stretching and not stretching) is done to give a nonuniform diameter to filaments. This modification affects the texture of fabrics and gives interesting variations in dyeing.

Modifications after Spinning

Filament tow can be cut into any staple length. Cold drawing or stretching after spinning is done to most fibers to improve fiber strength.

Man-Made versus Natural Fibers

A comparison of natural and man-made fibers is made in the following chart.

Comparison of Natural and Man-Made Fibers

Natural	Man-Made
Produced seasonally and stored until used	Continuous production
Vary in quality because they are affected by weather, nutrients, insects, or disease	Uniform in quality
Lack uniformity	Uniform or made purposely nonuniform
Physical structure depends on natural growth of plant or animal	Physical structure depends on fiber-spinning processes and after treatments
Chemical composition and molecular structure depend on natural growth	Chemical composition and molecular structure depend on starting materials
Properties are inherent	Properties are inherent
Properties conferred on fabrics can be changed by yarn and fabric finishes	Properties of fibers can be changed by varying spinning solutions and spinning conditions
	Properties conferred on fabrics can be changed by fabric finishes
Only silk is available in filament	Fibers can be any length
Less versatile	Versatile, changes can be made more quickly
Fibers are absorbent	Most (rayon and acetate are exceptions) have low absorbency
Not heat sensitive	Most (rayon is the exception) are heat sensitive
Require fabric finish to be heat-set	Most (rayon and acetate are exceptions) can be heat-set
Research, development, and promotion done by trade organizations	Research, development, and promotion done by individual companies as well as trade organizations

Man-Made Fiber Capacity

In 1928, man-made fibers accounted for 5 per cent of textile fiber consumption in the United States; today, the man-made fibers comprise 70 per cent of textile consumption. Ninety-one per cent of our carpets and 81 per cent of our blankets are made of man-made fibers, and much of our apparel is made of or contains man-made fibers. The capacity for man-made fibers in the United States is listed in the following chart.

U.S. Man-Made Fiber Capacity in Millions of Pounds in 1977*

Fiber	Filament	Staple and Tow
Acetate	399	18
Acrylic	0	865
Glass	893	0
Nylon	1866	910
Olefin	861	120
Polyester	2159	2355
Rayon	85	691

*1977 Man-Made Fiber Deskbook *Modern Textiles* Magazine (March 1977).

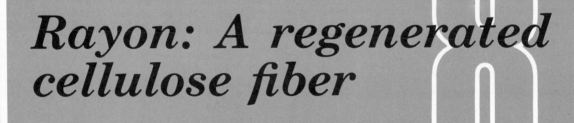

Rayon: A regenerated cellulose fiber

Rayon is a man-made cellulose fiber in which the starting material, wood pulp or cotton linters, is physically changed. Rayon, the first man-made fiber, was developed before scientists knew much about molecular chains—how they are built up in nature or how they can be built up in the laboratory. The developers of rayon were trying to make artificial silk. Three methods of manufacturing rayon were developed in Europe in the 1880s and 1890s.

Frederick Schoenbein discovered in 1846 that cellulose would dissolve in a mixture of ether and alcohol if it were first treated with nitric acid, but the resulting fiber was highly explosive.

In 1884, Count Hilaire de Chardonnet, in France, made the first successful rayon by changing the nitrocellulose fiber back to cellulose. This process was dangerous and difficult, and the nitrocellulose process has not been used anywhere in the world since 1949.

In 1890, Louis Despeissis discovered that cellulose would dissolve in a cuprammonium solution, and in 1919 J. P. Bemberg made a commercially successful cuprammonium rayon. It was produced in the United States from 1926 until 1976. In 1892 in England, Cross, Bevan, and Beadle developed the viscose method. This is the only process currently used in the United States.

Commercial production of viscose rayon in the United States started in 1911, and the fiber was sold as artificial silk until the name "rayon" was adopted in 1924. Viscose filament fiber, the first form of the fiber to be made, was a very bright, lustrous fiber. Because it had low strength, this fiber was used in the crosswise direction of the cloth; the lengthwise yarns were of silk, a fiber strong enough to withstand the tension of the loom. The double Godet wheel, invented in 1926, stretched the filaments and gave them strength (see page 47). Delustering agents, which were added to the spinning solution, made it possible to have dull as well as bright fibers. Solution-dyed fibers came later.

In 1932 machinery was designed especially for the making of staple fiber. Large spinnerets with ten times as many holes were used and the fibers from several spinnerets were collected as a rope called *tow*, which was then crimped and cut.

The first uses of rayon were in the clothing field, and its first success was in crepe and linen-like fabrics. The high twist that was required to make the crepe yarn reduced the bright luster of the fibers. "Transparent velvet" (made in France), sharkskin, tweed, challis, and chiffon were other fabrics made from these first rayons.

The physical properties of rayon remained about the same until 1940, when high-tenacity rayon for tires was developed. It proved to be superior to cotton, and by 1957 cotton had disappeared from the tire-cord market. After high-tenacity tire cord and heavy-denier carpet fiber were developed, 65 per cent of the rayon produced went into industrial and household uses and less went into apparel.

Continued research and development led to what has been considered the greatest technological breakthrough in rayon—the high wet modulus (HWM) or high performance (HP) rayon or polynosic rayon. Production in the United States started in 1955. This modified fiber made it possible for rayon to be used for *washable* fabrics, dresses, sheets, towels, and also in blends with cotton. High performance rayon stimulated a resurgence in the use of rayon in apparel.

In 1960, 12 companies were producing rayon in the United States; in 1977 there were four producers, only one of which produced filament rayon. It is estimated that the output of rayon will not be increased because of the high cost of replacement machinery. Rayon is no longer the inexpensive fiber it once was. A comparison of spun yarns on cones in March 1977 is given in the following table.

*Cost of Spun Yarns on Cones**

Fiber	Yarn Size	Cost/pound	Fiber	Yarn Size	Cost/pound
Carded Cotton	30s	1.46–.54	Polyester	30s	1.30–.32
Combed Cotton	30s	1.60–.66	Polyester	22s	1.22–.26
Rayon	30s	1.20–.25	50/50 Polyester/Cotton	30s	1.50–.58
Textile World (May 1977).					

Rayon fibers are highly absorbent, soft and comfortable, easy to dye, versatile and economical, and fabrics made of these fibers have good drapability.

Rayon fibers are used in nonwovens, apparel, home furnishings, and medical/surgical products.

Production

In the production of rayon, purified cellulose is chemically converted to a viscous solution that is pumped through spinnerets into a bath that changes it back to solid 100 per cent cellulose filaments. In the following chart the processes for making regular and high wet modulus rayon are

Spinning Processes for Viscose Rayon

Regular or Standard		High Wet Modulus
1. Blotterlike sheets of purified cellulose	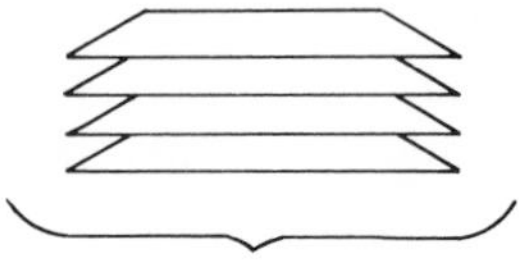	1. Blotterlike sheets of purified cellulose
2. Steeped in caustic soda		2. Steeped in weaker caustic soda
3. Liquid squeezed out by rollers		3. Liquid squeezed out by rollers
4. Shredder crumbles sheets to alkali crumbs		4. Shredder crumbles sheets to alkali crumbs
5. Crumbs aged 50 hours		5. No aging
6. Crumbs treated with carbon disulfide to form cellulose xanthate, 32% C_2S		6. Crumbs treated with carbon disulfide to form cellulose xanthate, 39–50% C_2S
7. Crumbs mixed with caustic soda to form viscose solution		7. Crumbs mixed with 2.8% sodium hydroxide to form viscose solution
8. Solution aged 4–5 days		8. No aging
9. Solution filtered	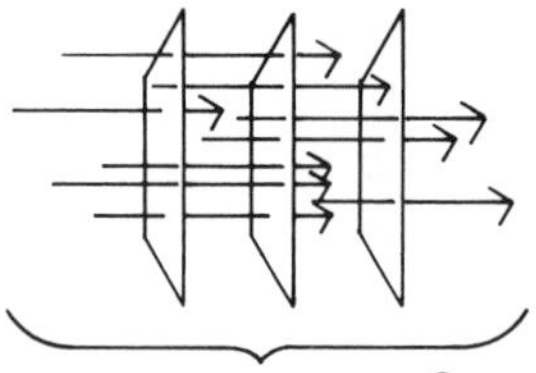	9. Solution filtered
10. Pumped to spinneret and extruded into sulfuric acid bath	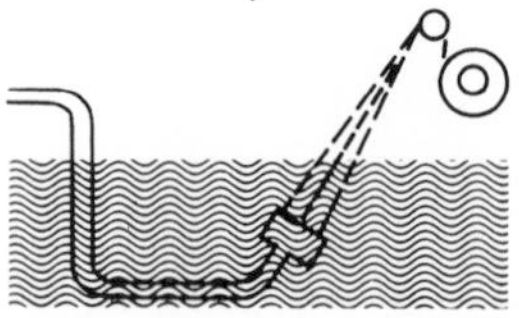	10. Pumped to spinneret and extruded into acid bath
10% H_2SO_4 16–24% Na_2SO_4 1–2% $ZnSO_4$	Spinning bath	1% H_2SO_4 4–6% Na_2SO_4
120 meters/minute	Spinning speed	20–30 meters/minute
45–50°C	Spinning bath temperature	25–35°C
25%	Filaments stretched	150–600%

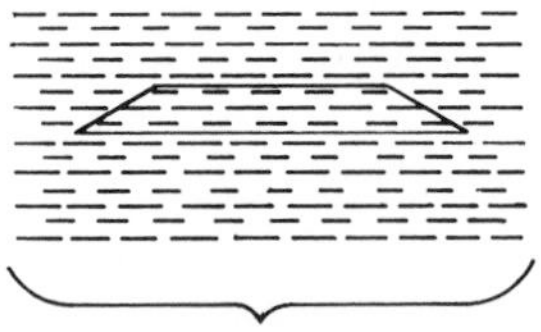

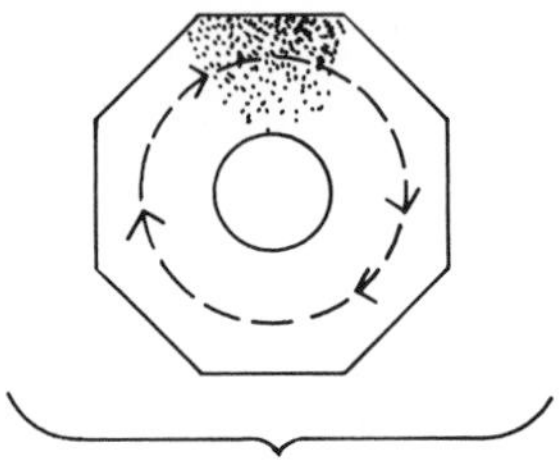

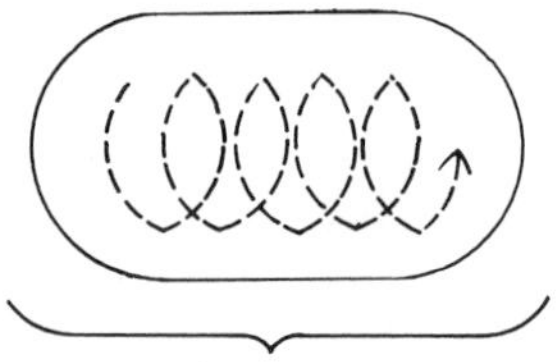

Properties	Cotton	Regular Rayon	High Wet Modulus Rayon*
Fibrils	Yes	No	Yes
Molecular chain length	800+	250±	500±
Swelling in water, %	6	26	18
Average stiffness	57–60	6–50	28–75
Tenacity, grams/denier			
Dry	4.0	2.0	4.5
Wet	5.0	1.0	3.0
Breaking elongation,† %	12	11	30

*High wet modulus is a measure of the wet breaking strength divided by the breaking elongation.
†Elongation with a load of 0.5 gram/denier.

Comparison of Cotton, Regular Rayon, and High Wet Modulus Rayon

described. The differences in the spinning process produce fibers with different properties. In the high wet modulus process the maximum chain length and fibril structure are maintained as much as possible.

Physical Structure

Regular viscose is characterized by lengthwise lines called *striations*. The cross section is a *serrated* circular shape (Figure 8-1). The shape of the fiber results from the presence of zinc sulfate in the spinning bath and from the liquid lost from the fiber during coagulation. The indented shape is an advantage in dye absorption.

High performance rayon that is spun into a bath with less zinc sulfate has a rounder cross section. Figure 8-2 shows the difference in cross sectional shapes of regular and high wet modulus rayon.

Filament rayon yarns have from 80 to 980 filaments per yarn and vary from 40 to 5,000 denier. Staple fibers and tow have a range of 1.5 to 15 denier, the 15 denier being carpet fiber. Staple fibers are usually crimped mechanically or by chemical means (Figure 8-3).

Rayon fibers are naturally very bright. This was one of the limitations to the use of the early fibers because bright filaments make very lustrous fabrics that are limited in use to dressy or luxury type garments. The addition of delustering pigments (see page 49) remedied this problem. Pigment colors can be added to the fiber spinning solution to make dull or colored—solution-dyed—fibers.

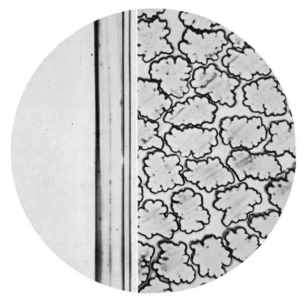

Fig. 8-1 Photomicrograph of viscose rayon: cross-sectional (*right*) and longitudinal (*left*) views. (*Courtesy of Du Pont Company.*)

Fig. 8-2 (*Left*) Stereoscan photograph of Fibro, regular rayon. (*Courtesy of* Modern Textiles Magazine.)

Fig. 8-2 (*Right*) Stereoscan photograph of Vincel, high wet modulus rayon. (*Courtesy of* Modern Textiles Magazine.)

Fig. 8-3 Crimp in viscose rayon staple.

Chemical Composition and Molecular Structure

Rayon is a manufactured fiber composed of regenerated cellulose, as well as a manufactured fiber composed of regenerated cellulose in which substituents have replaced not more than 15 per cent of the hydroxyl groups.—Federal Trade Commission.

Rayon is 100 per cent cellulose and has the same chemical composition as natural cellulose (see page 36). The molecular structure of rayon is also the same as cotton and flax except that the rayon molecular chains are shorter and do not form as many crystallites. The breakdown of the cellulose occurs when the alkali cellulose and the viscose solution are aged. In regular rayon the breakdown of the chains is quite severe. When the solution is spun into the acid bath, regeneration and coagulation take place very rapidly. Stretching aligns the molecules to give strength to the filaments. In high wet modulus rayon, since the aging is eliminated, the molecular chains are not shortened as much. Because the acid bath is less concentrated there is slower regeneration and coagulation so that more stretch and thus more orientation of the molecules can be made. The comparison chart shows the similarity between cotton and HWM rayon.

Properties

Aesthetic. Since the luster, fiber length, and diameter of the fiber can be controlled, rayon can be made into cottonlike, linenlike, woollike, and silklike fabrics. As a blending fiber, rayon can be given much the same physical characteristics as the other fiber in the blend. If it is chosen instead of cotton or to blend with cotton, rayon can give the look of mercerized long staple cotton to a fabric.

Durability. Regular rayon is not a very strong fiber and it loses about 50 per cent of its strength when wet. The breaking tenacity is 0.7–2.6 g/d. Rayon has a breaking elongation of 15 per cent dry and 20 per cent wet and has the lowest elastic recovery of any fiber. All of these factors are the result of the amorphous regions in the fiber. Water enters the amorphous areas very readily causing the molecular chains to separate as the fiber swells. This breaks the hydrogen bonds and permits distortion of the chains. When water is removed, new hydrogen bonds form but in the distorted state.

HWM rayon has a more crystalline and oriented structure so that the dry fiber is relatively strong. It has a breaking tenacity of 2.5–5.5 g/d, a breaking elongation of 6.5 per cent dry and 7 per cent wet and an elastic recovery that is greater than that of cotton.

Comfort. Both types of rayon make very comfortable fabrics. They are absorbent having a moisture regain of 13 per cent. This eliminates any static. They are smooth and soft.

Care. The chemical properties of rayon are like those of other cellulose fibers. They are harmed by *acids,* resistant to dilute *alkalis,* and are not affected by organic solvents, and can thus be safely dry cleaned. Rayon is attacked by silverfish and mildew.

Rayon is not greatly harmed by sunlight. It is not thermoplastic and thus can withstand a fairly high temperature for pressing. Rayon burns readily (see page 16).

Rayon has very poor *resiliency* especially when wet as a result of its molecular structure as has been explained. It accepts crease resistant finishes very well.

Regular rayon fabrics have limited washability because of the low strength of the fibers when wet. Unless resin treated, rayon fabrics have a tendency to shrink progressively. This shrinkage cannot be controlled by Sanforization.

HWM rayon fabrics have excellent washability. They have stability equal to cotton and strength equal to or better than cotton; they can be mercerized, and Sanforized and they wrinkle less than regular rayon in washing and drying.

Rayon	Trademark	Producer
Staple fiber	Fibro	Courtaulds
	Fibrenka	American Enka
Filament, staple, tow	Narco	Beaunit
Solution dyed	Coloray	Courtaulds
	Jetspun	American Enka
	Kolorbon	American Enka
	Skybloom	American Enka
Acid dyeable	Enkrome	American Enka
	Fibro-DD	Courtaulds
Varied cross section	Enkaire	American Enka
	Viloft	Courtaulds
Intermediate or high tenacity	Hi-Narco	Beaunit
	Super-Narco	Beaunit
	I. T.	American Enka
	Aviloc (adhesive treated)	Avtex
High wet modulus	Avril	Avtex
	Vincel	Courtaulds
	Zantrel	American Enka

Acetate: A derivative of cellulose

9

Acetate was the second man-made fiber produced in the United States: production began in 1924. The origin of acetate was in Europe and the process for making it was one of the techniques tried to make a spinning solution for a silklike fiber. The early experiments were not successful, because the treated cellulose was only soluble in an expensive, highly toxic solvent. It was later discovered that with further treatment, a nontoxic, less expensive solvent could be used. The Dreyfus brothers, who were experimenting with acetate in Switzerland, went to England during World War I and perfected the acetate "dope" as a varnish for airplane wings. After the war, they perfected the process of making acetate fibers.

More problems had to be solved with the acetate process than with the rayon processes, in which, unlike the acetate process, the treated cellulose was changed back to 100 per cent cellulose. The acetate fiber was a different chemical compound. In the original acetate or primary acetate there were no hydroxyl groups; in the modified or secondary acetate there were only a few hydroxyl groups. Thus, the fiber could not be dyed with any existing dyes. Disperse dyes were developed especially for acetate.

Acetate had better properties than rayon for use in silklike fabrics. It had natural body, which made it good for blends with rayon in staple form for woollike fabrics.

When a new fiber comes on the market, problems often arise. Because acetate was the first thermoplastic or heat sensitive fiber, consumers were confronted with fabrics that melted under a hot iron. This was a long time before durable press fabrics and homemakers were accustomed to washing and ironing all apparel. The problem was further confused because manufacturers introduced and named acetate as a kind of rayon.

Another problem with acetate was fume fading—a condition in which certain disperse dyes changed color (blue to pink, green to brown, gray to pink) as a result of atmospheric fumes. Solution dyeing was developed to correct this problem in 1951. This process is now used for all man-made fibers, if desired. In 1955, an inhibitor was developed that gave greatly improved protection to the dyes under all conditions that cause fading.

Acetate fabrics have a luxurious feel and appearance as well as excellent drapability. They are economical. Triacetate fiber was introduced in 1955; Celanese is the only company in the United States making this fiber, which is called Arnel.

Production

Two kinds of acetate are produced in the United States—acetate (chemically di-acetate or secondary acetate) and triacetate (triacetate or primary acetate). In 1960 six companies were producing acetate; in 1978 there are three. The manufacturing processes are listed in the accompanying chart, which indicates the two major differences in production. Triacetate is produced in both processes, but to make acetate, the solution is hydrolized (treated with water and aged) which causes some hydroxyl groups to reform. Triacetate is soluble in a different solvent than is acetate.

Manufacturing Process

Acetate	Triacetate
1. Purified cellulose from wood pulp or cotton linters	1. Same as acetate
2. Mixed with glacial acetic acid, acetic anhydride and a catalyst	2. Same as acetate
3. Aged 20 hours—partial hydrolysis occurs	3. No aging. Solution is ripened. No hydrolysis
4. Precipitated as acid resin flakes	4. Same as acetate
5. Flakes dissolved in acetone	5. Flakes dissolved in methylene chloride
6. Solution is filtered	6. Same as acetate
7. Spinning solution extruded in column of warm air. Solvent recovered	7. Same as acetate
8. Filaments are stretched a bit and wound onto beams, cones, or bobbins ready for use	8. Same as acetate

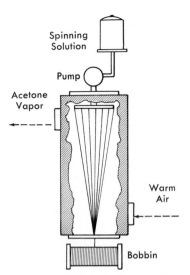

Fig. 9-1 Acetate spinning chamber. (*Courtesy of the Tennessee Eastman Company.*)

Physical Structure

Both kinds of acetate are produced as staple or filament. Much more filament is produced because of its silklike end use (see page 51). Staple fibers are crimped and usually blended with other fibers. Acetate and triacetate look alike under the microscope. The cross section is lobular or flower-petal shaped. (Lobular shape is characteristic of silklike fibers.) The shape results from the evaporation of the solvent as the fiber solidifies in spinning. Notice in Figure 9-2 that one of the lobes shows up as a false lumen.

The cross-sectional shape can be varied. Y-shaped fibers have been produced for fiberfill for

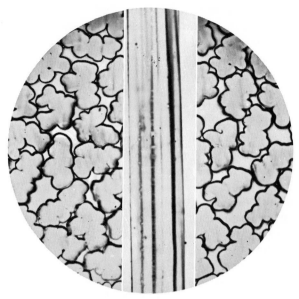

Fig. 9-2 Photomicrograph of acetate fiber: longitudinal and cross-sectional views. (*Courtesy of Du Pont Company.*)

pillows and battings; flat filaments have been produced to give glitter to fabrics.

Chemical Composition and Molecular Structure

Acetate is a manufactured fiber in which the fiber forming substance is cellulose acetate. Where not less than 92 per cent of the hydroxyl groups are acetylated the term triacetate may also be used as a generic description of the fiber.—Federal Trade Commission.

(Glucose)

Acetate

Triacetate

Acetate is an ester of cellulose and therefore has a different chemical structure than rayon or cotton. In triacetate all of the hydroxyl (OH) groups have been replaced by acetyl (CH_3COOH) groups. In acetate two of the hydroxyl groups have been replaced by acetyl groups. (In reality, 2.6 per cent of the hydroxyl groups are replaced.) The bulky acetyl groups tend to keep the molecules apart so they do not pack into regions of regularity (crystalline areas). There is less attraction between the molecular chains as a result of a lack of hydrogen bonding. Water molecules do not penetrate as readily, which accounts for the lower absorbency of acetate. The changed chemical structure also explains the different dye affinity of acetate.

Acetate is thermoplastic but the two kinds react differently. Triacetate molecules move easily to new positions when subjected to heat, whereas those of acetate, with its less symmetrical molecular structure, do not.

Properties

Acetate has a combination of properties that make it a valuable textile fiber. It is low in cost and has natural body to give it good draping qualities.

Aesthetics. Acetate has been promoted as the beauty fiber. It is widely used in satins, brocades, and taffetas in which luster and body and beauty of fabric are more important than durability or ease of care. Embossed finishes are durable on acetate. Triacetates can be heat-set so that fabrics can be permanently pleated. Acetate has, and keeps, a good white color. This is one of its advantages over silk, which yellows readily.

Durability. Both kinds of acetate are weak fibers having a breaking tenacity of 1.2–1.5 g/d. They lose some strength when wet. Other weak fibers have some compensating factor, such as good elastic recovery in wool or spandex, but acetate does not. Acetate has a breaking elongation of 25 per cent and an elastic recovery of 58 per cent. Acetate also has poor resistance to abrasion. A small percentage of nylon is often combined with acetate to make a stronger fabric.

Comfort. Acetate has a moisture regain of 6.0 per cent. Triacetate has a moisture regain of 3.2 per cent. They both are subject to static buildup.

Care. Acetates are resistant to weak acids and to alkalis. They can be bleached with hypochlorite or peroxide bleaches. Acetate is soluble in acetone; triacetate is soluble in chloroform and methylene chloride. Both kinds of acetate can be safely dry-cleaned. Triacetate is machine washable and dryable.

Effect of Heat. Both kinds of acetate are thermoplastic and heat sensitive, but to different degrees. Acetate becomes sticky at 350–375°F and melts at 446°F; triacetate has a sticking point of 482°F and a melting point of 550°F. Triacetate can be heat-set at a temperature high enough to give permanent shape to fabrics and to raise the safe ironing temperature. In this property, triacetate is like the synthetic fibers. Triacetate is promoted as an Ease of Care fiber. Acetate cannot be heat-set because the heat-setting temperature would have to be so low that it would not be effective. Figure 9–3 shows two fabrics, one acetate and the other triacetate, which were pressed with an iron set at cotton setting. The diacetate fabric softened and shrank, whereas the triacetate fabric showed only a slight imprint of the iron.

Acetate fabrics are not as resilient as triacetate fabrics and, when washed, they often develop wrinkles that are difficult to remove.

Effect of Sunlight. Triacetate is more resistant to sunlight than is acetate. Acetate has better resistance than silk or nylon but less than the cellulose fibers.

Flammability. Both kinds of acetate burn readily (see section on fiber identification.)

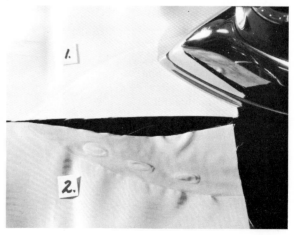

Fig. 9-3 Effect of heat on (1) Arnel and (2) acetate.

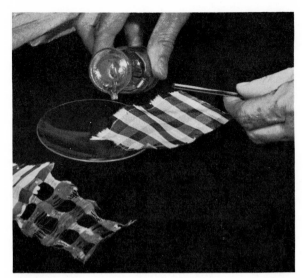

Fig. 9-4 Acetone test for identification of acetate fiber.

Effect of Fungi, Moths. Acetate is resistant to moths, mildew, and bacteria.

Fiber Identification

The *acetone test* is a specific identification test for acetate.[1] None of the other fibers will dissolve in acetone. Figure 9-4 shows a procedure for testing the acetate content of a fabric. Use a dropper bottle, a glass rod, watch glass, and cleaning tis-

[1]Triacetate is soluble in chloroform or methylene chloride.

sue. Test individual yarns first. The presence of other fibers, in blends or combinations with acetate, can be determined. The structure will not disintegrate if only a small amount of acetate is present, but it will feel sticky and will stiffen permanently when the solvent evaporates.

The *burning test* will also identify acetate. Acetate gives off an acetic—vinegarlike—odor that is specific for acetate. It burns freely, melts, and then decomposes to a black char. Diacetate and triacetate burn in a similar manner. Fire-resistant fiber types have been developed by the producers.

Comparison with Rayon

Rayon and acetate are the two oldest man-made fibers and have been produced in large quantities, filling a very important need for less expensive fibers in the textile industry. They lack the easy care, resilience, and strength of the synthetics and have had difficulty competing in uses where these characteristics are important. Rayon and acetate have some similarities because they are made from the same raw material, cellulose. The manufacturing processes differ, so the fibers have many individual characteristics and uses. Some of these are listed in the following table.

Types and Kinds

Types of acetate are solution dyed, flame retardant, sunlight resistant, fiberfill, textured filament,

Comparison of Rayon and Acetate

Rayon	Acetate
Differences	
Wet spun	Dry spun
Regenerated cellulose	Chemical derivative of cellulose
Serrated cross section	Lobular cross section
More staple produced	More filament produced
Scorches	Melts
High absorbency	Fair absorbency
No static	Static
Not soluble in acetone	Soluble in acetone
Industrial uses—tires	Very few industrial uses
Not used for fiberfill	Used for fiberfill
Color may crock or bleed	Color may fume fade
Mildews	Resists mildew
Similarities	
Low cost	Low cost
Low strength	Low strength
Low abrasion resistance	Low abrasion resistance
Chlorine bleaches can be used	Chlorine bleaches can be used
Flammable	Flammable

modified cross section, and thick-and-thin slub-like filament. Combination yarns are also produced. Arnel plus nylon is a coherent bundle of dissimilar filaments that is engineered to provide better bulk and create a textured surface (see Chapter 16).

Acetate	Trademarks	Producer
Regular	Celanese	Celanese
	Estron	Eastman Kodak
Solution dyed	Celaperm	Celanese
	Chromspun	Eastman Kodak
	Avicolor	Avtex
Modified cross section	Celafil	Celanese
	Celacloud (fiberfill)	Celanese
Textured or crimpable	Celacrimp	Celanese
	Celara	Celanese
	Loftura	Eastman Kodak
Flame retardant	Type ADA	Celanese
	Type 14 Estron	Eastman Kodak
	SayFR	Avtex
Triacetate, regular	Arnel	Celanese
	Type DDC	Celanese
Combinations		
Acetate/polyester core bulked yarn	Lanese	Celanese
Triacetate/nylon filament yarn	Arnel Plus	Celanese

Nylon: The first synthetic fiber

10

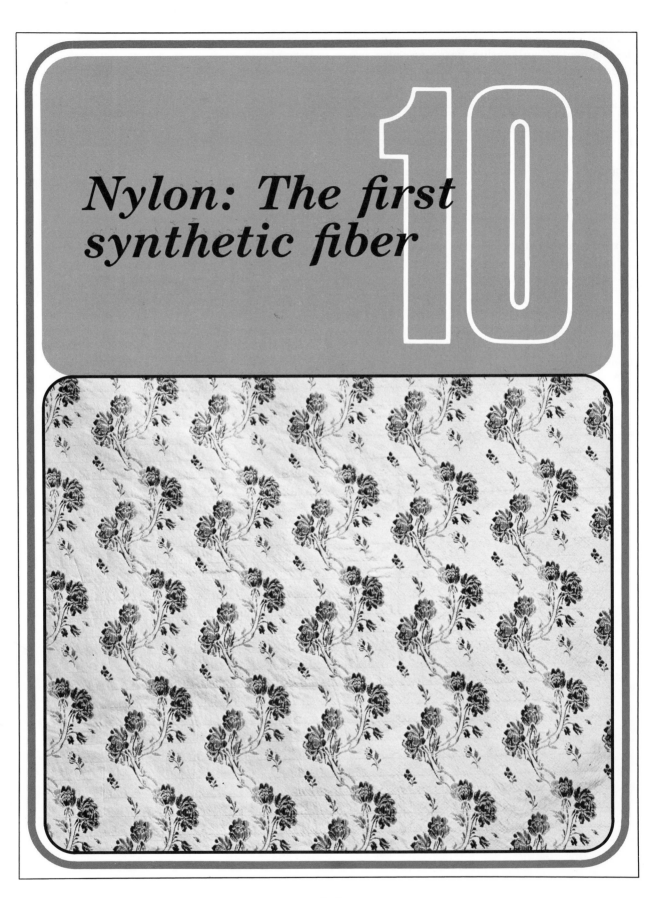

Synthetic Fibers

Synthetic fibers are made by putting together simple chemical elements (monomers) to make a complex chemical compound (polymers). They are also called chemical or noncellulosic man-made fibers. The fibers differ in the elements used, the way they are put together as polymers, and the method of spinning used. The synthetic fibers are polyamide, polyacrylic, polyester, polyolefin, polyurethane, and polyvinyl. The synthetic fibers have many properties in common which are listed in the following chart.

Properties Common to Synthetic Fibers

Properties	Importance to Consumers
Heat sensitive	If iron is too hot, fabric will shrink and then melt. Hole melting from cigarettes. Pleats, creases, etc., can be heat-set in fabrics. Fabric can be stabilized by heat setting. Yarns can be textured for high bulk. Guard-hair furlike fabrics can be produced.
Resistant to most chemicals	Can be used in laboratory and work clothing where chemicals are used.
Resistant to moths and fungi	Storage is no problem. Useful in sandbags, fishlines, tenting.
Low moisture absorbency	Clothes dry quickly. Resist waterborne stains. Stains can be sponged off. Lack comfort in humid weather. Increases possibility of static. Water does not cause shrinkage. Difficult to dye.
Oleophilic	Oil and grease absorbed into the fiber must be removed by dry-cleaning agents.
Electrostatic	Clothes cling to wearer. May cause sparks that can cause explosions or fires. Shocks in cold, dry weather are unpleasant.
Abrasion resistance good to excellent (acrylics lowest)	Good appearance retained longer because holes and worn places do not appear as soon. Color does not wear off as fast.
Strength good to excellent	Strongest fibers make good ropes, belts, women's hosiery, etc. Resist breaking when stress is applied.
Resilience excellent	Easy-care, wash-and-wear clothing. Clothing packable for travel. Less mussing during wear.
Sunlight resistance good to excellent (nylon modified to improve resistance)	Webbing for outdoor furniture. Indoor/outdoor carpet. Curtains and draperies. Flags.
Flame resistance	Varies from poor to excellent. Check individual fibers.
Density or specific gravity	Varies as a group but tend to be light in weight.
Pilling	May occur in staple length fibers.

Common Properties

Heat-Sensitivity. All man-made fibers, *except rayon,* are heat sensitive. *Heat-resistance* is the resistance of a fiber to heat exposure. The term *heat-sensitivity* is used with specific meaning for fibers that soften or melt with heat; those that scorch or decompose are described as being heat resistant. Heat-sensitivity is important in the everyday use and care of fabrics as well as in manufacturing processes. Heat is encountered in washing, ironing, and dry cleaning during use, and in dyeing, scouring, singeing, and other fabric-finishing processes.

The fibers differ in their *level* of heat-resistance. This difference is reflected in the table of safe ironing temperatures on page 14. The speed of ironing has been found by research to average about 40 inches per minute. This means that in normal ironing the fabric never gets as hot as the sole plate of the iron. If the iron is slowed down or allowed to stand in one spot, the heat will build up. If heat-sensitive fabrics get too hot, the yarns will soften and pressure from the iron will flatten them (Figure 10–1). This flattening will be permanent. Flattening of the surface is called *glazing*. This problem can be prevented by careful checking of the ironing temperature before starting to iron and by the use of a soft press pad that will permit edges and seams to sink down into the

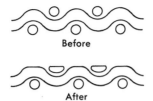

Before

After

Fig. 10-1 Heat and pressure cause permanent flattening of the yarn—glazing.

pad when pressure is applied by the iron. Garment alteration is difficult in heat-sensitive fabrics because creases are hard to press in or out. Fullness cannot be shrunk out of the top of a sleeve or other parts of the garment, so patterns have to be adjusted to remove some of the fullness in areas where fullness is usually controlled by shrinkage.

Heat Setting. *Heat setting* is a factory process that is more or less a baking or steaming finish to stabilize yarns or fabrics made of heat-sensitive fibers. (Acetate is heat-sensitive, but it does not take a true "set.") The yarn or fabric is heated to bring it almost to the melting point that is specific for the fiber. This temperature range is from 375 to 445°F. The fiber molecules can then move freely to become better arranged, thus dissipating stresses within the fiber. The fabric is kept under tension until it cools, to prevent shrinkage. After cooling, the fabric or yarn will be stable to any heat lower than that at which it was set, but changes can be brought about by higher temperatures. Heat setting may be done at any stage of finishing, depending on the level of heat-resistance of the fiber and other qualities. Figure 10-2 illustrates heat setting of flat fabric. Heat setting is both an advantage and a disadvantage to the consumer.

Pilling. The strength of fibers is a basic factor in the problem of fabric pilling. Pilling is the formation of bunches or balls on the surface of the

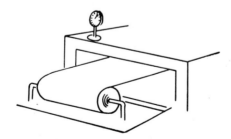

Fig. 10-2 Heat setting nylon flat fabric. (*Courtesy of Du Pont Company.*)

Advantages	Disadvantages
Embossed designs are permanent. Pleats and shape are permanent. Size is stabilized. Pile is crush-resistant. Knits do not need to be blocked. Clothing resists wrinkling during wear.	"Set" creases and wrinkles are hard to remove in ironing or in garment alteration. Care must be taken in washing or ironing to prevent the formation of set wrinkles.

fabric and occurs on fabrics that have free fiber ends when the ends get tangled by rubbing. The pills often break off before the garment becomes unsightly, but with nylon and the polyesters the fibers are so strong that none of the pills break off and they all accumulate on the surface of the garment. Pills are of two kinds: lint and fabric. Lint pills are more unsightly, because they contain not only fibers from the garment but fibers picked up in the wash water or through contact with other garments and even through static attraction. Figure 10-3 shows two socks, one having lint pills and the other fabric pills. Observe the difference in appearance.

The best single treatment to prevent pilling is *singeing.* Singeing is a necessity for polyester/

Fig. 10-3 Lint pills make an unattractive appearance.

cotton and polyester/worsted blends. Singeing consists of running the fabric between two gas flames or two hot plates so it will be singed on both sides at one pass. It should be done very rapidly. The ends of the polyester fibers melt and shrink into the core of the yarn, making it harder for the fibers to work to the surface and form pills. The tips of the fibers look like match heads under the microscope. Singeing should be done after dyeing because these fused ends will take a deeper dye.

The construction of the fabric is an important factor in the prevention of pilling. Close weave, high yarn twist or plied yarns, and longer staple fibers are recommended. Resin finishes of cotton and fulling of wool are finishes that help prevent pilling.

Static Electricity. Static electricity is generated by the friction of a fabric when it is rubbed against itself or other objects. If the electrical charge is not conducted away, it tends to build up on the surface. When the fabric comes in contact with a good conductor, a shock or transfer occurs. This transfer may produce sparks that, in a gaseous atmosphere, can cause explosions. Static electricity is always a hazard in such places as dry-cleaning plants and operating rooms. Nurses are forbidden to wear nylon or polyester uniforms in operating rooms because of the danger. Static tends to build up more rapidly in dry, cold regions. Other problems involving static include

1. Soil and lint cling to the surface of the fabric and dark colors become very unsightly. Brushing simply increases the problem.

2. Dust and dirt are attracted to curtains.

3. Fabrics cling to the machinery at the factory and make cutting and handling very difficult. Static is responsible for increased defects and makes a higher percentage of seconds.

4. Clothes cling to the wearer and cause discomfort and an unsightly appearance. Temporary relief can be obtained by the wearer if a damp sponge or paper towel is wiped across the surface to drain away the static. More permanent relief can be obtained by the use of *fabric softeners* available at the grocery store. These are effective when used as directed.

Antistatic finishes are applied to many of the fabrics at the factory, but they frequently wash out or come out in dry cleaning.

Oily Stains. Fibers that have low moisture absorption usually have an affinity for oils and greases. They are oleophilic. These stains are very difficult to remove and require prespotting with a concentrated liquid soap or a dry-cleaning solvent.

Nylon

Nylon was the first synthetic fiber and it was the first fiber conceived in the United States. The discovery of nylon was not planned, but resulted from a fundamental research program by Wallace Carothers that was designed to extend basic knowledge of the way in which small molecules are united to form giant molecules (polymers).

In 1928 the Du Pont Company decided to establish a fundamental research program. If anything was discovered it would be good for the company—a means of diversification. The slogan of Du Pont is "Better Things for Better Living through Chemistry." Du Pont hired Dr. Carothers, who had done research on high polymers, to head up a team of scientists. These people created many kinds of polymers starting with single molecules and building them up into long molecular chains. One of Carothers' assistants noticed that when a glass rod was taken out of one of the polyester stills the solution adhering to it stretched out into a solid filament. The filament could be stretched even further and it did not go back to its original length. This stimulated the group to concentrate on textile fibers. The polyester filaments lacked certain characteristics that seemed desirable at that time and they decided to develop polyamides that had fewer problems.

By 1939, Du Pont was making nylon 6,6 in a pilot plant. Nylon 6,6 was introduced to the public in women's hosiery where it was an instant success. The term *nylon* was chosen for the fiber. It had no special meaning but had a nice textile sound like cotton and rayon. (At this time there were no laws specifying generic names for fibers. Acetate was still considered a kind of rayon.)

Nylon was called the *Miracle Fiber* for several years. It had a combination of properties unlike any natural or man-made fiber in use in the 1940s. It was stronger and more resistant to abrasion than any fiber; it had excellent elasticity; it could be heat-set, and permanent pleats became a

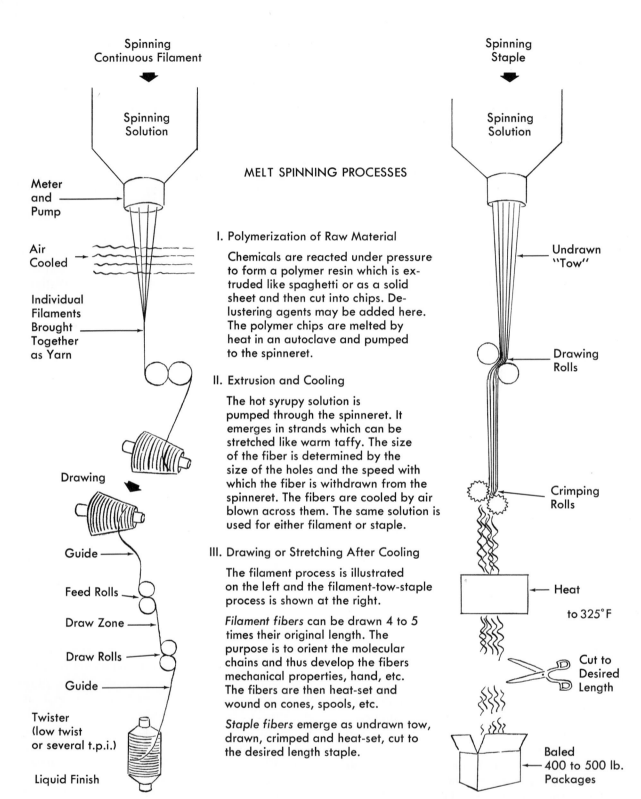

Spinning
Continuous Filament

Spinning
Solution

Meter and Pump

Air Cooled

Individual Filaments Brought Together as Yarn

Drawing

Guide

Feed Rolls

Draw Zone

Draw Rolls

Guide

Twister
(low twist or several t.p.i.)

Liquid Finish

Spinning
Staple

Spinning
Solution

Undrawn "Tow"

Drawing Rolls

Crimping Rolls

Heat
to 325°F

Cut to Desired Length

Baled
400 to 500 lb. Packages

MELT SPINNING PROCESSES

I. Polymerization of Raw Material

Chemicals are reacted under pressure to form a polymer resin which is extruded like spaghetti or as a solid sheet and then cut into chips. Delustering agents may be added here. The polymer chips are melted by heat in an autoclave and pumped to the spinneret.

II. Extrusion and Cooling

The hot syrupy solution is pumped through the spinneret. It emerges in strands which can be stretched like warm taffy. The size of the fiber is determined by the size of the holes and the speed with which the fiber is withdrawn from the spinneret. The fibers are cooled by air blown across them. The same solution is used for either filament or staple.

III. Drawing or Stretching After Cooling

The filament process is illustrated on the left and the filament-tow-staple process is shown at the right.

Filament fibers can be drawn 4 to 5 times their original length. The purpose is to orient the molecular chains and thus develop the fibers mechanical properties, hand, etc. The fibers are then heat-set and wound on cones, spools, etc.

Staple fibers emerge as undrawn tow, drawn, crimped and heat-set, cut to the desired length staple.

Fig. 10-4 Chart of melt spinning process.

reality. For the first time, gossamer-sheer, frilly lingerie was durable and machine washable. Nylon's high strength, light weight, and resistance to sea water made it suitable for ropes, cords, sails, and the like.

As nylon entered more end-use markets, its disadvantages became apparent—static buildup, poor hand and lack of comfort in skin contact apparel fabrics, and low resistance to sunlight in curtains. But fortunately as each problem appeared more was learned about fibers, and ways were found to overcome the disadvantages.

In 1960 five firms in the United States were producing nylon. In 1977 there were 31; eighteen of them producing nylon 6, twelve producing nylon 6,6, and one producing nylon 12.

Production

Polyamides are made from various substances. The numbers after nylon indicate the number of carbon atoms in the starting materials. For example, nylon 6,6 has 6 carbon atoms in hexamethylene diamene and 6 carbons in adipic acid; nylon 6 is made from a single substance, caprolactam, which has 6 carbons; nylon 12 is made from polylaurylamide, which has 12 carbon atoms. Nylon is melt spun (Figure 10-4): this process was also developed by Du Pont.

Melt Spinning. *Melt spinning* is essentially a simple process. It can be demonstrated by a laboratory experiment that is fun to do. A flame, a pair of tweezers, and a piece of nylon are all that are needed. An old nylon stocking serves very well. (The polyesters and the olefins can be tested the same way.) Allow the fabric to burn until quite a little melt has formed, then quickly draw out the fibers with tweezers as shown in Figure 10-5. Figure 10-6 shows commercial spinning of nylon.

Commerical melt spinning consists of forcing nylon melt through the holes of the stainless-steel plate of a heated spinneret. The fiber cools in contact with the air, solidifies, and is wound on a bobbin. (The melt spinning process, for both filament and staple nylon fiber, is shown in Figure 10-4). The chainlike molecules of the fiber are in random helter-skelter arrangement and the filament fiber must be *drawn* to develop the desirable properties of the fiber, such as strength, pliability, toughness, and elasticity. Nylon is *cold drawn* (Figure 10-4). (The polyesters must be hot

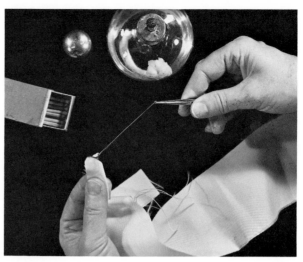

Fig. 10-5 Spinning a melt-spun fiber by hand.

drawn.) Drawing aligns the molecules, placing them parallel to one another and bringing them closer together. The fiber is also reduced in size. The amount of draw—the draw ratio—determines the decrease in fiber size and the increase in strength, and it varies with intended use.

Chemical Composition

Nylon is a manufactured fiber in which the fiber-forming substance is any long-chain, synthetic polyamide in which less than 85 per cent of the amide linkages (—C—NH—)
$$|$$
$$O$$
are attached directly to two aromatic rings.—Federal Trade Commission.

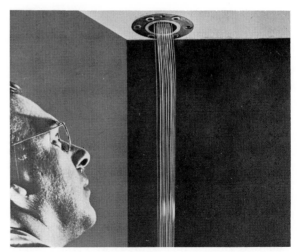

Fig. 10-6 Spinning nylon fiber. (*Courtesy of Du Pont Company.*)

The various nylons are all polyamides with recurring amide groups. They all contain CHON. They differ in their chemical arrangement and this accounts for slight differences in properties.

Nylon 6,6: Made of hexamethylene diamine and dibasic acid

$$HO-\left[\overset{\overset{O}{\|}}{C}\underset{CH_2}{CH_2}\underset{CH_2}{CH_2}\underset{\underset{O}{\|}}{C}\overset{H}{N}\underset{CH_2}{CH_2}\underset{CH_2}{CH_2}\underset{CH_2}{CH_2}\overset{\overset{O}{\|}}{\underset{\underset{H}{}}{C}}\right]_n$$

Advantages
Pleats, creases, etc., can be heat-set at higher temperatures
Softening point 482°F

Nylon 6: Made of caprolactum

hydrogen
bond →

$$H-\overset{H}{N}\underset{CH_2}{CH_2}\underset{CH_2}{CH_2}\underset{CH_2}{CH_2}\overset{\overset{O}{\|}}{C}-OH\Big]_n$$

Advantages
Better dye affinity
Better weathering properties
Softening point 428°F

Nylon has a proteinlike molecule and is related chemically to the protein fibers silk and wool. Both have amino dye sites that are important in the reaction of acid dyes. Nylon possesses only one such dye site for every 30 dye sites present in wool.

Physical Structure and Molecular Arrangement

Nylon is made as multifilaments, monofilaments, staple, and tow in a wide range of deniers and staple lengths. They are produced as bright, semidull, and dull lusters. They vary in degree of polymerization (D.P.) and thus in strength. They are available as partially drawn or completely finished filaments. Regular nylon has a round cross section and is perfectly uniform throughout the filament (Figure 10-7). At first, the uniformity of nylon filaments was a distinct advantage over the natural fibers—especially silk. Silk hose often had rings (thicker areas in yarns), which detracted from their beauty. The perfect uniformity of nylon produced woven fabrics with a

Fig. 10-7 Photomicrograph of nylon fiber. Inset is cross-sectional view. (*Courtesy of The Du Pont Company.*)

dead feel. They lacked the liveliness of silk. This condition was corrected by changing the shape of the spinneret holes. Trilobal fibers give a silklike hand to nylon fabrics. In nylon carpets, trilobal fibers and square fibers with voids give good soil-hiding characteristics (see Chapter 16).

The molecular chains of nylon vary in length. They are long, straight chains with no side chains or cross linkages. Cold drawing aligns the chains so that they are oriented with the lengthwise direction and are highly crystalline. High-tenacity filaments have a longer chain length than regular nylon. Staple fibers are not cold drawn after spinning and thus have fewer crystallites. They have lower tenacities than filaments.

Properties

Aesthetic. Regular nylon has been very successful in hosiery and in knitted filament fabrics because of its smoothness, light weight, and high strength. Nylon has a density of 1.14 g/cc compared to silk, acetate, and rayon, which have densities of 1.25, 1.32, and 1.50 g/cc, respectively. Staple nylon was not very satisfactory in woollike sweaters and carpeting because it pilled, because of the high strength of the fibers, and the pills did not break off during wear. By reducing the strength of the fibers or by using textured filaments, the pilling problems have been minimized.

Durability. Nylon has outstanding durability. High-tenacity fibers (6.0–9.5 g/d) are used in seat belts, tire cords, ballistic cloth, and the like. Regular tenacity fibers (3.0–6.0 g/d) are used in apparel. In addition to high strength and resistance to abrasion, nylon has good elastic recovery (100 per cent). Nylon carpet fibers outwear all others. Inexpensive nylon carpeting may lose its aesthetic appearance by pilling, pile flattening, or soiling in traffic lanes, but it will not become threadbare for many years.

No other fiber has been able to compete with nylon in hosiery. Filament nylon hose develop runs because the fine yarns break and the knit loop is no longer secure in the stocking, but the excellent resistance to abrasion has practically eliminated the need for darning hosiery.

Tire cord is another major end use of nylon. Nylon is used in replacement tires but has not yet penetrated the new equipment market because of "flat spotting." Flat spotting occurs when a car has been standing on nylon tires for some time and a flattened place forms. It causes the car to ride bumpily for the first mile or so until the tire recovers from flattening. Nylon has many other industrial uses, such as tents, sails for boats, and storage tanks.

Comfort. Nylon has a smooth, silky feel and low density, which makes it ideal for undergarments. High strength and low density make lightweight foundation garments possible.

Nylon has low absorbency (4.0–4.5 per cent moisture regain). One disadvantage of low absorbency of nylon was the discomfort of the early fabrics during wear. The smooth, straight fibers were packed together very compactly in yarns, impeding ventilation. The first nylon shirts, which failed for this reason, were said to feel like a film worn around the body.

The bad image of nylon was not changed until the advent of textured yarns. On the basis of this experience, fiber producers began to set up fabric quality-control programs through which they could exercise control over the final product and thus protect the image of their fibers.

Another disadvantage of low absorbency is the development of static electricity by friction. This disadvantage can be overcome by use of antistatic type nylon fibers, by antistatic finishes, and by blending with high-absorbency, low-static fibers. Comfort properties can be improved by use of the filament bulking process—texturing—without the necessity of resorting to blends with high-absorbency fibers.

Care. The *low water absorbency* of nylon contributes to good dimensional stability in laundering and rapid drying with little wrinkling if properly cared for. Nylon introduced the concept of "easy-care" garments.

The chemical resistance of nylon is generally good, similar to that of cotton. Nylon has excellent resistance to alkali and to chlorine bleaches but is damaged by strong acids. Soot from smoke in industrial cities contains sulfur, which on damp days combines with atmospheric moisture to form an acid that has been responsible for epidemics of runs in stockings. Certain acids, when printed on the fabric, will cause shrinkage that creates a puckered damask effect. Nylon will dissolve in formic acid and phenol.

Nylon is resistant to moths and fungi.

Nylon must be *heat-set*. The test for a well-set fabric is that is should not shrink more than 1 per cent when placed for $\frac{1}{2}$ hour in boiling water. The heat-settability of nylon is high enough to make it possible to heat-stabilize nylon fabrics permanently against shrinkage. Pleats, creases, and embossed designs will last for the life of the garment. Wrinkles acquired in hot wash water are also quite permanent. Home ironing temperatures are not high enough to press seams, creases, and pleats in home-sewn garments or to press out the wrinkles acquired in washing. Nylon knits do not acquire set wrinkles to the same degree as woven fabrics. Care labels for nylon recommend warm water because hot water may cause wrinkling in some constructions. Nylon can be ironed at 270 to 300°F. Nylon has low resistance to sunlight. Better resistance is achieved in curtain fabrics by using bright rather than delustered fibers, which absorb rather than reflect light.

Identification. The burning test is a very good way to identify nylon. Untreated nylon does not flash burn and does not readily support the spread of the flame after the ignition sources are removed. When exposed to a flame, nylon fuses and draws away from the flame before it will ignite. When it burns, the nylon fibers melt and drip and some of the flame is carried down with the drip. The odor is celerylike, and white smoke is given off. In untreated nylon the melt will harden as a tan bead. A black bead forms when dyes are present, and certain finishes will increase the flammability.

Comparison with Triacetate

Triacetate and nylon are compared in the following chart to show the differences and similarities of a cellulosic thermoplastic fiber and a synthetic thermoplastic fiber. Both fibers are frequently available in brushed nightgown fabrics, velour robes, and tricot blouses. In later chapters, the other synthetic thermoplastic fibers are compared.

Comparison of Triacetate and Nylon

Triacetate		Nylon
	Similarities	
	Thermoplastic	
	Can be heat-set	
3.2%	Low absorbency	4.0–4.5%
	Static buildup	
	More filament than staple	
	Differences	
Dry spun		Melt spun
Cellulose derivative		Polyamide
Low strength 1.2–1.5 g/d		High strength 3.0–9.5 g/d
Low abrasion resistance		Excellent abrasion resistance
Flammable		Melts and drips—does not flame

Types and Kinds of Nylon

It has been said that as soon as a new need arose, a new type of nylon was produced to fill the need. This has led to a large number of types of nylon that are identified by trademarks, many of them with roman numerals II, III, IV to indicate second or third-generation fibers. The types and kinds of nylon fibers are too numerous to list as was done for rayon and acetate. The following lists merely illustrate the many nylon fiber modifications.

Types and Kinds of Nylon

Cross Section	Dyeability	Crimp or Textured	Others
Round	Acid dyeable	Mechanical crimp	Antistatic
Heart-shaped	Cationic dyeable	Crimp-set	Soil hiding
Y-shaped	Disperse dyeable	Producer textured	Bicomponent
8-shaped	Deep dye	Undrawn	Biconstituent
Delta	Solution dye	Partially drawn	Faciated
Trilobal			
Triskelion			
Trinode			

Some Trademarks and Producers

Nylon 6,6		Nylon 6	
Trademarks	Producer	Trademarks	Producer
Antron, Antron II, Antron III, Cantrece, Cordura	Du Pont	Anso, Anso X, Caprolan, Captiva	Allied Chemical
Type numbers	Beaunit	Type numbers	Dow Badische
Type numbers	Celanese	Crepeset, Enkaloft I,	American Enka
Actionwear, Cadon, Cumuloft, Ultron	Monsanto	Enkaloft II, Enkalure II, III, Enkasheer	

Qiana Nylon

Qiana nylon deserves special consideration because of the research involved in its production and because of the unusual marketing approach used. Qiana is not a modified nylon but is a new kind of nylon made up of unique molecular units joined together by chemical linkages that are the same as those of regular nylon. It is made from an amine and a dibasic acid namely bis-para-aminocyclohexyl methane and dodecanedioic acid.

$$\left[-NH-\bigcirc-CH_2-\bigcirc-NHCO(CH_2)_2CO\right]_n$$

Qiana nylon

This new chemical structure plus the modification of regular nylon that had been perfected over the years resulted in a fiber that made fabrics as soft, supple, and lively as silk but with the ease-of-care properties of polyester.

Qiana is the most silklike of the man-made fibers. The fiber is nylon Type 472 and the name Qiana (pronounced Key-ah'-na) is Du Pont's trade name used on products that meet test standards. The name Qiana was chosen by computer and is one of a very few words in which the letter *Q* is not followed by the letter *U*. (Another is that of the musk-ox fiber, qiviut.) The developmental work on Qiana was kept secret until the product was ready to be introduced on the market. Efforts were concentrated on the filament form of the fiber. Experimental fabrics were woven by small weavers in France, Italy, and Switzerland, and the fabrics were made into dresses by top French and Italian designers. The news about the new fiber was announced simultaneously in eight cities around the world in 1968.

Qiana was introduced as a fiber of luxury and elegance that sold for $5 to $7 per pound. The entrance of Qiana into the volume market was with dresses at $70 and less. Commerical production of Qiana began in late 1971—up to that time it had been in pilot-plant production—about 5 million pounds per year. Du Pont plans to make it a major fiber.

Qiana is designed only for use in apparel and home furnishings. It has a trilobal cross section similar to silk. It takes dyes well giving clear bright colors and has excellent luster (comparable to silk). The properties of Qiana are given in the following comparison chart.

Comparison of Qiana and Nylon 6,6 and Nylon 6

Property	Qiana	Nylon 6,6	Nylon 6
Density	1.03 g/d	1.14	1.14
Tenacity (filament)	3.0–3.3 g/d	3.0–6.0	6.0–9.5
Elongation	30%	23	23
Moisture regain	2.0–2.5%	4.0–4.5	4.5
Melting point	275°C or 527°F	250°C or 482°F	212°C or 414°F
Sticking point	230°C or 446°F	229°C or 445°F	171°C or 340°F
Safe ironing temperature	185°C or 280–320°F	177°C or 340°F	149°C or 300°F
Sunlight resistance	Very good	Poor	Poor
Oleophilic	Absorbs oil readily	Same	Same
Static	Yes	Yes	Yes
Heat setting temperature	190°C	205°C	150°C

Polyester Fibers

11

The polyester polymers were part of the high-polymer research program of Wallace Carothers in the early 1930s. When work on the polyesters was discontinued by Du Pont in favor of the more promising nylon fiber, research on polyesters continued in England, and the first polyester fiber, Terylene, was produced there under a patent that controlled the production rights for the world. In 1946, Du Pont purchased the exclusive right to produce polyesters in the United States. The Du Pont fiber was given the trade name Dacron—a name that is commonly mispronounced. The correct pronunciation is "Daykron."

Dacron was first produced commercially in 1953. In 1958, Kodel, a different kind of polyester, was introduced by Eastman Kodak Company. In 1960 four companies were producing polyester; in 1977 there were 23 producers. It is the most widely used synthetic fiber. Polyester is sometimes referred to as the "workhorse" fiber of the industry. The filament form of the fiber has been said to be the most versatile fiber, and the staple

duced they were backed by quality control programs that limited the use of a trade name to those products that met standards set by the fiber producers. Consumers readily accepted polyesters.

The polyesters have probably undergone more research and developmental work than any other fiber. The polymer is "endlessly engineerable," and many physical and chemical variations are possible. These modified fibers are designed to improve the original polyester in areas where it has shown either a deficiency or a limitation in its use. One of the important physical changes has been that of changing from the standard round shape to a trilobal cross section that gives the fiber silklike properties. A chemical modification, high-tenacity staple, was developed for use in durable press fabrics. The strength of the polyester reinforces the cotton fibers, which are weakened by the finishing process.

The properties of polyester that make it the most widely used man-made fiber are listed in the following chart.

Properties of Polyester

Properties	Importance to Consumers
Resilient—wet and dry	Easy-care apparel, home furnishings, packable garments
Dimensional stability	Machine washable
Resistant to sunlight degradation	Good for curtains and draperies
Durable, abrasion resistant	Industrial uses, sewing thread, good for work clothes
Aesthetics superior to nylon	Blends well with natural or other man-made fibers, good silklike filaments

form has been called the "big mixer" because it can be blended with so many other fibers, contributing its good properties to the blend without destroying the desirable properties of the other fiber. Its versatility in blending is one of the unique advantages of polyester.

By the time the polyesters were synthesized much had been learned about high polymers and about the structure of fibers. Many of the problems of production had been solved—for example, controlled luster and strength, spinning methods, making of tow for staple fibers, and crimping of staple. Continuing research is being done on heat setting, high temperature dyeing, and static control. Man-made fibers were being promoted vigorously by their trade names. The generic names nylon, rayon, acetate, and acrylic had been agreed upon. When the polyesters were intro-

Production

Polyester is made by reacting an acid with an alcohol. The fibers are melt spun by a process that is very similar to that used to make nylon. The polyester fibers are hot drawn (nylon is cold drawn) to orient the molecules and make significant improvement in strength and elongation, and especially in the stress-stain properties. As the polyester fibers, like the nylons, have the ability to retain the shape of the spinneret hole, modifications in cross-sectional shape are possible.

Physical Structure

Polyester fibers are produced in many types—filament yarns, staple fibers, and tow. Filaments

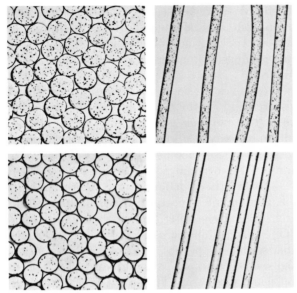

Fig. 11-1 Photomicrographs of Dacron and Terylene polyester: (*upper left*) Dacron (delustered) cross section; (*upper right*) Dacron (delustered) longitudinal view; (*lower left*) Terylene (bright) cross section; (*lower right*) Terylene (bright) longitudinal view. (*Courtesy of The Du Pont Company.*)

are high tenacity or regular, bright or delustered, white or solution dyed. Staple fibers are available in deniers from 1.5 to 10 and are delustered. They may be regular or low-pilling or high tenacity.

Regular polyester fibers, when seen under the microscope, are so much like nylon that identifi-cation is difficult. The smooth rodlike fibers have a circular cross section (Figure 11-1). The fibers are not as transparent as the nylon fibers. They are white, so they normally do not need to be bleached. However, whiter types of polyester fibers have been produced by the addition of optical whiteners (fluorescent compounds) to the fiber spinning solution.

A variety of cross-sectional shapes are produced: round, trilobal, octolobal, oval, hollow, voided, hexalobal, and pentalobal (star-shaped).

Chemical Composition and Molecular Structure

Polyester fibers are manufactured fibers in which the fiber forming substance is any long chain polymer composed of at least 85 per cent by weight of an ester of dihydric alcohol and terephthalic acid. (p $HOOC—O_6H_4—COOH$)—Federal Trade Commission.

Polyester fibers are made from two kinds of terephthalate polymers. The original fibers Terylene and Dacron were spun from polyethylene terephthalate (abbreviated PET). In 1958, Eastman Chemical Products, Inc., introduced a new type of polyester, Kodel, which is spun from 1,4 cyclohexylene-dimethylene terephthalate, commonly known as PCDT. The differences are listed in the following table.

Comparison of PET and PCDT Fibers

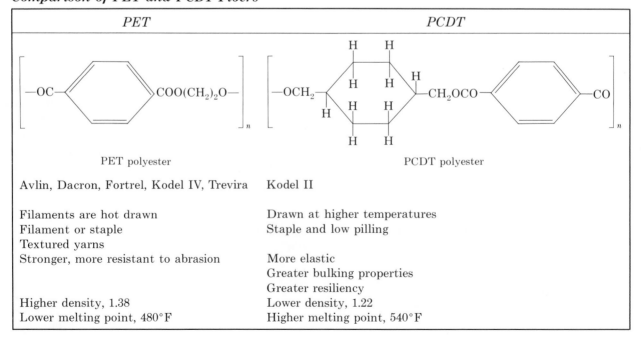

PET	PCDT
PET polyester	PCDT polyester
Avlin, Dacron, Fortrel, Kodel IV, Trevira	Kodel II
Filaments are hot drawn	Drawn at higher temperatures
Filament or staple	Staple and low pilling
Textured yarns	
Stronger, more resistant to abrasion	More elastic
	Greater bulking properties
	Greater resiliency
Higher density, 1.38	Lower density, 1.22
Lower melting point, 480°F	Higher melting point, 540°F

One should not assume from this chart that only Kodel II is low pilling. The PET spinning solutions may be homopolymers or copolymers. The copolymers are pill resistant, lower strength staple fibers used primarily in knits and carpets.

Polyester fibers have straight molecular chains that are packed closely together and are well oriented with very strong hydrogen bonds.

Properties

Polyester fibers are outstanding in their wet and dry resiliency. Because of polyesters ironing has almost been eliminated from apparel and bed and table linens, although many people still do touch-up pressing.

The first use of polyester filaments was in knit shirts for men and blouses for women. The filaments were also used in sheer curtains, where the excellent light resistance of the fibers and the fineness of denier made them particularly suitable for ninon and marquisette. The use of filament polyester increased tremendously when the "set" textured yarns were developed and used in double-knit and woven fabrics for suits, dresses, jackets, and lightweight coats. Both smooth and textured filaments have had wide use in career apparel such as uniforms for nurses and waitresses.

The first use of staple polyester was in tropical suitings for men's summer suits. The suits were light in weight and machine washable—something unique in men's clothing. The very low absorbency of the polyester fibers limited the comfort factors of these first garments, a disadvantage that was overcome by blending polyester with cotton and/or wool. In 1977 staple polyester began to be widely used in heavier cottonlike fabrics such as denim or gabardine.

More recent uses of polyester fibers have been in carpets and tires. The first polyester carpets suffered from a "walked-down" look after a period of wear in heavy traffic areas. This now has been corrected by autoclave heat setting the fibers. In tires, the polyesters do not "flat-spot."

Aesthetic. Polyester fibers accommodate themselves in blends so that a natural fiber look and texture are maintained with the advantage of easy care. Polyester double knits have a special "look" that is attractive to many people. Silklike polyesters have been very satisfactory in appearance and hand.

The trilobal polyester fibers were developed as the result of a study by Du Pont to find a man-made filament that would have the aesthetic properties possessed by silk. The study, made in cooperation with a silk finishing company, started with an investigation of the effect of the different stages of silk-finishing processes on the aesthetic properties of silk fabrics, since silk seemed to acquire added richness in the fabric form.

In silk fabric, sericin (gum) makes up about 30 per cent of the weight. The boil-off finishing process removes the sericin and creates a looser, more mobile fabric structure. If the fabric is in a relaxed state while the sericin is being removed, the warp yarns take on a *high degree of weave crimp*. This crimp and the *looser fabric structure* together create the liveliness and suppleness of silk. The suppleness has been compared to the action of the coil-spring "Slinky" toy. The properties are quite different when the boil-off is done under tension. The weave crimp is much less, and the response of the fabric is more like that of a flat spring; thus the supple nature is lost. This helps to explain the difference between qualities of silk fabric.

The results of the silk fabric study indicated that the unique properties of silk—liveliness, suppleness, and drape of the fabric; dry "tactile" hand; and good covering power of the yarns—are the result of (1) the triangular-like shape of the silk fiber; (2) the fine denier per filament; (3) the loose, bulky yarn and fabric structure; and (4) a highly crimped fabric structure.

The process was then applied to polyesters. The fibers were spun with a trilobal shape and made into fabrics that were processed by a silk-finishing treatment. The polyesters were particularly suited to this study. They are unique because they can be treated with a caustic soda to dissolve away the surface, leaving a thinner fiber, yarn, or fabric without changing the fiber basically.

Man-made fibers are normally processed under tension by a continuous method rather than by a batch method. Because of the results of the Du Pont research study of silk, the trilobal fabrics are processed in a *completely relaxed* condition. Finishing starts with a heat-setting treatment to stabilize the fabric to controlled width, remove any wrinkles, and impart resistance to wrinkling. The next step is a very important caustic soda (alkali) treatment, which dissolves away a controlled amount of the fiber. This step is similar to the degumming of silk and it gives the fabric structure greater mobility. All remaining finishes

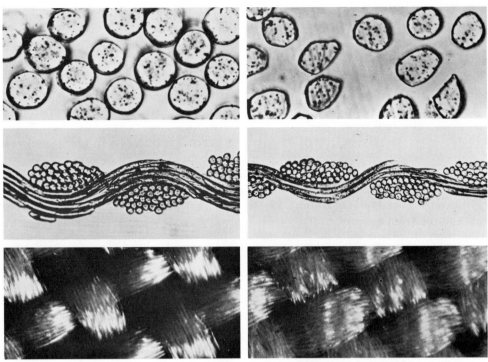

Fig. 11-2 Photomicrographs showing effect of heat-caustic treatment. (*Top*) Dacron polyester fiber cross section, 1,000×. (*Middle*) Fabric cross section, 200×. (*Bottom*) Fabric surface, 50×. (*Courtesy of The Du Pont Company.*)

are done with the fabric *completely relaxed* to get maximum weave-crimp. (Antron nylon is finished in the same way except that there is no caustic treatment.) Figure 11-2 shows the effect of the alkali treatment on a fabric made of a circular-cross-section polyester.

Some adverse problems rarely mentioned by the producers of polyesters are pilling, soiling, bacterial odor, and discomfort in humid weather.

Pilling was a severe problem with the fabrics made from the standard polyesters. Pilling changes the appearance of fabrics making them look shabby before they are worn out. Polyester fabrics did not pill more than wool fabrics, but the pills held on and did not break off as they did with wool. Pilling is a problem with all smooth round fibers of high strength. Low-pilling fiber types have been developed to minimize the problem and to make them more suitable to use in blends with wool and cellulose and in napped and pile fabrics.

Durability. The strength and abrasion resistance of polyesters are quite high, and the wet strength is comparable to the dry strength. The high strength is developed by hot-drawing or stretch-

ing to develop crystallinity and also by increasing the molecular weight. The breaking tenacity of polyester varies from 4.0 to 5.5 in regular filament, 6.3 to 9.5 in high tenacity filament, and 2.5 to 5.5 in staple fiber. High-tenacity filaments are used in tire cords and industrial fabrics. The higher tenacity staple fibers are used in durable press goods.

A need for a strong sewing thread that had good resistance to damage by resin finishes was created by the synthetic fabrics and durable press. Cotton thread was weakened by resin finishes so it was not resistant to abrasion, and it also lacked "give" and would break when the seams stretched. Thread shrinkage caused unsightly puckering of seams and zipper areas—especially those on the straight grain of the fabric.

Two kinds of polyester thread are available for use with synthetic and durable press fabrics.

Polyester/Cotton Core-Spun Thread. The thread has a high-strength filament polyester core around which is spun a sheath of high-quality cotton fiber. This thread combines the good characteristics of polyester and cotton fibers. The cotton outer cover gives the thread excellent sew-ability, and the polyester core provides high strength and resistance to abrasion and degradation. Polyester/cotton thread also provides the slight "give" that is necessary in knits.

One Hundred Per Cent Spun Polyester Thread. The thread is produced in much the same manner as is cotton thread, with short staple-length fibers. Spun polyester thread is stronger than cotton, providing "give" without breaking, and is more resistant to abrasion and chemical degradation. This thread performs satisfactorily in home-sewing situations.

Comfort. *Absorbency* is quite low for the polyesters, ranging from 0.4 to 0.8 per cent moisture regain. Fabrics are resistant to waterborne stains and are quick drying. Polyester upholstery fabrics have more stability in humid weather than nylon, which has a higher moisture regain. Poor absorbency lowers the comfort factor of skin-contact apparel. The *soil-release* finishes have improved the wicking characteristics of the polyesters, thus improving the breathability and comfort of the fabrics. Blends of polyester/cotton are more comfortable in humid weather.

Polyesters are more *electrostatic* than the other fibers in the heat-sensitive group. Static is characteristic of fibers that have low absorbency. Static is a definite disadvantage because lint is attracted to the surface of fabrics and it is difficult to keep dark-colored fabrics looking neat. Curtains soil more rapidly. New fabrics usually have an antistatic finish, but it is often removed by washing or dry cleaning. The fabric softeners as a laundry aid are good antistatic agents. Temporary relief from static can be gained by running a damp sponge over a garment or by using an antistatic spray.

Care and Related End-Use Properties. *Resiliency* relates to tensile work recovery and refers to the extent and manner of recovery from deformation. The table indicates that polyester has a high recovery when the elongation is low, an im-

Tensile Recovery from Elongation of:

Fiber	1%	3%	5%	15%
Polyester 56 (regular)	91	76	63	40
Nylon 200 (regular)	81	88	86	77

Source: E. I. du Pont de Nemours & Company, *Technical Bulletin X-142* (September 1961).

portant factor in the suiting market. Only small deformations are involved in the wrinkling of a suit, and Dacron recovers better than nylon. The recovery behavior of Dacron at the elongation percentages given in the table is similar to that of wool at the higher elongations. Nylon shows better recovery at the higher elongations, however, so it would perform better in garments that are subject to greater elongation—hosiery, for example.

The other polyesters are similar to Dacron in their wet and dry wrinkle recovery. This has given them an advantage over wool in tropical suitings, since wool has poor wrinkle recovery when wet. Under conditions of high atmospheric humidity and body perspiration, polyester suits do not shrink and are very resistant to wrinkling. However, when polyester garments do acquire wear wrinkles, as often happens at the waist of a garment where body heat and moisture "set" the wrinkles, pressing is necessary to remove them.

Resiliency and quick drying make the polyesters especially good for fiberfill batts in quilted fabrics,—for example quilts, bedspreads, parkas and robes.

Resistance to Chemicals and Biological Attack. Polyester fibers are generally resistant to both acids and alkalis and can be bleached with either chlorine or oxygen bleaches. This is very important because the largest single use of the polyesters is in blends with cotton for durable press. They are resistant to biological attack and to sunlight damage. The polyester fibers are the most important filaments for sheer glass curtains.

Effect of Heat. Polyesters are thermoplastic. They must be heat-set to obtain stability and permanent pleats in garments. Washing in warm water followed by tumble drying is recommended, but polyesters may be safely washed in hot water to remove greasy and oily stains or to remove a buildup of body oils. Hot water may cause them to wrinkle more and may cause color loss.

The heat properties of the polyesters are used to advantage in the production of fiberfill for pillows, quilts, and linings. The fiber is flattened on one side or made asymmetrical while it is softened by heat, and it will then take on a tight spiral curl of outstanding springiness. Fiberfill can be made of a blend of fiber deniers to give three distinct levels of support. Lumpiness in pillows can be prevented by spot-welding the fibers to each other by running hot needles through the pillow bat. The jumpsuits in Figure

Fig. 11-3 Jump suit. Eastman Kodel polyester fiberfill. (*Courtesy of the Rowland Company, Inc.*)

Fig. 11-4 Furlike coat. Eastman Kodel polyester 60 percent and acrylic 40 percent. (*Courtesy of the Rowland Company, Inc.*)

11-3 have unquilted nylon shells over Kodel fiberfill insulation. The *specific gravity* of the polyesters varies from 1.22 to 1.38; they are heavier than the nylons and acrylics but compare favorably with the acetates, which are also used for quilted linings but are less washable.

The *heat shrinkage* of the polyester fibers can be controlled so they can be used in furlike fabrics. Figure 11-4 is a coat of furlike fabric of 60 per cent polyester and 40 per cent acrylic. Type 414 Kodel is a polishable fiber for pile fabrics. (See electrifying finish in Chapter 28.)

In 1970, Du Pont reported experimental work on heat molding of polyester to make a man's vestlike garment.

> Tailoring to fit the shoulders was accomplished by shaping the fabric on a hot head press heated to 350°F and by using a fusible interliner in the front panels . . . Resulting garments are home launderable. Also described is making a pair of slacks from only two pieces of fabric.—*Textile Industries,* **134:**33 (December 1970).

Identification. *Burning Test and Flammability.* The polyesters, like nylon, withdraw from the flame before igniting, so they do not flash burn. They also melt and drip and the flame is carried down with the drip. A black bead forms when the melt hardens. The polyesters can be distinguished from the nylons by the odor and the smoke. The polyesters have an aromatic odor and give off a heavy black smoke that contains pieces of soot. The fabric must burn briskly before black smoke and soot are evolved, so an adequate sample must be tested to make the identification positive.

Types and Kinds of Polyester

The following chart lists the terminology used to describe the types and kinds of polyester. Each company has a large variety of specific fibers or yarns that combine one or more of these many variables.

Types and Kinds of Polyester

Filament, staple, tow, fiberfill, staple for non-wovens
Modified cross section
Producer textured, partially oriented, undrawn filament
Disperse dyeable, cationic dyeable, solution dyed, optically whitened
Regular tenacity, high tenacity
High shrinkage, normal shrinkage, low shrinkage, heat stabilized
Pill resistant, normal pilling
Homopolymer, copolymer
Bicomponent—cospun (homopolymer/copolymer)
Polished high luster

Trademarks and Producers

Trademarks	Producer
A.C.E.	Allied Chemical
Avlin	Avtex Fibers
Dacron	Du Pont
Encron	American Enka
Fortrel	Fiber Industries
Golden Touch	American Enka
Kodel	Eastman Chemical Products
Quintess	Phillips Fibers
Spectran	Monsanto
Strialine	American Enka
Trevira	Hoechst Fibers Industries

Olefin Fibers

12

Many attempts were made to polymerize ethylene in the 1920s. Ethylene was polymerized and used as an important plastic during World War II but filaments made from it did not have sufficient strength or a high enough melting point for use in textile fibers. In 1954 Karl Ziegler in Germany developed a process in which the melting point of polymerized ethylene filaments was raised but it still was too low for apparel fibers. Polyethylene fibers were used in some industrial end uses. In Italy, Giulio Natta worked with polypropylene and was successful in making linear polymers of high molecular weight that proved to be suitable for textile applications. By 1957, Italy was producing olefin fibers; U.S. production of olefin fibers started in 1960 with the production of Herculon by the Hercules Powder Company Inc.

Olefin fibers have a combination of properties that make them good for home furnishings, apparel that does not need ironing, and for industrial uses. Olefin fibers are strong and resistant to abrasion, inexpensive, chemically inert, and thermoplastic but static resistant.

There are 39 producers of polypropylene in the U.S.

Production

The term *olefin* is derived from the Latin *oleum*, meaning oil. (Oleum is also the root of the word *oleomargarine*.) The olefin fibers are melt-spun from polypropylene, an inexpensive crude-oil cracking product. Extrusion is almost the same as for nylon and polyester. After extrusion the filaments are drawn to orient the molecules and to develop crystallization. Olefins differ from polyester and nylon in that the solution crystallizes very rapidly (undrawn fibers are crystalline) so that the spinning conditions and after treatments greatly affect the fiber properties.

Physical Structure

Olefins are produced as monofilament, multifilament, staple fiber, and tow with variable tenacities. The fibers are colorless, usually round in cross section, and have a somewhat waxy feel (Figure 12–1).

Chemical Composition and Molecular Structure

Olefin fibers are manufactured fibers in which the fiber forming substance is any long chain synthetic polymer composed of at least 85 per cent by weight of ethylene, propylene or other olefin units except amorphous (noncrystalline) polyolefins qualifying as rubber. (CH_2CH_2:$CH_3CH_2CH_2CH_3$) —Federal Trade Commission.

The process used to obtain polypropylene fibers was a remarkable development. Polypropylene is a three-dimensional structure with a backbone of carbon atoms and methyl groups standing out from the chain. Natta observed that three configurations could be developed when propylene was polymerized and that when all the methyl groups were on one side of the chain, the molecular chains could pack together and crys-

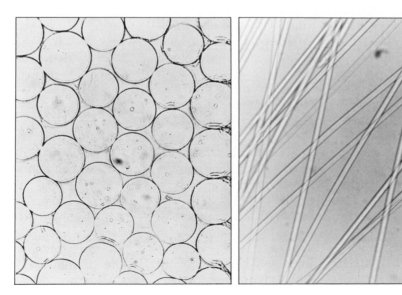

Fig. 12-1 Photomicrograph showing cross-sectional (*left*) and longitudinal (*right*) views of Herculon (Hercules registered trademark). (*Courtesy of Hercules Incorporated.*)

tallize. Natta developed the process in which polymerization would take place in this manner, and, together with Ziegler, received the Nobel Prize in 1963 for his achievement.

Karl Ziegler's work on catalysts to polymerize ethylene and Giulio Natta's discovery of steriospecific polymerization made it possible to obtain high-molecular-weight crystalline polypropylene polymers. Steriospecific polymerization means that all the molecules are specifically arranged in space so that all the *methyl groups have the same location* and there are no polar groups. Natta called this phenomenon *isotactic*. In the atactic form, the methyl groups are randomly oriented, resulting in an amorphous polymer that would qualify as rubber.

Methyl groups

Olefin fibers have no polar groups. The chains are held together by crystallinity alone. The absence of polar groups makes the dyeing of the fiber a problem. Solution dyeing is expensive and not as versatile as piece dyeing and printing.

Properties

Aesthetic. Olefin fibers are the lightest textile fibers with a specific gravity of 0.91. This provides more fiber per pound for better cover. If other problems with olefins could be solved, they should be good for warmth-without-weight fabrics for sweaters and blankets. Olefins do not build up static as do the other melt-spun fibers.

Durability. Olefin fibers are produced with different strengths suited to the end use. For ropes the breaking tenacity is 9.0 g/d ±. Tenacities up to 13 g/d can be achieved. Regular fibers have strengths of 4.5 to 6.0 g/d. Olefin fibers have excellent abrasion resistance. Elongation ranges from 15 to 30 per cent. Elastic recovery varies but is comparable to nylon. Olefin fibers have 0.01 moisture regain so their strength is as good wet as dry.

Comfort. Olefins are not widely used in apparel fabrics. The low density (0.91) is an asset in fiber-fill for sleeping bags or in blankets. Olefins have a unique wicking characteristic that is desirable in apparel.

Care. Olefins have easy care characteristics that make them suited to a number of end uses. They are not affected by moisture; they have excellent *resistance* to *acids, alkalis, insects, microorganisms.* Olefins are affected by sunlight but stabilizers can be added to correct this disadvantage. Indoor/outdoor carpeting made of olefin fibers can be hosed off.

Olefins have a low melting point (325–335°F), which limits their use in apparel. Warm or cold water should be used for spot cleaning or washing. Olefin fabrics should be air dried. Olefins are more oleophilic than nylon.

Identification. Polypropylene melts as do other melt-spun fibers. It will burn with a blue and yellow flame in continued contact with flame.

Split-Fiber Olefins

Extrusion—forcing a liquid through a spinneret to form fine strands—is the standard method of spinning fibers. The *split-fiber method* was developed in 1965 at the Shirley Institute in England. The method is less expensive than the traditional extrusion process and can be done by small industry. However, some fiber polymers cannot be processed by the split-fiber method. Polypropylene is used extensively because of its ease of processing and economic factors.

Production

Pellets of polypropylene are melted, extruded as a film 0.005 to 0.020 inch thick, and cooled quickly by quenching in water. The film is slit into tapes 0.1 inch wide. The slit tapes are then heat-stretched to orient the molecular chains, and the stretching is carried to a point where the film develops a tendency to fibrillate (split into fibers). Twisting or other mechanical action completes the fibrillation. Split-fiber yarns have high strength.

Uses

Yarns as low as 250 denier have been made from split fibers, but these are coarse for clothing uses. Carpet backing, rope, cord, fishnets, and bagging are the big uses.

Continued research and refinement of the process may result in a wholly new generation of fibers in the future. One of the interesting outgrowths of split-film research may be the development of a new process for making nonwovens. Some of the early work with fibrillation of nylon film gave lacelike sheets that suggested possibilities in the nonwoven area.

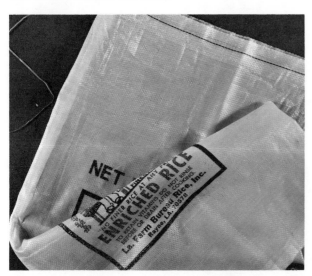

Fig. 12-2 Bag woven with slit olefin yarns.

Olefin films are slit into yarns that are used for the same textile products as split-fiber olefin (Figure 12-2).

Types and Kinds of Olefin Fibers	
Heat stabilized	Acid dyeable
Light stabilized	Solution dyed
Modified cross section	Bicomponent
Pigmented	Fibrillated

Some Trade Names and Producers	
Fibralon, Fibrilawn	Fibron, Inc.
Herculon, Herculon II, IV	Hercules, Inc.
Marvess, Marvess III	Phillips Fibers Corp.
Patlon	Amaco Fabrics
Polybloom	Chevron Chemical
Vectra	Vectra Corp.

Major end uses
- Industrial   Bags, fishnets, ropes, twines, filter fabric
- Home furnishings   Upholstery, primary and secondary carpet backings, indoor/outdoor carpets, carpet face fiber, substrate for coated fabrics

Comparison of Melt Spun Fibers

	Nylon	Polyester	Olefin
Mill capacity, 1977	1866–filament	2159–filament	861–filament
(Million pounds)	910–staple	2355–staple	120–staple
Breaking tenacity	3.5–9.5 g/d filament	4.0–9.5 filament	4.8–6.0 filament
	2.5–6.0 g/d staple	2.5–6.5 staple	
Specific gravity	1.14	1.22 or 1.38	0.91
Moisture regain	4.5	0.2–0.8	0.01
Melting point	482° or 414°F	540° or 482°F	325°–350°F
Safe ironing temperature	300°–350°F	325°–350°F	250°F–lowest setting
Effect of light	Poor resistance	Good resistance	Poor resistance

Acrylic Fibers, Modacrylic Fibers, and Other Vinyl Fibers

13

Acrylic Fibers

Acrylonitrile, the substance from which acrylic fibers are made and from which the generic name is derived, was first made in Germany in 1893. It was one of the chemicals used by Carothers and his team in the fundamental research done on high polymers for The Du Pont Company.

Du Pont developed an acrylic fiber in 1944 and started commercial production of this fiber in 1950. The fiber was given the trade name Orlon. Three other companies began to produce acrylics; Chemstrand Corp. (Monsanto) introduced Acrilan in 1952, Dow Chemical (Dow-Badische) began the production of Zefran in 1958, and American Cyanimid began the production of Creslan in 1958. Only these same four companies were producing acrylic fibers in 1977.

Acrylic fibers are soft, warm, light in weight and resilient and they make easy care fabrics. They are resistant to sunlight and weathering. They are produced as staple fiber and used primarily in woollike end uses.

Production

Some acrylic fibers are dry or solvent spun and others are wet spun. In *solvent spinning* the polymers are dissolved in a suitable solvent such as dimethyl formamide, extruded into warm air, and solidified by evaporation of the solvent. After spinning, the fibers are stretched hot, three to ten times their original length, and then crimped, and marketed as cut staple or tow. In *wet spinning* the polymer is dissolved in solvent, extruded into a coagulating bath, dried, crimped, and collected as tow for use in the high-bulk process or cut into staple and baled.

Acrylonitrile is relatively cheap but the solvents are expensive making the spinning process more expensive than that of other synthetic fibers.

Physical Structure

One of the most important features of the acrylic fibers is the cross-sectional shape that results from the spinning method (Figure 13-1). *Dry spinning* gives a dog-bone shape. Differences in cross-sectional shape affect physical and aesthetic properties and thus are a factor in determining end use. Round and lima-bean shapes are better for carpets because of high bending stiffness, which contributes to resiliency. Dog-bone shape and flatness give the softness and luster desirable for apparel uses. Creslan, Zefran, and Acrilan are wet spun.

All of the production of acrylic fibers in the United States is staple fiber and tow. Staple fiber is available in deniers and lengths suitable for all spinning systems. Acrylic fibers also vary in shrinkage potential. Bicomponent fibers were first produced as acrylics.

Chemical Composition and Molecular Structure

Acrylic fibers are manufactured fibers in which the fiber forming substance is a synthetic polymer of at least 85 per cent by weight of acrylonitrile.—Federal Trade Commission.

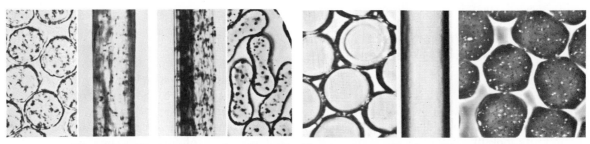

Fig. 13-1 Photomicrographs of acrylic fibers: cross-sectional and longitudinal views. (*Left to right*) Acrilan, Orlon, Creslan, Zefran. (*Photomicrograph of Acrilan courtesy of the Chemstrand Corporation; photomicrograph of Orlon courtesy of The Du Pont Company; photomicrograph of Creslan courtesy of American Cyanamid Company; photomicrograph of Zefran courtesy of the Dow Badische Company.*)

$$CH_2\!-\!\overset{\displaystyle H}{\underset{\displaystyle CN}{\overset{|}{\underset{|}{C}}}}\!-$$

The acrylonitrile monomer was discovered in 1893, and the polymer was first patented in 1929. The pure polymer was extremely insoluble until dimethyl formamide was discovered.

Fibers of 100 per cent polyacrylonitrile have a compact, highly oriented internal structure that makes them virtually undyeable. Therefore, most acrylics are made as copolymers with up to 15 per cent additives, which give a more open structure and which permit dyestuffs to be absorbed into the fiber. The additives furnish dye sites and are cationic for acid dyes and anionic for basic dyes. This makes cross dyeing possible.

Zefran is a graft polymer. In graft polymerization, the additive does not become a part of the main molecular chain but is fastened as side chains. The difference between polymers, copolymers, and graft polymers is as follows:

```
××××××××××××××××××××××××    Polymer
○×○×○×○×○×○×○×○×○×○×○×○×    Copolymer
××××××××××××××××××××××××    Graft polymer
 | | | | | | |
 C  C  C  C  C  C  C
```

The copolymer acrylics are not as strong as the homopolymers or graft polymer acrylics. Since the end uses for acrylics are mostly apparel and home furnishings, the reduced strength is not very important.

Properties

The acrylic fibers have been most successful in end uses that have previously been dominated by wool. Because of their low specific gravity and high bulk properties, the acrylics have been called the Warmth Without Weight fibers. They are superior to wool in their easy-care properties and they are nonallergenic.

Aesthetic. Acrylic fibers are the most woollike of the man-made fibers. Carpet fibers look like wool, and baby knits look like wool but are softer and more easily cared for. Jerseys, challis, and other fine wool fabrics can be duplicated in acrylics. The cost of acrylic fabrics and apparel is comparable with good quality wool but the acrylics are especially good for people who are allergic to wool. The first acrylic fibers were subject to pilling and bulky knits stretched and bagged (instead of shrinking as wool did), but these problems were solved by using proper yarn and knit structures.

Acrylic fibers cannot be given a "permanent set" like that of the nylons and polyesters. However, acrylics have the ability to take a *set* such as a pleat or crease in skirts or trousers that will not be affected by wear, laundering, or dry cleaning. Also, the acrylic fibers have the ability to develop a *latent shrinkage potential* and retain it indefinitely at room temperature. The pleat and the latent shrinkage fiber represent a *metastable* heat stage. The application of heat and/or steam will easily remove the pleat and restore the fiber to its original condition. This potential for returning to the original state is referred to as "memory."

Latent shrinkage in a fiber is achieved by heating, stretching, and then cooling while in the stretched condition. These heat-stretched fibers are called *high-shrinkage fibers*. (High-shrinkage fibers are processed on the Turbo-Stapler; see Chapter 18.) High-shrinkage fibers are combined with nonshrinkage fibers in the same yarn, which is then made into a garment. Heat treatment of the garment will cause the high-shrinkage fibers to relax or shrink, forcing the *nonshrinkage fibers* to bulk. This makes high-bulk sweaters and similar garments. Knitting yarns are sometimes made the same way. High-shrinkage fibers tend to migrate to the center of the yarn. Thus, if fine-denier nonshrinkage fibers are combined with coarse-denier high-shrinkage fibers, the fine-denier fibers will end up on the outer surface of the yarn. The amount of bulk can be controlled by regulating the amount of heat stretching. Zefran fibers cannot be modified for heat shrinkage and are not made into high-bulk yarns.

The high-bulk principle can be used to achieve interesting effects, such as "guard hairs" in synthetic furs and sculptured high-low effects in carpets. Carpet pile or furlike fabrics can be made more dense by using a high-shrinkage type fiber for the ground yarns. When the yarns shrink, the fibers are brought much closer together.

Durability. Acrylics are not as durable as nylon, polyester, or olefin fibers but in apparel and household textiles the strength of acrylics is satisfactory. The first Orlon was produced in filament form with strength almost as good as nylon. Because of its exceptional resistance to weathering it was thought that acrylics would be widely used in awnings, outdoor furniture, and curtains. (Filament yarn acrylic is found in imported drapery fabrics.) The resistance of acrylics to dyes and the high costs of production limited its use in these end uses. Success was later achieved for acrylics with staple fibers of lesser strengths. The following chart shows that acrylic fibers are comparable to wool in their durability properties.

Comparison of Acrylic Fibers with Wool—Durability

Fiber Property	Acrylic	Wool
Breaking tenacity	2.0–3.5 g/d dry	1.5 g/d dry
	1.8–3.5 g/d wet	1.0 g/d wet
Elastic recovery	92%	99%
Elongation at break	20%	25%
Abrasion resistance	Good	Fair

Comfort. Acrylic fibers are soft and nonallergenic. They have a density of 1.14–1.15 g/cc, which makes them much lighter in weight than wool. The moisture regain varies from 1.0–3.0 per cent. Static charges develop but not to the same extent as with polyesters. High-bulk acrylic fibers make fabrics that give warmth without weight.

Care. The acrylics have good resistance to most chemicals except strong alkalis and chlorine bleaches. (Fibers containing nitrogen are usually susceptible to damage from alkali and chlorine.) Except for the furlike fabrics, acrylic fabrics have good wash-and-wear characteristics. They do not wrinkle if handled properly and if directions on the label are followed. Sweaters made of acrylic fibers do not need to be blocked to shape as is the case with wool sweaters.

Acrylics can be dry-cleaned; on some fabrics the finish is removed, which results in a harsh feel. Care labeling should be followed. Acrylics are resistant to moth damage and to mildew. Acrylics have excellent resistance to sunlight.

The *burning* characteristics of the acrylics are similar to those of the acetates. The fibers soften, burst into flame and burn freely, then decompose to a black crumbly residue. There is a chemical aromatic odor that is different from the vinegarlike odor of the acetates. Differences in the flammability of the acrylics and the modacrylics is the result of the high acrylonitrile content of the acrylics. The modacrylics, which have a much lower acrylonitrile content, are self-extinguishing.

Many acrylic fibers are used in napped or pile fabrics, so fire retardancy is necessary to comply with safety requirements. Acrylic fibers have been modified for fire retardancy. Types 78 Acrilan and Type 84 Creslan are examples of fibers with flame-retardancy.

The following chart compares properties related to care of acrylic fiber with wool.

Comparison of Acrylics and Wool—Care

Fiber Property	Acrylic	Wool
Effect of alkalis	Resistant to weak	Harmed
Effect of acids	Resistant to most	Resistant to weak
Effect of solvents	Can be dry-cleaned	Dry cleaning recommended
Effect of sunlight	Excellent resistance	Low resistance
Stability	Can be heat-set for shape retention	Subject to felting, shrinkage
Permanence of creases	Creases can be set and removed by heat	Creases set by heat and moisture—not permanent
Effect of heat	Thermoplastic—sticks at 450–490°F	Scorches easily. Becomes brittle at high temperature
Resistance to moths and fungi	Resistant	Harmed by moths. Mildew will form on soiled stored wool

Modacrylic Fibers

Modacrylic fibers are modified acrylics. They are also made from acrylonitrile but have a larger proportion of other polymers added to make the copolymers.

Production of modacrylic fibers started in the United States in 1949 with Dynel produced by Union Carbide Corp. Production of Dynel was discontinued in 1977. Verel was introduced by Tennessee Eastman in 1956. In 1971, Monsanto began production of SEF modacrylic.

Modacrylics do not support combustion, are very difficult to ignite, are self-extinguishing, and do not drip. This innate fire retardance makes them good for end uses in which compliance with the Flammable Fabrics Act is required. Modacrylics are widely used in children's sleepwear, contract draperies, fake furs, and wigs.

Production

The modacrylic fibers are produced by polymerizing two components, dissolving the copolymer in a suitable solvent (acetone) and pumping the solution into a column of warm air, and stretching while hot.

Physical Structure

The modacrylics are creamy white and are produced as staple or tow. They have a dog-bone or irregular cross section (Figure 13–2). Various deniers, lengths, crimp levels, and shrinkage potentials are available to fabric producers.

Chemical Composition and Molecular Structure

Modacrylic fibers are manufactured fibers in which the fiber forming substance is any long chain synthetic polymer composed of less than 85 per cent but more than 35 per cent acrylonitrile units.—Federal Trade Commission.

The chemicals other than acrylonitrile are vinyl chloride (CH_2CHCl), vinylidene chloride ($CHCCl_2$), or vinylidene dicyanide (CH_2CCN_2).

Properties

Modacrylics are similar to the acrylics in their properties—the major differences being fire retardance and effect of heat.

Aesthetic. Furlike fabrics, wigs and hairpieces, and fleece-type pile fabrics are important end uses for modacrylic fibers. Verel is produced with different amounts of crimp and shrinkage potential. By mixing different fiber types it is possible to obtain fibers of different pile heights, long, polished fibers (guard hairs) and soft, highly crimped undercoat fibers much like real fur (Figure 13–3). Fabrics can be sheared, embossed, and printed to resemble fur.

Durability. Modacrylics have adequate durability for their end uses. A comparison of durability factors of modacrylics and acrylics is listed.

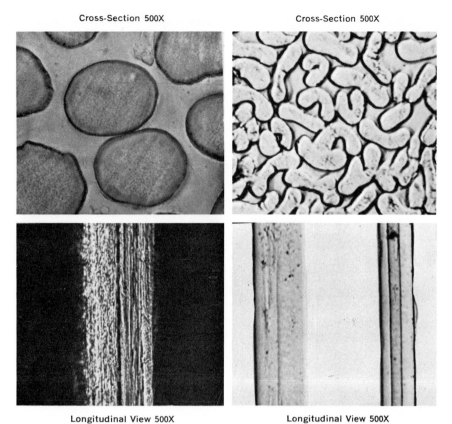

Cross-Section 500X Cross-Section 500X

Longitudinal View 500X Longitudinal View 500X

Fig. 13-2 Photomicrographs of modacrylic fibers. (*Courtesy of American Association of Textile Chemists and Colorists.*)

Comfort. Modacrylics are poor conductors of heat. Fabrics are soft, warm, and resilient. Fabrics have a tendency to pill. Their absorbency is low, varying from 2 to 4 per cent moisture regain.

Care. Modacrylics are resistant to acids, weak alkalis, and most organic solvents. Most modacrylics dissolve in boiling acetone. They are resistant to mildew and moths. They have very good resistance to sunlight. They have very good flame resistance.

Modacrylics can be washed or dry-cleaned but special care must be taken. Excessive rubbing may cause fabrics to pill. Fibers are heat sensitive; they shrink at 250°F and stiffen at temperatures over 300°F. If machine washed, warm water should be used. Tumble dry at low setting. Most fabrics need little ironing; lowest setting should be used if ironed. The furlike fabrics vary in methods used for cleaning. Some are dry-cleanable; some require special care in dry cleaning (no steam, no tumble, tumble cold; some should be cleaned by furrier method). Look for instructions on labels (Figure 13-4).

Fig. 13-3 Furlike fabric. Notice long sleek guard hairs and soft fine undercoat.

Comparison of Modacrylic and Acrylic Fibers

Factor	Modacrylic	Acrylic
Strength	1.7–3.5 g/d	2.0–3.5 g/d
Elongation	30–60%	20%
Elastic recovery	88%	92%
Sunlight resistance	Excellent	Excellent

Fig. 13-4 Label giving directions for cleaning furlike fabric.

Types and Kinds of Modacrylic

Verel	SEF
Controlled shrinkage	Staple
Very low nonperma-	Producer blend of
nent crimp	65% SEF/35% polyester
High crimp	
Very high crimp	
Ribbon cross section	

Trademarks and Producers

SEF	Monsanto
Verel	Eastman Kodak
Zefran	Dow Badische

Other Vinyl Fibers

In 1958, when The Textile Fiber Products Identification Act was passed, generic names were given to the various vinyl fibers based on their chemical composition.

Saran

Saran is a manufactured fiber in which the fiber forming substance in any long chain synthetic polymer composed of at least 80 per cent by weight of vinylidene chloride units. (CH_2CCl_2)—Federal Trade Commission.

Saran is a vinylidene chloride/vinyl chloride copolymer developed in 1940 by the Dow Chemical Company. The raw material is melt-spun and stretched to orient the molecules. Both filament and staple forms are produced. Much of the filament fiber is produced as a monofilament for seat covers, furniture webbing, screenings, luggage, shoes, and handbags. Monofilaments are also used in doll's hair and wigs. The staple form is made either straight, curled, or crimped. The curled form is unique in that the curl is inherent and closely resembles the curl of natural wool. The staple is used in rugs, draperies, and upholstery. In addition to its use as a fiber, saran has wide use in the plastics field.

Saran has good *weathering properties, chemical resistance,* and *resistance to stretch.* It is an unusually tough, durable fiber. The fiber as seen under the microscope is perfectly round and smooth. It does not catch and hold gritty dirt particles that, when embedded in a rug, set up and abrasive shearing action. Saran absorbs little or no moisture, so it dries rapidly. It is difficult to dye, and for this reason, solution dyeing is used. Saran does not support combustion. When exposed to flame, it will soften, char, and decompose.

Vinyon

Vinyon is a manufactured fiber in which the fiber forming substance is any long chain synthetic polymer composed of at least 85 per cent by weight of vinyl chloride units. (CH_2CHCl)—Federal Trade Commission.

A patent for making fiber from a copolymer of vinyl chloride (86 per cent) and vinyl acetate (14 per cent) was obtained by the Union Carbide Corporation in 1937. The raw material is dissolved in acetone and dry-spun. The name "vinyon" was adopted as a trade name and later released for generic usage.

Vinyon is very sensitive to heat. The fibers soften at 150 to 170°F, shrink at 175°F, and do not withstand boiling water or normal pressing and ironing temperatures. They are unaffected by moisture, chemically stable, resistant to moths and biological attack, poor conductors of electricity, and *do not* burn. These properties make vinyon especially good for bonding agents for rugs, papers, and nonwoven fabrics. The fibers have a tenacity of 0.7 to 1.0 gram/denier, which indicates that they are not stretched after spinning. These fibers, which are amorphous, have a warm, pleasant hand.

Vinal

Vinal—a manufactured fiber in which the fiber-forming substance is any long-chain synthetic polymer composed of at least 50 per cent by weight of vinyl alcohol units ($-CH_2-CHOH$) and in which the total of the vinyl alcohol units and any one or more of the various acetal units is at least 85 per cent by weight of the fiber.

No vinal fibers are produced in the United States. Modified vinal fibers are imported for use in children's sleepwear because of their inherent flame-retardant properties. Cordelan, a biconstituent vinal/vinyon fiber imported from Japan, is the major one used.

Nytril—Production Discontinued in United States

Nytril—a manufactured fiber containing at least 85 per cent of a long-chain polymer of vinylidene dinitrile ($-CH_2C(CN)_2$) in which the vinylidene content is no less than every other unit in the polymer chain.

Spandex and Rubber

14

Elastomeric or stretch fibers are those that have elongations of 450 to 700 per cent and recovery that is instantaneous and complete. Rubber and spandex are the two elastomers produced in the United States.

Kinds of Stretch

Every apparel covering of the body needs some stretch or elasticity. Skin is very elastic and will stretch when the body turns, twists, and bends. The amount of stretch in stretch fabric should be adequate for this elongation.

There are two kinds of stretch: power stretch and comfort stretch. *Power stretch* is important in end uses where holding power and elasticity are needed. Elastic fibers that have a high retractive force must be used to attain this kind of stretch. Some end uses are foundation garments, surgical support garments, swimsuits, garters, belts, and suspenders. Power stretch garments have about 200 per cent extensibility and support muscles and body organs, reduce apparent body size, and firm and shape body flesh.

Comfort stretch is important in outerwear where elasticity only is desired. Comfort stretch garments look no different than garments made from nonstretch fabrics. They have 10 to 15 per cent extensibility and provide comfort as well as fit and neatness retention. Comfort stretch fabrics are usually lighter in weight than power stretch fabrics.

Spandex is used to achieve both kinds of stretch (see the following table.)

New fibers are usually compared with natural fibers that they resemble. Compared with rubber, which has almost been replaced in apparel, spandex is lighter in weight and stronger. Spandex is also more resistant to body secretions and it can be dyed.

Rubber

Natural rubber is the oldest elastomer and the least expensive. It is obtained by coagulation of the latex from the rubber tree. (Do not confuse latex with Lastex, a core yarn made of any of the elastic fibers.) In 1905 sheets of rubber were cut into strips that made the yarns used in foundation garments and the like. Previous to this time, whalebone and lacings had been used for corsets. In the 1930s a technique was developed for making fine, round rubber fibers of unlimited length by extruding liquid latex through spinnerets into a coagulating bath. The fibers were then washed and vulcanized.[1] In 1950 rubber was produced as a white fiber.

Although antioxidants are incorporated in the spinning solution, rubber still does not have good resistance to oxidizing agents and is damaged by aging, sunlight, oil, and perspiration. Rubber's resistance to alkali is generally good, but it is damaged by heat, chlorine, and solvents, so it should be washed with care and should *not* be dry-cleaned.

Rubber has *good elasticity,* but its recovery force and tensile strength are not high enough so that it can be used in lightweight garments. The

[1] A manufactured fiber in which the fiber forming substance is a hydrocarbon such as natural rubber, polyisoprene, polybutadiene, copolymers of dienes and hydrocarbons or amorphous (noncrystalline) polyolefins:

$$\begin{array}{cc} CH_2 & CH_2 \\ \| & \| \\ C & \!\!=\!\! C \\ | & | \\ CH_3 & H \end{array}$$

Spandex	*Major End Uses*	*Important Properties*
	Athletic apparel	Power stretch, washability
	Foundation garments (Power net, tricot)	Power stretch, washability, lightweight
	Bathing suits	Power stretch, resistance to salt and chlorine treated water, dyeability
	Golf jackets	Comfort stretch
	Ski pants	Comfort stretch
	Support and surgical hose	Power stretch, lightweight
	Elastic webbing	Power stretch

finest rubber yarns must be three times as large as spandex yarns to be comparable in strength. *Dye acceptance* of rubber is low. Yarns are always covered (see page 97) to give better hand, comfort, and appearance.

Spandex

After many years of research Du Pont introduced the first man-made elastic fiber, Lycra, in 1958.

There was much interest in spandex fibers; they were superior to rubber in strength and durability. By 1965 eight companies were producing spandex. It was assumed that spandex would be widely used in all apparel to make fabrics more comfortable. At this time durable press was introduced. Both durable press and spandex fabrics required special or different cutting, sewing, and pressing techniques and the ready-to-wear industry could only cope with one completely new development at a time. Efforts were concentrated on durable press. At this time also, knitted fabrics were being made in greater quantity and often with textured stretch yarns (see Chapter 17). Knits have comfort stretch because of their fabric construction. In 1977 there were only three producers of spandex: Glospan and Cleerspan by Globe Manufacturing, Lycra by Du Pont, and Numa by Ameliotex.

Production

Spandex fibers are made by reacting preformed polyester or polyether molecules with di-isocyanate and then polymerizing into long molecular chains. Filaments are obtained by wet or solvent spinning. Like all man-made fibers, the spinning solution may contain delustering agents, dye receptors, whiteners, and lubricants.

Physical Structure

Spandex is produced as monofilament or multifilament yarns. Monofilaments are round in cross section whereas multifilaments are coalesced or partly fused together at intervals (Figure 14–1). A pin inserted in the yarn cannot be pulled through the entire length but will be stopped by the joinings. Companies that make multifilaments say that the advantage of these yarns in sewing

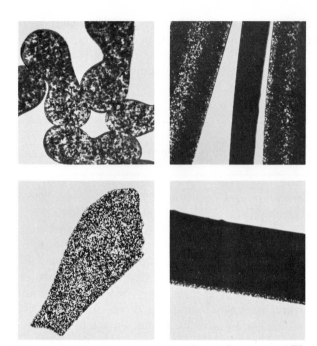

Fig. 14–1 (*Top*) Lycra spandex fiber. (*Courtesy of The Du Pont Company.*) (*Bottom*) Vyrene spandex fiber (*Courtesy of Uniroyal, Inc.*)

fabrics is that the machine needle will go between the fine filaments and thus there is no danger of breaking the filaments. Companies making monofilaments say that when a ball point needle is used it will push the monofilament aside, so there is no danger of rupture.

Spandex fibers are delustered and white. The exception is Cleerspan, which is transparent. Deniers range from 20 to 4,300.

Chemical Composition and Molecular Structure

Spandex is a manufactured elastomeric fiber in which the fiber forming substance is a long chain polymer consisting of at least 85 per cent segmented polyurethane—Federal Trade Commission.

Spandex is a generic name but it is not derived from the chemical nature of the fiber as are most of the man-made fibers (rayon and nylon are the exceptions), but was coined by shifting the syllables of the word *expand*.

Spandex is made up of rigid and flexible segments in the polymer chain; the soft segments provide the stretch and the rigid segments hold the chain together. When force is applied, the

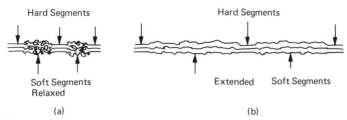

Fig. 14-2 Spandex molecular chains: (a) relaxed (b) extended.

folded or coiled segments straighten out; when force is removed they go back to their original positions (Figure 14-2). Varying proportions of hard and soft segments are used to control the amount of stretch.

Properties

Aesthetic. Spandex is never used alone in fabrics. Other yarns (or fibers) are used to give the desired hand and appearance to fabrics. Even in power stretch fabrics for foundation garments and surgical hose where beauty is not of major importance, nylon or other yarns are used. The characteristics of spandex that contribute to beauty in fabrics are the dyeability of the fiber and good strength making it possible to have fashion in color and prints and sheer garments. Rubber does not take dye, which previously limited the use of color in foundation garments. *Covered yarns* were necessary not only to absorb dye but also to protect the rubber from body oils and secretions and to ensure the degree of stretch.

Covered yarns consist of a central core of rubber or spandex covered with yarns. There are two kinds: single covered and double covered. Covered yarns are wrapped with yarn. The yarn may be filament or spun and may be of any suitable fiber content. Single-covered yarns have a single yarn wrapped around them. Unless the torque is controlled, the yarns may be unbalanced. They are lighter, more resilient, and more economical than double-covered yarns and can be used in satin, batiste, broadcloth, and suiting as well as for lightweight foundation garments. Most ordinary elastic yarns are double-covered to give them balance and better coverage. Fabrics made with these yarns are heavier. A double-covered yarn is shown in Figure 14-3. Covered yarns are subject to "grin-through," which happens as the fabric gets older and the elastic core gets weaker or when the covering sheath is disturbed and lets the core show through.

Spandex needs no cover since it will take dye.

Eliminating the cover yarn reduces the cost and results in lighter weight garments. This is not only important for beauty but also for comfort.

Core-Spun Yarns. Core spinning is a technique of spinning a sheath of staple fiber—*roving*—around an elastomer core while the core is stretched. Any kind of fiber or blend of fibers can be used. The core is completely hidden and does not change the fabric surface. The sheath gives aesthetic properties to the yarn, and the core gives just enough stretch for comfort. Core-spun yarns can be used to give woven fabrics, such as batiste, broadcloth, and suiting, an elasticity more like that of the knits. It was thought that garments made of core-spun yarns would be less apt to require alterations—one of the big costs in retail apparel.

In the core-spinning process, Figure 14-4, a spandex filament is stretched before it is fed to a modified conventional spinning frame where it is combined with a roving that is wrapped around it. The tension on the spandex causes it to keep to the center of the bundle. The core must be completely covered to prevent "grin-through," which makes the core visible.

Biconstituent Fibers. Monsanto introduced a new fiber Monvelle, in 1974 for use in support hose (see Chapter 25). Monvelle is a biconstituent fiber composed of 50 per cent spandex and 50 per

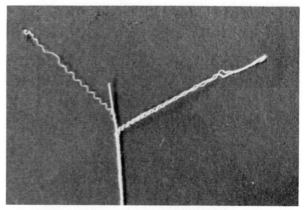

Fig. 14-3 Double-wrapped elastic yarn.

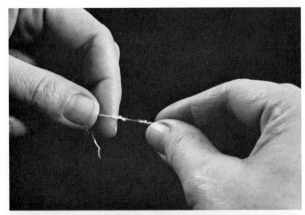

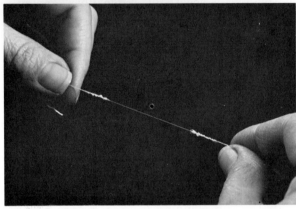

Fig. 14-4 Core-spun spandex (*Top*): relaxed yarn, cotton fibers removed to show core. (*Bottom*): extended.

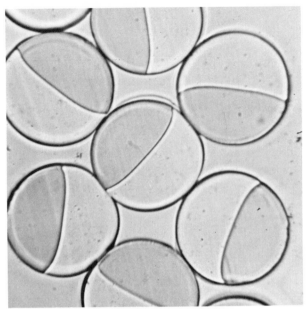

Fig. 14-5 Photomicrograph of Monvelle biconstituent. (*Courtesy of the Monsanto Textiles Company.*)

cent nylon. When dyed the nylon component of the fiber takes the color and the spandex portion remains colorless (Figure 14-5). Monvelle gives the strength and durability of support hose but has the sheerness of regular nylon hose. The transparent portion of the monofilament gives the appearance of sheerness. The fiber was phased out in 1977 because it did not meet Monsanto's objectives for long-term growth.

Durability. Spandex is more durable than rubber because it is not deteriorated by aging. Durability factors are compared in the following chart. Nylon is included in the chart because it has

more stretch than other man-made filaments and illustrates the difference between a hard fiber and an elastomeric fiber.

Spandex is resistant to body oils, perspiration, and cosmetics, which cause degradation of rubber. It also has good shelf life, that is, it does not deteriorate with age.

Comfort. Spandex fibers have a moisture regain of 0.75–1.3 per cent, making it uncomfortable for skin-contact apparel. Power stretch garments are uncomfortable to most people but some feel better psychologically in tight garments. Lighter weight foundation garments of spandex have the same holding power as heavy garments of rubber.

Care. Spandex is resistant to dilute acids and to alkalis. It has good resistance to cosmetic oils and lotions. Most spandex fibers are resistant to bleaches. They have good resistance to dry-cleaning solvents. Spandex is thermoplastic with a melting point of 446–518°F.

Durability Factors

Fiber Property	Spandex	Rubber	Nylon
Breaking tenacity	0.6–0.9	0.34	3.0–9.5
Breaking elongation	400–700%	500–600%	23%
Flex life	Excellent	Fair	Excellent
Recovery from stretch	99%	97%	100%

Other Elastomers

Anim 8, an anidex[2] fiber, was produced by Rohm and Haas Co. between 1970 and 1975. Lastrile[3] was a generic name established by the Federal Trade Commission for an elastomeric fiber. Rohm and Haas experimented with lastrile but did not produce it commercially.

[2] A manufactured fiber in which the fiber-forming substance is any long chain synthetic polymer composed of at least 50 per cent by weight of one or more esters of a monohydric alcohol and acrylic acid.

$$(CH_2{=}CH{-}COOH)$$

[3] A manufactured fiber in which the fiber forming substance is a copolymer of acrylonitrile and a diene (such as butadiene) composed of not more than 50 per cent but at least 10 per cent by weight of acrylonitrile units:

$$-CH_2-\underset{\underset{CN}{|}}{CH}-$$

Other Textile Fibers: Aramid, glass, metal and metallic, novoloid

15

Aramid

Nylon is a polyamide fiber; aramid is an *aromatic* polyamide fiber. When researchers at the Du Pont Company were working on nylon variants they produced a fiber that had exceptional heat and flame resistance. Du Pont introduced this fiber in 1963 under the trade name Nomex nylon. Another variant of nylon was introduced by Du Pont in 1973 as Kevlar. This fiber had exceptional strength in addition to fire resistance. In response to a petition by Du Pont for a new generic name classification for these fibers that were uniquely different from nylon, the Federal Trade Commission (FTC) established the generic classification of *aramid* in 1974.

Aramid—a manufactured fiber in which the fiber forming substance is a long chain synthetic polyamide in which at least 85 per cent of the amide linkages $\left(\begin{array}{c} -C-NH \\ \parallel \\ O \end{array}\right)$ are attached directly to two aromatic rings.

Aramid fibers do not melt at any temperature. Aramid fibers also have high strength and flame resistance, and they are unaffected by moisture and by most chemicals. Kevlar fibers have a combination of high strength and toughness that had never before been attained either in nature or in man-made fibers. Fibers are round or dog-bone depending on spinning method (Figure 15-1).

Glass

Glass is an *incombustible* textile fiber; it cannot burn. This makes it especially suitable for end uses where the danger of fire is a problem such as in draperies for motels, nursing homes, public buildings, and homes. Glass fibers have also been used in bedspreads and tablecloths and in interlinings for coats and mittens. The possibility of severe skin irritation from tiny broken fibers has limited the use of glass fibers in wearing apparel.

The process of drawing out glass into hairlike strands dates back to ancient history. It is

Properties of Aramid

Property	Normal Tenacity	High Tenacity
Breaking tenacity	4.3–5.1 g/d–filament 3.7–5.3 g/d–staple	21.5 g/d
Specific gravity	1.38	1.44
Moisture regain	4.5%	3.5–7.0%
Effect of heat	Carbonizes above 800°F Very resistant to flame Does not melt	Same
Resistance to acids	Better than nylon	
Resistance to alkalis	Good	
Resistance to organic solvents	Good	
Resistance to sunlight	Poor	
Oleophilic	Yes, unless special finishes are used	
Static buildup	Yes, unless special finishes are used	

Types and Kinds of Aramid

Nomex	Kevlar
Staple, tow, filament Color sealed—olive green, sage green, international orange End uses: space program, cubical curtains, pillows, sheets, robes, ironing board covers, draperies, carpeting	High tenacity—low elongation Very high modulus Tire cords, hoses, belting

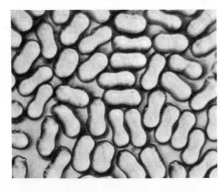

Longitudinal View 600X

Fig. 15-1 Photomicrograph of aramid. (*Courtesy of American Association of Textile Chemists and Colorists.*)

thought that Phoenician fishermen noticed small pools of molten material among the coals of the fires they built on the sands of the Aegean beaches and while poking at the strange substances, they drew out a long strand—the first glass fiber.

The raw materials for glass are sand, silica, and limestone, combined with additives of feldspar and boric acid. These materials are melted in large electric furnaces (2400°F). For *filament* yarns, each furnace has holes in the base of the melting chamber. Fine streams of glass flow through the holes and are carried through a hole in the floor to a winder in the room below. The winder revolves faster than the glass comes from the furnace, thus stretching the fibers and reducing them in size before they harden. The round rodlike filaments are shown in Figure 15–2. When *staple* yarn is spun, the glass flows out in thin streams from holes in the base of the furnace, and jets of high-pressure air or steam yank the glass into fibers 8 to 10 inches long. These fibers are collected on a revolving drum and made into a thin web, which is then formed into a sliver, or soft, untwisted yarn.

Beta Fiberglas was introduced by the Owens-Corning Fiberglas Corporation in 1964. It has one sixth the denier of common glass fibers. The extremely fine filaments are resistant to breaking and thus more resistant to abrasion. Beta Fiberglas has about half the strength of regular glass fiber, but its tenacity of 8.2 is still greater than most fibers.

Coronizing. Coronizing is a process for heat setting, dyeing, and finishing glass fiber in one continuous operation. Since glass is *low in flexibility,* the yarns resist bending around one another in the woven fabric. Heat setting at a temperature of 1100°F softens the yarns so that they will bend and assume yarn crimp. Coronized fabrics have greater wrinkle resistance and softer draping qualities.

After heat setting the glass fabric is treated with a lubricating oil; then color and a water-repellent finish are added. For this treatment the Hycar–Quilon process is used. Hycar is an acrylic latex resin, which, with the colored pigment, is padded on the fabric and then cured at a temperature of 320°F. This is followed by a treatment with Quilon, a water-repellent substance, and the fabric is again cured. The resin used in the color treatment increases the flexibility of the fiber but is damaged by chlorinated dry-cleaning solutions, so dry cleaning should be done with Stoddard solvent.

Screen printing as well as roller printing can be done by the Hycar–Quilon process, since the color paste dries fast enough to allow one screen to follow another rapidly. The Hycar–Quilon process gives good resistance to rubbing off (crocking),

Fig. 15-2 Photomicrograph of fiberglass. (*Courtesy of the Owens-Corning Fiberglas Corporation.*)

which is one of the disadvantages of other coloring methods.

Glass fiber is extensively used in the decorator field for curtains and draperies. Here the fiber performs best if bending and abrasion can be kept at a minimum. Curtains or draperies should not be used at windows that will be kept open, allowing the wind to whip the curtains. The bottom of the curtains or draperies should not be allowed to touch the floor or windowsills.

The weight of the fabrics may mean that special rods are necessary, especially if large areas are draped.

Glass fiber has wide industrial use where noise abatement, fire protection, temperature control (insulation), and air purification are needed.

Glass-Fiber Properties Important in Draperies	
Flexibility	Breaks easily
Specific gravity	Heavy
Absorbency, percent of moisture regain	None
Effect of sunlight	None
Effect of acid and alkali	None
Effect of heat	Flameproof

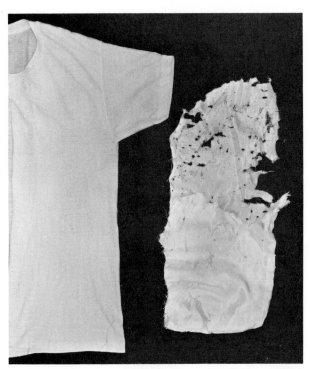

Fig. 15-3 Glass-fiber laundry bag after being washed with regular family wash.

Care. Hand washing is preferred to machine washing, which causes excessive breaking of the fibers. Figure 15-3 shows the remnants of a fiberglass laundry bag that was machine washed. A residue of tiny glass fibers in the washing machine will contaminate the next load and cause severe skin irritation for those who wear that clothing. Even with hand washing, severe skin irritation can occur. The Federal Trade Commission proposed in 1967 that the label should disclose the possibility of severe skin irritation.

Curtains should not require frequent washing since glass fibers *resist soil,* and *spots and stains can be wiped off* with a damp cloth. No ironing is necessary. Curtains can be smoothed and put on the rod to dry. Oils used in finishing have caused graying in white curtains. Oil holds the dirt persistently and also oxidizes with age. Washing has not proved to be a very satisfactory way to whiten the material, and dry cleaning is not recommended unless Stoddard solvent is used.

Metal and Metallic Fibers

The Federal Trade Commission definition of metallic fibers is as follows: Metallic: a manufactured fiber composed of metal, plastic-coated metal, metal-coated plastic, or a core completely covered by metal.

Gold and silver have been used since ancient times as yarns for fabric decoration. More recently, aluminum yarns, aluminized plastic yarns, and aluminized nylon yarns have taken the place of gold and silver.

Stainless-steel fibers were developed in 1960, and other metal fibers have also been made into fibers and yarns. Stainless steel has had the most extensive development.

The use of stainless steel as a textile fiber was an outgrowth of research for fibers to meet aerospace requirements. Superfine-stainless-steel filaments (3 to 15 microns) are made by the following process. A bundle of fine wires (0.002 inch) is sheathed with dissimilar alloys and drawn to its final diameter, pickled in nitric acid to remove the sheath, and the yarn of several filaments is then ready for sizing, warping, and weaving. The early fibers were costly, $25 per pound. Several problems had to be solved, one of which involved twist. Each filament tended to act like a tiny coil spring, so the yarns required special treatment to deaden the twist.

Stainless-steel fibers are produced as both filament and staple. They can be woven or knitted and can be used as either the wrap or core of core yarns. The staple fiber can be blended with other textile fibers to *reduce static* permanently. Only 1 to 3 per cent of the stainless-steel fiber is needed. The limitation on the use of stainless steel in clothing is its inability to be dyed, although some producers claim that such a small amount will not affect the color of white fabrics. Stainless steel has been used in carpets to reduce static and has been used, experimentally, in men's suits. It is also suitable for this purpose for use in upholstery, blankets, and work clothing, but until the cost of stainless-steel fibers is reduced, its use in such articles will not be practical. Stainless-steel fibers are used for industrial purposes such as tire cord and missile nose cones, and in corrective heart surgery.

Metals do not have many of the properties usually attributed to textile fibers. They are much heavier than the organic materials that compose most fibers—specific gravity of metal fibers is 7.88 grams/denier as compared to 1.14 for nylon. They cannot be folded and unfolded without leaving permanent crease lines, have very little or no drape characteristics, and do not have the hand associated with textiles. Reduction in the denier of the fiber improves its properties, but the finer fibers are more expensive.

Novoloid

Novoloid is the generic name for a manufactured fiber containing at least 85 per cent by weight of a cross-linked novolac. Kynol is the only novoloid fiber produced in the United States. Kynol was introduced by the Corborundum Company (now American Kynol) in 1969 with commercial production beginning in 1972.

Kynol shows outstanding flame resistance to a blaze of 2500°C from an oxyacetylene torch, and it can meet any flammability requirements that might be legislated. The yarns do not melt, burn, or fuse but turn to carbonized yarns that main-

Cross-Section 500X

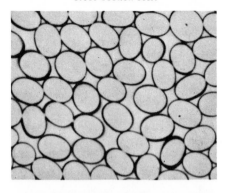

Longitudinal View 500X

Fig. 15-4. Photomicrograph of novoloid. (*Courtesy of American Association of Textile Chemists and Colorists.*)

tain their construction. Pile fabrics made of Kynol have four times the no-burn qualities of asbestos.

Kynol fiber is gold in color, so its dyeing possibilities are somewhat limited—darker shades present no problem. It can be bleached to a good white. It was first produced as staple and later as filament. The starting price was $5 per pound.

Properties

Cross section	Round
Tenacity (grams/denier)	1.5–2.5 g/d
Specific gravity (grams/cc)	1.25
Moisture regain (per cent)	5.5
Chemical resistance	Excellent
Uses	
Fireproof clothing and fabrics	
Chemical filters	
Blankets and draperies	
Institutional bedding, carpets, and household furnishings	

Fiber Modifications

16

(Delustered fibers, solution-dyed fibers, optically whitened fibers and high wet modulus rayon are discussed in previous chapters.)

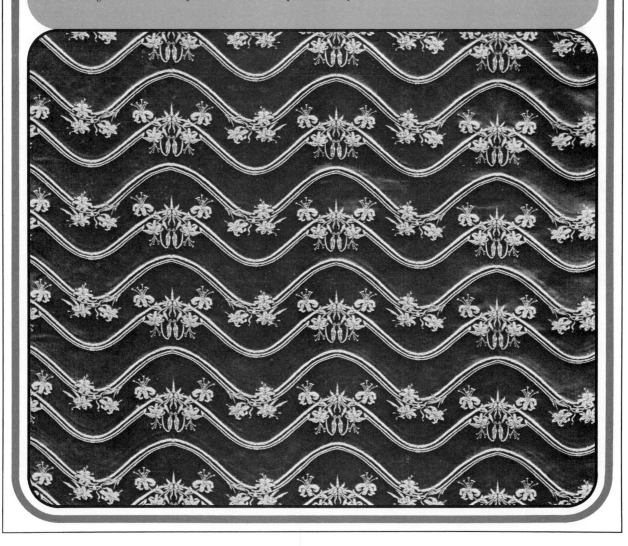

One advantage of the man-made fibers is that each step of the production process can be precisely controlled to "tailor" or modify the parent fiber. These modifications are the result of a producer's continuing research program to correct any limitations, to explore the potential of its fibers, and to develop properties that will give greater versatility in the end uses of the fibers.

The *parent fiber* is the fiber in its simplest form. It is often sold as a "commodity fiber" by generic name only, without benefit of a trade name. The parent fiber has been called by the following names: regular, basic, standard, conventional, or first-generation fiber.

Modifications of the parent fiber are usually sold under a brand or trade name. Modifications are also referred to as types, variants, or second-generation fibers.

Fiber modifications of the second generation are

1. Modification of fiber shape:
Cross section, thick-and-thin, hollow

2. Modification of molecular structure and crystallinity:
High-tenacity, low-pilling, low-elongation

3. Additives to polymer or fiber solution:
Cross dye, antistatic, sunlight-resistance, fire retardant

4. Modifications of spinning procedures:
Crimp, fiberfill.

Complex modifications have been engineered to combine two polymers of the same generic family or two polymers from different generic groups as separate entities within a single fiber or yarn. These have been referred to as third-generation fibers.

1. Bicomponent fibers
2. Biconstituent fibers
3. Blended filament yarns

Modification of Shape

Nonround Fiber Types

Changing the cross-sectional shape is the easiest way to alter the mechanical and aesthetic prop-

Fig. 16–1(a) Stereoscan photograph of trilobal nylon. (*Courtesy of The Du Pont Company.*)

erties of a fiber. This is usually done by changing the shape of the spinneret hole to produce the fiber shapes desired. All kinds of shapes are possible: flat, trilobal, quadralobal, pentalobal, triskelion, cruciform, clover leaf, and alphabet shapes such as Y and T.

The *flat shape* was one of the first variations produced. "Crystal" acetate and "Sparkling" nylon were ribbonlike fibers that were extruded through a long, narrow spinneret hole. Flat fibers tend to catch and reflect light much as a mirror does, so fabrics have a glint or sparkle. *The trilobal shape* has been widely used in both nylon and polyester fibers (Figure 16–1). It is spun through a spinneret with three triangularly arranged slits. Antron Nylon, 501 carpet nylon, and T62 Dacron were the first trilobal fibers. The trade name Antron now designates selected round, trilobal, and pentalobal fibers made by Du Pont. Some of the advantages of trilobal shape are

- Beautiful silklike hand (depending on end use requirements)
- Subtle opacity
- Soil-hiding (cloaks dirt)
- Built-in bulk without weight
- Moisture-heightened wicking action
- Silklike sheen and color
- Crush resistance in heavy deniers
- Gives good textured crimp.

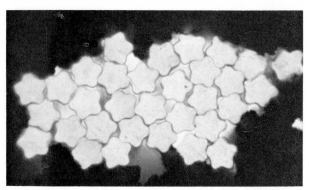

Fig. 16–1(b) Trevira polyester pentalobal cross section 312×. (*Courtesy Hoechst Fibers Industries.*)

Cadon is a *triskelion*-shaped fiber (a three-sided configuration similar to a boat propeller) carpet nylon by Monsanto. Trevira is a *pentalobal* polyester fiber produced by Hoechst. Encron 8 is octolobal. "Touch" nylon has a *Y-shaped* cross section. All these fibers have characteristics similar to the trilobal fibers. Dacron Type 83 is a *cruciform*-shaped staple fiber (shaped like a cross) with a crisper, more cottonlike hand. It has been optically whitened. It has been suggested that the cruciform shape might be the perfect shape for a fiber.

Thick-and-Thin Fiber Types

Thick-and-thin fiber types have variations in diameter along their length as a result of uneven drawing after spinning. When woven into cloth, these yarns give the effect of a duppioni silk fabric or give linenlike texture. The thick areas or nubs will dye a deeper color to create interesting tone-on-tone color effects. Speckelon and Stryton nylon upholstery fibers are bright filaments used for color and surface effects. Barré in knits can be eliminated by thick-and-thin yarns. Many surface textures are possible by changing the size and length of the nubs or slubs.

Hollow or Multicellular Fiber Types

The hair or fur of many animals contains air cells which provide insulation in cold weather. The feathers of birds are hollow to give them buoyancy. Similar air cells and hollow filaments are possible in man-made fibers by the use of gas-forming compounds added to the spinning solution, by air injection at the jet face as the fiber is forming, or by the shape of the spinneret holes. Bubblefil was a viscose rayon fiber developed by the American Viscose Company to replace kapok, a natural hollow fiber, during World War II. Several hollow or multicellular viscose fibers have been developed by the Japanese. Hollow acrylic fibers have been made by gas-forming techniques. Viloft (Courtaulds, Ltd.) is an inflated rayon fiber made to collapse and give a more cottonlike hand to fabric (Figure 16–2).

Hollow melt-spun fibers can be formed by pyrolizing a portion of the polymer flowing to the spinneret to form gas and then extruding the bubble containing polymer as hollow filaments.

Nylostraw is a hollow nylon fiber that is extruded round and flattened into continuous strips $\frac{3}{16}$ inch wide. It has excellent abrasion and scuff resistance. It is used in shoes, hats, and handbags. Poly-Slim is a spun-bonded Reemay that has been needle punched with hollow polyester fibers. It is used for clothing and outerwear.

The spinneret hole can be shaped to produce hollow fibers. One of the earliest of these, Estron Type 50, was a donut-shaped acetate fiber that was extruded through a C-shaped hole. The fiber closed immediately upon extrusion. Other spinneret holes spin the fiber as two halves that immediately close to make the hollow fiber.

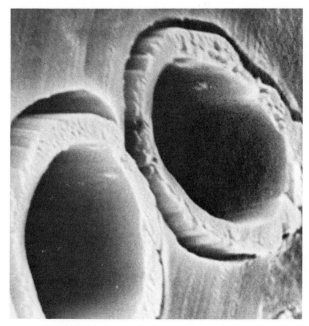

Fig. 16–2 Stereoscan photograph of Viloft. (*Courtesy of* Modern Textiles Magazine.)

Modifications of Molecular Structure and Crystallinity

High-Tenacity Fiber Types

Stretching a fiber changes its stress–strain curve that is the basis of high tenacity (and low tenacity). Fiber strength is increased by (1) drawing or stretching the fiber to align or orient the molecules, thus strengthening the intermolecular forces, and/or by (2) chemical modification of the fiber polymer to increase the degree of polymerization.

High-tenacity rayon results from the rate of coagulation, the spinning speed, and/or modifiers added to the spinning solution. The spinning speed for regular *rayon* is quite high and the coagulation and regeneration occur almost simultaneously. This results in the formation of an oriented skin and amorphous core. In high-tenacity *rayon* the spinning speed is reduced and the zinc sulfate content of the bath is increased, so there is an increase in the proportion of skin and a decrease in the core to the point where the core may disappear and the fiber will be an all-skin structure. The increase in orientation of an all-skin fiber increases tensile strength. Stretching is done by passing the fibers around two Godet wheels, one of which rotates faster than the other. After the high-tenacity fiber emerges from the coagulating bath, it is then given a high degree of stretch in a hot-water or dilute acid bath. This stretching increases orientation and strength. Figure 16–3 is a photomicrograph of a high-tenacity all-skin rayon. Amino compounds may be added to the spinning solution to increase the viscosity and produce a higher degree of polymerization.

High-strength rayons are suitable for blending with nylons and polyesters. They are widely used for industrial purposes such as in conveyor belts and tire cord. Comiso is a high-strength apparel fiber made by Beaunit. Tyrex, Dynacor, and Suprenka are trade names for tire cord.

High-Tenacity Synthetic Fibers. Molecular chain length can be varied in the melt-spun fibers at the polymer stage by changes in time, temperature, pressure, and chemicals. Long molecules are harder to pull apart than short molecules. Hot drawing of polyester and cold drawing of nylon align the molecules in such a way that the intermolecular forces are strengthened. Some of the high-tenacity (low-elongation) nylons and polyesters were designed to strengthen cotton blends for durable press. Polyester's stress/strain curve more closely matches that of cotton, so they "pull together" to give greater durability.

High-tenacity polyester is now used in tire cord. Nylon has always had its widest use in industrial items such as tires for cars, trucks, and planes. Beaunit's polyester for carpets and durable press is promoted under the label Tough Stuff. Aramid fibers are the strongest and toughest fibers that have ever been made.

Low-Pilling Fiber Types

Low-pilling fiber types are engineered to reduce the flex life by reducing the molecular weight as measured in terms of intrinsic viscosity. When flex abrasion resistance is reduced, the fiber balls (pills) break off almost as soon as they are formed and the fabric retains its attractive appearance. These low-pilling fibers are not as strong as other types but are durable enough for apparel uses and are particularly suited to soft knitting yarns. (Review the discussion of molecular weight, page 9.)

Dacron Type 35 is a higher-modulus, low-pilling staple fiber for blending with cotton. Type 65 is an extremely low-pilling, basic-dyeing staple for knitted garments; Dacron 107-W and Trevira Type 350 are optically brightened pill-resistant staple for cotton/polyester blends in underwear.

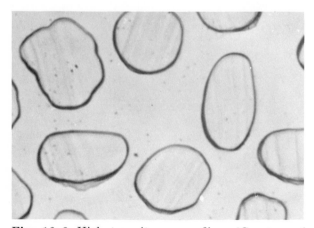

Fig. 16-3 High tenacity rayon fiber. (*Courtesy of American Viscose.*)

Binder Staple

Binder staple is a semidull, crimped polyester with a very low melting point. (Melting point relates to molecular structure.) It was designed to develop a thermoplastic bond with other fibers under heat and pressure. It sticks at 165°F and will shrink 55 to 75 per cent at 200°F; Type 450 Fortrel is a fiber of this type.

Low-Elongation Fiber Types

Low-elongation fiber types are designed as reinforcing fibers to increase the strength and abrasion resistance of cotton and cellulosic fabrics. Nylon 420 was the first one developed. It has been called the most striking example of a fiber developed to fit a need. It is a high-strength fiber with a low elongation much like that of cotton. The low elongation results from changing the balance of tenacity and extension. High-tenacity fibers have lower elongation properties, as shown in the table.

Elongation Properties of Nylon and Cotton

Fiber	Tenacity (grams/denier)	Elongation at Break (per cent)
Nylon Type 200 (regular)	4.0	40
Cotton ($1\frac{1}{16}$ inch)	3.0	8
Nylon Type 420	6.5	23

Source: E. I. du Pont de Nemours & Company, *Bulletin n-163* (October 1963).

Nylon 420 is more costly than regular nylon, so it is used to increase the strength of the warp yarns in end use fabrics that have more warp

Fig. 16-4 Nylon 420 appears on the label. Durable-press trousers are shown in the picture.

than filling yarn exposed on the surface (Figure 16-4). A strength increase of 20 per cent can be achieved by adding only 25 per cent Nylon 420 in the warp. End uses are mainly in work clothing—items that get hard wear. Kodel 421 is a low-elongation fiber for use in blends with cotton.

Additives to the Polymer or Spinning Solution

Cross-Dyeable Fiber Types

Cross-dyeable fiber types are very different from solution-dyed fibers. Solution-dyed fibers have colored pigment added to the spinning solution, so they are colored as they emerge from the spinneret.

Cross-dyeable fiber types are made by incorporating dye-accepting chemicals into the molecular structure. Some of the parent fibers are nondyeable or have poor acceptance of certain classes of dyes; the cross-dyeable types were developed to correct this limitation. Cross-dyeable types are white when spun, but will react with dyes later when the fabric is to be colored.

Two or more of these cross-dyeable fiber types can be used in a fabric that is then immersed in a suitable dye-bath mixture, and each fiber type reacts to pick up a different color. As many as five colors have been achieved in one dyebath. Designs may be heather, tone-on-tone, floral, or geometric, depending on the arrangement of the fiber types within the fabric. Solution-dyed fibers may be combined with cross-dyeable fiber types to increase color possibilities. Some of the cross-dyeable fiber types are

- basic dyeable
- acid dyeable
- disperse dyeable
- acid-dye resist, basic dyeable
- nondyeable.

Antistatic Fiber Types

Static is a result of the flow of electrons. Fibers conduct electricity according to how readily electrons move in them. If static builds up in a fiber so that it has an excess of electrons, it is negatively charged and it will be attracted to something that is positively charged—something that has a deficiency of electrons. This attraction is illustrated by the way clothing clings to the body. *Water will dissipate static.* Because the heat-sensitive fibers, especially the synthetics, have such low water absorbency, static charges will build up rapidly during cold dry weather, and they are slow to dissipate. If the fibers can be made *wettable,* the static charges will dissipate quickly and there will be no annoying static buildup.

For the person whose clothes are clinging, an immediate but temporary solution is that of using a wet sponge or paper towel and rubbing it over the garment or slip to drain away the static. The benefits will last much longer if one of the fabric softeners is used in place of plain water.

Much of the progress in the field of antistatic finishes and new fiber types resulted from the research on soil-release finishes for durable press in 1966 and 1967. Most of the antistatic sprays and finishes are effective, but temporary. Finishes are applied to the surface of the fiber and are lost during washing and wear.

The *antistatic fiber types* give durable protection because the fiber is made *wettable* by incorporating an antistatic compound—a chemical conductor—in the fiber so that it becomes an integral part of the fiber. The compound is added to the fiber polymer raw material so that it is evenly distributed throughout the fiber dope or

Fig. 16-5b Antistatic polyester. (*Courtesy of The Du Pont Company.*)

spinning solution. It changes the fiber's hydrophobic nature to a hydrophilic one and raises the moisture regain so that static is dissipated more quickly. The moisture content of the air in the home should be kept high enough to provide moisture for absorption. Even "bone-dry" cotton will build up static. Static control is also achieved by incorporating a conductive filament into the filament (Figures 16–5a and 16–5b.) In the chart, Antistatic Fiber Variants, trade names and end uses are listed.

The *soil-release* benefits of the antistatic fiber types has been outstanding. The antistatic fibers retard soiling by minimizing the attraction and retention of dirt particles, and the opacity and luster in the yarn have soil-hiding properties. Soil redisposition in laundry is dramatically reduced. Oily stains, even motor oils, are released easily.

Sunlight Resistant Types

Ultraviolet light is the source of fiber degeneration as well as color fading. When ultraviolet light is absorbed, the damage results from an oxidation-reduction reaction between the radiant energy and the fiber or fiber dye. Stabilizers such as nitrogenous compounds may be added to the fiber to increase their light resistance. These sta-

Fig. 16-5a Antistatic nylon. (*Courtesy of The Du Pont Company.*)

Parent Fiber	Trademark	Fiber Modification	End Use	Producer
Nylon	Antron III (Figure 16-5a)	Three filaments of carbon black core surrounded by sheath of nylon	Apparel Carpets	Du Pont
Nylon	X-Stat	Seven silver coated nylon filaments	Carpets	
Nylon	Ultron	Conjugate spun 95% nylon 6,6 and 5% nylon/carbon black polymer stripe	Carpets	Monsanto
Nylon	Bodyfree		Apparel	Allied Chemical
Nylon	Enkalure	Fine denier–anticling	Apparel	American Enka
Polyester	Dacron III (Figure 16-5b)	Polymeric conductive core	Carpets	Du Pont

bilizers must be carefully selected for the fiber and the dye. Estron SLR is an acetate fiber.

Bacteriostatic Viscose Rayon

These fibers are still in the experimental stage. They would be used for sanitary and disposable products.

Flame-Resistant Fiber Types

Flame-resistant fibers give better protection to consumers than do topical flame-retardant finishes (see Chapter 37).

The man-made fibers that are always flame resistant are aramid, novolid, modacrylic, glass, saran, and vinyon. Other man-made fibers can be modified by changing their polymer structure or by adding water-insoluble compounds to the spinning solution. These fiber modifications make the fibers inherently flame resistant. The fibers vary in their resistance to flame.

The following chart lists both the naturally fire-resistant and modified fibers. Fibers that are not produced in the United States are included in the chart because they are imported for use in fabrics in this country.

Flame-Resistant Fibers[1]

Trade Name	Producer	Chemical Nature	End Uses
Fiberglas	Owens-Corning	Glass	Curtains, industrial work clothes
Nomex III	Du Pont	Aramid	Industrial fabrics, airline upholstery, protective apparel
Durette	Fire Safety Products, Inc.	Aramid	Space program, race drivers' apparel
Kynol	American Kynol Co.	Novoloid	Industrial fabrics, speciality products
Verel	Tenn. Eastman	Modacrylic	Interior furnishings
SEF	Monsanto	Modacrylic	Apparel, draperies, industrial fabrics
Orlon FR	Du Pont	Modacrylic	Apparel
Teviron	Teijin (Japan)	Vinyon	Apparel, interior furnishings
Trevira 271	Hoechst	Polyester	Apparel
Leavil	Montedison	Vinyon	Apparel, interior furnishings
Clevyll T	Rhone-Poulenc	Vinyon	Apparel, interior furnishings
Cordelan®	Kohjin (Japan)	Vinal-vinyon matrix	Apparel, interior furnishings Blends with cotton, polyester, nylon modacrylic
SayFR	Avtex	Acetate with additive	Apparel, 100% acetate or blends with polyester
Arnel FR	Celanese	Triacetate with additive	Apparel, blends with polyester

[1]Textile Industries, February 1976.

Modifications of Spinning Procedure

When producers started to make staple fiber, mechanical crimping was done to broken filaments and later to filament tow to make the fibers more cohesive and thus easier to spin into yarns. Other techniques were developed to give permanent crimp to rayon and acetate and to provide bulk or stretch to all fibers—filaments as well as staple.

Crimping of fibers is important in many end uses for cover and loft in bulky knits, blankets, carpets, battings for quilted items, pillows, and the like, and for stretch and economy in hosiery and sportswear. One of the first crimping techniques was developed for use with rayon.

Viscose rayon fiber with latent or potential crimp is produced by coagulating the fiber in a bath of lower acid and higher salt concentration. A skin forms around the fiber and then bursts. A thinner skin forms over the rupture. The crimp develops when the fiber is immersed in water. Avicron is a latent crimp rayon fiber made by American Viscose. It is a heavy-denier novelty filament fiber used in pile fabrics (Figures 16–6 and 16–7).

Celanese Type TY (Celacrimp) is a hot-water crimpable continuous filament. Crimpable acetate is specifically engineered in 600 and 900 de-

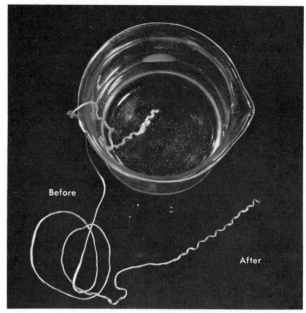

Fig. 16–7 Avicron self-crimping fiber curls when immersed in water.

nier for chenille-type bedspreads. Celanese Type F, a Y-cross-section acetate that is sold as Celafil, is a staple fiber used for battings in quilted items.

Crimped polyester fibers are used for *fiberfill* batting for pillows, furniture, carpets, sleeping bags, and quilted apparel. The fiberfill used for furniture is made into bats that are needle-punched to prevent lumping. Helically (spiral) crimped fibers are produced by cooling one side of the fiber faster than the other side as the melt-spun fiber is extruded. This uneven cooling causes a curl to form in the fiber. The same effect can be achieved by heating one side of the fiber during the stretching or drawing process. This helical crimp has more springiness than the conventional mechanical sawtooth crimp, and these fibers are used where high levels of compressional resistance and recovery are needed.

Dacron 108 for pillow battings comes already encased in a marquisette covering ready for the insertion of the pillow. A mix of different deniers is used and may be varied to give pillows with three distinct levels of support. Fortrel Type 470 fiberfill staple and Vycron Type 2950 (Tough Stuff) are other polyester fiberfill fibers.

Beka is one example of a textured high bulk yarn. Half of the filaments are drawn after spinning to give low shrinkage while the other half are undrawn to give high shrinkage. When wet finished, the low shrinkage filaments float out to the

Fig. 16–6 Cross section of Avicron rayon. Note the difference in thickness of the skin on the two sides. (*Courtesy of the FMC Corporation, American Viscose Division.*)

surface and wave while the high shrinkage filaments become the core. Heat setting stabilizes the yarn in this configuration.

Textured yarns were developed by throwsters to make stretch fabrics about 1950 (see Chapter 17). In the 1970s fiber producers started texturizing yarns. Undrawn and partially drawn yarns are sold for texturizing.

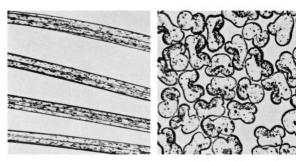

Fig. 16-9 Photomicrograph of semidull Orlon Sayelle: longitudinal (*top*) and cross-sectional (*bottom*) views. (*Courtesy of The Du Pont Company.*)

Third Generation Fiber Types

Bicomponent Fibers (*Self-Crimping, Postbulkable Fibers*)

Bicomponent fibers are composed of two polymers of different chemical or physical structures arranged in layers side by side or one enveloping the other.

The original discovery that the two sides of a fiber can react differently when wet was made during studies of wool in 1886. In 1953 it was discovered that the difference in reaction was the result of the bicomponent nature of wool, which results from a difference in growth rate and in chemical composition. The first procedure for spinning man-made bicomponent fibers—conjugate spinning—was developed by American Viscose in 1940. Two viscose solutions—one aged and one unaged—were spun through spinneret holes, each of which was separated into two halves by a divider through the center (Figure 16-8). The resulting fiber had a side-by-side or bilateral arrangement. This fiber is straight as it is spun but will crimp when immersed in hot or cold water

and will retain its crimp after it dries. Crimp potential of this kind is referred to as *latent* or *inherent crimp*. When the latent crimp of a bicomponent, bilateral fiber is developed by heat and/or moisture, it is a three-dimensional helical crimp with the shorter component on the inside. Helical crimp (or curl) gives more bulk and stretch than other types of crimp.

The pipe-in-pipe procedure is another way to spin bicomponent fibers. In this case a sheath-core structure is formed, one component forming the sheath and the other the core (Figure 16-8).

Conjugate spinning was used in 1959 to produce Orlon 21 (Figure 16-9), the first acrylic bicomponent bilateral structure that would respond to wetting and drying in the same manner as the wool fiber. The fiber is spun straight and made into a garment such as a sweater, which is then exposed to heat, which causes one side of the fiber to shrink and the fiber takes on a helical (curl) crimp. The reaction of the fibers to water occurs during laundering. As the fiber gets wet, one side swells and the fiber uncrimps. As the crimp relaxes, the sweater increases in size. The crimp will return as the sweater dries and it will regain its original size *if properly handled*. The sweater should not be drip-dried or placed on a towel to dry because the weight of the water and the resistance of the towel will prevent the sweater from regaining its original size. The right way to dry the sweater is to either machine dry it at low temperatures or place it on a smooth, flat surface and "bunch-it-in" to help the crimp recover. This Orlon bicomponent fiber is called a *reversible crimp fiber* because of the uncrimping and crimp recovery action during the laundry process. When Orlon 21 is used in quality products, the trade name Sayelle is used on the label.

Other bicomponent acrylic fibers are Orlon

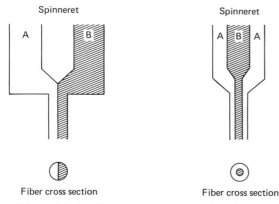

Fig. 16-8 Bilateral and sheath-core bicomponent fiber structure.

Type 27, Orlon Type 33 for carpets, Acrilan Type 45 for carpets, Creslan Type 68-B, and Creslan Type 83 CF-5 carpet fiber. Civona is a bicomponent Orlon that was created for worsted spun machine knitting yarns having a fine, Merino woollike handle. Bi-loft is a bicomponent acrylic made by Monsanto for apparel.

The bicomponent fibers have been classified as latent-crimp-water (viscose) and latent-crimp-heat types. Nylon bicomponents are of the latter type. Nylon was the first of the synthetics to be made as a bicomponent fiber. Cantrece was the trade name adopted by Du Pont for hosiery made of its monofilament bicomponent fiber. Cantrece I was introduced in 1963, but it lacked the elastic recovery needed to prevent bagging at the knees. After a period of research, Cantrece II was introduced successfully. Like the other synthetic bicomponent fibers (Types 880, 881, 882, and 890 are used in Cantrece products), the two sides of the fiber differ in their reaction to heat. One side will shrink, causing the fiber to curl helically.

Bicomponent polyester and olefin fibers have been developed for use in the clothing, upholstery, and carpet fields.

Biconstituent Fibers

The traditional way of capitalizing on the good properties of a fiber—or minimizing its poor properties—has been to blend fibers from two or more generic groups to make a yarn. A newer approach is to *blend two generically different polymers* one polymer dispersed as a mechanical micromixture of fibrils embedded in a matrix of the other polymer. (The mixture is not a solution of one polymer within another.) The fiber with the lower percentage forms the fibrils, and the other forms the matrix (Figure 16-10). The compounds must be compatible, have a similar melting point, and be spun by the same method. The first biconstituent fiber was Source, by Allied Chemical. It is a 70 per cent nylon/30 per cent polyester blend, but 120 different combinations are possible. It was originally designed for tire cord to eliminate the flat spotting of nylon tires but is now used primarily in carpets. This biconstituent fiber is a reflecting fiber with the dyeability of nylon. The carpets have a silklike look and many are designed for the Oriental-rug market. The strength and melting point of the nylon are relatively unaffected by the addition of the polyester; but the fiber modulus, important in nearly all end uses, is doubled by the addition of 30 per cent polyester. This increases the effectiveness of the nylon in certain industrial end uses where its strength alone was not sufficient. Sheen and better texturing properties are advantages that the fiber has.

Cordelan is a vinal/vinyon biconstituent flame-resistant fiber. It is made of three polymers: polyvinyl chloride, polyvinyl alcohol, and a copolymer of PVC/PVA. It is a matrix fibril-type fiber.

Biconstituent fibers may also be conjugate spun as bilateral or as sheath-core filaments. See Monvelle, page 98.

Blended Filament Yarns

Blended filament yarn differs from bicomponent and biconstituent fibers in that the blending takes place *after the fibers are spun* (Figure 16-11). This is a less complex combination than the other two and can be made from a wider range of materials; the combinations can be tested very quickly in fabric form.

The first successful blended filament yarn was Arnel plus nylon. It comes in five blends in several different deniers. It can be engineered to provide better bulk and create a textured surface without using a textured fiber. The differential shrinkage rates of Arnel plus nylon create this subtle texture and bulk. The nylon fiber contributes strength to the blend and the Arnel triacetate contributes aesthetic silklike qualities. Arnel plus nylon is not a trade name.

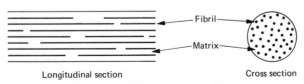

Longitudinal section   Cross section

Fig. 16-10 Biconstituent fiber.

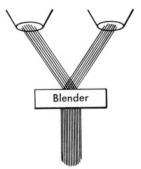

Blender

Fig. 16-11 Blended filament.

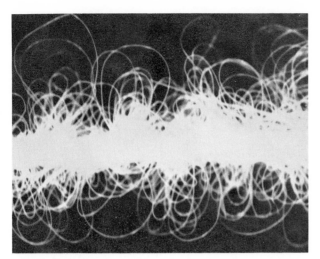

Fig. 16-12 Lanese yarn. (*Courtesy of Celanese Fibers Marketing Company.*)

Lanese is Celanese's trademark for its acetate/polyester core-bulked filament yarn used in apparel and home-furnishing fabrics (Figure 16–12). Creslan 67A, 67AB, and 710 are blends of monocomponent and bicomponent Creslan acrylic staple fibers. SEF modacrylic types SX6 and SX7 are producer blends of 65 per cent SEF modacrylic and Spectran polyester.

Rotofil or Faciated Yarns

The purpose of these yarns is to give better texture and hand to fabrics. The yarns are combinations of coarse filaments for strength and fine broken filaments for softness. They are made by a combination of crimping and twisting. Trevira *Dawn* by Hoechst Fibers Industries is a polyester rotofil yarn.

Carpet Fibers

Carpeting is an end use in which a large volume of fiber or yarn is needed. Carpeting also requires a specific combination of fiber properties for satisfactory appearance and performance. The ideal carpet is durable, resilient (shows no traffic pattern), resistant to soil, and is easily cleaned. The major portion of a carpet consists of the fiber that forms the face. Fibers with high abrasion resistance make the most durable carpets, but the useful life of the carpet is also dependent on appearance retention—shedding, fading, "walked-down" areas, pilling, and soil and static resistance. Some carpets may need to be replaced before they are worn out. Wool was, at one time, the standard carpet fiber; but the amount of carpet wool produced throughout the world has declined, whereas the need for carpet fiber has increased tremendously. Throughout the 1960s and 1970s, nylon was the most widely used carpet fiber. By 1976, polyester accounted for 15 per cent of the market.

Abrasion Resistance. Abrasion resistance is the major factor in wear performance or durability. Durability has been defined as the time required to wear out the face fibers. The thickness of the yarn tufts, the denseness of the pile, and the kind of fiber are major factors in durability. In resistance to abrasion the carpet fibers are rated as follows: nylon (unexcelled); polyester and olefins (very good); acrylics, modacrylics, and wool (good).

Compressional Resiliency. Compressional resiliency is the tendency of a carpet fiber to spring back to its original height after being bent or otherwise deformed. This is particularly important in areas of heavy traffic or under the crushing force of the legs of heavy furniture. Nylon is unexcelled in overall recovery. Wool and the acrylics and polyesters are very satisfactory and have better immediate recovery. The cellulose fibers have poor recovery. As finer denier fibers were used to achieve a softer hand in the late 1970s, the autoclave heat setting process was developed so that these finer yarns performed with comparable resiliency.

Carpet fibers are larger in diameter (Figure 16–13) than apparel fibers. This larger size gives the fiber more resistance to bending or crushing. A combination of different deniers is often used in a carpet. Man-made carpet fibers are used in most rugs and carpeting today (see the following chart).

Fiber Consumption in Carpet and Rug Face Yarns (Million Pounds)

	Year		
Fibers	*1966*	*1971*	*1976*
Man-made	622.0	1227.5	1482.4
Wool and cotton	144.9	92.5	15.2

Fiber Characteristic	Wool	Man-Made
Fiber diameter	Coarse—blends of various wools	15–18 denier or blend of various deniers
Fiber length	Staple	Staple or filament blend of various lengths
Crimp	3D Crimp	Sawtooth crimp, 3D crimp, bicomponent, textured filament
Cross-section	Oval	Round, trilobal, multi-lobal, square with voids
Resiliency and resistance to crushing	Good	Medium to excellent depending on fiber
Resistance to abrasion	Good	Good to excellent
Resistance to water-borne stains	Poor	Good to excellent
Resistance to oily stains	Good	Poor
Fire retardancy	Good	Modified fiber or topical finish
Static resistance	Good	Poor to good depending on fiber

Soiling. Soiling is a strongly fiber-dependent property. It may be *real* or *"apparent."* Soil retention is a function of fiber cross-sectional shape. "Apparent" soiling is a function of fiber color and optical properties, such as transparency or opacity, as well as fiber shape. Smooth circular fibers retain the minimum quantity of soil. However, when circular fibers are transparent, as nylon is, the soil shows through and the circular shape tends to magnify it, so the "apparent" soil seems much worse.

Fibers can be made more opaque by changing the cross-sectional shape from circular to non-round. Light is reflected by the angles of the indented surfaces of nonround fibers, giving them greater opacity. For this reason (as well as bulk), the trilobal and Y-shaped fibers are often used (Figure 16–14). However, in areas of heavy, oily soil, circular fibers may be better, as they have fewer crevices where soil can be deposited and from which it must be removed. The delustering

Fig. 16–13 (*Left*) Carpet wool. (*Right*) Carpet rayon. (*Courtesy of Bigelow-Sanford, Inc.*)

Fig. 16–14 Trilobal carpet fiber. (*Courtesy of The Du Pont Company.*)

Fig. 16-15 Nylon fiber with voids. (*Courtesy of The Du Pont Company.*)

agent, titanium dioxide, will increase the opacity of a fiber and thus reduce the apparent soiling, but it makes the carpet look dull and chalky and it affects dyeing properties. Nylon fibers have now been spun in such a way as to leave voids in the fiber that scatter light, thus giving the same effect as the delusterant (Figure 16–15). Soil retention of a carpet is affected by the electrostatic properties of the fiber. Fibers with high static buildup will attract and hold dust particles. High room moisture will reduce the tendency toward static buildup.

Static. Static is one of the annoying problems associated with carpets. Some fibers generate more static than others. Cut pile generates more static than loop pile. Some carpet backings are better conductors than others. Conductive carbon black can be added to the latex adhesive to reduce carpet static. The shoes worn by the individual have an effect on the amount of static produced. Shoes with leather soles and rubber heels generate more static than others.

Metallic fibers can be used in a limited way to control static. Brunsmet, a *stainless steel* fiber from 2 to 3 inches long, can be mixed throughout any kind of spun yarn to make the yarn a good conductor. Only one or two fibers per tuft will carry the static from the face fiber to the backing. So far, this kind of carpet yarn has been used in places in which static is a special problem, such as hospitals and rooms where sensitive computer equipment is kept. Zefstat, an acrylic or nylon spun yarn by Dow Badische, contains an especially treated strip of aluminum blended in so that it is invisible. As little as 2 per cent aluminum will dissipate static as fast as it is generated.

Summary of Fiber Properties Important in Carpets*

	Durability	Crush Recovery	Natural Fire Retardancy	Resistance to Waterborne Soil	Resistance to Oily Soil
Wool	Very Good	Good	Excellent	Fair	Good
Nylon	Very High	Exceptional	Good	Fair	Poor
Acrylic	Very Good	Good	Poor	High	Poor
Modacrylic	Very Good	Good	Excellent	High	Poor
Olefin	High	Medium	Good	High	Poor
Polyester	High	Good to Medium	Good	High	Poor

*Static, soil resistance, luster, and light resistance can be regulated by additives.

Filament Yarns: Smooth and textured

17

Yarn is the generic name for an assemblage of fibers that is laid or twisted together. There are two general classes of yarns: *spun yarns* made from staple fibers and *filament yarns* made from long continuous filaments. A wide variety of yarns in both categories is available to the fabric manufacturer. Yarns play a very important part in determining the hand and performance of the fabric. For example, yarns with very high twist are used to create the crinkle in true crepe fabrics, and yarns with very low twist are used in fabrics that are to be napped. Yarn may enhance good fiber performance or compensate for poor fiber performance. The effectiveness of a finish may depend on the proper choice of yarn. Most yarns can be easily recognized and identified.

Filament yarns are primarily man-made since silk is the only natural filament and accounts for less than 1 per cent of fiber and yarn production. Man-made filament yarns are made by chemical spinning, the process in which a polymer solution is extruded through a spinneret, solidified in fiber form, and then the individual filaments are immediately brought together with or without a slight twist (Figure 17-1). The bringing together of the filaments and/or the addition of twist *creates the filament* yarn. The spinning machine winds the yarn on a bobbin. The yarn is then rewound on spools or cones and is a finished product unless some additional treatment is required, such as crimping, twisting, texturing, or finishing.

Throwing was originally a process for twisting silk filaments but evolved into the twisting of man-made fibers and then into texturing (page 120). Throwing provides the weaver or knitter with the kind of yarn needed for a particular product; high twist for crepe or ply yarns for men's suit fabrics are examples. The throwster performs a service for the industry and, until the

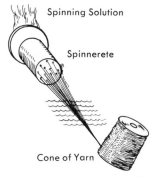

Fig. 17-1 Chemical spinning of filament yarn.

advent of textured yarns, did not use a trademark for his products. Some throwsters now have trademarks, such as Ban-Lon, which are used on garments made from their yarns. The consumer sometimes incorrectly assumes that these names represent new fibers, but the trademark simply indicates the yarn-texturing process. The yarns are made of nylon, polyester, acetate, and other fibers. Recently there has been a trend for the fiber producer to texture his own yarns as a final step in the spinning process. A texturing device is installed as part of the fiber spinning machine.

Smooth Filament Yarn

In the development of a new fiber, filament yarn production usually precedes production of tow for staple. Filament yarns are more expensive in price per pound; however, the cost of making tow into staple and then spinning it into yarn by the mechanical spinning process usually makes the final cost about the same. The number of holes in the spinneret determines the number of filaments in the yarn.

Regular or conventional filament yarns are smooth and silklike as they come from the spinneret. Their smooth nature gives them more *luster* than spun yarns, but the luster varies with the amount of delustering agent used in the fiber spinning solution and the amount of twist in the yarn. Maximum luster is obtained by the use of bright filaments, which are laid together with little or no twist. Crepe yarns, of very high twist, were developed as a means of reducing the luster of the filaments. Filament yarns are generally used with either *high twist or low twist.* The addition of twist increases bulk.

Filament yarns have no protruding ends, so they do not shed lint; they resist pilling; and fabrics made from them tend to shed soil. Filaments of round cross section pack well into compact yarns that give little bulk, loft, or cover to fabric. Compactness is a disadvantage in some end uses, where bulk and absorbency are necessary for comfort. Nonround or lobal filaments create more open space for air and for moisture permeability and give greater cover.

The *strength* of a filament yarn depends on the strength of the individual fibers and on the number of filaments in the yarn. Filament fiber strength is usually greater than that of staple fibers. For example:

Tensile Strength

Polyester Filament	Polyester Staple
5–8 grams/denier	3–5.5 grams/denier

The strength of each filament is fully utilized. In order to break the yarn, all the filaments must be broken. Therefore, it is possible to make hosiery and very sheer fabrics of fine filaments that have good strength. Filament yarns reach their maximum strength at about 3 to 6 turns per inch; then strength remains constant or decreases.

Fine filament yarns are soft and supple. However, they are not as resistant to abrasion as coarse filaments, so for durability it may be desirable to have fewer, but coarser, filaments in the yarn. Filament yarns are made with a denier (size) designed for a particular end use. For example:

Denier	Use
15	Sheer hosiery
40–70	Tricot lingerie, blouses, and shirts
140–520	Outerwear
520–840	Upholstery
1040	Carpets, some knitting yarns

Textured Filament Yarns

The texturing process discussed in this unit are mechanical texturing methods based on the use of thermoplastic fibers and heat. Turn to page 113 for a discussion of chemical methods of achieving texture by means of bicomponent fibers.

"Textured" is a general term for any continuous filament yarn whose smooth straight fibers have been displaced from their closely packed, parallel position by the introduction of some form of crimp, curl, loop, or coil (Figure 17-2).

Textured yarns have characteristics that are quite different from smooth filament yarns. Texturing gives slippery filaments the aesthetic properties of spun yarns by altering the surface characteristics and creating space between the fibers. This gives the fabric more breathability

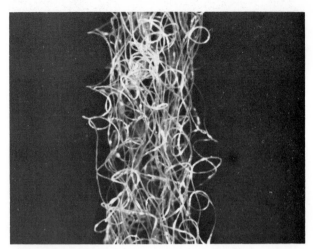

Fig. 17-2 Typical textured yarn. (*Courtesy of the Monsanto Textiles Company.*)

and more permeability to moisture, and the fabric is more absorbent, more comfortable, and has less static buildup. Bulk, cover, and elasticity or stretch are increased. Excellent ease of care (dependent on fiber content) is an advantage for the consumer, and for the manufacturer there is tremendous flexibility. Textured filament yarns can have spunlike qualities without the pilling and shedding that occurs with spun yarns. The first textured nylon, Helanca, was produced in the United States in 1952 and was used in stretch hosiery for men. The stretch eliminated the need for garters.

Three classes of textured filament yarns are made:

1. Bulk textured yarn:
Any kind of fiber

2. Stretch textured yarn:
Primarily nylon fiber

3. "Set"—modified stretch—textured yarns:
Polyester (major), acetate, and acetate fiber.

Bulk Textured Yarns

(No-torque—a yarn has torque if, when held by one end, the free end tends to rotate.)

Bulk-type texturing processes can be used with any kind of filament fiber—or spun yarn. The yarns have less stretch than either the stretch or "set" textured yarns. Bulk texturing is done by

1. Gear crimping—sawtooth crimp

2. Stuffer-box process—sawtooth crimp

3. Air-jet process—loops in individual fibers.

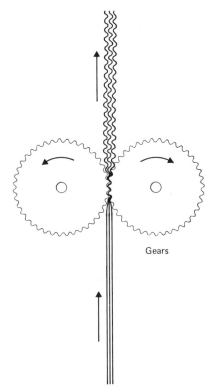

Fig. 17-3 Gear crimp.

Gear Crimp. The filament yarn passes between the teeth of two heated gears that mesh and thus give the yarn the shape of the gear teeth—sawtooth crimp (Figure 17–3). The bends are angular in contrast to the rounded waves and bends of natural crimp. This method has been used in the past to increase the crimp of carpet wools. When it is used with thermoplastic fibers, the crimp is permanent. Spunized is a trademark for gear-crimped yarns.

The Stevetex[1] crimping process crimps multiple filament yarns *arranged in warp formation* rather than one yarn at a time. Crimp is uniform along the whole warp length and the yarns are free of torque. The number of crimps can be controlled—increased or decreased. Some end uses are tricot for lingerie, blouses, pajamas, and dresses.

Stuffer Box. The stuffer box produces a sawtooth crimp of considerable bulk. Straight filament yarns are literally stuffed into one end of a heated box (see Figure 17–4) and are then withdrawn at the other end in crimped form. Bulked single yarns are usually plied to hold the fila-

[1] J. P. Stevens and Company developed the process.

ments together and to minimize snagging. The apparent volume increase is 200 to 300 per cent. The yarns have some elasticity but not enough to be classified as stretch yarns. The stuffer box is a fast method and one of the least costly. It is the most widely used bulking process.

End products of yarns crimped by this process are carpets, upholstery, sweaters, and knitted dresses. Textralized, Ban-lon and Spunized are registered trademarks for such yarns.

Air-Jet. The air-jet process produces loop-type displacement of the fibers. Conventional filament is fed over an air jet (Figure 17–5) at a faster rate than it is drawn off. The blast of air forces some of the filaments into very tiny loops; the velocity of the air affects the size of the loops. This is not a high-speed process and is relatively costly.

Volume increase in the yarn is between 50 and 150 per cent. A fabric made from these yarns may seem to have more texture or luster change than it has change in bulk. The process is very versatile. Any kind of fiber can be used and styling possibilities are unlimited—silklike, worsted, heather, slub, and blends with spun or textured.

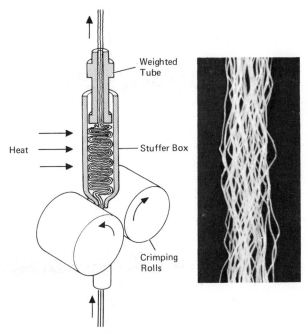

Fig. 17-4 (*Left*) "Stuffing-box" process. (*Right*) Textralized yarn used in Ban-lon garments. Textralized and Ban-lon are trademarks for end products and continuous-filament yarns modified by a process licensed by Joseph Bancroft and Sons. (*Courtesy of the Chemstrand Corporation.*)

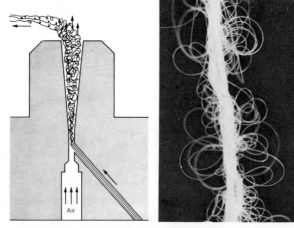

Fig. 17-5 (*Left*) Air-jet process. (*Right*) Taslan textured yarn. Taslan is Du Pont's registered trademark used to designate textured yarns made in accordance with quality standards set by Du Pont. (*Courtesy of the Chemstrand Corporation.*)

Air-jet yarns will maintain their size and bulk under tension, because the straight sections of the fiber bear the strain and allow the loops to remain relatively unaffected. The yarns have little or no stretch. Heat setting is not necessary, so the process can be used for non-heat-settable yarns. The yarn under magnification looks like a novelty yarn. Registered trademarks for yarns made by this process include Taslan, Skyloft, and Lofted acetate. Some end uses for these yarns are shirts, blouses, women's wear, shoelaces, and household furnishings.

Stretch Textured Yarns

Stretch-type textured yarns are characterized by high elongation—300 to 500 per cent, rapid recovery, and moderate bulk per unit of weight. The original or "classical" method of producing a stretch yarn was developed by the Heberlein Co. of Switzerland. It was done in three separate steps, which involved twisting the yarn 60 to 130 turns per inch, heat setting in an autoclave, and untwisting the yarn. The process made an excellent stretch yarn, but it was costly and has been largely replaced by the false-twist method.

Stretch yarns are made primarily of nylon fiber and have been used extensively in men's and women's hosiery, panty hose, leotards, swimwear, ski pants, football pants, and jerseys. Stretch yarns make it possible to manufacture fewer sizes, as one-size items will fit wearers of different sizes.

Stretch yarns are made as:

1. False-twist coil type
2. Edge-crimped curl type
3. Knit-de-knit crinkle type

False-Twist Coil-Type Yarns. The false-twist spindle is an ideal device for making stretch yarns. (It is also used for "set" textured yarns.) The spindle whirls at 600,000 revolutions per minute and generates sound comparable to a jet engine. The effect of this sound on health and hearing has been a matter of concern in the industry. The process is continuous; the yarn is twisted, heat-set, and untwisted as it travels through the spindle (Figure 17–6). As the false-twist spindle turns, there will be an S-twist in the yarn on one side and a Z-twist in the yarn on the other side (Figure 17–6). When the yarn untwists, the filaments are essentially in the form of a helical coil distorted by the untwisting (Figure 17–7). If the yarn is pulled at each end the coils will straighten out—thus the stretch.

A wide range of stretch yarn properties can be achieved by differences in the amount of false twist and differences in the degree of tension on the feed roll. The spindle can be twisted to the right or the left and can twist alternately to the

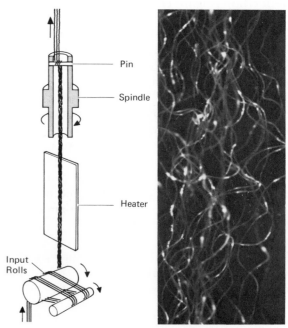

Pin

Spindle

Heater

Input Rolls

Fig. 17-6 (*Left*) "False-twist" process. (*Right*) Fluflon yarn. Fluflon is a registered trademark of Marionette Mills, Inc. (*Courtesy of the Chemstrand Corporation.*)

Fig. 17–7 False-twist spindle.

Round Filament   Flattened

Fig. 17–9 Edge-crimping flattens one side of the filament.

right or left by reversing at controlled time intervals. The yarn can be used as singles or can be plied by combining singles of right and left twist. They are usually made of nylon fiber. False-twist is the most widely used method of texturizing.

Some trademarks for false-twist yarns are Helanca,[2] Fluflon, Superloft, Saaba.

The Duo-Twist process by the Turbo Machine Company is similar to the false-twist method but uses no spindle and yarns have lower twist and torque. Two yarns are twisted together, heat-set and untwisted, and then wound on individual spools.

Edge-Crimp Curl-Type Yarns. Curl-type stretch yarns are made by drawing heated filaments over a knifelike edge (Figure 17–8), which flattens the filaments on one side and causes the

yarn to curl, with an effect like that obtained by pulling a Christmas ribbon over scissors to curl it. The filament cross section changes from round to flattened on one side (Figure 17–9). The flattened side is shortened, so differential shrinkage of the sides causes a nontorque curl. The effect is similar to that of bicomponent stretch.

The process is low cost and speedy. It can be used on monofilaments as well as multifilaments. The primary end use is hosiery. Agilon is a trademark of the Deering-Milliken Research Corporation.

Knit-de-Knit Crinkle Type Yarns. *Knit-de-knit* was one of the older methods but was not used much until 1965, when it became very popular. A small-diameter tube like a seamless stocking is knit at a rapid speed (Figure 17–10), (Figure 17–11). It is then heat-set, unraveled, and wound on cones (Figure 17–12). Crimp size and frequency can be varied by difference in stitch size and tension. The knitting stitch used to make the garment must be of different gauge than that of the knit-de-knit tube or pinholes will form where

[2] Helanca trademarks are sometimes followed by code letters: Helanca SW, for example, means sweater weight.

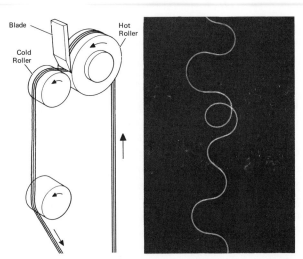

Fig. 17–8 (*Left*) Edge-Crimp yarn process. (*Right*) Agilon yarn. (*Photograph courtesy of Deering-Milliken Research Corporation.*)

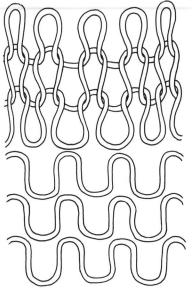

Fig. 17–10 Knit-de-knit crimp.

Fig. 17-11 KDK Knitting Machine knitting tubes for crinkle type yarns. (*Courtesy of Scott & Williams, Inc.*)

the crimp gauge snd knit gauge match. Knit-de-knit produces a bouclé or crepe effect and is used in outerwear, swimwear, and upholstery.

Set Textured Yarns

Set textured yarns, primarily polyester, comprise more than half of all yarns used in apparel. They are used in both knit and woven fabrics. They have true wash-and-wear characteristics and give an excellent hand and drape to fabrics.

Set textured yarns are stabilized stretch yarns—they have bulk and some comfort stretch.

Fabrics made from these yarns maintain their original size and shape during wear and care.

Set textured yarns are made from (1) flat drawn yarn (thermoplastic filaments drawn after spinning), (2) undrawn or unoriented filament yarns, and (3) partially drawn or oriented (POY) yarn. Texturing and stabilizing are done by (1) a double heater false-twist machine or (2) by a double heater friction-twist machine.

Flat Drawn Set-Textured Yarns. These yarns are made by a machine that is essentially the same as that shown in Figure 17–6 with a second

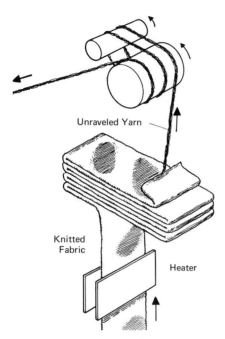

Fig. 17-12 Knit-de-knit.

heating zone. The false-twisted yarn is stretched slightly and stabilized at a temperature higher than that used for texturing.

Draw Textured Yarns. Prior to 1971 all set textured polyester yarn was produced by throw-sters by this process. In 1970 fiber producers developed a process by which the drawing and texturing could be done in one process. In the traditional melt-spinning process filaments from the spinneret are gathered together into a yarn and wound on spools.

Polyester and nylon yarns are then stretched to orient the molecules and develop fiber strength and are finally heat-set to stabilize them. These are the flat yarns used in the traditional texturing process.

In the draw-texturing process the unoriented filaments or partially oriented filaments are fed directly through the double heater false-twist spinner. This eliminates the separate stretching process.

Draw texturing is a much faster and cheaper way of making set textured yarns and the finished yarns are as good as, or better than, those done by conventional means. Throwsters are changing from the conventional process and are modifying their machines and buying POY yarns from fiber producers.

Friction Textured Yarns. Friction texturing is a process in which POY yarns (partially oriented yarns) are fed into machines that put twist into the yarns by friction surfaces rather than false twisters or spindles.

Spun Yarns

18

Spun yarns are made from staple fibers that are twisted together. They are suited to clothing fabrics in which absorbency, bulk, warmth, or cotton-like or woollike textures are desired.

Spun yarns are characterized by *protruding fiber ends*. The fiber ends hold the yarn away from close contact with the skin; thus a spun yarn is more comfortable on a hot humid day than a fabric of smooth-filament yarns. *Carded yarns,* made of short fibers, have more protruding fiber ends than *combed yarns,* which are made of long-staple fibers. Protruding ends contribute to a dull fuzzy appearance, to the shedding of lint, and to the formation of pills on the surface of the fabric. Fuzzy ends can be removed from the yarn or from the fabric by singeing (page 261).

The *strength* of the individual staple fiber is less important as a factor in yarn strength than it is in filament yarns. Instead, spun-yarn strength is dependent on the cohesive or clinging power of the fibers and on the points of contact resulting from pressure of twist. The greater the number of points of contact, the greater is the resistance to fiber slippage within the yarn. Fibers with crimp or convolutions make a greater number of points of contact. The friction of one fiber against another gives resistance to lengthwise fiber slippage. A fiber with a rough surface—wool scales, for example—creates more friction than a smooth fiber.

The spinning of staple fibers into yarns is one of the oldest manufacturing arts and has been described as an invention as significant as that of the wheel. The first yarns—spun yarns—were made from flax, wool, and cotton, all of which are staple fibers. The basic principles of spinning are the same now as they were when man first made yarn.

The earliest primitive spinning consisted of drawing out the fibers, which were held on a stick called a distaff, twisting them by the rotation of a spindle, which could be spun like a top and then winding up the spun yarn (Figure 18-1). The

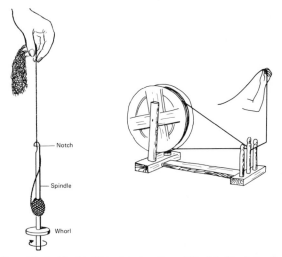

Fig. 18-1 (*Left*) Hand spinning. (*Right*) Early spinning wheel.

spinning wheel was invented by the spinners of India and was introduced into Europe in the fourteenth century. The factory system began in the eighteenth century when spinning was done by a class distinct from the weavers. In 1764 an Englishman named James Hargreaves invented the first spinning jenny—a machine that could turn more than one spinning wheel at a time. Other inventions for improving the spinning process followed and led to the Industrial Revolution, when power machines took over hand processes and made mass production possible. Machines were developed for each separate step in the spinning process.

Spinning is currently in a process of evolution. Progress in *conventional ring spinning* has been in the area of reduction in the number of steps involved in the combination of individual steps—continuous spinning. Several steps have been automated. Other spinning methods have excited a great deal of interest as being faster, simpler, and more economical than ring spinning. Spun-yarn processes are shown in the chart.

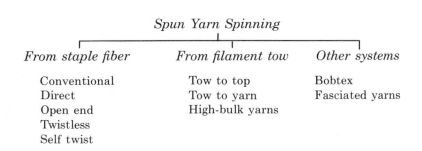

Spun Yarn Spinning

From staple fiber	From filament tow	Other systems
Conventional	Tow to top	Bobtex
Direct	Tow to yarn	Fasciated yarns
Open end	High-bulk yarns	
Twistless		
Self twist		

Operations	Purpose
Opening	Loosens, blends, cleans, forms *lap*.
Carding	Cleans, straightens, forms *carded sliver*.
Drawing	Parallels, blends, forms *drawn sliver*.
Combing	Parallels, removes short fibers, forms *combed sliver* (used for long staple cotton only).
Roving	Reduces size, inserts slight twist, forms *roving*.
Spinning	Reduces size, twists, winds the finished yarn on a bobbin.
Winding	Rewinds yarn from bobbins to spools or cones.

Spinning Staple Fibers

Conventional Spinning

Conventional spinning has traditionally consisted of a series of operations performed by individual machines and has involved a great deal of hand labor. Although continuous spinning and some automation have come into use, spinning is still a long and expensive process. The different operations are designed to (1) clean and parallel staple fibers, (2) draw them out into a fine strand, and (3) twist them to keep them together and give them strength. Spinning may be done by any one of five conventional systems[1] that are adapted to the characteristics of the fiber—length, cohesiveness, diameter, elasticity, and surface contour. Because the cotton system is representative of the rest, it is discussed here in detail.

Opening. Opening loosens, cleans, and blends the fibers. The fibers have been compressed very tightly in the bale and may have been stored in this state for a year or more. Machine-picked

[1] Conventional spinning systems are: Cotton, Woolen, French, Bradford, and American.

Fig. 18-2 Karousel opener-picker machine. (*Courtesy of the American Reiter Company, Inc.*)

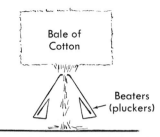

Fig. 18-3 Beaters (pluckers) pull fibers from the bale.

cotton contains a much higher percentage of trash and dirt than does hand picked cotton; consequently, the work of cleaning has become more complicated. Part of it is done at the gin. Cotton varies from bale to bale, so the fibers from several bales are blended together to give yarns of more uniform quality. Two types of opening units are used. One is a chute-feed system and the other (Figure 18-2) is a merry-go-round-like unit. In both systems the bales travel over bale pluckers (Figure 18-3) that pull small tufts of fiber from the underside of the bales and drop the tufts on a screen or lattice. High-velocity air removes dirt and trash. The loosened cleaned fibers are fed to the carding machine in sheet form.

Carding. Carding partially straightens the fibers and forms them into a thin web, which is brought together as a soft rope of fibers called a *carded sliver* (Figure 18-4). The carding machine consists of cylinders covered with heavy fabric embedded with especially bent wires.

Drawing. Drawing increases the parallelism of the fibers and combines several carded slivers into

Fig. 18-4 Carding. (*Courtesy of Coats & Clark Inc., New York, N.Y.*)

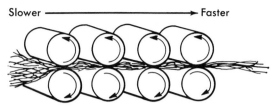

Slower ——————→ Faster

Fig. 18-5 Drawing rolls.

one *drawn sliver*. This is a blending operation that contributes to greater yarn uniformity. Drawing is done by sets of rollers, each set running successively faster than the preceding set (Figure 18-5).

Combing. If long staple fibers are to be spun, carding and drawing will be followed by combing. The fundamental purpose of combing is to parallel fibers and *to remove any short fibers* from the long staple so that the combed fibers will be more uniform in length. Fibers emerge from the combing machine as *combed sliver*. The combing operation and the long staple fiber are costly and as much as one fourth of the fiber is combed out as waste.

Roving. Roving reduces the drawn sliver, increases the parallelism of the fibers, and inserts a small amount of twist (Figure 18-6). The product is called a *roving*. It is a softly twisted strand of fibers about the size of a pencil. Successive roving operations that gradually reduce the size of the strand may be used.

Spinning. Spinning[2] adds the twist that makes the yarn—a single spun yarn. Ring spinning draws, twists, and winds in one continuous operation. The traveler (Figure 18-7) carries the yarn as it slides around the ring, thus inserting the twist. Because ring spinning is a slow textile process in terms of productivity per unit produced—it has been limited in traveler speed, package size, and adaptability to automation—much interest has been shown in *open-end* spinning (page 131), which in many ways resembles whorless primitive spinning.

Figure 18-8 shows a ring spinning frame—a multiple spinning machine that holds a number of individual units.

[2] Mule spinning is an intermittent action used in the woolen spinning system. The yarn is drawn out and twisted, then the twisting stops while the twisted portion of yarn is wound on the bobbin. This intermittent action is the basic fault of mule spinning, which may cease to be used in the future.

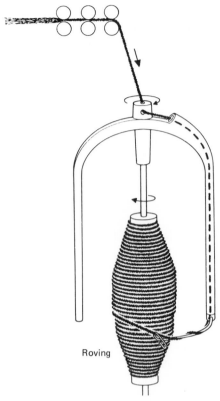

Fig. 18-6 Roving.

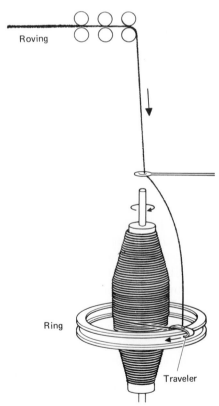

Fig. 18-7 Ring spinning.

Fig. 18-8 A spinning frame holds multiple ring spinners.

Comparison of Carded and Combed Yarns

The length and parallelism of fibers in spun yarns is a major factor in the *kind* of fabric, the *cost* of the yarns and fabrics, and the *terminology* used to designate these characteristics.

Yarns made from carded sliver are called *carded* yarns. Carded sliver of short wool fibers is made into *woolen* yarns and the fabrics are called *woolen* fabrics. (*Note:* The term *woolen* has a specific meaning and should not be used as a synonym for wool, the name of the fiber. For example, if one says "This is a woolen dress," it means that the dress fabric is made from the shorter wool fibers.)

Yarns made from combed sliver are called *combed* yarns except in the case of wool, in which case combed sliver is referred to as *top* and the yarns made from top are called *worsted* yarns. The short fibers that are combed out are called *noils* and are a source of fiber supply for carded yarns. Fine combed cotton yarns are made from the fibers that measure more than $1\frac{1}{8}$ inches. In many fabrics combed cotton is being replaced by long staple high performance rayon or polyester fibers.

Carded and combed yarns are compared in the chart and in Figure 18-9.

Much research has been done to develop a spinning system for staple fibers that will shorten or simplify yarn spinning by eliminating or bypassing some of the steps in the conventional system.

Carded and Combed
Yarn Comparison

	Carded	Combed
Fibers used:	Short staple	Long staple
Yarns:	Medium to low twist	Medium to high twist
	More protruding ends	Fewer protruding ends
	Bulkier, softer, fuzzier	Parallel fibers; finer count
		Longer wearing, stronger
Fabrics:	May become baggy in areas of stress	Smoother surface, lighter weight
		Do not sag
	Fabrics may be soft to firm	Take and hold press
	Blankets always carded	Fabrics range from sheers to suitings
	Wide range of uses	

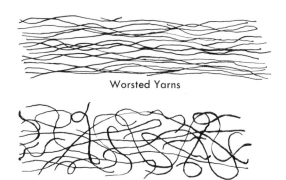

Worsted Yarns

Woolen Yarns

Fig. 18-9 Woolen and worsted yarns. (*Top*) Long parallel wool fibers in combed yarn. (*Bottom*) Short staple wool fibers in carded or woolen yarn.

The goal of most of the current developmental work is to use fiber directly from the card machine, thus eliminating drawing, roving, ring spinning, and rewinding. Some of these goals have been achieved.

Direct Spinning

The Mackie direct spinner[3] (1960) eliminates the roving but still uses the ring-spinning device for inserting the twist. Notice in Figure 18-10 that the sliver is fed directly to the spinning frame. This machine is used to make heavier yarn for pile fabrics and carpets.

Open End Spinning

Open end spinning eliminates the roving and twisting by the ring. Knots are eliminated, larger packages of yarn are formed, less operator super-

[3] Do not confuse this machine with the direct spinner for processing filament tow (page 132).

Fig. 18-10 Mackie direct spinner turns *sliver* into finished yarn—eliminates roving. (*Courtesy of James Mackie & Sons Ltd.*)

vision is needed, and higher production speeds (about four times that of ring spinning) are achieved.

In this process, fibers from a sliver are fed through rollers or over a spiked roller that breaks up the sliver so that individual fibers are fed by an air stream and deposited on the inner surface of a rotating device driven at high speed. As the fibers are drawn off, twist is inserted by the rotation of the rotor making a yarn (Figure 18-11).

Twistless Spinning

Twistless spinning eliminates the twisting process. A roving is wetted, drawn out, sprayed with sizing, and wound on a package. The package is steamed to gelatinize the starch and bond the fibers together (Figure 18-12).

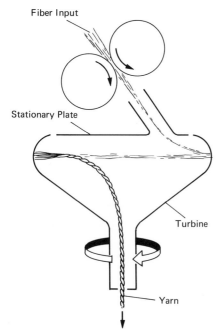

Fig. 18–11 Open-end or break spinning.

The yarns are flat and ribbonlike in shape and are quite stiff because of their size. They lack strength as individual yarns but gain strength in the fabric from the pressure between the warp and filling. The absence of twist gives the yarns a softness and good luster after the sizing is removed. The notable feature of the twistless yarns is their opaqueness. The yarns are open to dye and have very good durability but are not suitable to very open weaves.

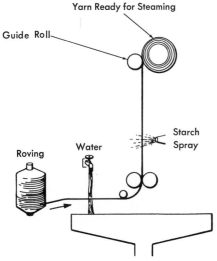

Fig. 18–12 Twistlers spinning.

Self-Twist Spinning

Self-twist spinning is a process in which two strands of roving are carried between two rollers that move forward to draw out the roving and sideways to put in twist. The yarns have areas of S-twist and areas of Z-twist. When the two twisted yarns are brought together they intermesh and entangle, and when pressure is released the yarns try to untwist and this causes them to ply over each other (Figure 18–13).

Spinning Filament Tow into Spun Yarns

Any kind of man-made fiber in filament tow form can be processed by the direct spinning process. Filament tow can be made into spun yarns, without disrupting the continuity of the strand, by either the tow-to-top system or by the direct-spun tow-to-yarn system.

Tow-to-Top (Sliver) System

The tow-to-top system bypasses the opening, picking, and carding steps of conventional spinning. In this system the filament tow is reduced to staple and formed into sliver (or top) by either diagonal cutting on a Pacific Converter or break stretching on a Perlock machine. The sliver from either machine is made into regular spun yarn by conventional spinning.

The *diagonal cutting stapler* changes tow into staple of equal or variable lengths and forms it into a crimped sliver (Figure 18–14). Yarn spinning is completed later on the conventional spinning system.

The *break-stretch stapler* operates on the principle that, when tow is stretched, the fibers will break at their weakest points (random breakage) without disrupting the continuity of the strand. The resultant staple will be of various lengths.

Tow-to-Yarn System

Tow-to-yarn spinning is done by a machine called a *direct spinner*. Light tow (4,400 denier) is fed into the machine through leveling rolls, passes between two nip rolls, and then passes across a conveyor belt to a second pair of nip rolls, which

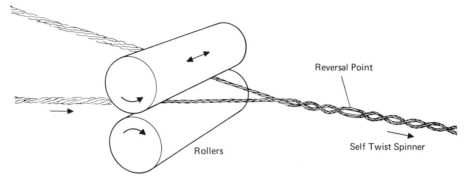

Fig. 18-13 Self-twist spinning.

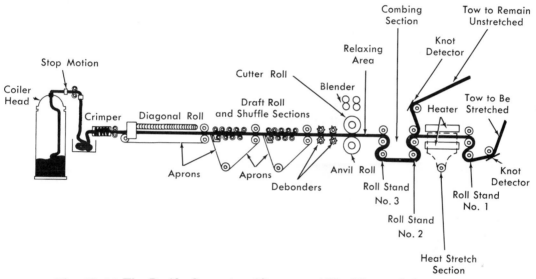

Fig. 18-14 The Pacific Converter. (*Courtesy of The Warner & Swasey Co.*)

travel at a faster rate of speed and create tension that causes the fibers to break at their weakest points. The strand is then drawn out to yarn size, twisted, and wound on a bobbin (Figure 18–15).

High-Bulk Yarns

High-bulk yarns are made from filament tow on these machines by the addition of a heating element. Part of the tow is heat-stretched and the other part is not. The two parts are then brought together and diagonally cut and spun by conventional means. On the Perlock or Turbo-Stapler (Figure 18–16) the tow is heat stretched and passed through the breaker zone. The fibers are crimped, a portion of the top is relaxed by steam, and the two portions are brought together and

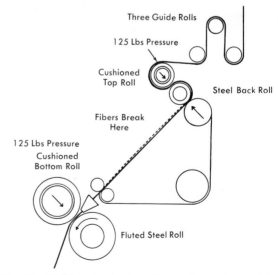

Fig. 18-15 Direct spinning of yarn from filament tow.

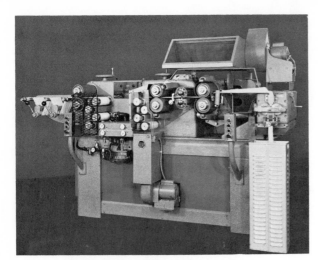

Fig. 18-16 The Turbo-Stapler.

spun into yarns. Both of these methods make yarns that are composed of high- and low-shrinkage fibers. The yarns containing high-shrinkage and low-shrinkage fibers are first made into a garment such as a sweater. The garment is then immersed in boiling water and the high-

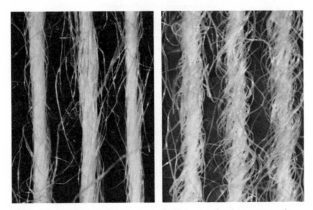

Fig. 18-17 High-bulk yarn before and after steaming.

shrinkage component of the yarn contracts—shrinking as much as 20 per cent—and draws in toward the center causing the low-shrinkage fibers to buckle and create loft and bulk (Figure 18-17). The heat treatment will stabilize the garment and no further shrinkage will occur in use.

Other Systems

In other spinning systems the yarns have a core of filaments or polymer and a sheath of staple fibers. They look like spun yarns and are either stronger or less expensive to produce.

Bobtex

The Bobtex system, developed in Canada, produces a yarn by pressing staple fibers of any length or generic class into a molten polymer stream. As the polymer solidifies, the fibers that are partially embedded become firmly attached and form a sheath of staple fiber. The resultant yarn is about $\frac{2}{3}$ fiber and $\frac{1}{3}$ polymer. The polymer, which is extruded as man-made fibers are, is a less expensive product than other melt-spun filaments.

Fasciated Yarns

Fasciated yarns, developed by Du Pont, consist of parallel filaments bound together by broken filaments or fibers (Figure 18-18). The yarns are produced by feeding filaments through a device similar to a false-twist machine. The yarns are stronger than conventional spun yarns.

Fig. 18-18 Fasciated yarn.

Yarn Classification

19

Yarns are classified and can be identified by type of yarn, size, amount of twist, and number of parts. Each of these classifications contributes to fabric performance.

Yarn Types

Type or kind of yarn is based on fiber length and parallelism, appearance, and special end use. The names of yarns are usually based on type.

Regular filament, textured filament, and spun yarns were discussed in Chapters 17 and 18. The

following chart summarizes the properties that these yarns give to fabrics.

Yarn Size

Yarn Number. *Spun yarn size* is referred to as *count* or *number* and is expressed in terms of length per unit of weight. It differs according to the kind of fiber. The cotton system is given here. Weaving yarns and sewing thread are numbered by the cotton system. It is an indirect system; the finer the yarn, the larger is the number. The

Comparison of Spun, Regular Filament, and Textured Filament Yarns

Spun Yarns	Plain Filament Yarns	Textured Filament Yarns
I. Fabrics are cottonlike or woollike.	I. Fabrics are silklike.	I. Fabrics have the strength of filament yarns and the appearance of spun yarns.
II. Strength of fibers is not completely utilized.	II. Strength of fiber is completely utilized.	II. Strength may or may not be completely utilized.
III. Short fibers twisted into continuous strand, has protruding ends.	III. Long continuous, smooth, closely packed strand.	III. Long continuous, irregular, porous, flexible strand.
1. Dull, fuzzy look.	1. Smooth, lustrous.	1. Fuzzy, dull.
2. Lint.	2. Do not lint.	2. Do not lint.
3. Subject to pilling.	3. Do not pill readily.	3. Pilling depends on fabric construction.
4. Soil readily.	4. Shed soil.	4. Soil more easily than plain filament.
5. Warm (not slippery).	5. Cool, slick.	5. Warmer than plain filament.
6. Loft and bulk depend on size and twist.	6. Little loft or bulk.	6. Loft, bulk and/or stretch.
7. Do not snag readily.	7. Snagging depends on fabric construction.	7. Snag easily.
8. Stretch depends on amount of twist.	8. Stretch depends on amount of twist.	8. Stretch depends on method of processing.
9. More cover (more opaque).	9. Less cover (less opaque).	9. More cover (more opaque).
IV. Are absorbent.	IV. Absorbency depends on fiber content.	IV. More absorbent than plain filament yarns of same fiber content.
1. Good for skin contact (most absorbent).	1. Thermoplastics are low in absorbency.	1. Most manufacturing processes require thermoplastic fibers.
2. Less static buildup.	2. Static buildup high in thermoplastics.	2. Static buildup.
V. Size often expressed in yarn number.	V. Size in denier.	V. Size in denier.
VI. Various amounts of twist used.	VI. Usually very low or very high twist.	VI. Usually low twist.
VII. Most complex manufacturing process.	VII. Least complicated manufacturing process.	VII. Manufacturing process is more complex than plain filament.

count is based on the number of hanks (1 hank is 840 yards) in 1 pound of yarn (see the table). Some examples that show how the size of the weaving yarn affects the weight of the fabric are given in the second half of the table.

Cotton System

Number or Count of Spun Yarn	Hanks	Weight (pounds)
No. 1	1 (840 yards)	1
No. 2	2 (1,680 yards)	1
No. 3	3 (2,520 yards)	1
etc.		

Examples of Fabric Weight	Yarn Size	
	Warp	Filling
Sheer lawn	70s*	100s
Dressweight percale	30s	40s
Suiting-weight Indian Head	13s	20s

* The "s" after the number means that the yarn is single.

The woolen and worsted systems are similar to the cotton system except that hanks are of different lengths.

Denier. *Filament yarn size* is dependent partly on the size of the holes in the spinneret and partly on the rate at which the solution is pumped through the spinneret and the rate at which it is withdrawn. The size of filament yarns (and filament fibers) is expressed in terms of weight per unit of length—denier (pronounced "den-yer"). In this system the unit of length remains constant. The numbering system is direct because the finer the yarn, the smaller is the number.

Filament Yarn Size

1 denier	9,000 meters weigh 1 gram
2 denier	9,000 meters weigh 2 grams
3 denier	9,000 meters weigh 3 grams

Tex System. The International Organization for Standardization had adopted the Tex system,

Tex System

Tex System	
1 Tex	1,000 meters weighs 1 gram
2 Tex	1,000 meters weigh 2 grams
3 Tex	1,000 meters weigh 3 grams

which determines yarn count or number in the same way for all fiber yarns and uses metric units.

Number of Parts

A simple yarn is alike in all its parts. A novelty yarn has unlike parts; it is irregular at regular intervals.

Simple Yarns

Simple yarns are classified as single, ply, and cord.

A *single yarn* is the product of the first twisting operation that is performed by the spinning machine (Figure 19–1a).

A *ply yarn* is made by a second twisting operation, which combines two or more singles (Figure 19–1b). Each part of the yarn is called a *ply*. The twist is inserted by a machine called a *twister*. Most ply yarns are twisted in the opposite direction to the twist of the singles from which they are made; thus the first few revolutions tend to untwist the singles and straighten the fibers somewhat from their spiral position and the yarn becomes softer. Plying tends to increase the diameter, strength, and quality of the yarn. Terms indicating quality, such as combed or worsted, may be used on the label. Ply may or may not be on the label. If simple ply yarns are used in one

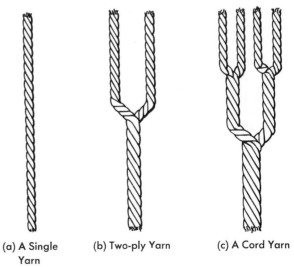

(a) A Single Yarn   (b) Two-ply Yarn   (c) A Cord Yarn

Fig. 19–1 Parts of a yarn. (a) Single yarn. (b) Two-ply yarn. (c) Cord yarn.

direction only and are in the filling direction, they are used for some fabric effect other than strength.

A *cord* is made by a third twisting operation, which twists ply yarns together (Figure 19-1c). Some types of sewing thread and some ropes belong in this group. Cord yarns are seldom used in apparel fabrics.

Yarn Twist

Twist is defined as the spiral arrangement of the fibers around the axis of the yarn. Twist is produced by revolving one end of a fiber strand while the other end is held stationary. Twist binds the fibers together and gives the yarn strength. It is a tool for varying fabrics and fabric design.

The number of twists is referred to as *turns per inch.* They have a direct bearing on the cost of the yarn because higher twist yields lower productivity.

Direction

The direction of twist is described as S-twist and Z-twist.[1] A yarn has S-twist if, when held in vertical position, the spirals conform to the direction of slope of the central portion of the letter "S." It is called Z-twist if the direction of spirals conforms to the slope of the central portion of the letter "Z." Z-twist is the standard twist used for weaving yarns (Figure 19-2).

Amount

The amount of twist varies with (1) the length of the fibers, (2) the size of the yarn, and (3) the

[1] These terms have largely replaced the terms *regular, reverse, right,* and *left,* which are used with opposite meaning by various segments of the textile industry.

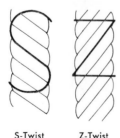

S-Twist   Z-Twist

Fig. 19-2 S- and Z-twists.

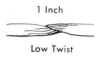

1 Inch

Low Twist

High Twist

Fig. 19-3 Low and high turns per inch.

intended use. Increasing the amount of twist up to the point of perfect fiber-to-fiber cohesion will increase the strength of the yarns. Too much twist places the fibers at right angles to the axis of the yarn and causes a shearing action between fibers and the yarn will lose strength (Figure 19-3).

Combed yarns with long fibers do not require as much twist as carded yarns with short fibers, since they establish more points of contact per fiber and give stronger yarn for the same amount of twist. Fine yarns require more twist than coarse yarns. Knitting yarns have less twist than the filling yarns used in weaving. The chart and discussion that follow give examples of different amounts of twist.

Amount of Twist

Amount	Example
Low twist	Filament yarns: 2–3 tpi*
Napping twist	Blanket warps: 12 tpi
	Filling: 6–8 tpi
Average twist (usually spun yarn)	Percale warps: 25 tpi
	Filling: 20 tpi
	Nylon hosiery: 25–30 tpi
Voile twist	Hard twist singles: 35–40 tpi
	are plied with 16–18 tpi
Crepe twist	Singles; 40 to 80 or more tpi
	are plied with 2–5 tpi
*Turns per inch.	

Low twist in spun yarns results in lofty yarns. It is used in filling yarns of fabrics that are to be napped. The low twist permits the napping machine to tease out the ends of the staple fibers and create the soft fuzzy surface. (See "Napping," page 268.)

Average twist is frequently used for yarns made of staple fibers and is very seldom used for filament yarns. The amount of twist that gives warp yarns maximum strength is referred to as *standard warp twist.* Warp yarns need more twist than filling yarns because warp yarns are under

Fig. 19-4 Twist-on-twist yarn.

high tension on the loom and they must resist wear caused by the abrasion of the shuttle moving back and forth. The lower twist of the filling yarns makes them softer and less apt to kink.

Hard twist (voile twist) yarns have 30 to 40 turns per inch. The hardness of the yarn results when twist brings the fibers closer together and makes the yarn more compact. This effect is more pronounced when a twist-on-twist ply yarn is used. Twist-on-twist means that the direction of twist in the singles is the same as that of plying twist (Figure 19-4). This results in a buildup of the total amount of twist in the yarn (see "Voile," page 166).

Crepe yarns are made of either staple or filament fiber. They are made with a high number of turns per inch (40 to 80) inserted in the yarn. This makes the yarn so lively and kinky that it must be twist-set before it can be woven or knitted. *Twist-setting* is a finishing process in which the yarns are moistened and then dried in a straightened condition. After weaving, the cloth is moistened and the yarns become lively and kinky once more and thus produce the crinkle characteristic of true crepe fabrics. All the common *natural* fibers and rayon can be used in crepe twist yarns because they can be twist-set in water. The thermoplastic fibers are twisted and set by heat. They do not have as much stretch as other crepe yarns, and fabrics made from them do not shrink. Increasing the amount of crepe yarn twist and alternating the direction of twist will increase the amount of crinkle in a crepe fabric. For example,

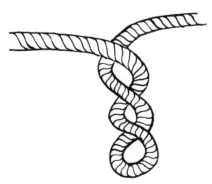

Fig. 19-5 Kink in crepe yarn.

6S and 6Z will give a more prominent crinkle than 2S and 2Z.

To identify crepe yarns, ravel adjacent sides to obtain a fringe on each of the two edges. Test the yarns that are removed by pulling on the yarn and then letting one end go. The yarn will "kink up" as shown in Figure 19-5. Do not confuse kink with yarn crimp. Examine the fringe of the fabric. If yarns other than crepe yarns are used in the fabric, they will probably be of very low twist. The majority of crepe fabrics have crepe yarns in the crosswise direction, although some are in the lengthwise direction and some have crepe yarns in both directions. Crepe fabrics are discussed in Chapter 24.

Novelty and Specialty Yarns

Novelty yarns are made on twisters with special attachments for giving different tensions and rates of delivery to the different plies (parts) and thus allow loose, curled, twisted, or looped areas in the yarn. Slubs and flakes of color are introduced into the yarn by special attachments also.

Novelty yarns may be defined as *yarns that are irregular at regular intervals.* Knots or slubs, for example, are made at regular cycles of the machine operation (Figure 19-6).

A typical novelty yarn has three basic parts:

- The ground or foundation or core.
- The fancy or effect.
- The binder.

Some facts about novelty yarns:

1. Novelty yarns are usually ply yarns, but they are not used to add strength to the fabric.

2. If novelty yarns are used in one direction only, they are usually in the filling direction. They "go further" there and are subject to less strain and are easier to vary for design purposes.

3. Novelty yarns add interest to plain weave fabrics at lower cost than if effects were obtained from weave. Novelty yarn effects are permanent.

4. Novelty yarns that are loose and bulky give crease resistance to a fabric but they make the fabric spongy and hard to sew.

Fig. 19-6 Knot or spot novelty yarn, showing the three basic parts.

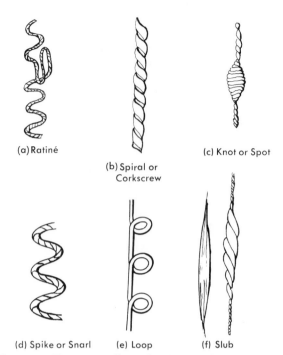

Fig. 19-7 Fancy or effect ply of several kinds of novelty yarns.

5. The durability of novelty yarn fabrics is dependent on the size of the novelty effect, how well the novelty effect is held in the yarn, and on the firmness of the weave of the fabric. Generally speaking, the smaller the novelty effect, the more durable the fabric is, since the yarns are less affected by abrasion and do not tend to catch and pull out so readily.

Typical novelty yarns are:

Ratiné is a typical novelty yarn. The effect ply is twisted in a somewhat spiral arrangement around the ground ply; but at intervals a longer loop is thrown out, kinks back on itself, and is held in place by the binder (Figure 19–7a).

The *spiral or corkscrew yarn* is made by twisting together two plies that differ in size or in twist. These two parts may be delivered to the twister at different rates of speed (Figure 19–7b).

The *knot, spot, nub, or knop yarn* is made by twisting the effect ply many times in the same place (Figure 19–7c). Two effect plies of different colors may be used and the knots arranged so the colored spots are alternated along the length of the yarn. A binder is added during the twisting operation.

In the *spike or snarl,* the effect ply forms alternating unclosed loops along both sides of the yarn (Figure 19–7d).

The *loop, curl, or bouclé yarn* has closed loops at regular intervals along the yarn (Figure 19–7e). These yarns are used in woven or knit fabrics to create a looped pile that resembles caracul lambskin and is called *astrakhan cloth.* They are used to give textured effects to other coatings and dress fabrics. Mohair makes the best loop. Rayon and acetate are good also.

Slub effects are achieved in two ways (Figure 19–7f). True slubs are made by varying the tightness of the twist at regular intervals. Intermittently spun flake or slub effects are made by incorporating soft, thick, elongated tufts of fiber into the yarn at regular intervals. A core or binder is needed in the latter.

Metallic yarns have been used for thousands of years. The older yarns were made of pure metal (lamé) and were heavy, brittle, expensive, and had the disadvantage of tarnishing.

Two processes are now used to make metallic yarns. The *laminating process* seals a layer of aluminum between two layers of acetate or polyester (mylar) film, which is then cut into strips for yarn (Figure 19–8). The film may be colorless, so the aluminum foil shows through, or the film and/or the adhesive may be colored before the laminating process. The *metalizing process* vaporizes aluminum under high pressure and deposits it on the polyester film.

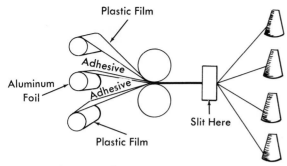

Fig. 19-8 Laminating metal yarn.

Fabric containing a large amount of metal can be embossed. Ironing is a problem when metallic film yarns are used with cotton, because a temperature high enough to take the wrinkles out of cotton will melt the plastic. The best way to remove wrinkles is to tip the iron on its side and draw the edge of the sole of the iron across the fabric.

Chenille yarns are novelty yarns used primarily in upholstery fabrics. They are discussed in Chapter 28, Pile Fabrics.

Blends

A *blend* is an intimate mixture of fibers of different composition, length, diameter, or color spun together into a yarn. A *mixture* is a fabric that has yarn of one fiber content in the warp and yarn of a different fiber content in the filling. A *combination* yarn has two unlike fiber strands twisted together as a ply. Blends, mixtures, and combinations give properties to fabrics that are different from those obtained with one fiber only. The following discussion relates to blends, although most of the facts are true for mixtures and combinations as well.

Fig. 20-1 Viyella, the oldest fiber blend.

Fiber Blends

Blends are not new, but in the past 20 years they have become very important. *Viyella*[1] *flannel* (Figure 20–1) is one of the oldest blends. It is a 55 per cent cotton and 45 per cent wool fabric that has been woven in England for many years. It feels like a lightweight wool but does not felt and is washable. Long Johns were made from a combination of wool and cotton. Covert, a fabric specially designed for hunting, was originally a blend of cotton and wool. Today it is possible to obtain all basic fabrics in fiber blends.

There is no perfect fiber. All fibers have good, fair, and poor characteristics. Blending enables the technician to combine fibers so that the good qualities are emphasized and the poor qualities minimized. Blending requires knowledge of both science and art.

[1] Registered trademark of William Hollins & Company, Ltd., London.

Blending is done for several reasons:

1. To obtain cross-dyed effects or create new color effects such as heather, when fibers with unlike dye affinity are blended together and then piece-dyed.

2. To improve spinning, weaving, and finishing efficiency for uniformity of product, as with self-blends of natural fibers to improve uniformity.

3. To obtain better texture, hand, or fabric appearance. A small amount of a specialty wool may be used to give a buttery or slick hand to wool fabrics, or a small amount of rayon may give luster and softness to a cotton fabric. Fibers with different shrinkage properties are blended to produce bulky and lofty fabrics or furlike fabrics with guard hairs.

4. For economic reasons. Expensive fibers can be extended by blending them with more plentiful fibers. This use is sometimes unfair to the consumer, especially when the expensive fiber is used in small amounts but advertised in large print; for example, CASHMERE and wool.

Fiber Properties

Properties	Cotton	Rayon	Wool	Acetate	Nylon	Polyester	Acrylic	Modacrylic	Olefin
Bulk and loft	−	−	+ + +		−	−	+ + +	+ + +	
Wrinkle recovery	−	−	+ + +	+ +	+ +	+ + +	+ +	+ +	+ +
Press (wet) retention	−	−	−	+	+ +	+ + +			
Absorbency	+ + +	+ + +	+ + +	+	−	−	−	−	−
Static resistance	+ + +	+ + +	+ +	+	+	−	+	+	+ +
Resistance to pilling	+ + +	+ + +	+	+ + +	+				+ +
Strength	+ +	+	+	+	+ + +	+ + +	+	+	+ + +
Abrasion resistance	+	−	+ +	−	+ + +	+ + +	+	+	+ + +
Stability	+ +	−	−	+ + +	+ + +	+ + +	+ + +	+ + +	+ + +
Resistance to heat	+ + +	+ + +	+ +	+ +	+	+	+ +	−	−

+ + +, excellent;   + +, good;   +, fair;   −, deficient.

5. To produce fabrics with better performance. This is perhaps the most important reason for blending. In end uses where durability is very important, nylon or polyester blended with cotton or wool provide strength and resistance to abrasion, while the wool or cotton look is maintained. A classic example is in durable press garments, where 100 per cent cotton fabrics are not as durable as polyester/cotton blends.

In the chart some fiber properties are rated. Notice that each fiber is deficient in one or more important property. Try different fiber combinations to see how a blend of two fibers might give different performance than either fiber used alone.

Blend Levels

For a specific end use, a blend of fibers that complement each other will give more satisfactory all-round performance than a 100 per cent fiber fabric.

M. J. Caplan[2] in his article "Fiber Translation in Blends" used the following example to show that a blend will yield a fabric with intermediate values. He took two fibers, A and B, each of which could be used to make a similar fabric, measured five performance properties of each of these 100 per cent fabrics, and then predicted the performance of a blended fabric 50/50 A and B by averaging the values of each fabric in the blend.

Notice that the predicted value for the blend is lower than the high value of one fabric, and is greater than the low value of the 100 per cent fabric. By blending them, a fabric with intermediate values is obtained. Unfortunately, the real values do not come out in the same proportion as the respective percentage in a blend.

Property	Known Values		Predicted Values 50/50 A and B
	A	B	
1	12	4	8
2	9	12	10.5
3	15	2	8.5
4	7	9	8
5	12	8	10

Much research has been done by the fiber manufacturers to determine just how much of

[2] M. J. Caplan, "Fiber Translation in Blends," *Modern Textiles Magazine,* **40**:39 (July 1959).

each fiber is necessary in the various fiber constructions. It is very difficult to generalize about percentages, because the percentage varies with the kind of fiber, the fiber construction, and the expected performance. For example, a very small amount of nylon (15 per cent) improves the strength of wool, but 60 per cent nylon is needed to improve the strength of rayon. For stability, 50 per cent Orlon blended with wool in a woven fabric is satisfactory, but 75 per cent Orlon is necessary in knitted fabrics.[3]

Fiber producers have controlled blend levels fairly well by setting standards for apparel or fabrics identified with their trademark. For example, the Du Pont Company recommends a blend level of 65 per cent Dacron polyester/35 per cent cotton in light- or medium-weight fabrics, whereas 50/50 Dacron/cotton is satisfactory for suiting weight fabrics. This assures satisfactory performance of the fabric and maintains a good fiber "image" for Dacron. The fabric manufacturer profits from large-scale promotion carried on by the fiber producer.

If fiber trademarks become less important and fabric or apparel producers are willing to use generic names only, they can set their own blend levels. These should be satisfactory to most consumers, however, because fabrics will have to meet minimum standards to compete in the retail market.

By using specially designed fiber variants it is possible to obtain desired performance and appearance in fabrics. For example, fading, shrinking, and softening in time are desirable characteristics to the people who buy Indigo denim Levi's and jeans. (These characteristics are undesirable in most apparel). Du Pont has developed a Dacron polyester variant that, when blended with cotton, will fade, shrink uniformly, and become softer. In Levi Strauss' fabric, a blend of ring-spun 75 per cent cotton/25 per cent Dacron X17 is used in the warp and open-end spun 50 per cent cotton/50 per cent Dacron X17 is used in the filling. The polyester fibers migrate to the center of the yarn and the cotton fibers migrate to the surface. The cotton absorbs the dye.

Blending Methods

Blending can be done at any stage prior to the spinning operation. Blending can be done during

[3] E. I. du Pont de Nemours & Company, *Bulletin X–21* (no date).

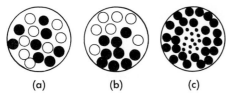

Fig. 20-2 Cross section of yarn showing the location of the fiber in the blend.

opening-picking, drawing, or roving. One of the disadvantages of direct spinning is that blending cannot be done before the sliver is formed.

The earlier the fibers are blended in processing, the better is the blend. Figure 20-2 shows a cross section of yarn (a), in which the fibers were blended in opening, and yarn (b), a yarn in which the fibers were blended at the roving stage.

Variations occur from spot to spot in the yarn and also from inside to outside. Long, fine fibers tend to move to the center of a yarn, whereas coarse, shorter fibers migrate to the periphery of yarn (c). The older methods of blending involve much hand labor.

Opening-Picking. In one method, several bales of fiber are laid around the picker and an armful from each bale is fed alternately into the machine. Another method is called *sandwich blending.* The desired amounts of each fiber are weighed out and a layer of each is spread over the preceding layer to build up a sandwich composed of many layers. Vertical sections are then taken through the sandwich and fed into the picker. *Feeder blending* is an automatic process in which each type of fiber is fed to a mixing apron from individual hoppers (Figure 20-3).

Blending on the Drawing Frame. When the physical properties of two fibers differ, it is not always practical to blend them before carding, so they are picked and carded separately and then blended in the drawing frame. The problem of mixed wastes is eliminated with this process.

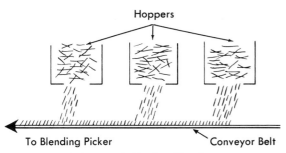

Fig. 20-3 Feeder blends.

Blending on the Roving and Spinning Frame. Both these operations combine fiber strands to reduce size and increase amount of twist until the final size and twist are achieved. Blending colors is the primary purpose at this stage (see page 129).

Blending is a complicated and expensive process, but it makes it possible to build in a combination of properties that are permanent. Not only are blends used for better functionability of fabrics but they are also used for beauty of appearance and hand.

Other Blends

Blended Yarns

A blended yarn is one in which unlike filaments are blended together. This is usually done to improve performance and appearance of fabrics. Arnel plus nylon has nylon for strength and durability and Arnel for absorbency (see page 114).

Composite Yarns

A *composite yarn* has two or more elements one of which is a continuous filament. These yarns look like spun yarns but are stronger. *Core spun* spandex is one type of composite yarn (see page 97).

Fasciated Yarns

Fasciated yarns consist of a bundle of filaments wrapped with staple fibers. They are produced by running the filaments and stretch-broken tow through a device that spins the staple around the bundle of filaments. Production of these yarns is

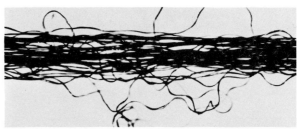

Fig. 20-4 Trevira polyester Dawn. Trevira® Registered Trademark Hoechst A.G. (*Courtesy Hoechst Fibers Industries.*)

very fast. Trevira "Dawn" is a bicomponent polyester yarn composed of high-strength and low-strength polymers. The yarn is crimped and twisted causing the low-strength component to break. The broken portion of the yarn is $\frac{2}{3}$ whereas the core is $\frac{1}{3}$ of the filament (Figure 20–4).

Polymer Staple Yarns

Polymer staple yarns are made by passing filament yarns through a polymer or copolymer resin and bonding staple fiber to it; or a polymer may be extruded and staple fibers superimposed on it.

Introduction to Fabric Construction

21

Fabric Construction Processes

A fabric is a planelike structure, which is pliable enough to be made into garments and household textiles, and for industrial uses in which some shaping or flexibility is needed. Fabrics are made from solutions, directly from fibers, from yarns, and from combinations of these elements often with a previously made fabric or cloth. Fabrics are usually available to the consumer by the yard or meter.

The fabric-forming process helps determine the appearance and texture, the performance during use and care, and the cost of a fabric. The process often determines the name of the fabric; for example, felt, lace, double knit, jersey. The cost of fabrics in relation to the construction process depends on the number of steps involved and the speed of the process; the fewer the steps and the faster the process the cheaper is the fabric.

The illustrated chart that follows provides brief descriptions of the fabric-construction processes and outstanding characteristics of typical fabrics.

Fabrics Made from Solutions

Films

- Solution is extruded through narrow slits into warm air or cast onto a revolving drum. Molding powders may be pressed between hot rolls.
- Waterproof. Low cost. Resistant to soil. Nonfibrous.
- May lack permeability.
- May lack strength unless supported by a fabric back.
- Low drapability.
- Finished to look like every other fabric as well as having its own characteristic appearance.

Foam

- Made by incorporating air into an elasticlike substance. Rubber and polyurethane are most commonly used (see Figure 21-9).
- Lofty, springy, bulky material. Combined with

Fig. 21-1 Films.

fashion fabric in apparel to give warmth without weight at low cost.

Fabric Made Directly from Fibers

Felt

- Wool fibers are carded (and combed), laid down in a thick batt, sprayed with water, and run through hot agitating plates, which cause the fibers to become entangled and matted together.
- No grain. Does not fray or ravel.

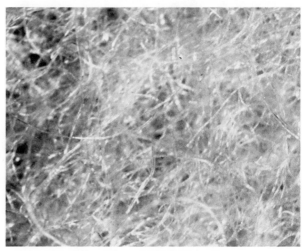

Fig. 21-2 Felt. (Magnified)

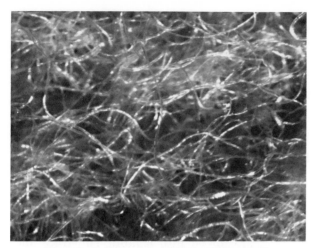

Fig. 21-3 Nonwoven fabric. (Magnified)

- Absorbs sound. Lacks pliability, strength, and stretch recovery.

Nonwoven

- Produced by bonding and/or interlocking textile fibers by mechanical, chemical, thermal, or solvent means, or combinations of these processes.
- Cheaper than woven or knitted fabrics. Widely used for disposable or durable items. May have grain but usually do not.

Fabrics Made from Yarns
Braid

- Yarns are interlaced diagonally and lengthwise. Fabrics are narrow. Used primarily for trim. Made circular for shoelaces.

Fig. 21-4 Braid.

- Stretchy.
- Easy shaping.

Knitting

- One or more yarns are formed into a series of interlocking loops.

Fig. 21-5 Knit.

- Faster technique than weaving. Requires more yarn per unit of cover.
- Stretchy, elastic fabrics.
- Porous. Resilient.

Lace

- Yarns are knotted, interlaced, interlooped, or twisted to form open-work fabrics—usually with some figures.

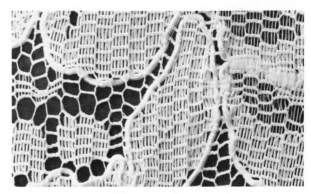

Fig. 21-6 Lace.

- Decorative edgings or entire fabric.
- Open porous structure.
- Made by hand or machine.

Weaving

- Two or more sets of yarns are interlaced at right angles to each other.
- Most widely used construction technique.
- Many different interlacing patterns give interest to fabric.

Fig. 21-7 Plain weave fabric.

- Fabrics can be raveled from adjacent sides.
- Fabrics have grain.
- Rigid fabrics—do not stretch much in warp or filling.

Composite Fabrics (Nonseparable)

Coated Fabric

- Application of semiliquid material to a fabric substrate. Rubber, polyvinyl chloride, and polyurethane are usual coating materials.

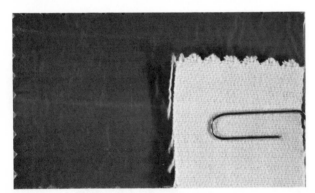

Fig. 21-8 Coated fabric.

- Stronger and more stable than unsupported films.
- Widely used for upholstery, handbags, and leatherlike apparel.

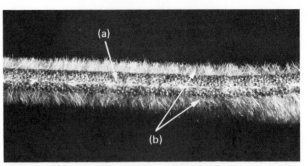

Fig. 21-9 Flocked fabric. (a) Foam; (b) Fiber.

Flocked Fabric

- Fibers are forced into a fabric substrate and held by an adhesive or electronic bonding to make a pile figure or overall pile on fabric.
- Widely used pile figures on dress fabrics, Vellux blankets, and automotive fabrics.

Foam and Fiber Fabric

- Fibers and polyurethane solution are mixed together, cast on a drum, or forced through a slit to make fabric. Napped on both sides. Fibers used are polyester, nylon, and rayon.

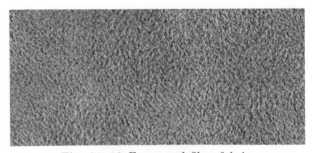

Fig. 21-10 Foam and fiber fabric.

- Looks and feels like suede.
- Machine washable and dry cleanable.
- Uniform in thickness and quality and sold by the yard or meter.

Tufting

- Yarns carried by needles are forced through a fabric substrate and formed into cut or uncut loops.
- Cheaper than woven or knitted pile fabrics.
- Widely used in rugs and carpets, upholstery, coat liners, and bedspreads.

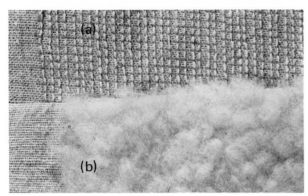

Fig. 21-11 Tufted fabric. (a) Reverse side; (b) Right side.

Multicomponent Fabrics

Bonded or Laminated

- Two or more fabrics are made to adhere together by an adhesive or flame-foam process.

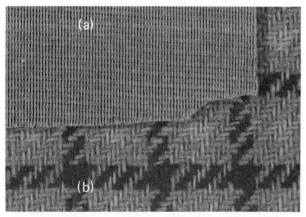

Fig. 21-12 Bonded fabric. (a) Reverse side—Tricot; (b) Right side—wool plaid.

- Lower cost than double woven or double knit.
- Warmth without weight.
- Makes possible the use of lightweight fabrics for outerwear.
- Fabrics have body.
- Do not hold sharp creases.
- May be laminated off grain, and may come apart (delaminate).

Quilted

- One or two fabrics and wadding, batting, or foam are stitched together by machine or hand or welded by sonic vibrations.

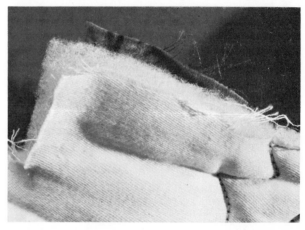

Fig. 21-13 Quilted fabric; reverse side in picture.

- Bulky, warm, and decorative. Stitches may break.
- Widely used in ski jackets, robes, comforters, quilts, and upholstery.

Weaving and the Loom

22

Woven fabrics are made with two or more sets of yarns interlaced at right angles to each other. The yarns running in the lengthwise direction are called *warp* yarns and the yarns running crosswise are called *filling* or *weft*. Warp yarns are also called *ends* and filling yarns are also called *picks*. The right-angle position of the yarns gives the cloth more firmness and rigidity than yarn arrangements in knits, braids, or laces. Because of this structure, yarns can be raveled from adjacent sides. Woven fabrics vary in interlacing pattern, count (number of threads per square inch), and balance (ratio of warp to filling yarns).

Woven fabrics are widely used and weaving is one of the oldest methods of making cloth. Names were given to fabrics based on the end use, the town in which the fabric was woven, or for the person originating or noted for that fabric. For example: hopsacking (cloth used in bags for collecting hops), tobacco cloth (used to give shade to tobacco plants), cheese cloth (to wrap cheeses), ticking (cloth used to cover mattresses which were called "ticks") are named for their original end use; Bedford cord (New Bedford, Mass.); calico (Calcutta, India); chambray (Cambrai, France); shantung (Shantung, China) were named for the town in which they were first woven; batiste (Jean Baptiste, a linen weaver) and Jacquard (Joseph Jacquard) are named for people. Fabrics that look like the woven basic fabric but are constructed differently often carry the name of the woven fabric. Denim, for example, is a yarn-dyed woven twill fabric, but denim-looking fabrics are also made by knitting.

The Loom

Weaving is done on a machine called a *loom*. All the weaves that are known today have been made by the primitive weaver. The loom has changed in many ways, but the basic principles and operations remain the same. Warp threads are held between two beams, and filling threads are inserted and pushed back to make the cloth.

In primitive looms the warp threads were kept upright or horizontal (Figure 22–1a and b). In back-strap looms, which are still used for hand weaving in many countries, the warp threads are kept taut by attaching one beam to a tree or post and the other beam to a strap that fits around the weaver's hips as the weaver squats or sits to weave (Figure 22–1c). Filling threads were inserted over and under the warp by the fingers and later by a shuttle batted through raised warp yarns. To separate the warp yarns and make hand weaving faster, alternate warp yarns were attached to wooden bars that could be raised bringing half of the warp yarns up. A comb, very much like a hair comb, was used to beat up the yarns. The wooden bar mechanism developed into headles and harnesses that were attached to foot pedals so that the weaver could separate the warp yarns with his feet and leave the hands free for inserting the filling yarns.

The Industrial Revolution and mass production caused changes in looms, all of which were aimed at achieving high-speed production. The basic modern loom consists of two beams, a warp beam and a cloth beam, holding the warp yarns between them (Figure 22–2). The warp is raised and lowered by a harness-headle arrangement. A *harness* is a frame to hold the headles. A *headle* (heddle) is a wire with a hole in its center through which the yarn goes. There are as many headles as there are warp yarns in the cloth and the headles are held in two or more harnesses. As can be seen in the diagram of a two-harness loom as one harness is raised, the yarns form a *shed* through which the filling can be inserted. A shuttle carries the filling yarn through the shed. A *reed* or *batten* beats the filling yarn back into the cloth to make the weave firm. A reed is a set of wires in a frame, and the spaces between the wires are called *dents*.

Weaving consists of the following steps:

1. *Shedding:* the raising of one or more harnesses to separate the warp yarns and form a shed.

2. *Picking:* passing the shuttle through the shed to insert the filling.

3. *Beating up:* the reed pushing the filling yarn back into place in the cloth.

4. *Take-up:* the finished cloth is wound on the cloth beam.

Additional harnesses are used to make more intricate designs. The number of harnesses that a loom can operate efficiently is limited. When the repeat of the woven pattern requires more than six harnesses, an attachment is added to the loom to control the raising and lowering of the warp yarns.

Fig. 22-1 Primitive Looms. (*Left*) Upright rug loom. (*Center*) Horizontal loom. (*Right*) Back-strap loom. (*Courtesy of Prodesco, Inc.*)

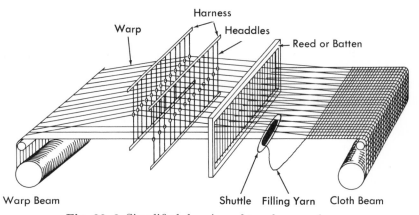

Fig. 22-2 Simplified drawing of two-harness loom.

Preparation of Yarns for Weaving

Winding. The spun yarn as it comes from the spinning frame is a *single* yarn that must be rewound on spools. As it is rewound, the spun yarn can be given more twist or combined with other singles to make ply yarn.

Creeling. Spools of yarn are placed on a large creel (Figure 22–3) and wound onto a warp beam. The yarn from the warp beam will be run through a "slash" bath, dried, and rewound on the warp beam before it is put on the loom for weaving. The "slash" solution is a sizing to protect the yarns from mechanical action in weaving. After weaving, the cloth is removed from the cloth beam, washed to remove the slashing, finished to specification, and wound on bolts or tubes for sale to cutters or consumers.

Loom Developments

Loom developments over the years have centered on (1) devices to separate the warp to make intricate weave designs, (2) the use of computers and electronic monitoring systems, and (3) speedier methods of inserting the filling.

Warp Shedding. Warp-shedding devices have included the dobby, doup, lappet, and leno attachments and the Jacquard loom. These have become so sophisticated that pictures can be woven in cloth (see Chapter 29).

Computer and electronic devices play an important part in developing design tables for setting up "maximum weavability" properties, such as tightness and compactness in wind-repellent fabrics or tickings. The computer plays a part in textile designing. Designs can be programmed by

Fig. 22-3 Creeling. Spools of yarns are placed on a large creel and wound onto a warp beam.

means of punched tapes that control the operation of individual warp yarns.

Shuttleless Looms. Shuttleless looms were developed as a way to replace the shuttle. In the simple loom a "flying" shuttle is "batted" back and forth through the warp shed by picker sticks at both sides of the machine. The speed with which the shuttle is sent back and forth is limited—usually about 200 picks per minute. Manufacturers have long sought a way to replace the shuttle and increase the speed of weaving.

Three different types of shuttleless looms have been developed—water jet, air jet, and the rapier loom. They give higher weaving speeds and reduced noise levels—a factor of great importance to the worker. In all three types of looms the filling yarns are measured and cut, thus leaving a fringe along the side. This fringe may be fused to make a selvage, if the yarns are thermoplastic, or the ends may be turned back into the cloth. These selvages are not always as usable as conventional selvages because of a tendancy toward puckering that requires slitting.

Water-Jet Loom. The water-jet loom uses a high-pressure jet of water to carry the filling yarn across the warp (Figure 22–4). It works on the

principle of continuous feed and minimum tension of the filling yarns, so it can weave fabrics without barré or streaks. The filling yarn comes from a stationary package at the side of the loom, goes to a measuring drum that controls the length of each filling, and continues through a guide to the water nozzle, where a jet of water

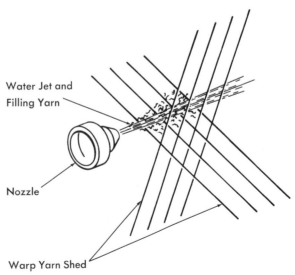

Water Jet and
Filling Yarn

Nozzle

Warp Yarn Shed

Fig. 22-4 Water jet carries filling through warp shed.

carries it across through the warp shed. After the filling is beaten back, it is cut off. If the fibers are thermoplastic, a hot wire is used to cut the yarn, fusing the ends so they serve as a selvage.

The water is removed from the loom by a suction device. Water from the jet will dissolve regular warp sizings so one of the problems has been that of developing water-resistant sizings that can be removed easily in cloth finishing processes. The fabric is wet when it comes from the loom and must be dried—an added expense. The water-resistant sizings may reduce the wettability of the yarns and help solve this problem. The water-jet loom has proved ideal for fashion fabrics using both smooth and textured filaments and for men's slacks and shirtings. It will use practically every natural or synthetic fiber in several different deniers. The loom is more compact, less noisy, and takes up less room than the conventional loom. It can operate at 400 to 600 picks per minute—two or three times faster than the conventional loom. Maintenance is relatively easy.

Air-Jet Loom. The air-jet loom or pneumatic method was developed in Sweden by a textile engineer who got the idea while sailing. He noticed the short regular puffs that came from the exhaust of a diesel motor. His first loom used a bicycle pump to furnish the compressed air. The filling is premeasured and guided through a nozzle, where a blast of air sends it across. The loom can operate at 320 picks per minute and is suitable for spun yarns. There are limitations in fabric width because of diminution of the jet of air as it passes across the loom.

Rapier-type Loom. The rapier-type loom weaves (primarily) spun yarns at 300 picks per minute. It has two metal arms, about the size of a small penknife, called carriers or "dummy shuttles," one on the right side and the other on the left side of the loom. A measuring mechanism on the right side of the loom measures and cuts the correct length of filling yarn to be drawn into the shed by the carriers. The two carriers enter the warp shed at the same time and meet in

the center. The left-side carrier takes the yarn from the right-side carrier and pulls it across to the left side of the loom. After each insertion the filling threads are cut near the edge and protruding ends tucked back into the cloth to reinforce the edge. Figure 22-5 shows the carrier arms. This loom has found wide acceptance for use with basic cotton and woolen/worsted fabrics.

Multished Loom. Several weft carriers insert the precut weft that are stored inside them in a continuous process instead of the intermittent process of single-shed weaving. Beating up and shedding arrangements are different and the process is said to put less stress on warp and filling yarns and to decrease the noise level and energy consumption. In this continuous weaving process the picks per minute (ppm) is doubled.

Circular Loom. Because most looms are flat machines and weave flat fabrics, few people realize that circular looms have been developed that make tubular fabric. The circular loom in Figure 22-6 weaves sacks of split-film polypropylene. Pillowcases are also tubular woven.

New Weave Systems

Triaxial Loom. A new weaving system, Do-weave, has been developed that weaves three sets of yarns at 60-degree angles to each other (Figure 22-7). The resulting fabric is *triaxial*. The outstanding property of these fabrics is their stability in all directions—horizontally, vertically, and on the bias. Biaxial woven fabrics, in which the sets of yarns are woven at right angles to each other, do not have stability on the bias.

In triaxial weaving all of the yarns are usually alike in size and twist. Two thirds of the yarns are warp and one third are filling. Fabrics can be produced more quickly than other weaves because there are fewer picks per inch and speed of weaving is based on the number of picks per minute.

The weaving mechanism used in triaxial weav-

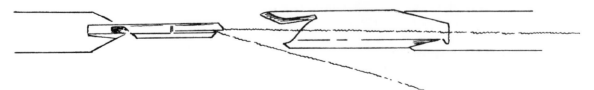

Fig. 22-5 Carrier arms of a rapier-type shuttleless loom.

Fig. 22-6 Circular loom used to weave bagging. (*Courtesy of Textile Industries.*)

ing differs from that of a regular loom in the following ways:

1. Warp yarns are wound on eight small warp beams (Figure 22–8).

2. Headles, carrying the warp yarns, are slid into two guide bars in a horizontal position. The headles have an eye at one end. The guide bars are positioned opposite each other.

3. Shedding is achieved as the headles move forward (Figure 22–9).

4. Filling yarns are inserted by rapiers.

Basic Basket Weave

Fig. 22-7 Triaxial Weave Pattern. (*Courtesy of Modern Textiles Magazine.*)

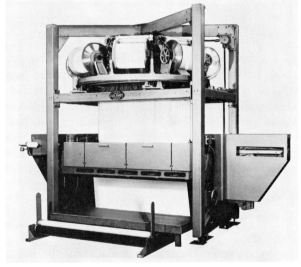

Fig. 22-8 Triaxial Weaving Machine. (*Courtesy of Modern Textiles Magazine.*)

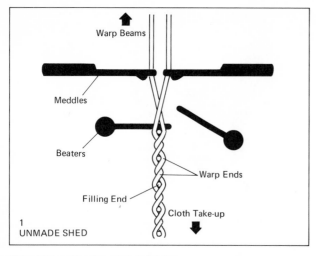

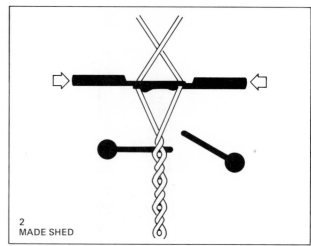

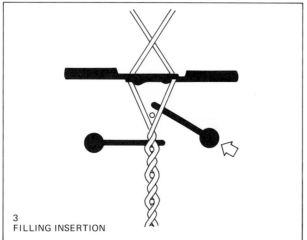

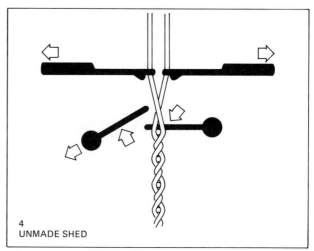

Shed Formation

Fig. 22–9 Shed formation in Triaxial weaving. (*Courtesy of Modern Textiles Magazine.*)

5. Two reeds work from opposite sides to beat up the filling.

6. To obtain the 60° angles of the warp yarns, the guide bars move horizontally one to the right and one to the left alternately after pick insertion. One headle is transferred from the end of the one guide bar to the end of the opposite guide bar.

More complicated mechanisms are used for other weave patterns. Some advantages are

1. Strength and stiffness can be controlled in all directions from rigid to stretchiness close to that of knits.

2. Open-weave constructions are stable.

3. Slippage is no problem—yarns are locked in place.

The end uses of triaxial fabrics include balloons, air structures, sailcloth, diaphragms, truck covers, and outerwear apparel. Some projected end uses of this fabric are upholstery, filter cloth, shoe uppers, canvas shoes, foundation garments, slacks, swimsuits, and athletic uniforms.

Characteristics of Woven Fabrics

All yarns in woven fabrics interlace at right angles to one another (Figure 22–10). An *interlacing* is the point at which a yarn changes its position from the surface of the cloth to the underside and

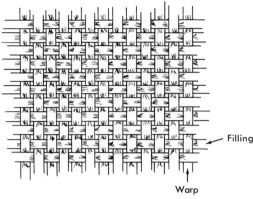

Fig. 22-10 Yarn arrangement in weaving.

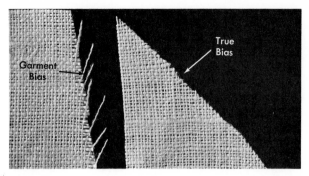

Fig. 22-11 Cut edges show two grain positions of cloth.

vice versa. When a yarn crosses over more than one yarn at a time, *floats* are formed and the fabric has fewer interlacings.

Yarns

Warp and filling yarns have different characteristics, and the cloth performs differently in the warp and filling directions. The warp must resist the high tensions of the loom and the abrasion of the shuttle as it flies back and forth, so the warp yarns are stronger, of better quality, and have higher twist. Filling yarns are more apt to be the decorative or special-function yarns, such as high-twist crepe yarns or low-twist napping yarns.

Following are ways to recognize warp and filling:

1. The selvage always runs in the lengthwise (warp) direction of all fabrics.

2. Most fabrics stretch less in the warp direction.

3. The warp yarns lie straighter in the fabric because of loom tension. They show less crimp.

4. Decorative or special-function yarns are usually the filling.

5. Specific characteristics may indicate the warp and filling directions. For example; poplin always has a filling rib, satin always has warp floats, and flat crepe has high-twist yarns in the filling and low-twist yarns in the warp.

Grain

Grain is a term used to indicate the warp and filling positions in a woven fabric. Figure 22–11

shows why a garment bias edge will ravel more than any of the other grain positions.

The grain positions are as follows:

• Lengthwise grain is a position along any warp yarn.

• Crosswise grain is a position along any filling yarn.

• True bias (Figure 22–11) is the diagonal of a square.

• Garment bias is any position on the cloth between true bias and either lengthwise or crosswise grain (Figure 22–11).

Off-Grain. "Off-grain" fabrics have been a troublesome problem for the industry and for the consumer. At the factory, off-grain causes reruns and lower fabric quality. For the consumer it means that garments will not drape properly or hang evenly and that printed designs will not be straight. If the fabric has a durable press finish or is made of heat-sensitive fibers, the home sewer will not be able to straighten the fabric, so it is on-grain. Wool fabrics can be straightened, but only with much extra work. The fabric must be dampened and allowed to stand until it relaxes and then pressed carefully so that the yarns are at right angles. Figure 22–12 shows a plaid design that has been printed about 5 inches off grain— the printed lines do not follow the threads or a torn edge. Bed sheets used to be torn and then hemmed so the hems were always straight with the grain. Now they are cut and the fabric must be very straight or the sheets will be off-grain.

There are two kinds of off-grain. *Skew* cloth results when one side of the fabric travels ahead of the other. The fabric in Figure 22–12 is "skewed." *Bow* occurs when the center of the fabric lags behind but the two sides keep even as

Fig. 22-12 "Off-grain" fabric.

Fig. 22-14 Thread counter. (*Courtesy of the Alfred Suter Company.*)

the fabric travels through the tenter frame. The consumer should always examine a fabric or garment to see if the cloth is off-grain.

Cloth Straighteners. It is now possible for the manufacturer to control the straightness of the fabric to within 0.25 inch. This is done by cloth straighteners—sensitive detectors attached to the tenter frame that gently ride on the cloth and "feel" the bowed or skewed threads (Figure 22-13).

Thread Count

Thread or cloth count is the number of warp and filling per square inch of gray goods (fabric as it comes from the loom). This may be changed by shrinkage during dyeing and finishing. Thread count is written with the warp number first, for example 80 × 76; or it may be written as the total of the two, as 156. (Thread count should not be

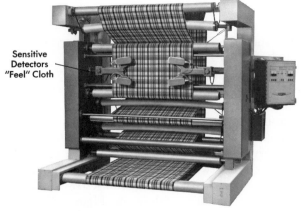

Sensitive
Detectors
"Feel" Cloth

Fig. 22-13 Cloth straightener. (*Courtesy of Coltron Industries, Inc.*)

confused with yarn count or number, which is a measure of yarn size. See the discussion on page 136.)

Thread count is an indication of the quality of the fabric—the higher the count, the better is the quality for any one fabric—and can be used in judging raveling, shrinkage, and durability. Higher count also means less potential shrinkage and less raveling of seam edges. Catalogs frequently give the thread count since the customer must judge the quality from printed information rather than from the fabric itself.

A standard method of making a thread count may be found in the American Standards for Testing Materials. The count is made with a thread-counting instrument (Figure 22-14). It is possible to use a "hand" method by which the area is measured by a ruler and counted by sight or yarns raveled off and counted.

Percale fabrics have, in the past, had a standard thread count of 80 × 80 and were called 80-square fabrics. In February, 1960, *Women's Wear Daily* announced that, as a result of cost factors, a 78 × 78 fabric would be the basic print cloth used. (Print cloth is the percale fabric as it comes from the loom before any finishing has been done.)

Balance

Balance is the *ratio* of the warp yarns to filling yarns in a fabric. A well-balanced fabric has approximately one warp yarn for every filling yarn, or a ratio of 1:1. Examples of typical unbalanced fabrics are cotton broadcloth, with a thread count of 144 × 76 and a ratio of about 2:1, and nylon satin, with a thread count of 210 × 80 and a ratio of about 3 : 1.

Balance is helpful in recognizing and naming fabrics and in distinguishing the warp direction of a fabric. Balance is *not always* related to quality. Balance plus thread count is helpful in predicting slippage. If the count is low, there seems to be more slippage in unbalanced fabrics than there is in balanced fabrics.

Selvages

A *selvage* is the self-edge of a fabric formed by the filling yarn when it turns to go back across the fabric. The conventional loom makes the same kind of selvage on both sides of the fabric but the new shuttleless looms have different selvages because the filling yarn is cut and the selvage looks like a fringe. In some fabrics stronger yarns, or a basket-weave arrangement, are used.

Plain selvages are similar to the rest of the fabric. They do not shrink and can be used for seam edges in garment construction. *Tape selvages* are made of larger and/or ply yarns to give strength. They are wider than the plain selvage and may be of basket weave for flatness. An example is the selvage on sheets. *Split selvages* are used when narrow items such as towels are made by weaving two or more side by side and cutting them apart after weaving. The cut edges are finished by a machine chain stitch or a hem. *Fused selvages* are the heat-sealed edges of ribbon or tricot yard goods made from wide fabric and cut into narrower widths.

Fabric Width

The loom determines the width of the fabric. Handwoven fabrics are usually 27 to 36 inches wide. Before the 1950s, machine-woven cottons were traditionally 36 inches wide. However, wider fabrics are more economical to weave and the garment cutter can lay out patterns to better advantage. The new looms weave cotton 45 or more inches wide. Wool fabrics are 54 to 60 inches wide and silk-type fabrics are 40 to 45 inches wide. Double knits are usually about 60 inches wide.

Properties

Fabric properties resulting from weaving variables are summarized in the following chart.

The type of weave or interlacing pattern influences fabric properties as well as fabric appearance. The chart, Basic Weaves, is an introduction to the various weaves and also a summary which may be used as a reference. In the text, the three basic weaves are discussed in one chapter. The other weaves are discussed in fabric chapters which include weaves as well as other construction processes.

Properties of Woven Fabrics

Fabric Type	Properties
High-thread count	Firmness, strength, cover, body, compactness, stability, wind repellency, water repellency, fire retardancy, reduced raveling of seams.
Low-thread count	Flexibility, permeability, pliability, better drape, higher shrinkage potential, more seam raveling.
Balanced	Less seam slippage, warp and filling wear evenly resulting in holes.
Unbalanced (usually more warp)	Seam slippage in low count, warp yarns wear out first leaving strings (common in upholstery fabrics). In plain weave crosswise ribs give interesting surface.
Floats	Luster, smoothness, flexibility, resiliency, tendency to ravel and snag, seam slippage in low count.

Name	Interlacing Pattern	General Characteristics	Typical Fabrics	Page Reference
Plain $\frac{1}{1}$	Each warp interlaces with each filling.	Most interlacings per square inch. Balanced or unbalanced. Wrinkles most. Ravels most. Less absorbent.	Batiste Voile Percale Gingham Broadcloth Crash Cretonne	166–168
Basket $\frac{2}{1}$ $\frac{2}{2}$ $\frac{4}{4}$	Two or more yarns in either warp or filling or both woven as one in a plain weave	Looks balanced. Fewer interlacings than plain weave. Flat looking. Wrinkles less. Ravels more.	Oxford Monk's cloth	169
Twill $\frac{2}{1}$ $\frac{2}{2}$ $\frac{3}{1}$	Warp and filling yarns float over two or more yarns from the opposite direction in a regular progression to the right or left.	Diagonal lines. Fewer interlacings than plain weave. Wrinkles less. Ravels more. More pliable than plain weave. Can have higher count.	Serge Surah Denim Gabardine Herringbone	171–172
Satin $\frac{4}{1}$ $\frac{1}{4}$	Warp and filling yarns float over four or more yarns from the opposite direction in a progression of two to the right or left.	Flat surface. Most are lustrous. Can have high count. Fewer interlacings. Long floats—subject to slippage and snagging.	Satin Sateen	173–174
Momie or Crepe	An irregular interlacing of yarns. Floats of unequal lengths in no discernable pattern.	Rough-looking surface. Crepe looking	Granite cloth Moss crepe Sand crepe	178
Dobby	Special loom attachment allows up to 32 different interlacings.	Small figures. Cord-type fabrics.	Shirting madras Huck toweling Waffle cloth Pique	227
Jacquard	Each warp yarn controlled individually. An infinite number of interlacings is possible.	Large figures	Damask Brocade Tapestry	226
Pile	Extra warp or filling yarns are woven in to give a cut or an uncut three-dimensional fabric.	Plush or looped surface. Warm. Wrinkles less. Pile may flatten.	Velvet Velveteen Corduroy Furlike fabrics Wilton rugs Terry cloth	214–218
Slack-tension	A type of pile weave. Some warp yarns can be released from tension to form raised areas in the cloth or a pile surface.	Crinkle stripes or pile surface. Absorbent. Nonwrinkling.	Seersucker Terry cloth Friezé	179 218 218

Basic Weaves (*Cont.*)

Name	Interlacing Pattern	General Characteristics	Typical Fabrics	Page Reference
Leno	A doup attachment on the loom causes one of two warp yarns to be carried over the other on alternate passings of the filling yarns.	Meshlike fabric. Lower thread count fabrics that are resistant to slippage	Marquisette Curtain fabrics	244
Swivel	An attachment to the loom. Small shuttles carrying extra filling yarns weave in small dots.	Dots on both sides of fabric as filling floats	Dotted swiss	229

The Three Basic Weaves

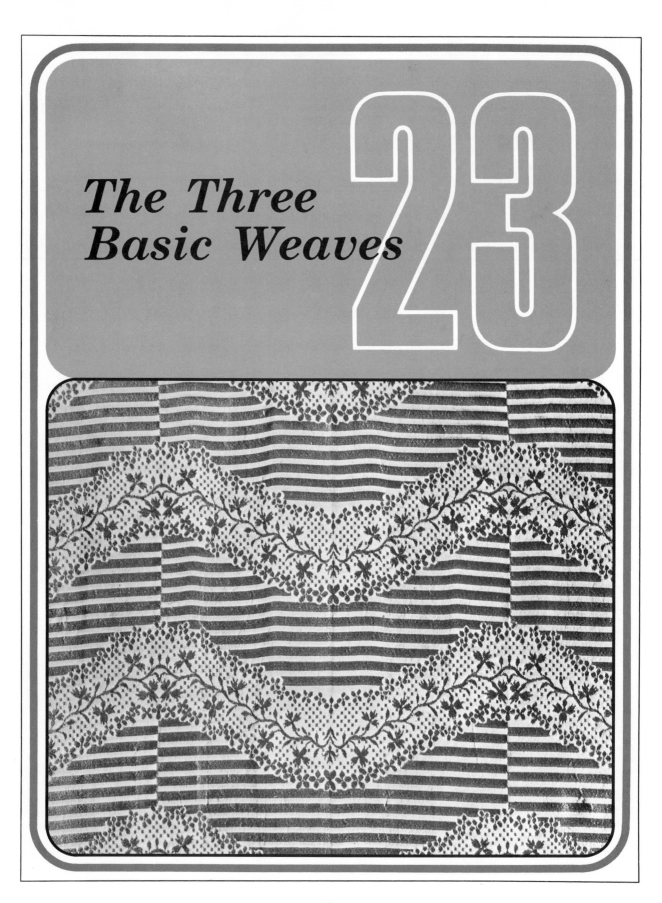

The three basic weaves—plain, twill, and satin—can be made on the simple loom without the use of any attachment.

Plain Weave

Plain weave is the simplest of the three basic weaves that can be made on a simple loom. It is formed by yarns at right angles passing alternately over and under each other. Each warp yarn interlaces with each filling yarn to form the maximum number of interlacings (Figure 23-1). Plain weave requires only a two-harness loom and is the least expensive weave to produce. It is described as a $\frac{1}{1}$ weave: one harness up and one harness down when the weaving shed is formed.

Plain weave fabrics have no right or wrong side unless they are printed or given a surface finish. Their plain, uninteresting surface serves as a good background for printed designs, for embossing, and for puckered and glazed finishes. Because there are many interlacings per square inch, plain

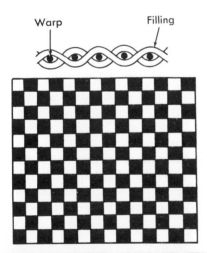

Warp   Filling

Fig. 23-1 Three ways to show the yarn-interlacing pattern of plain weave: (*top*) cross section, (*center*) checkerboard, (*bottom*) photograph.

weave fabrics tend to wrinkle more, ravel less, and be less absorbent than other weaves. Interesting effects can be achieved by the use of different fiber contents, novelty or textured yarns, yarns of different sizes, high- or low-twist yarns, filament or staple yarns, and different finishes.

The simplest form of plain weave is one in which warp and filling yarns are the same size and the same distance apart so they show *equally* on the surface—balanced plain weave. Other forms have warp yarns so numerous as to *cover the filling* that are obvious only in the form of ridges called *ribs*—unbalanced plain weave, and variations that have two or more yarns interlaced as *one*—basket weave.

- Balanced plain weave
- Unbalanced plain weave
- Variations: basket weave

Balanced Plain Weave

Plain-weave balanced fabrics have a wider range of end uses than fabrics of any other weave and are, therefore, the largest group of woven fabrics. They can be made in any weight, from very sheer to very heavy.

Sheer Fabrics.[1] Sheer fabrics are very thin, lightweight, transparent, or semitransparent. *High-count sheers* are characterized by transparency as a result of the fineness of yarns. Lawn, organdy, and batiste are finished from the same gray goods (lawn gray goods). They differ from one another in the *way* they are finished. The better qualities are made of combed cotton or cotton/polyester yarns.

Sheer fabrics are used for glass curtains (which give privacy but let in light); for summer-weight shirts, blouses, and dresses; and for baby dresses. Short wash cycles and low ironing temperatures are required. They dry faster, so they may need to be redampened during ironing. Small hems and enclosed seams are used to enhance the daintiness of the fabric and to prevent pulling out during use and care.

---

[1] *Low-count sheers*—cheesecloth and crinoline—are characterized by open spaces between the yarns. They are made of carded yarns of size 28s and 30s in the warp and 39s and 42s in the filling. Thread count ranges from 10 × 12 to 48 × 44. They are neither strong nor durable, are seldom printed, and differ in the way they are finished. See the Glossary.

High-Count Sheers

Fabric	Typical Thread Count	Yarn Size, Number, or Count	
		Warp	Filling
Lawn	88 × 80	70s*	100s*
Organdy	Similar to lawn	Similar to lawn	
Batiste	Similar to lawn	Similar to lawn	

*The "s" after the number means that the yarn is a single thread. If a ply yarn is used in the fabric, it is indicated by writing the number as 38/2 or 44/2, etc.

Organdy is the sheerest cotton cloth made. Its sheerness and crispness are the result of an acid finish (see page 267). Because of its stiffness, it wrinkles badly. *Lawn* is a crisp fabric that is often printed. *Batiste* is the softest of the three. It is highly mercerized and often used in whites or pastels. Batiste fabrics are also made of wool, polyester, and polyester/cotton fiber. *Tissue ginghams and chambray* are similar in weight to lawn but are yarn-dyed.

Filament yarn sheers are often designated by the fiber content; for example, polyester sheer or nylon sheer, or they may be called by the name of the cotton fabric they resemble. *Ninon* is a filament sheer that is widely used for curtains. *Georgette* and *chiffon* are made with crepe yarns, the latter being smoother and more lustrous.

Voile is a sheer made with special high-twist or twist-on-twist yarns (see page 139). Voile was originally a cotton or wool fabric, but it is now found on the market in other fiber contents.

Medium-Weight Fabrics. This is the largest group of woven fabrics, because medium-weight fabrics have many more uses than either lightweight or heavyweight fabrics. These fabrics have medium-sized yarns, a medium thread count and carded or combed yarns, and they may be finished in different ways or woven from dyed yarns.

The carded yarn fabrics in this group are converted from a gray-goods cloth called *print cloth.* Most print cloth is made into *percale,* a smooth, slightly crisp, printed or plain-colored fabric. It is called *calico* if it has a small quaint printed design, *chintz* if it has a printed design, and *glazed chintz* if it is given a glazed resin finish. Glazed chintz is made in solid colors as well as prints. The name chintz comes from the Hindu word meaning "spotted." These fabrics are often made with blends of cotton and polyester or high wet modulus rayon. They are used for shirts, dresses, blouses, pajamas, and aprons.

Any plain woven, balanced fabric ranging in weight from lawn to heavy bed sheeting may be called *muslin.* This is also a specific name for medium-weight fabric that is unbleached or white.

Ginghams are yarn-dyed fabrics with checks, and plaids, or they may appear to be solid in color. Chambrays appear to be solid color but have white filling and colored warp yarns, or they may have darker yarns in the filling (iridescent chambray), or they may have stripes. Some chambray is unbalanced with high warp count, which produces a filling rib similar to that of broadcloth and poplin.

Ginghams and chambray are made of cotton or cotton blends and are usually given a durable-press treatment. When they are made of fiber other than cotton, the fiber content is included in the name, for example, silk gingham. In filament rayon these fabrics are given a crisp finish and called *taffetas.* In wool, similar fabrics are called wool checks, plaids, and shepherd's checks.

The construction of gingham and chambray is a more costly process than the making of converted goods because the loom must be re-threaded for each new design, and threading a loom for yarn-dyed fabrics requires more skill than threading it with undyed yarns. It is necessary also for the manufacturer to carry a larger inventory, which requires more storage space.

Stripes, plaids, and checks present problems that are not present in solid colored fabrics. Crosswise lines must be parallel to the floor in draperies, must be lined up with the edges of furniture, and must be properly balanced in apparel. Ginghams may have an up and down, a

Converted (Finished) Fabrics*

Fabrics	Range in Thread Count	Yarn Size	
		Warp	Filling
Percale, carded (muslin, plissé. calico, chintz, etc.)	80 × 80 to 44 × 48	30s	42s
Combed cottons	96 × 80	40s	50s

*Other fabrics, such as pigment taffeta, challis, and dress linen, are given in the Glossary.

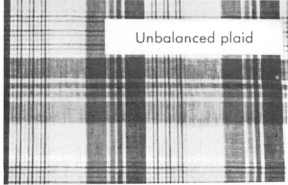

Fig. 23-2 Gingham: yarn-dyed fabric.

right and left, or both. These are called *unbalanced plaids*. Compare the unbalanced plaid in the picture in Figure 23–2 with the balanced plaid. More time is needed to cut out a garment in plaid than in plain material, and more attention must be given to the choice of design. Plaids in inexpensive garments seldom match except at the center front and back seams, places where failure to match is more noticeable.

Imitations of gingham are made with printed designs. There is, however, a right and a wrong side to the print, whereas true gingham is the

Yarn-Dyed Fabrics

Fabrics	Range in Thread Count	Yarn Size	
		Warp	Filling
Gingham, cotton	64 × 76	Same as percale	
Carded	to		
	48 × 44		
Combed	88 × 84		
	to		
	84 × 76		
Chambray and gingham madras are similar to gingham.			

same on both sides. Lengthwise printed stripes are usually on-grain, but the crosswise stripes are frequently off-grain (see page 160).

Suiting-Weight Fabrics. Suiting-weight or bottom weight fabrics are heavy enough to tailor well. Filling yarns are usually larger than the warp yarns because of slightly lower twist. Because of their weight, they are more durable and more resistant to wrinkling than sheer or medium-weight fabrics, but they tend to ravel more because of their low thread count.

Cotton suiting is converted from a gray goods called *coarse narrow sheeting.* Kettlecloth is a manufacturer's trade name. Cotton suiting is plain in color or printed. *Cretonne* is similar to cotton suiting except that it has large floral designs.

Crash is made with yarns that have thick-and-thin areas that give it an uneven nubby look. It shows wrinkles less than a plain surface does.

Butcher rayon is a crashlike fabric of 100 per cent rayon or rayon/acetate blends. In heavier weights it looks like linen suiting.

Tweed is made of any fiber or mixture of fibers and is always characterized by nubs of different colors. The name comes from the Tweed River in Scotland. Harris tweed is handwoven in the Outer Hebrides Islands, and Donegal tweed is handwoven in Donegal County, Ireland.

Suiting-Weight Fabrics*

Fabric	Typical Thread Count	Typical Yarn Size
Cotton suiting	48 × 48 to 66 × 76	13s to 20s

* Tropical worsteds, linen suitings, cretonne, crash, Butcher rayon, flannel, tweed, sailcloth, homespun, etc., are suitings that vary in yarn construction and fiber content. (See the Glossary for those not discussed here.)

Unbalanced Plain Weave

Increasing the number of warp yarns in a plain woven fabric until the count is about *twice* that of the filling yarns creates a crosswise ridge called a *filling rib,* as well as a warp surface in which the warp yarns completely cover the filling yarns. Small ridges are formed when the warp and filling yarns are the same size, and larger ridges are

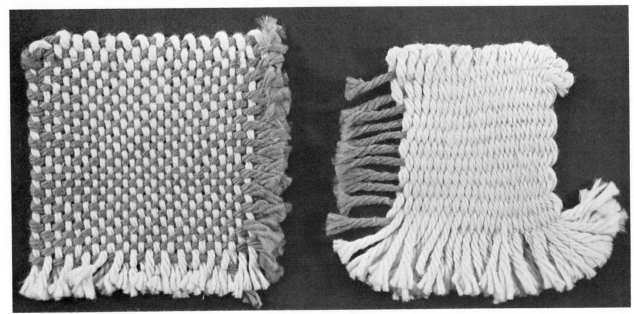

Fig. 23-3 Comparison of plain balanced and unbalanced weave.

formed where the filling yarns are larger than the warp. Yarn sizes are given in the fabric chart (see page 169).

If the yarns are of different colors, the only color showing on the surface will be that of the warp yarns. Figure 23-3 shows the high warp count, the warp surface, and a difference in color in a ribbed fabric.

Ribbed fabrics such as broadcloth look very much like percale. If the following technique of analysis is used, the difference between the two fabrics will become evident.

1. Use a 2-inch square of broadcloth and of percale.

2. *Ravel* adjacent sides of each fabric to make a $\frac{1}{4}$-inch fringe.

3. Observe the difference in the number of yarns in each fringe. Broadcloth will have a very thick fringe of warp yarns (144 × 76); whereas in the percale fabric (80 × 80) the fringe of warp yarns will be about the same as the fringe of filling yarns.

Slippage is a problem in ribbed fabrics made with filament yarns, especially those of lower quality and lower count, as shown in Figure 23-4. This occurs at points of wear and of tension such as at seams and buttonholes. If the yarns are of different colors, as they are in iridescent taffeta with black warp and bright red filling, a bright red streak would show along a seam where slip-

page had occurred, and the main portion of the garment would remain black. Wear always occurs on the top of the ribs. The warp yarns wear out first and splits occur in the fabric. The filling yarns, which are covered by the warp, are protected from wear.

Ribbed fabrics with fine ribs are softer and more drapable than comparable balanced fabrics—broadcloth is more drapable than percale. Those with large ribs have more body and less drapability and are good for garments where a bouffant look is desired. There are few sheer rib fabrics except those used in glass curtains.

Medium-Weight Ribbed Fabrics. Medium weight is the largest group of ribbed fabrics.

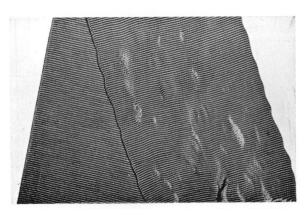

Fig. 23-4 Slippage of yarns in a ribbed fabric.

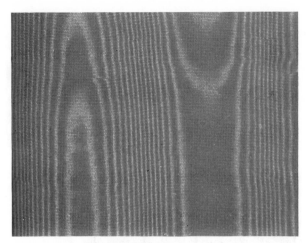

Fig. 23-5 Acetate moiré.

Fabric	Thread Count	Yarn Size Warp	Yarn Size Filling
Rep	88 × 31	30/2	5s
Bengaline	92 × 40	150 denier	15s spun
Shantung	140 × 44	150 denier	30/2

Broadcloth has the finest rib of any of the staple fiber fabrics because the warp and filling yarns are the same in size. The better qualities are made of long-staple cotton, ply yarns, and are usually mercerized for luster. They have a very silky appearance. The term "Pima Broadcloth" on a label refers to the use of long-staple fiber. Combed broadcloth will cost from two to four times as much as carded broadcloth. *Slub broadcloth* is made with a yarn that contains slubs at regular intervals. *Silk broadcloth* has filament warp and staple filling. *Poplin* is similar to broadcloth, but the ribs are heavier because of larger filling yarns. Polyester/cotton blends are widely used.

Taffeta is a fine rib, filament yarn fabric with crispness and body. In acetate taffeta, crispness is produced by the fiber and the finish, and in rayon taffeta it is produced by the finish only. *Moiré taffeta* has a watermarked embossed design that is durable on acetate taffeta but temporary on rayon taffeta unless resin treated (Figure 23–5).

Faille (pronounced *file*) is made of filament warp and staple filling yarns. The filament yarns are usually acetate, rayon, polyester, or nylon.

Shantung has an irregular rib surface produced by long irregular areas in the yarn. It may be made in medium or suiting weight and of various kinds of fiber.

Rep is a heavy coarse fabric with a pronounced rib effect. *Bengaline* is similar to faille and is often made with rayon warp and cotton filling. It is sometimes woven with two warps at a time to emphasize the rib. *Grosgrain* (pronounced *grow'-grane*) has a rounder rib than faille. Grosgrain ribbon may shrink as much as 2 to 4 inches per yard. It is often used at the button closure of sweaters and causes an unsightly appearance when it shrinks.

Poplin, rep, and bengaline are usually bottom weight fabrics.

Plain Weave Variation: Basket Weave

Basket weaves are made with two or more warps used as one, and with two or more fillings placed in the same shed. The most common basket weaves are 2 × 2 and 4 × 4, but other combinations are 2 × 1, 2 × 3, and so on. These fabrics

Medium-Weight Unbalanced Ribbed Fabrics

Fabric	Thread Count*	Yarn Size Warp	Yarn Size Filling
Staple Fiber			
Combed broadcloth	144 × 76	100/2	100/2
Carded broadcloth	100 × 60	40s	40s
Filament Fiber			
Rayon taffeta	60 × 15	10/2	3s
Acetate taffeta	140 × 64	75 denier	150 denier
Faille	200 × 64	75 denier	200 denier

*Counts may be high for polyester/cotton and durable press fabrics.

Fig. 23-6 A 2 × 2 basket weave.

have flexibility and wrinkle resistance because there are few interlacings per square inch. The fabrics have a flatter appearance than a comparable plain weave fabric would have. Long floats will snag easily. Figure 23–6 shows a 2 × 2 basket weave.

Monk's cloth, friar's cloth, druid's cloth, and mission cloth are some of the oldest basket weave fabrics. They are usually brownish white or oatmeal color.

Oxford is a 2 × 1 or 3 × 2 basket weave. It may have a yarn-dyed warp and white filling and be called an oxford chambray. Oxford looks like a balanced fabric because the warp yarns are finer and have higher twist than the filling. Because of soft yarns and loose weave, yarn slippage occurs at the seams and within the fabric itself. Loose-weave fabrics will snag and pill. Filling yarns have a little higher breaking strength than the warp. Oxford fabrics are soft, porous, and lustrous. Like most cotton fabrics, oxford is usually made of polyester/cotton today.

Hopsacking is an open basket weave fabric made of cotton, linen, or wool. It is primarily used for coats and suits. It gets its name from the sacks used to gather hops.

Twill Weave

Twill weave is one in which each warp or filling yarn floats across two or more filling or warp yarns with a progression of interlacings by one to the right or left to form a distinct diagonal line or *wale*. A *float* is that portion of a yarn that crosses over two or more yarns from the opposite direc-

Fig. 23-7 A $\frac{2}{1}$ twill weave.

tion. Twill weaves vary in the number of harnesses used. The simplest twill requires three harnesses. The more complex twills may have as many as 18 picks inserted before repeating and are woven on a loom with a dobby attachment. Twill weave is the second basic weave that can be made on the simple loom.

Twill weave is often designated by a fraction (for example $\frac{2}{1}$ in which the numerator indicates the number of harnesses that are raised and the denominator indicates the number of harnesses that are lowered when a filling yarn is inserted. The fraction $\frac{2}{1}$ would be read as "two up, one down." A $\frac{2}{1}$ twill is shown in Figure 23-7. The floats on the surface are warp yarns, making it a warp surface—warp-faced twill.

Characteristics. Twill fabrics have a right side and a wrong side. If there are warp floats on the right side, there will be filling floats on the wrong side. If the twill wale goes up to the right on one side, it will go up to the left on the other side. Twill fabrics have no up and down. Check this fact by turning the fabric end to end and then examining the direction of the twill wale.

Sheer fabrics are seldom made with a twill weave. Printed designs are seldom used, except in silk and lightweight twills, because a twill surface has interesting texture and design. Soil shows less

Fig. 23-8 Twill wales in lapel look unbalanced.

on the uneven surface of twills than it does on smooth surfaces.

Fewer interlacings permit the yarns to move more freely and give the fabric more softness, pliability, and wrinkle recovery than a comparable plain-weave fabric. When there are fewer interlacings, yarns can be packed closer together to produce a higher count fabric (Figure 23–8). If a plain-weave fabric and a twill-weave fabric had the same kind and number of yarns, the plain-weave fabric would be stronger because it has more interlacings. It is, however, possible to crowd more yarns into the same space in twill in which case the twill fabric would be stronger.

The *prominence* of a twill wale may be increased by the use of long floats, combed yarns, ply yarns, hard-twist yarns, or twist of yarns opposite to the direction of the twill line, and by the use of high thread count. Fabrics with prominent wales, such as gabardine, may become shiny because of flattening caused by pressure and wear. If the ridges have been flattened by pressure, steaming will raise them to remove the

shine. Pure white vinegar (5 per cent) or sandpaper may be used to remove shine caused by pressure or wear. Dip a piece of terry cloth in the vinegar, wring it out, and rub hard and fast in both directions of the cloth in the shiny area. As the cloth dries, the vinegar odor will disappear.

The *direction* of the twill wale usually goes from lower left to upper right in wool and wool-like fabrics—right-hand twills—and from lower right to upper left in cotton or cottonlike fabrics—left-hand twills. This fact is important only in deciding which is the right and wrong side of a twill fabric. In some fabrics that have a very prominent wale or are made with white and colored yarns, the two lapels of a coat or suit will not look the same (Figure 23–8). This cannot be avoided, and if it is disturbing, a garment of a different design should be chosen.

The *degree of angle* of the wale depends on the balance of the cloth. The twill line may be steep, regular, or reclining. The greater the difference between the number of warp and filling yarns, the steeper the twill line will be. Steep twill fabrics have a high warp count and, therefore, are stronger in the warp direction. The importance of the angle is that is serves as a guide in determining the strength of a fabric. Figure 23–9 is a diagram that shows how the twill line changes in steepness when the number of warp yarns changes and the filling yarns remain the same in number.

Even-Sided Twills

Even-sided twills[1] have the same amount of warp and filling yarn exposed on both sides of the fab-

[1] Filling-faced twills are not discussed in this text because they are usually reclining twills and are less durable than the others.

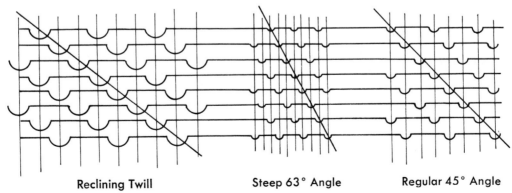

Reclining Twill   Steep 63° Angle   Regular 45° Angle

Fig. 23-9 Twill angle depends on ratio of warp to filling.

Even-Sided Twills*

Fabric	Thread Count	Range in Yarn Size	
		Warp	*Filling*
Serge	48 × 34 to 62 × 58	Vary with fiber content	
Flannel	56 × 30 to 86 × 52	Vary with fiber content	
*See the Glossary for other twill fabrics.			

Warp-Faced Twills*

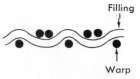

Fabric	Thread Count	Range in Yarn Size	
		Warp	*Filling*
Jean	84 × 56 to 100 × 64	21s to 24s	24s to 30s
Denim (work)	60 × 36 to 72 × 44	7s to 16s	8s to 23s
Gabardine	110 × 76 to 130 × 80	15s to 39/2	15s to 26s
*See Glossary for Whipcord, Cavalry twill.			

ric. They are sometimes called *reversible twills* because they look alike on both sides although the direction of the twill line differs. Better quality filling yarns must be used in these fabrics than in the warp-faced twills since both sets of yarn are exposed to wear. They are $\frac{2}{2}$ twills and have the best balance of all the twill weaves (see the chart).

Serge is a $\frac{2}{2}$ twill with a rather subdued wale, and a clear finish. Cotton serge of fine yarn and high count is often given a water-repellent finish and used for jackets, snowsuits, and raincoats. Heavy-yarn cotton serge is used for work pants. Wool serge gets shiny from abrasion and repeated pressing but is not subject to flattening of the wale.

Surah is a printed filament twill fabric of $\frac{2}{2}$ construction which is used on silklike dresses, linings, ties, and scarves.

Twill flannel is a $\frac{2}{2}$ or $\frac{2}{1}$ twill. The filling yarns are low-twist, larger yarns, specially made for napping. They may be either woolen or worsted. Worsted flannels have less nap, will take and hold a sharp crease, and are less apt to show wear or to get baggy.

Warp-Faced Twills

Warp-faced twills have a predominance of warp yarns on the right side of the cloth. Since warp yarns are made with higher twist, they are stronger and more resistant to abrasion.

Gabardine is a warp-faced *steep* twill with a very prominent, distinct wale. It has a 63° angle or greater and always has many more warp than filling. Cotton gabardine is made with 11, 13, or 15 harnesses. Rayon and wool gabardine are some-

Fig. 23-10 Herringbone.

times made with a three-harness arrangement in which the warp yarns are crowded close together, giving a steep twill.

Denim was traditionally a yarn-dyed cotton twill made in two weights: for sportswear and for overalls. Its use in jeans has increased tremendously and the nature of denim has also changed. It is often napped, printed, and made with stretch yarns.

Jean is a medium-weight twill used for children's playclothes, draperies, slipcovers, and work shirts. Jean is not heavy enough for work pants.

Herringbone Fabrics. Herringbone fabrics have the twill line reversed at regular intervals to give a design that resembles the backbone of a fish (Figure 23-10).

Fig. 23-11 Warp-faced satin weave: $\frac{4}{1}$ yarn arrangement.

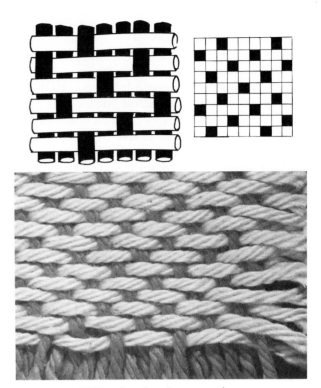

Fig. 23-12 Filling-faced satin weave: $\frac{1}{4}$ yarn arrangement.

Satin Weave

Satin weave is one in which each warp yarn floats over four filling yarns ($\frac{4}{1}$) and interlaces with the fifth filling yarn, with a progression of interlacings by two to the right or the left (Figure 23–11). (Or each filling yarn floats over four warps and interlaces with the fifth warp ($\frac{1}{4}$) with a progression of interlacings by two to the right or left (Figure 23–12). In certain fabrics, such as double damask and slipper satin, each yarn floats across seven yarns and interlaces with the eighth yarn. Satin weave is the third basic weave that can be made on the simple loom, and the basic fabrics made with this weave are *satin* and *sateen*.

Satin-weave fabrics are characterized by luster because of the long floats that cover the surface. Note in the checkerboard designs that (1) there are few interlacings; thus the yarns can be packed close together to produce a very high count fabric; and (2) no two interlacings are adjacent to one another, so no twill effect results from the progression of interlacings unless the thread count is low.

When warp yarns cover the surface, the fabric is a warp-faced fabric—satin—and the warp count is high. When filling floats cover the surface, the fabric is a filling-faced fabric—sateen—and the filling count is high. These fabrics are, therefore, unbalanced, but the high count compensates for the lack of balance.

All these fabrics have a right and wrong side. A high yarn count gives them strength, durability, body, firmness, and wind repellency. Fewer interlacings give pliability and resistance to wrinkling but may permit yarn slippage and raveling.

Sateen

Sateen is a lustrous fabric made of spun yarns. In order to achieve luster with staple fibers, low twist must be used in the yarns forming the float surface. These yarns are the *filling* yarns because if warp yarns were made with twist low enough to

Typical Sateen Fabrics

| Fabric | Count | Kind of Yarn | |
		Warp	Filling
Filling sateen	60 × 104 carded	32s	38s
	84 × 136 carded	40s	50s
	96 × 108 combed	40s	60s
Warp sateen	84 × 64 carded	12s	11s
	160 × 96 carded	52s	44s

produce luster, the yarns would not be strong enough to resist the tensions of weaving. A resin finish is used also on the woven cloth to enhance the luster and make it durable.

Filling sateen is a smooth lustrous cotton fabric used for draperies and dress fabrics. It is often made with carded yarns with a high filling thread count. Yarns are similar in size to those used in print cloth, but the filling yarns have a low twist and are larger in size than the warp yarns. (This factor can be used to help identify the warp and filling direction of the fabric.)

Luster is obtained by the Schreiner finish (see page 266). *Schreinering* is a mechanical finish in which fine lines, visible only under a hand lens, are embossed on the surface. Unless a resin finish is applied at the same time, the finish is only temporary. Combed sateens are usually mercerized as well as Schreinered. Carded sateens are Schreinered only, because short fibers are used; mercerization would not produce enough luster to justify the cost.

Warp sateens are cotton fabrics made with warp floats in $\frac{4}{1}$ interlacing pattern. They have a rounded wale effect that makes them resemble a twill fabric. They are stronger and heavier than filling sateens because of the high warp count. They are less lustrous than filling sateen and are used where durability is more important than luster. Large amounts of warp sateens are used in slacks, skirts, pillow and bed tickings, and sometimes in draperies.

Satin Fabrics

Satin fabrics are usually made of bright filament yarns with very low twist. Warp floats completely cover the surface. Because of the bright fibers, low twist, and long floats, satin is one of the most

Typical Satin Fabrics

Fabric	Count	Kind of Yarn	
		Warp	Filling
Satin	200 × 65	100-denier rayon	100-denier rayon
Nylon satin	320 × 140		
Slipper satin	300 × 74	75-denier acetate	300-denier acetate
Crepe-backed satin	128 × 68	100-denier acetate	100-denier rayon crepe

lustrous fabrics made. It is made in many weights (see the table) for use in dresses, linings, lingerie, draperies, and upholstery. It seldom has printed designs. It is especially good for linings because the high count makes it very durable and the smooth surface makes the garment easy to slip on and off. Satin makes a more pliable lining than taffeta and thus does not split as readily at the hem edges of coats and suits. Quality is particularly important in linings. The higher the count, the better the quality is. Low-count satins will pull at the seams, rough up in wear, and the floats will shift in position to make bubbly areas and wrinkled effects on the surface of the cloth. Satin upholstery should be applied so that one "sits with" the floats.

In crepe-back satin, the crepe yarns are used in the filling and the low-twist warp floats give the smooth satiny surface to the fabric. The crepe yarns give softness and drapability.

Care of satin fabrics should be directed toward maintenance of luster and the prevention of distortion of the floats. Wash or dry clean as indicated by the fiber content, and press on the wrong side or iron with the direction of the floats.

Crepe Weave and Crepe Fabrics

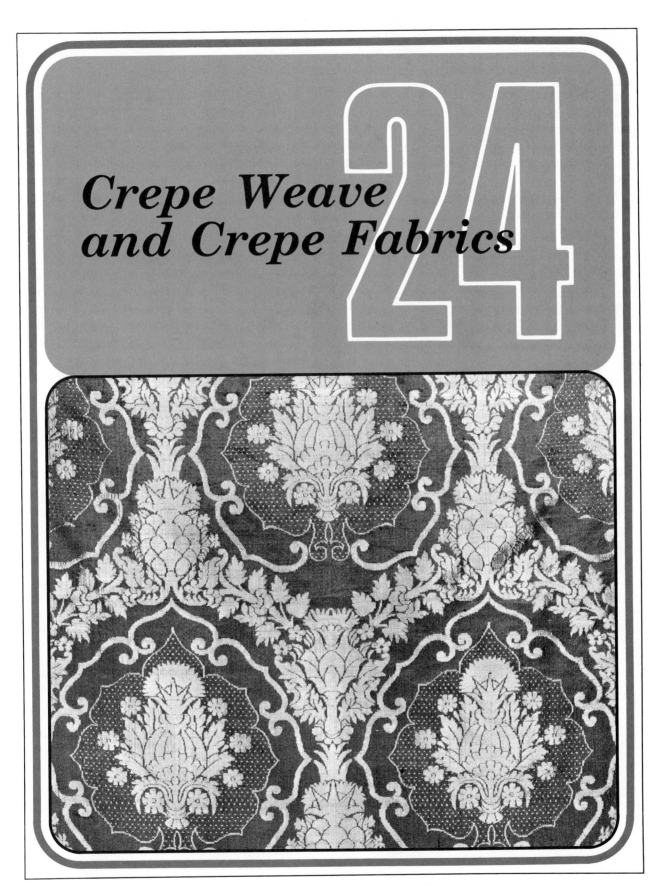

Crepe is a French word meaning "crinkle." A crepe crinkle is obtained in several ways so this chapter deals with a *family* of crepe fabrics, including crepe weave. True crepes and crepe effects are compared in the chart below. Crepe fabrics are classified according to the way the crinkle is obtained.

1. True crepe—crinkle is achieved by high-twist yarns.

2. Crepe effect—crinkle is achieved by
   (a) textured yarns
   (b) weave
   (c) finish.

True Crepe

True crepe fabrics are fabrics containing high-twist yarns. They are made on a loom with a box attachment that can insert alternating groups of S- and Z-twist yarns to enhance the amount of crinkle. The high-twist crepe yarns are made of rayon, cotton, flax, wool, and silk fibers, because the liveliness of the high twist can be "set" by wetting and drying before weaving. Thermoplastic fibers must be set by heat.

The warp yarns of a true crepe fabric are often low-twist yarns of acetate fiber. Low twist in the warp enhances the crinkle achieved by the crepe yarns in the filling.

Gray-goods crepe fabric is smooth as it comes from the loom. It is woven wide and then shrunk to develop the crinkle. Immersion in water causes the crepe-twist yarns to regain their liveliness and contract or shrink. For example, the fabric is 47 inches wide on the loom, contracts to 30 to 32 inches in boil-off, and is finished at 39 inches. This explains why a crepe fabric will shrink when it gets wet and why garment size is so much more easily controlled by dry cleaning than by washing.

True crepe fabrics are classified, by the position of the crepe yarn, as filling crepes, warp crepes, balanced crepes, and variations.

Comparison of Crepe Fabrics

True Crepe By High-Twist Yarns (40–80 tpi)	Crepe Effect		
	By Textured Yarn	By Weaving	By Finish
Permanent crinkle. Will flatten during use. Moisture will restore it	Permanent crinkle. Does not sit out or need ironing	Crinkle does not flatten in use	Crinkle may sit out or be less prominent after washing
High potential shrinkage	Low potential shrinkage	Lower potential shrinkage	Lower potential shrinkage
Good drapability	Less drapable	Less drapable	Less drapable
Stretches	Low stretch	Low stretch	Low stretch
Resilient, recovers from wrinkles	Does not wrinkle	Wrinkles do not show because of rough surface	Wrinkles do not show because of rough surface
Dry cleaning preferable	Wash-and-wear	Washable unless fiber content requires dry cleaning	Washable unless fiber content requires dry cleaning
Typical fabrics* French crepe Flat crepe Wool crepe Crepe de chine Matelassé Chiffon Georgette	Typical fabric Whipped cream†	Typical fabrics Sand crepe Granite cloth Seersucker	Typical fabrics Plissé Embossed crepe

*Some of the less commonly used crepes are described in the Glossary.
†Trade name of Burlington/Klopman.

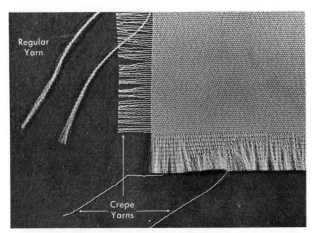

Fig. 24-1 Flat crepe. Notice crimp of regular yarn caused by pressure of crepe yarn when fabric was pressed.

Filling-Crepe Fabrics

Filling-crepe fabrics have high-twist crepe yarns in the *filling* direction and low-twist yarns in the warp direction (Figure 24–1).

Multifilament and *French crepe* are the smoothest and most lustrous of the true crepe family. Because they are smooth, they are washable and are used in lingerie and sometimes in blouses. They contain crepe yarns of the lowest twist.

Flat crepe is the most widely used filling crepe. It has a dull crepelike surface. A rayon/acetate fiber combination is frequently used. The acetate is very low-twist filament used in the *warp* and the rayon is the crepe yarn filling. The rayon crepe yarns alternate with S- and Z-twist or with 2S- and 2Z-twist. A high warp count and low filling count give a crosswise *rib* effect. Low count in the filling gives the crepe yarns room to contract, so the amount of crinkle will be greater. Figure 24–1 shows a filling crepe. Analysis of a filling-crepe fabric will show that it is easy to distinguish between the warp and filling yarns (see page 139). Polyester and nylon crepes do not shrink when wet and thus may be laundered.

When sewing with crepe it is *not advisable to preshrink* the cloth with the hope that it will then be completely relaxed. If crepes are completely relaxed, they will stretch too much during pressing and use. True crepes present some problems in pressing, but the secret is to work quickly with as little pressure and moisture as is necessary to obtain good results. It is best to dry clean crepes that have enough crinkle to present pressing or shrinkage problems.

Warp-Crepe Fabrics

Warp-crepe fabrics are made with crepe yarns in the warp and regular yarns in the filling direction. Very few warp crepes are on the market, possibly because they tend to shrink more in the warp direction and it is, therefore, difficult to keep an even hemline in washable fabrics. Bemberg sheer and some wool crepes belong in this group (Figure 24–2).

Balanced-Crepe Fabrics

Balanced-crepe fabrics have crepe yarns in both directions and are usually balanced in thread

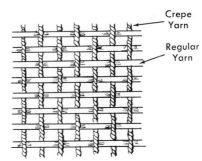

Fig. 24-2 Warp crepe.

Typical Filling Crepe Fabrics*		Denier			
Kind of Crepe	Thread Count	Warp	Filling	tpi
Multifilament or	250 × 104	55†	75	30
French crepe	150 × 94	75	75	38 S- and Z-twist
Flat crepe	150 × 76	75	75	50 S- and Z-twist

*"American Rayon Crepes and Their Construction," *Modern Textiles*, **34**:90 (September 1945).
†Yarn has 50 filaments. High number of filaments gives softness.

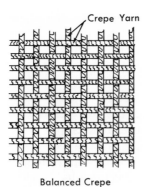

Balanced Crepe

Fig. 24-3 Balanced crepe.

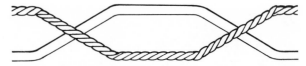

Fig. 24-5 Criss-crossing of yarns in matelassé.

count. They are often made in sheers and the crepiness of the yarns in both directions helps prevent yarn slippage. Figure 24-3 shows a balanced crepe. *Chiffon* is a very sheer crepe made with alternate S and Z twist yarns in a plain weave. *Georgette* is a sheer crepe originally made with two S and two Z twist yarns alternating. It is duller and heavier than chiffon.

Variations

Other forms of true crepes are the crepe seersuckers and the double-cloth crepes.

Puckered rayons (seersucker) are made in plain weave with alternating groups of regular yarns and crepe yarns in the filling direction. Warp yarns are regular yarns. When the fabric is wet in finishing, the crepe yarns shrink, which causes crosswise puckers in the regular yarn stripe (Figure 24-4).

Matelassé is a double-cloth construction with either three or four sets of yarns. Two of the sets are always the regular warp and filling yarns and the others are crepe yarns. They are woven together so that the two sets criss-cross, as shown in Figure 24-5. It is as if the two fabrics were inter-

Fig. 24-4 Rayon crepe seersucker.

laced with each other. The crepe yarns shrink during wet finishing and create puffy areas in the regular-yarn part of the fabric. Matelassé is usually a rayon/acetate combination.

Crepe-Effect Fabrics

The crinkled effect of a true crepe can be simulated by the use of textured polyester yarns in the filling direction of the fabric, by weave, and by finishes.

Crepe Effect by Textured Yarns

Filament polyester yarns textured by the false-twist process (page 122) are woven as the filling yarns in a plain weave fabric with standard filament yarns in the warp.[1] These textured filament yarns are *low twist*. The warp yarns are low-twist polyester or triacetate filament fibers. The crepe effect forms during the wet finishing of the cloth when the textured polyester shrinks.

The finished fabric has a high level of crinkle, good hand, and exceptional performance for the consumer. It packs well and never needs ironing. The fabric is relatively stiff or crisp when compared with true crepes—it does not drape well. One of the first textured yarn crepes on the market was Whipped Cream by Burlington/Klopman.

Crepe Effect by Weaving

Two kinds of weaves are used: the crepe weave and slack-tension weave.

Crepe Weave. Crepe is the name given to a class of weaves that present no twilled or other distinct weave effect but give the cloth the appearance of being sprinkled with small spots or seeds.[2] The

[1]R. W. Jackle, "Properties and Uses of Polyester Fibers," *American Dyestuff Reporter,* **54**:17 (December 6, 1965).
[2]G. H. Oelsner, *A Handbook of Weaves* (New York: Dover Publications, Inc., 1969), pp. 175–218.

Fig. 24-6 Crepe weave—irregular interlacings.

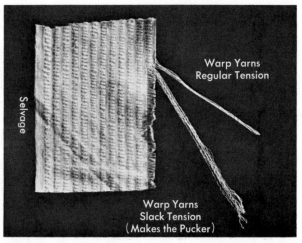

Fig. 24-7 Seersucker, showing the difference in length of slack- and regular-tension yarns.

effect is an imitation of true crepe, which is developed from yarns of high twist. Fabrics are made on a loom with a dobby attachment. Some are variations of satin weave, with filling yarns forming the *irregular* floats. Some are even-sided and some have a decided warp effect. Crepe weave is also called *granite* or *momie weave*. Fibers that do not lend themselves to true crepe techniques are often used in making crepe-weave fabrics. Wool and cotton fibers are also used frequently because the crepe-effect fabric is easier to care for than the true crepes. For a comparison of characteristics, refer to the table on page 176. An irregular interlacing pattern of crepe weave is shown in Figure 24–6.

Sand crepe is one of the most common crepe weave fabrics. It has a repeat pattern of 16 warp and 16 filling and requires 16 harnesses. No float is greater than two yarns in length. It is woven of either spun or filament yarns. The silklike acetate sand crepe (Magic Crepe, for example) is widely used.

Granite cloth is made with granite weave, based on the satin weave, and is an even-sided fabric with no long floats and no twilled effect. It is used in ginghams, draperies, and for other purposes.

Moss crepe is a combination of true crepe yarns and crepe weave. The fiber content is usually rayon and acetate. The yarns are ply yarns with one ply made of crepe-twist rayon fiber. Regular yarns may be alternated with the ply yarns or they may be used in one direction while the ply yarns are used in the other direction. This fabric should be treated as a true crepe fabric. Moss crepe is used in dresses and blouses.

Polyester crepe fabrics are frequently used in blouses and dresses. They are crepe weave fabrics made with textured yarns.

Slack-Tension Weave. In slack-tension weaving, two warp beams are used. The yarns on one beam are held at regular tension and those on the other beam are held at slack tension. As the reed beats the filling yarn into place, the slack yarns crinkle or buckle to form the puckered stripe and the regular-tensioned yarns form the flat stripe. (Loop-pile fabrics are made by a similar weave; see page 218.) *Seersucker* is the fabric made by slack-tension weave (Figure 24–7). The yarns are wound onto the two warp beams in groups of 10 to 16. The crinkle stripe may have slightly larger yarns to enhance the crinkle, and this stripe may also have a 2 × 1 basket weave. The stripes are always in the warp direction. Seersucker is produced by a limited number of manufacturers. It is a low-profit, high-cost item to produce because of slow weaving. Most seersuckers are made in 45-inch widths in plain colors, stripes, plaids, and checks. Cotton, polyester, acetate, and triacetate fibers are used singly or in blends. Seersucker is used in large amounts in the men's-wear trade for suiting and for women's and children's dresses and sportswear.

Crepe Effect by Finish

This effect is usually achieved by plisséing or embossing a plain woven fabric. The pucker is permanent or durable.

Plissé is converted from either lawn or print cloth gray goods by printing sodium hydroxide

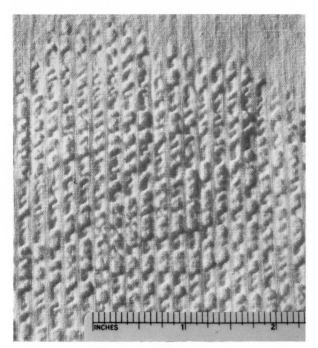

Fig. 24-8 Plissé crepe.

(caustic soda) on the cloth in the form of stripes or designs. The chemical causes the fabric to shrink in the treated areas. As the treated stripe shrinks, it causes the untreated stripe to pucker. Shrinkage causes a slight difference in thread count between the two stripes. The treated or flat stripe increases in thread count as it shrinks. The upper portion of the cloth in Figure 24-8 shows how the cloth looks before finishing, and the lower portion shows the crinkle produced by the caustic soda treatment. This piece of goods was found on a remnant counter and was defective because the roller failed to print the chemical in the unpuckered area.

Embossed crepe is made by pressing a crinkled design onto the surface of the cloth. Cotton cloth must be given a resin finish also to make the design durable. Thermoplastic fibers can be heat-set to make the design permanent.

Both plissé and embossed fabrics will retain their original appearance best if they are tumble dried and *not* pressed.

Knitting: Weft knitting and hosiery

25

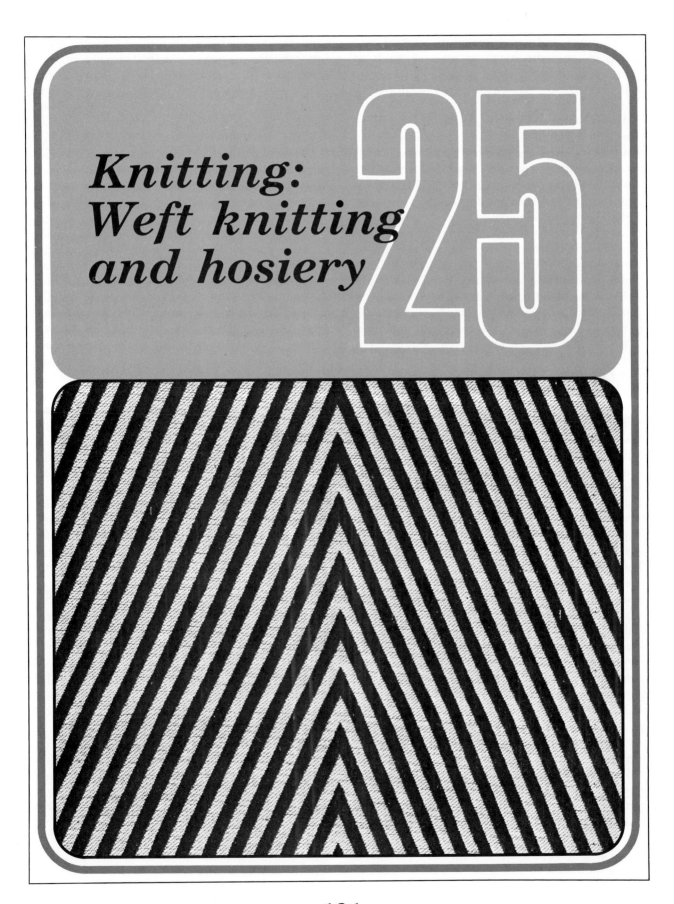

Knitting has traditionally been a standard construction for some items of apparel, such as sweaters, underwear, and hosiery but, for many years, knit goods represented only a small part of the apparel market.

The technique of knitting is not as old as that of weaving. Remnants of knit fabrics dating back to A.D. 250 were found near the borders of ancient Palestine. Knitting was a hand process until 1589, when the Reverend William Lee of England invented a flat-bed machine for knitting cloth for hosiery. This machine could produce cloth at 10 times the rate of hand knitting. The circular knitting machine and the warp knitting machine came about 200 years later. There is no evidence that warp knitting was ever a hand technique.

A unique advantage of the knitting industry is that it can produce—or "fashion"—a *completed garment* directly on the knitting machine. Sweaters and hosiery are good examples. The knitting of a completed garment was made possible in 1863 when William Cotton invented a machine that could shape garment parts by adding or dropping stitches.

The rate of production of knitting machines is relatively high—about four times as many square yards or meters per hour as for looms. A wider knitting machine will run as fast as a narrow one, whereas the wider the loom, the slower it weaves. This rate of speed should be an economic factor in favor of knitting as a method of cloth manufacture, but the increased cost of the yarn more than offsets any savings in the cost of manufacture. There are several reasons for this. First, because the looped position of the yarn imparts bulk, more yarn is required to produce a knit cloth than to produce a comparable woven cloth. Second, the looped structure is porous—has holes or spaces—and as a result, provides less *cover* than a woven fabric in which yarns lie side by side so, in order to achieve an equal amount of cover, the knitter must use smaller stitches (finer gauge) and finer yarns that are more expensive. Also, all knitting yarns are more expensive to make because they must be very uniform to prevent the formation of thick-and-thin places in the fabric.

Knitting is a very efficient and versatile method of making fabric. This versatility has resulted from the use of computerized systems wherein electronic patterning mechanisms[1] permit rapid adjustment to fashion changes. Fabric pattern designs can be changed quickly, so profitable items can be made as soon as their fashion appeal becomes evident. There is now a knitted counterpart for every woven fabric—knitted seersucker, piqué, denim, crepe, satin, terry cloth, velour, and furlike fabrics are examples.

Other knitting-machine technological developments helped broaden the range of knit-goods end uses. The double knits used in women's wear, for example, lacked the lighter weight, finer gauge, and stability needed for men's wear, so knitting machines had to be modified to make the kind of fabrics needed for men's wear. These modifications led to the development of attachments that made the knitting machine capable of producing a combination *knit-weave* fabric with stability more like that of wovens. The *weft-insertion* knitting machine introduced filling yarn for more crosswise stability and the *warp-insertion* machine added warp yarns for greater lengthwise stability. The Co-We-Nit machine gave a true combination of knitting and weaving by inserting both warp and filling into the knitted structure.

Knits, like weaves, can be made from any kind of fiber or yarn and can have many textures—soft as cashmere or boardy as felt, loose or tight, inert or elastic, and rough or smooth. They can also be opaque or transparent.

The fibers that predominate in knits are polyester, nylon, and acrylic. The use of cotton in knitting has diminished. Its strength now lies mainly in shirting fabrics where it is frequently blended with polyester. Wool is used in sweaters and in better dresses and suits. Single knits and medium weight interlocks gain popularity where styles are soft and drapey. When fashion calls for fabrics with more body, heavier double knits or bonded single knits are more popular.

Prior to 1920 most knitted items except silk hosiery were made of spun yarns. Man-made filament yarns created interest in knit goods of silk-like nature and they soon became widely used in women's lingerie. However, men objected to the filament yarn knits as being too soft, slippery, and cool. Filament tricot shirts and sheets appeared on the market in the 1950s but were unsuccessful

---

[1] The Moratronik system is an example. In this system the pattern design is drawn on special graph paper. The paper is scanned horizontally by photography and the pattern is recorded vertically on 35-mm photographic film as a transparent "hole" or blank. Each hole or blank will control the action of individual needles on the knitting machine. The needle signals that were stored on the tape are retrieved by electronic scanning and are transmitted to electromagnetic selectors built into the cam boxes of the knitting machine.

because of poor hand, static, and a clammy feel in hot weather. (Both items were improved and re-introduced, static free and with a luxury feel, in the 1970s).

The invention of the yarn texturing process brought about expanded use of filament yarns in knit goods. The textured yarns were first used in *stretch* nylon hosiery, leotards, and ski wear. The textured polyester *double knits,* however, sparked the most spectacular growth in the knitting in-dustry. By the mid 1970s, knit goods' share of the apparel, household, and industrial market had risen to about 50 per cent and for the first time, knitting became a serious competitor of weaving. Since that time the usage of woven fabrics has been increasing.

The major advantages of knitted garments to the wearer are comfort and neatness retention. Comfort in clothing is based on the ability of the garment to adapt to body movement without binding or inhibiting the wearer. The loop struc-ture provides the fabric with outstanding elastic-ity (stretch/recovery) that is distinct from any elastic properties of the fibers and yarns that are used. The loop can change shape by lengthening or widening to give stretch in either direction of the cloth (Figure 25–1).

The elasticity can be controlled from a mini-mum to a maximum by means of the stitch con-struction. Unfortunately, all knits are not con-structed properly for the end use and may sag, bag, or snag, thus disappointing the consumer. Knitted fabrics have higher potential shrinkage than woven fabrics. The accepted standard is 5 per cent for knits whereas 2 per cent is standard for wovens. This seems reasonable because a knitted garment will stretch, and although it may look a bit tight it is still wearable.

Warmth and coolness are also factors of com-fort. The bulky structure of a knit provides many dead air cells for good insulation in *still air* but a wind-repellent outer layer is needed to prevent chill winds from penetrating. On a warm, humid day, knits may be too warm because they tend to

fit snugly and keep warm air close to the body. Knits of 100 per cent polyester, however, make rather cool fabrics for winter wear and need to be blended with wool, rayon, or acrylic to alleviate this problem.

Neatness retention means lack of wrinkles during wear, care, and packing or storage. Wrin-kle recovery is based somewhat on the loop struc-ture, but it is also strongly influenced by fiber content and kind of yarn. A combination of poly-ester fiber, textured filament yarn structure, and loop stitch will produce an easy-care fabric, such as the double knits, that rarely wrinkle under any circumstances.

The chart summarizes some of the major dif-ferences between the processes of knitting and weaving and the fabrics made by these processes.

Knitting Terminology

Definition. Knitting is a cloth manufacturing process in which needles are used to form a series of interlocking loops from one or more yarns or from a set of yarns.

Methods of Knitting. Weft or filling knit is a process in which one yarn is carried back and forth (or around) and under needles to form a fabric. Yarns run horizontally in the fabric. *Warp* knit is a process in which a warp beam is set into a machine and yarns are interlooped to form a fabric. Yarns run vertically in the fabric. These names were borrowed from the weaving tech-niques and refer to the way the loops are formed.

Needles. Knitting is done by spring beard needles or by latch needles which are shown in Fig-ure 25–2. Spring beard needles are usually used with fine yarns, whereas latch needles are used in making coarse fabrics. A double latch needle is used to make purl loops.

Stitches. Stitches are the loops made by the needles. They are given various names depending on the way they are made.

Wales and Courses. Wales are vertical rows of loop stitches in the knit fabric. Courses are hori-zontal rows of loops. In machine knitting, each wale is formed by a single needle. Wales and courses show clearly on filling knit jersey, wales on the face and courses on the back (see Fig-ures 25–3, 25–4).

Loop Lengthened   Loop Widened   Loop Normal

Fig. 25–1 Loop can change its shape to give stretch.

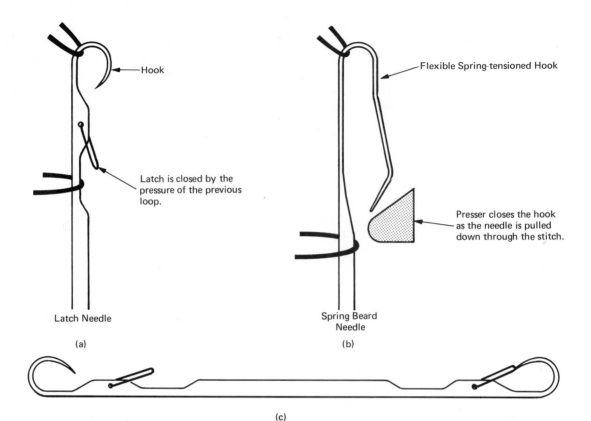

Fig. 25-2 Knitting needles. (a) Latch needle; (b) Spring beard needle; (c) Double latch needle.

Gauge, or cut, indicates the fineness of the stitch and is measured as the number of needles in a specific space on the needle bar. The number of needles representing gauge differs.

- Full-fashioned hosiery   needles/1.5″ = gauge
- Circular-knits   needles/1″ = gauge
- Tricot   needles/1″ = gauge
- Raschel   needles/2.0″ = gauge

The higher the gauge or cut the finer is the fabric. The finished fabric may not have the same cut or gauge as the machine that made it because of shrinkage or stretching during finishing.

Face or Right Side of the Fabric

1. Has a better finish.

2. Twill lines usually run to the right when present.

3. If two kinds of yarn or fiber are used, the more expensive one is used on the face side.

4. If floats are present, the least snaggable ones are on the face.

5. Finer yarns are on the face.

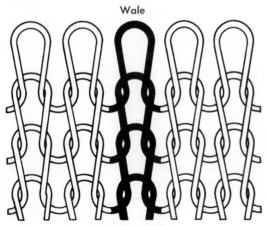

Wale

Fig. 25-3 Wale.

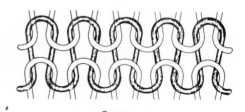

Course

Fig. 25-4 Course.

Comparison

Knitting	Weaving
Comfort and Neatness Retention	
Mobile, elastic fabric. Adapts easily to body movement. Good recovery from wrinkles.	Rigid to stress (unless made with stretch yarns). Varies with the weave.
Cover	
Porous, less opaque. More open spaces between yarns let chill winds penetrate.	Provides maximum hiding power. Maximum cover per weight of yarn.
Fabric Stability	
Less stable in wear and care. Many shrink more than 5% unless synthetic fibers have been heat-set.	More stable in wear and care. Many shrink less than 2%.
Versatility	
Sheer to heavyweight fabrics. Plain and fancy knits. Can be made to look like weaves, lace, and other fabrics.	Sheer to heavyweight fabrics. Many different textures and designs.
Economics	
Design patterns can be changed quickly to meet fashion needs. Process is less expensive but is offset by expensive raw material costs. Speedier regardless of fabric width.	Machinery less adaptable to rapid changes in fashion. Most economical method of producing a unit of cover.* Wider looms weave slower.

*Lower costs do not necessarily ensure higher profits. Fashion and supply are important factors. When double knits were first produced, higher prices could be charged, and the economic returns, yard for yard, were higher in double knits than in wovens.

6. If the two sides differ, the design is the face and the solid color is the back.

Technical face refers to right side of fabric as knitted. This may not be the side used as the right side in a garment.

Weft (or Filling) Knitting

Knitting is essentially two different industries—one is the production of finished garments and the other is the production of piece goods for cut and sewn garments.

Weft knitting can be either a hand or a machine process. In *hand knitting,* a yarn is cast (looped) onto one needle, another needle is in-serted into the first loop, the yarn is thrown around the needle, and by manipulating the needle the new loop is taken off onto the second needle. The process is repeated with all the loops being taken off from one needle to the other. In *machine knitting* many needles (one for each wale) are set into a machine; the yarn is carried under the needles (much like a shuttle inserts a yarn in weaving) that move down, back, and up to form new loops and a knitted cloth. Both hand and machine knitting can be flat, in which the yarn is carried back and forth, or circular, in which the yarn is carried around helically like the threads in a screw. In hand knitting many kinds of stitches can be made by varying the way the thread is placed around the needle (in front or behind) and by knitting stitches together, dropping stitches, or transferring stitches. Special mechanisms have to be used to obtain all of these variables in machine knitting.

Weft Knitting Machines and Fabrics

	Jersey—Flat	Jersey—Circular	Rib—Flat	Rib—Circular	Purl—Flat	Purl—Circular
Description	Straight bar holding latch needles. Yarn carried back and forth. Purpose is to shape garments	See Figure 25-7 latch needles. Yarn carried around. Electronic control patterns make range of designs	Two flat needle beds formed in ∧ position, see Figure 25-13. Yarn carried back and forth. Stitch transfer carriage can switch from one bed to another to make variety of stitches	See Figure 25-14. One set of needles mounted on dial, one set on cylinder. Multiple feed-yarn carried around needle selection mechanism	Two needle beds with double latch needles working between. See Figure 25-2. Yarn carried back and forth. Jacquard selection mechanism	Two cylinders, one above the other. Double latch needles. Yarn carried around. Jacquard selection mechanism
Kinds of knits and end uses	Basic knit stitch. Loops pulled to face of fabric. Fabric has different appearance on face and back. Full-fashioned garments. Ban-lon type pullover	Workhorse of knitting industry. Loops pulled to face. Fabric has different appearance face and back. High-volume production. Seamless hose. Jersey, velour, terry	Face wales and back wale. Same appearance face and back. Used when fabric must have finished edge. Collars, trims	Double knits—plain. Jacquard double knits. Interlock (requires special needles usually made on special machine)	Face and back loops in same wale. Same appearance face and back. Irish fisherman's knit. High-priced quality dresses. Sweater fronts of fancy knit stitches	Face and back loops in same wale. Same appearance face and back. Coarse gauge used for outerwear. Garment bodies. Some yardage
Advantages	Economical use of yarn. Garments always on grain. Can have some design	Least complicated. Fastest method	Less waste than circular rib	High-speed production. Excellent design flexibility. Versatile in yarn usage	Can knit plain, purl, rib stitches	Higher speed than flat purl. Can knit plain, purl, rib stitches
Limitations	Quite slow in production. Higher priced end product. Single feed system	Limited pattern possibilities	Slow speed	Complex machine. Downtime can be a problem	Very slow production	Slow production
Future	Affluent markets are increasing	Men's dress shirts. Draperies (9-foot cylinder could make room size draperies)	Increasingly important in trims	Men's wear potential	Can produce well-shaped, richly patterned goods	High-volume sweaters

Machines Used in Weft Knitting

Machine knitting is done on three types of circular and three types of flat-bed machines. The chart provides a comparison of the various machines and products made on them. Notice the following differences:

The machines are classified according to the kinds of stitches made—jersey, rib, purl.

The circular machines are faster in production. They make yardage primarily but are also used to make sweater bodies, panty hose, and socks.

The flat-bed machines knit full-fashioned garment parts and have much slower operating speeds.

Weft Knit Structures—Stitches

Weft knit fabrics are classified according to the stitches used. *Single jersey* has face loops only. *Rib fabrics* have face loops and back loops in the same course but not in the same wale. *Purl fabrics* have face loops and back loops in the same wale. *Interlock fabrics* consist of two ribs knitted alternately so that the two structures intermesh.

Figure 25-5 is a hand-knit sample in which the same number of stitches was used to knit each different section. Notice that the sections differ in length and width as well as in appearance. The plain or single jersey has a different appearance on face and back but the rib and purl look the same on both sides.

Plain or Single Jersey. Single jersey fabric has all the loops drawn to the face side of the fabric. The fabric has a definite right and wrong side. The face side has prominent wales—columns of loops running lengthwise. The back has prominent courses—rows of stitches running crosswise (see Figure 25-6). Stretch a swatch of jersey crosswise and it will curl to the wrong side at the lengthwise edges. The ends will curl toward the face. Ravel out a yarn. It will ravel crosswise because

Fig. 25-6 Plain jersey stitch.

the yarns run horizontally in the fabric. A run can be created by pulling on a cut edge of the fabric or by cutting or breaking a yarn. The run then forms vertically when the broken or cut loop drops loops above and below it. Single jerseys made of staple fiber yarns tend to resist running because of fiber cohesiveness. Fabrics formed by the plain jersey stitch tend to be flatter than other knits. They stretch more widthwise than crosswise.

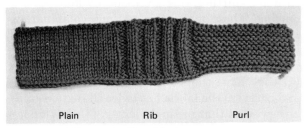

Fig. 25-5 Hand-knit structure.

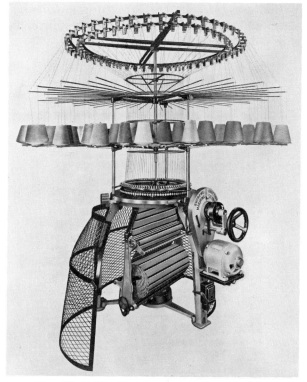

Fig. 25-7 Circular jersey knitting machine.

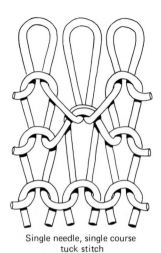

Single needle, single course
tuck stitch

Fig. 25-8 Tuck stitch. (*Courtesy of* Knitting Times, *official publication of National Knitted Outerwear Association.*)

The word *jersey* comes from the Isle of Jersey in the English Channel. It is applied to (1) the plain weft-knit stitch, (2) a single-knit fabric—either warp or weft knit, and (3) a pullover sweater.

The single jersey structure or plain knit is widely used because it is the fastest method of weft knitting and is made on the least complicated knitting machine.

End uses for plain knit structures include hosiery, underwear of cotton or blends, shirts, T-shirts, dresses, and sweaters.

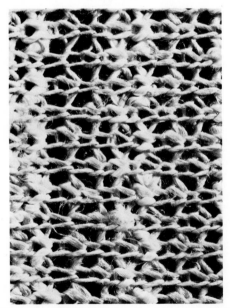

Fig. 25-9 Fabric knitted with tuck stitch.

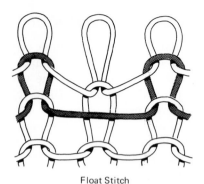

Float Stitch

Fig. 25-10 Float or miss stitch. (*Courtesy of* Knitting Times, *official publication of National Knitted Outerwear Association.*)

Variations in plain knit are made by programming the machines to knit stitches together, to drop stitches, and to use colored yarns to form patterns or vertical stripes. Extra yarns or slivers are used to make terry cloth, velour, and fake fur fabrics.

Two stitches commonly used to make jersey variations are tuck stitch and miss stitch. *Tuck stitch* receives a new yarn on a needle but does not lose its old loop and the accumulated yarns are knitted off later (Figure 25–8). Fabrics have a lofty appearance and soft hand. Fabrics are less extensible. Tuck stitch is used to create blisters or special effects and to secure laid-in yarns or long floats of yarns on the wrong side of the fabric. Figure 25–9 shows tuck stitches in fabric. *Miss stitch* or float stitch results when a needle is held in a nonworking position as the yarn is placed on the working needles. As the yarn is carried past the working needles a float (much like that in woven fabrics) is made (Figure 25–10). It is used to carry colored yarn on the back of fabric for knitted-in designs. Miss stitches make fabrics much less extensible.

Rib Structure. A rib structure is made of face wales and back wales. The lengthwise ridges are formed on both sides of the fabric by pulling loops first to the face and next to the back of the cloth. In hand knitting, ribs are made by knitting and purling. These may be in various combinations 1×1, 2×2, 2×3, and so on (Figure 25–11). Figure 25–12 shows a T-shirt fabric in rib knit.

Rib knits have the following properties: (1) they have the same appearance on the face and back, (2) the fabric has twice the extensibility crosswise as that of single jersey, (3) they do not curl at the edges, (4) they run, (5) they unravel

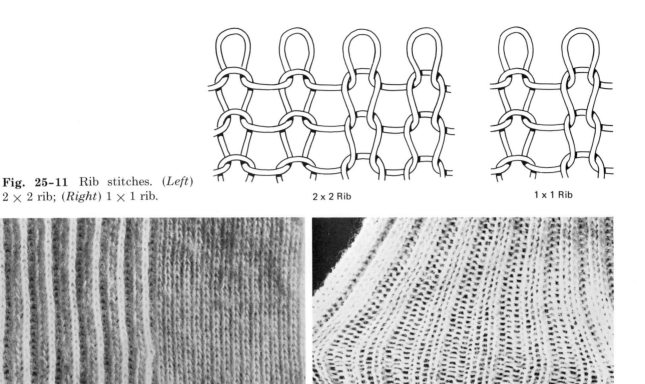

Fig. 25-11 Rib stitches. (*Left*) 2 × 2 rib; (*Right*) 1 × 1 rib.

2 x 2 Rib

1 x 1 Rib

Fig. 25-12 Rib knit fabric. (*Left*) Fabric relaxed, left side 2 × 2 rib, right side 1 × 1 rib. (*Right*) Fabric stretched to show difference in stitches.

from the end knit last, and (6) they are twice as thick as single jersey.

Single-rib knits are widely used for underwear and in the neckbands and wristbands of sweaters and T-shirts. Rib knits can be varied by tucking on the back wales to produce thicker, bulkier fabrics.

Rib fabrics are made on circular or flat-bed machines with two sets of needles (see chart page 186). In the flatbed machine the needle beds are in an inverted V position. Needles from one bed pull the loops to the back and those in the other bed pull the loops to the front (Figure 25-13). In the circular machine the loops are pulled to the face and back by setting one set of needles vertically in a cylinder and the other set of needles horizontally in a dial. The needles from each bed are placed opposite each other (Figure 25-14).

Purl Structure. Purl structure has the loops pulled to the face in one crosswise course and then to the back in the next course. Face loops and back loops are in the same wale (Figures 25-15 and 25-16).

Fabrics produced by the purl stitch are thick, wide, and short as compared to single jersey with the same number of plain stitches. Fabrics are highly extensible both crosswise and lengthwise. Fabrics do not curl but they do run and may be made to unravel from both ends.

The two major end uses for purl structures are children's and infant's wear and golf sweaters. Purl stitches are often used at the shoulder seams of sweaters to stabilize the garment since they have less crosswise stretch than plain knit.

Fancy purl knits are made by knitting groups of face loops and back loops to form a pattern. The areas curl in opposite directions giving very puffy designs.

The purl machine always moves to the left so it is sometimes called a links-links machine. The term *links* is a German word meaning "leftward."

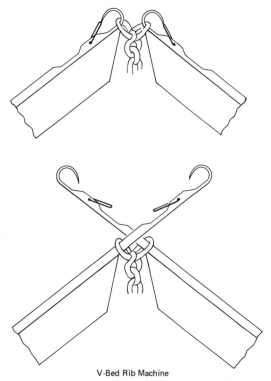

V-Bed Rib Machine

Fig. 25-13 Needle action in flat bed machine. (*Courtesy of* Knitting Times, *official publication of National Knitted Outerwear Association.*)

The stitch is rounder and puffier than most other weft-knit stitches and is said to resemble a pearl. The purl machine has two needle beds that lie in the same plane and one set of *double-hook* needles that can transfer from one needle bed to the other.

Purl is generally the slowest form of knitting but it is also the most versatile. The purl is the only weft-knitting machine that can produce all three types of weft-knit fabrics—plain, rib, and purl—although as a rule not as economically. Thus, a knitter can use a purl machine to make a garment that is part plain, part rib, and part purl.

Interlock Structure. Interlock fabrics are composed of two 1 × 1 rib stitches intermeshed. Interlock machines have long and short needles alternating in the dial and cylinder. Where there is a long needle in the dial there is a short needle in the cylinder and vice versa. Needles are aligned directly opposite each other so that the wales in the fabric are one on top of the other (Figure 25–17 is offset for clarity).

Both sides of the fabric are alike and resemble the face side of single jersey. Interlock stretches like plain jersey but the fabric is firmer. Inter-

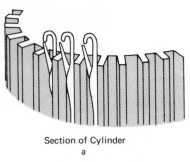

Section of Cylinder
a

Cylinder

b

Fig. 25-14 (a) Needle beds and (b) knitting action in circular knitting machine. (*Courtesy of* Knitting Times, *official publication of National Knitted Outerwear Association.*)

locks do not curl and fabrics *run* and unravel from one end only. Most interlock fabrics are plain or printed. Colored yarns can be knitted to give spot effects or horizontal or vertical stripes.

Double-Knit Structures. Double-knit fabrics are made on machines that have two sets of needles and are knit with tuck or float loops in addition to knit loops. They are somewhat like two fabrics interlocked into one.

Fabrics have two-way stretch and relatively high dimensional stability—especially the polyester double knits. They do not curl at the edges, and are less apt to "sit out" than single knits. They do not run. Double knits can be made to look like any woven structure and they are often given the woven fabric name—denim, seersucker, double piqué, and the like.

Weft or Filling Knit Fabrics

Single Knit Fabrics. *Single knits* are made on one complete set of needles (they may be in two

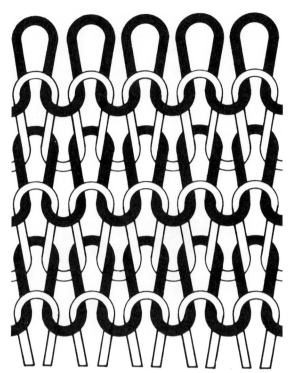

Fig. 25-15 Purl fabric. (*Courtesy of* Knitting Times, *official publication of National Knitted Outerwear Association.*)

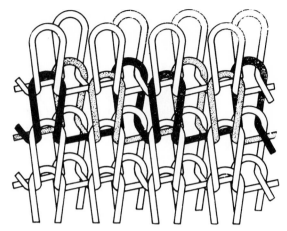

Fig. 25-17 Interlock. (*Courtesy of* Knitting Times, *official publication of National Knitted Outerwear Association.*)

needle beds). Single knits can be plain color or printed, striped or patterned, gossamer thin or heavy enough for use in winter sweaters. They are less stable than double knits, tend to curl at the edges, and run or ladder readily if made of filaments. Fabric names for knits are not as specific as for woven fabrics. Some fabrics are listed.

Jersey is a light-to-medium weight fabric knitted on a circular jersey machine and sold in tubular form or cut and sold as flat goods. When tubular fabrics are pressed at the factory in the

Fig. 25-16 Purl stitch: looks the same on both sides.

finishing operation, the creases are seldom parallel to the wales of the fabric—they are off-grain. To straighten these fabrics, put a basting thread or line of pins along one of the lengthwise wales. Then refold the cloth along the basting line and steam press to straighten but avoid creasing the folds; press them lightly. The tubular cloth does not need to be cut and opened out, when cutting out the garment, unless there is a specific reason for doing so. If it is to be cut, be sure to follow a wale. It may be best to avoid cutting along a course of the tubular fabric to straighten it crosswise. In some of the multiple-feed machines this may result in cutting strips spirally around the tube.

Figure 25-18 shows a child's top that was cut from tubular cotton jersey with crosswise stripes (wales are crosswise in the garment instead of lengthwise as knitted in the fabric). When the garment was purchased the stripes were vertical and the side seam was perpendicular to the lower edge. After washing, the fabric assumed its normal position causing the side seams to twist and the stripes to spiral.

Stockinette is another name for jersey. Wool, acrylic, polyester spun yarns, cotton, and polyester/cotton blends are widely used in jersey.

Single figured jerseys are made by a Jacquard mechanism on circular jersey machines. Printed jerseys are more commonly used.

Intarsia designs in jersey are made by laying in colored yarns. True intarsia designs have a clear pattern on both the right and wrong side of the cloth with no bird's-eye backing that is characteristic of Jacquard designs. Fabrics have no extra

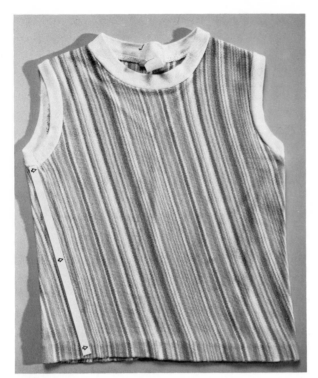

Fig. 25-18 Child's knitted top. Side seam is shown by white strip with arrows.

weight, and the stretch is not impaired. Mock intarsia designs are made by knitting and miss-knitting (miss or float stitch), which results in a heavier weight fabric with floating yarns on the reverse side. These floating yarns reduce the elasticity of the fabric and may snag readily.

Pile Knit Jersey (see page 219).

La Coste knit is made with a tuck stitch course alternating with a plain jersey course. Fabrics are used mainly in sportswear.

Double Knit Fabrics. Double knits are made on machines with two sets of needles and with two or more yarns that are knitted separately and together as the design requires.

Double-knit jersey, like *interlock jersey,* looks the same on both sides. It differs in that the needles from the cam and cylinder are not opposite each other but are positioned so that the needles from one bed work between the needles from the other bed. They also knit a 1 × 1 rib. To distinguish between interlock and rib double knit in a fabric, cut along a course and stretch the edge widthwise. Examine the edge. If it is interlock there will be a back loop opposite each front loop; if it is rib double knit the back loops will alternate between the front loops.

Rib-Jacquard Double Knits. These fabrics have almost limitless design possibilities. The intermeshing of the two yarns is the same as the double-knit jersey but have added needle-selecting mechanisms—pattern wheels, pattern drums, punched tapes or cards, or photographic electronic film (Figure 25-19).

Bourdelet is a ripple stitch or corded fabric produced by knitting and tucking. *Double piqué* has a fine diamond-shaped pattern on both sides of the fabric. Names of woven fabrics are often

Fig. 25-19 (*Top*) Tape punching machine prepares pattern tape. (*Bottom*) Circular knitting machine using pattern tapes. (*Courtesy of North American Rockwell.*)

used for double knits that resemble them but more often the term *polyester double knit* is the only name needed to identify this type of fabric.

Polyester double knits have had a tremendous impact on the knitting industry as well as on home sewing and the ready-to-wear (RTW) industry. The development of textured set yarns, proper dyeing techniques, and electronic patterning devices helped the "overnight success" (1967) of polyester double knits.

The first textured "set" polyester double knits were made for women's wear and were of fall or winter weight—standard weight was $14\frac{1}{2}$ ounces in a 16 to 18 gauge because this was what the existing machinery could produce. Development of finer gauge machinery made it possible to make double knits that were compact and that more closely resembled woven fabrics. These fabrics were 6 to 7 ounces in 24 to 28 gauge (interlock machines could make 32 gauge) and were suitable for summer dresses and blouses. Finer-gauge fabrics had the advantage of less pilling and snagging.

Snagging is probably the single most serious problem encountered in the use of knit fabric. When a yarn is snagged so it pulls out and stands away from the surface of the fabric, "shiners" or tight threads are formed on either side of the snag. If snags are cut off (rather than being worked back into original position) a run may start in some knits—particularly in weft knits. Incorrect amount of twist and improper knitting are major reasons for cloth snagging.

The mace test is a particularly tough test for snagging. It consists of running a round spiked iron ball a specified number of times along the surface of the cloth to test its resistance to snags (Figure 25–20). Finer yarns, smaller stitches, and higher twist all contribute to snag resistance. This test has been found to give good results in terms of correlation with what happens in actual wear. Antisnag, antistatic, and soil finishes release can be applied to knit fabrics. If these finishes are present, they should be identified on the label.

Double Knits in Men's Wear. Interest in knits for men's wear began to develop in 1969. One of the problems was that of getting the hand and feel of worsteds. In woven fabrics, men's wear traditionally has been either plain weave or twill weave, and styling is achieved through the kind of yarn used—colored, large or fine, novelty, high-twist, or soft blends and combinations of different fibers.

Fig. 25-20 Spiked iron ball used in mace test.

Requirements for men's wear are more rigid than those for women's clothing. Shrinkage is intolerable and must be controlled to within 2 per cent. One big snag could ruin a man's suit and be a costly accident. A suit must be capable of being worn several days in succession without requiring care and must be capable of being hung on a hanger in the normal manner. Men's wear must wear better, must be able to stand up under greater stress, and must not mold to the body. Some women's slacks have tended to cling to the body and reveal the lines of the underwear. (Wovens, on the contrary, provide desirable hiding power.)

One of the most critical specifications for men's wear is fabric weight—generally lower for any season than women's wear. The first men's knits were made of the double knits designed for women and did not meet this requirement. It was necessary to develop knitting machines that could use spun yarns, finer yarns, and knit finer gauge. The chart compares the first women's wear double knits with the fabrics developed for men's wear.

Men's wear is usually made of polyester/wool blends now because polyester double knits are cool in winter. The chart gives yarn and fiber characteristics.

First Women's Wear Double Knits	Double Knit Developed for Men's Wear
11–14½ ounces/yard	8–8½ ounces/yard
18 gauge	22 to 24 gauge
150-denier textured filament	100- to 120-denier textured filament
4.2–4.5 denier/filament	5 denier/filament
Higher number of filaments to give softer hand	Dull-luster fibers
Round cross-section fibers	Low-pill polyester variant
	Multilobal fibers for less shine

Knitting Garment Parts

Garment parts—sweater bodies, fronts, backs, sleeves, skirts, and collars can be knitted to shape on flat-bed machines. The stitch used for shaping is called *loop transfer*. A knit loop is transfered from one needle to another, usually near the end of a course, so that the width of the fabric is decreased. The process is called *fashioning* and is done to make armholes, neckline curves, collar points, and the like. Garment parts have finished edges.

A *looping machine* is used to join the shoulders and sleeves of the shaped parts with an effect of continuous knitting rather than of seams. This machine is also used to join collars to cut-and-sewn knit garments.

To identify fashioned garments look for "fashion marks" accompanied by an increase or decrease in the number of wales (Figure 25–21). Mock fashion marks are sometimes put in the garment but they are not accompanied by an

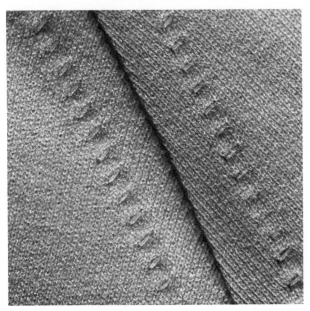

Fig. 25-22 Raglan sleeve portion of cut and sewn sweater. Notice mock fashion marks.

increase or decrease in the number of wales, so no shaping is done by the mock fashion marks (Figure 25–22). Full-fashioned sweaters are almost always made with a jersey stitch. Circular jersey sweaters are cut and sewn.

Full-fashioned garments do not necessarily fit better than cut-and-sewn garments because this depends on the size and shape of the pieces. But full-fashioned garments are always on grain and look better to the discerning eye and they should not become misshapen during washing—no twisted seams.

Fig. 25-21 Raglan sleeve portion of full-fashioned sweater. Notice that stitches are dropped.

Hosiery

Before the advent of knitting, people wore ill-fitting stockings that were cut and sewn from woven cloth. In the fifteenth and sixteenth centuries hand knitting of wool stockings was a cottage industry in England and in Scotland. Hand-knit silk stockings, very heavy and coarse by our present day standards, were imported from Italy in the latter part of the sixteenth century. In 1589, William Lee, an English clergyman, invented a flatbed machine for knitting wool stockings. Queen Elizabeth I refused to grant Lee a patent because she feared it would prevent the wool hand knitters from earning a living; she encouraged him to adapt his machine for silk. Lee was then invited to come to France and it was there that he perfected his machine.

Fashion and man-made fibers have been responsible for many of the developments in hosiery. Women's legs were shown in public for the first time in the twentieth century. Dress lengths gradually went from the floor in 1900 to far above the knee in 1970, creating a need for sheer, well-fitting women's hose and finally panty hose. Stretch nylon caused a change in construction methods. In all hosiery, sizing has been revolutionized; instead of many sizes, small, medium, and large fit most everyone's feet and legs.

Yarns Used for Hosiery

Spun yarns. Spun yarns are used for socks. They may be of any fiber content, acrylic and nylon blends are most commonly used. Cotton and wool are not as widely used as previously; wool is often blended with acrylic and nylon is commonly used as reinforcement in the heels and toes of socks. Two-ply mercerized cotton, called *lisle,* is stronger and more durable than regular cotton. Spandex is used in the tops of socks.

Filament nylon yarns. Filament nylon yarns are used in women's hosiery and lighter weight socks. They may be monofilament or multifilament.

When nylon was introduced in 1939, women were wearing silk hosiery—2 or 3 thread for dress weight and 6 to 8 thread for service weight. The first nylons were 30 denier, a service-weight stocking that was extremely durable. As nylon hose became more sheer, durability decreased. Finer yarns do not wear as well as heavier yarns. Most nylon hosiery is now 15 denier. Nylon stockings were first made of conventional nylon fiber (Figure 25–23), and elasticity and fit were dependent on the knit loop and the fiber's elasticity. In 1954, textured stretch yarns made by false

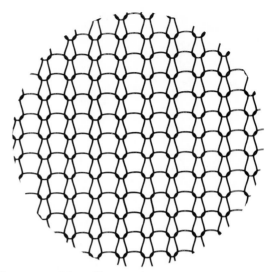

Fig. 25-23 Monofilament hosiery yarn. (*Courtesy of the Du Pont Company.*)

twist and edge crimping (see Figures 17–6 and 17–8) methods were introduced. Textured stretch yarns give better fit and better wear and make it possible for retailers to carry fewer sizes.

Bicomponent, self-crimping filaments are also used in hosiery. Cantrece II made by Du Pont is advertised as fitting like a second skin (Figure 25–24).

Biconstituent fibers, spandex, and rubber are used in support and surgical hose. *Support hose* are worn by both men and women for comfort. People who work in jobs that require them to be on their feet most of the time wear support hose (or support panty hose) to prevent muscular fatigue. Support hose are also beneficial to preg-

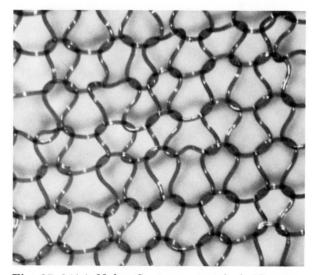

Fig. 25-24(a) Nylon Cantrece: stretched. (*Courtesy of the Du Pont Company.*)

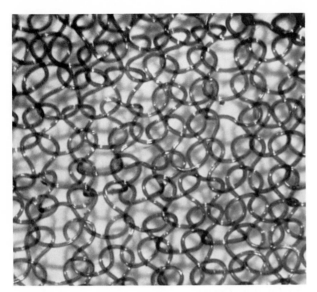

Fig. 25–24(b) Nylon Cantrece: relaxed. (*Courtesy of the Du Pont Company.*)

nant women. They are available in nylon and spandex or biconstituent nylon/spandex. Monvelle biconstituent, which combines spandex and nylon in one monofilament, is shown in Figure 25–25c. See Figure 14–5 for cross section.

Surgical hose are prescribed by doctors for leg disorders such as varicose veins and are worn by hospital patients to prevent blood clots after an operation. They may be purchased singly or in pairs, with or without heels and toes, and in various lengths—ankle, knee, or over the knee. It is very important to choose the correct size of surgi-

cal hose so that the support from the stocking is placed to give support where it is needed. The yarns are spandex, or rubber for the elastic core, and cotton and nylon are used as the wrap. Surgical hose are quite expensive and can be made to order. Figure 25–25b shows a wrapped spandex and nylon construction.

Construction

All hosiery is filling knit. The stitches used are plain (or jersey), rib, mesh, and micromesh. The plain knit has stretch in both directions, and hose can be very sheer if made of fine denier monofilaments. Plain knit has the disadvantage of running readily when a loop is broken. Mesh hose are lacelike knits that do not run, but they snag and holes will develop. Micromesh has loops knitted so that a run goes up only. Mesh and micromesh stockings are not as elastic or as smooth as plain jersey. Rib stitches as well as jersey are used in socks. Fancy knits such as cables and argyles are often used. Children's knee-high socks may be transfer printed (see page 294).

Full Fashioned. *Full-fashioned hose* are made on flat-bed machines and are shaped by dropping stitches at the appropriate places between top and knee, between knee and ankle, and to shape instep, heel and toe. The flat knit stocking is removed from the machine and the edges are stitched together from toe to top resulting in a

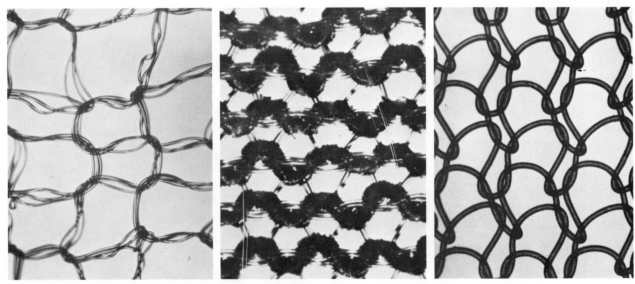

Fig. 25-25 Hosiery yarns. (*Left*) Textured nylon. (*Above*) nylon and spandex. (*Right*) Monvelle biconstituent. (*Courtesy of Monsanto Textiles Company.*)

seam down in the back and under the foot. When silk was the major fiber used in women's hose, 95 per cent of hosiery production was full-fashioned. It was the only way to really fit the leg and foot. With the introduction of nylon, which is thermoplastic and can be heat-set, seamless hose became more important and by 1956 full-fashioned hosiery had almost disappeared from the market.

Seamless. *Seamless hose* have the same number of stitches from top to toe and are knit on circular machines. Shaping may be done by decreasing the size of the loop gradually from top to toe. If shaping is done at toe and heel, a circular fashioning mechanism that drops stitches is used. Heavier yarn can be knit into toe and heel to give greater comfort and durability. Seamless hosiery is knit in one piece as a continuous operation. When knitting is finished, the toe is closed and the stocking is turned right side out.

Long hose of regular nylon and socks with shaped heels are *preboarded,* a process in which stockings are placed on metal leg forms of the correct size and shape and then steamed to press. Tube socks and stockings do not have shaped heels. They are seamed across the toe end.

Panty hose are usually made from textured stretch nylon. The panty portion is heavier than the stocking portion. Panty hose are knitted in tube shape with a guide for slitting. After slitting the panty section, two tubes are stretched together in a U-shaped crotch seam with a firm, serged stitch. A separate crotch section is often inserted for better fit. The crotch section is of a double layer of nylon or nylon and cotton. Control top panty hose may have spandex or bicomponent nylon/spandex in the panty portion, or a separate panty of cut and sewn power net (see page 204) may be stitched to stockings.

Sizing

Proper fit is extremely important to the durability of hosiery and panty hose. Hosiery is well marked, usually with information telling the consumer how to choose the correct size. *Stockings* knitted with regular yarns are sized according to foot length and height and range in size from $8\frac{1}{2}$ to 12 in short, average, long, and queen lengths. *Panty hose* are always knitted with stretch yarns. Their sizes are based on height and weight. A chart on the back of the package includes height and weight (sometimes hip or panty) measurements grouped into short, average, long, extra long, queen short, or queen long sizes, making it easy to choose the correct size. Sock sizes are usually related to shoe sizes.

Care of Hosiery

To avoid snagging, take off rings and bracelets before putting on stockings or pantyhose. Make sure that nails and cuticles are smooth.

To launder hose safely, sort according to color and wash in a basin of warm water and mild soap suds. Rinse in warm water. Dry over a smooth rack, roll loosely, and keep in a compartmented drawer-organizer or stocking case or in individual plastic sandwich bags.

Warp Knitting

26

Warp knitting is unique in that it developed as a machine technique without ever having been a hand technique. Warp knitting started about 1775 with the invention of the tricot machine by Crane of England. The tricot machine (pronounced tree-ko') is sometimes called a warp loom because it uses one or more sets of yarns that are wound on warp beams and mounted on the knitting machine (Figure 26–4). The first tricot machine made fabric 16 inches wide for silk-stocking cloths. In 1880, Kayser established the first warp knitting mill in the United States.

Warp knitting provides the fastest means of making cloth. It has been said that warp knits fall between double knits and wovens, combining the best qualities of both. Warp knits can duplicate wovens in many respects while, at the same time, offering the performance and easy care of the knits. Warp knit fabrics tend to be less resilient and lighter in weight than weft knits. They can have stability in both directions of the cloth or exhibit a degree of stretch, as determined by the control of the knitting stitch. This stability-stretch control is an important factor in the ability of warp knits to compete with double knits in men's wear.

Warp knitting produces a vertical-loop construction, as shown by the line of loops in Figure 26–1. It is a machine process of making fabric in flat or sheet form using one or more *sets* of warp that are fed from warp beams to a row of knitting needles extending across the width of the machine. Each set of warp is controlled by yarn guides (Figure 26–2) mounted in a guide bar that also extends across the width of the machine. If there is one set of warps, the machine will have one warp beam and one guide bar; if there are two

sets of warps, there will be two warp beams and two guide bars, and so on: hence the terms *one-bar tricot* and *two-bar tricot*. All guide bars feed yarn to the *same* set of *needles*. Each yarn guide on the bar guides one yarn to the hook of one knitting needle. Chains with links of various heights control the movement of the guide bars. More guide bars give greater design flexibility. The loops of one course are all made simultaneously when the guide bar raises and moves sideways to lay the warp around the needles to form the loops, which are then pulled down through the loops of the preceding course. Yarn from the front bar usually predominates on the surface whereas yarn from the back bars provides run resistance, elasticity, and weight.

Machines Used in Warp Knitting

Several types of warp knitting machine are listed in the chart on page 200. Tricot and Raschel machines, however, account for the manufacture of about 95 per cent of all warp-knit goods.

Warp Knits versus Weft Knits

The two kinds of knits differ because of the different knitting techniques and machines used in their manufacture. The major differences are summarized in the chart on page 201.

Fig. 26–3 Two-bar tricot. (*Top*) Face side. (*Bottom*) Reverse side.

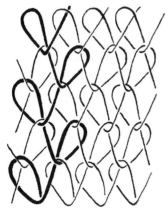

Fig. 26–1 Warp knitting stitch.

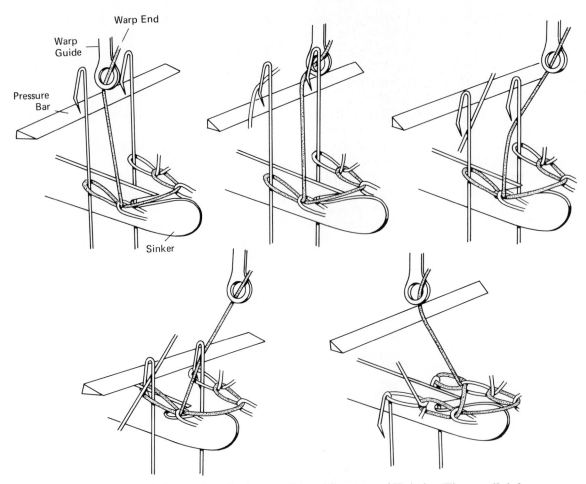

Fig. 26-2 Knitting action of tricot machine. (*Courtesy of* Knitting Times, *official publication of Knitted Outerwear Association.*)

Warp Knitting Machines

Tricot	Raschel	Simplex	Milanese
Single bed. Spring beard needles	One or two needle beds. Latch needles	2 sets of needles. Spring beard needles	Flat—spring beard needles Circular—latch needles
2-3-4 bars indicate number of sets of warp yarns	May have as many as 30 guide bars		Yarn travels diagonally from one side of material to the other
High-speed, high-volume. Usually filament yarns	Great designing possibilities		
End Uses			
Plain, patterned, striped, brushed fabric. Underwear Outerwear	Sheer laces and nets Draperies Power net Thermal cloth Outerwear	Warp double-knits Gloves	Underwear Outerwear

Comparison of Weft (Filling) and Warp Knits

Weft Knits	Warp Knits
Yarns run horizontally	Yarns run vertically
Loops joined one to another in the same course	Loops joined one to another in adjoining courses
Connections are horizontal	Connections are diagonal
More design possibilities	Higher productivity
Two-way stretch	Crosswise stretch, little lengthwise stretch
Run, most ravel	Do not run or ravel
Hand or machine process	Machine process
Flat or circular	Flat
Can have finished edges	
Can knit shaped garments garment pieces or yardage	Produced as yardage

Tricot Warp Knits

The name *tricot* has been used as a generic name for all warp-knit fabric; specifically, it is the fabric produced on the tricot machine using the *plain jersey stitch*. This fabric is called jersey, tricot, or tricot jersey. Tricot comes from the French word *tricoter,* meaning "to knit."

The plain jersey stitch is shown in Figure 26–3. The face of the fabric (top photo) is formed of vertical wales and the back (lower photo) has horizontal courses. The face has a much finer appearance than the back. Tricot is runproof and nonraveling. The fabric will curl just as weft-knit jersey does. Tricot fabric has high tear strength, high resiliency, and elasticity, which is greater in the crosswise direction. Some important end uses of tricot fabrics include

- Lingerie
- Sleepwear
- Loungewear
- Men's shirts
- Bonding
- Uniforms for nurses, waitresses, and the like
- Jersey dresses and blouses
- Other outerwear
- Automotive fabrics (upholstery)

The Tricot Machine The first tricot machines, which used spring-beard needles, were designed to use the finer yarns for blouses, underwear, and loungewear. Spun yarns were not knit on these machines, because the increased friction from the fuzzy ends and the irregularities that are typical of spun yarns caused excessive yarn breakage. Until the early 1970s, only 2 per cent of the warp knits were made of spun yarns. Then tricot machines, such as the Reading Spunwarp machine that used a latch needle, were developed for knitting spun yarns and novelty yarns as well as for textured yarns.

The modern tricot machine is the mainstay of the warp knitting industry (Fig. 26–4). It is a high-speed machine that can knit flat fabric up to 160 inches wide. The machine makes a plain jersey stitch or can be modified to make tuck stitch, clipped dot, Jacquard, and other designs. Another modification is the attachment for laying in weft (filling) yarn in a tricot structure. This is expected to play an important part in fabrics for men's wear (see page 207).

Tricot Fabrics. Plain tricot jersey is made on a machine employing one set of needles and two guide bars. Filament yarns of acetate, triacetate, polyester, and nylon are used in either smooth or textured form. Acetate is the least expensive yarn and is used extensively for tricot backing of bonded fabrics and for textured yarn dress fabrics.

Few if any methods of cloth manufacture can produce anything comparable to nylon tricot in the standard ranges of 15 to 40 denier. Nylon tricot is light in weight (17.5 to 6.5 yards/pound), has exceptional strength and durability, and can be heat-set so that it is dimensionally stable. One of the unique features of nylon tricot is that the same piece of gray goods can be finished under

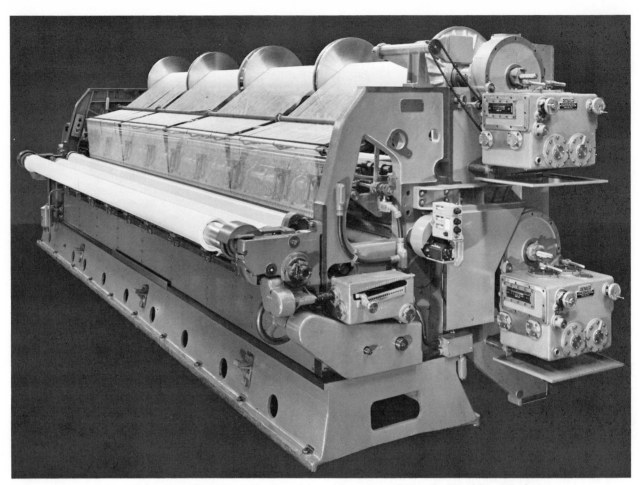

Fig. 26-4 Warp knitting tricot machine. (*Courtesy of Textile Machine Works.*)

different tensions to different widths that have different appearances; for example, 168-inch gray goods can be finished at 98, 108, 120, 180, or 200 inches wide.

Clipped dot tricot is basically the two-bar nylon tricot jersey with a third bar knitting in a heavy-denier *rayon* yarn where the spot is to be and then floating to the next spot. The floats are sheared off, so there is considerable waste. A good cross dye can be achieved with the rayon/nylon combination.

Brushed tricots are one of the most unusual applications of warp-knit fabrics. The velvetlike surface consists of loops raised from the surface. Heat-set nylon must be used, so it is possible to raise the loops without breaking them. The fabric is versatile and has several end uses such as sleepwear, evening gowns, shoes, slacks, upholstery, and draperies. Velcro closures with loops acting as catches for hooks are another end use.

Napped velours are Arnel/nylon combinations

with Arnel on the back or acetate/nylon combinations. Goods can be dyed, dried, heat-set, and then napped on a double-action napper, heat-set again to proper width, and then sheared.

The acetate knit stitches have long underlaps. One set of yarns is carried over 3 to 5 yarns to form floats; the second set of yarns interloops with adjacent yarns. Nylon is used for the adjacent looping to provide strength and durability. The weak acetate floats are broken when the fabric is run through the napper. The napped side is used as the right side of the fabric even though it is the technical back (Figure 26–5).

Satinlike tricots are made in the same way as napped tricots except that the fabric is Schreinered (see page 266) instead of napped. These fabrics are usually 100 per cent nylon or polyester and the floats are shorter.

Tricot net fabric can be made by skipping every other needle so only half as much yarn is used.

Tricot strips for trim can be made by cutting

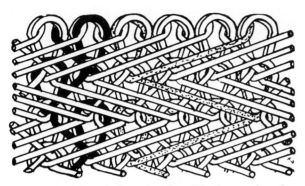

Fig. 26-5 Velour before napping. Black yarn is nylon; white and gray yarns are acetate. (*Courtesy of* Knitting Times, *official publication of Knitted Outerwear Association.*)

on a slitter or by knitting in an acetate thread that is later dissolved.

Striped tricot is made by using acetate yarn on the second and/or third bars and pulling the heavier acetate yarn to the face in alternating horizontal rows. Cross dyeing gives the difference in color.

Tuck effects use the same yarns as in the striped fabrics, but a change in the yarn arrangement forms a "lip" or tuck. The tucks may be straight, wavy, irregular, intermittent, wide, or narrow.

Automotive tricot upholstery—all nylon 2- to 3-bar tricot of 100-denier and 140-denier nylon 72 inches wide finished with a Scotchgard treatment—(Fig. 26-6) has been introduced.

Tricot Finishing. Nylon and polyester require heat setting to stabilize the fabric against shrinkage, to improve the hand, to give good stitch definition and desirable cutting properties, and to

Fig. 26-6 Tricot car upholstery with moiré finish.

improve the yield. Most heat setting is done on the pin tenter frame. Either radiant heat or superheated steam is used. Shrinkage can be controlled to within 1 per cent. If the tricot is dry-heat-set on the tenter frame with 15 per cent extension in width, improved crease resistance during wear is achieved.

The Schreiner finish (see page 266) was first used on tricot in 1957. Called Satinette, the finish causes a permanent flattening of the yarns, thus filling in the open spaces of the knit structure to give more cover and make the fabric more opaque. The fabric has a satiny smoothness.

Flocking imparts a softened lofty effect and can be used for a wide variety of designs from dots to large area designs.

Pleating is a natural for nylon tricot and is done with a pleating machine, which folds the fabric with pleating paper in the form desired. The fabric is steamed and the paper is removed. (A pleated effect can be achieved during the knitting process by leaving out threads in alternate areas.)

Bonding is usually done with single tricot jerseys. (Double knits are not bonded.) Acetate tricot is commonly used for the backing of bonded woven goods. Occasionally nylon, which is more costly, is used. Bonding provides greater stability and gives body to the fabric. "Leatherknit" is a product made with two layers of nylon tricot foam-bonded together. It has a leatherlike surface that is often embossed and is permanent. This process is known by the tradename Kalon by Wedgewood. The product is machine washable and dryable. It has *good porosity* and can be Zepel-treated for water and stain repellency.

Antistatic, antisnag, flame-retardant, and cross-dyed finishes are also used for tricot fabrics.

Raschel Warp Knits

The Raschel warp knitting machine, which is believed to be named for the mistress of the designer of the machine, has one or two needle beds with latch needles set in a vertical position and as many as 30 guide bars. The fabric comes from the knitting frame almost vertically instead of horizontally as in the tricot machine. The various Raschel machines knit a wide variety of fabrics from gossamer sheer nets and veilings to very heavy carpets.

The three greatest growth areas of Raschel knits are women's dresses, sportswear, and men's tailored suits. Raschel knits may be better suited for use in men's wear than the double knits because of their patterning possibilities, hand, and appearance.

Raschel knits are used industrially in laundry bags, fish nets, dye nets, safety nets, and covers for swimming pools.

Raschel fabrics. Crochet-type fabrics have rows of chainlike loops called *pillars* with laid-in yarns in various lapping configurations (Figures 26–7 and 26–8). These fabrics can be identified by raveling the laid-in yarn and noticing that the fabric splits or comes apart lengthwise. Curtain fabrics and outerwear fabrics are knitted on this standard type machine.

Carpets have been knitted since the early 1950s. Since their production is faster, knitted carpets are cheaper to make than woven carpets. Tufted carpets, being still much cheaper to produce, have captured most of the carpet market. Knitted carpets have 2- or 3-ply cotton or filament nylon warps for lengthwise stability; laid-in jute crosswise yarns for body and crosswise stability; and pile yarns of wool, acrylic, or nylon. Knitted carpets can be identified by looking for chains of stitches on the underside. They seldom have a secondary backing.

Lace and curtain nets of the kind made on

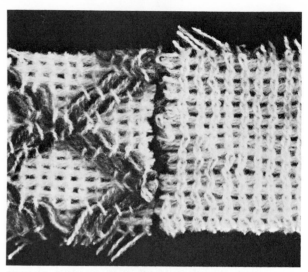

Fig. 26-8 Raschel knit with extra yarn. (*Left*) Right side of fabric. (*Right*) Reverse side of fabric.

Leavers lace machines (see page 242) can be made at much higher speeds on a Raschel machine. The Raschel machine has a single needle bed and 18 to 24 guide bars. Curtain nets, which can have square, diamond, or hexagonal meshes, are made on simpler machines. Laces are usually made of nylon or polyester (Figure 26–9).

Thermal cloth has pockets to trap heat from the body knitted in; it looks like woven waffle cloth. Brynje is the name given to this fabric, which is much like the Norwegian fisherman's vest. This knit is also used for thermal blankets.

Power net is an elasticized fabric used for foundation garments and bathing suits. Nylon is used for the 2-bar ground construction and spandex is laid in by two other guide bars (Figure 26–10).

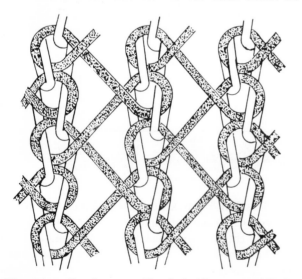

Fig. 26-7 Crochet-type Raschel. (*Courtesy of* Knitting Times, *official publication of Knitted Outerwear Association.*)

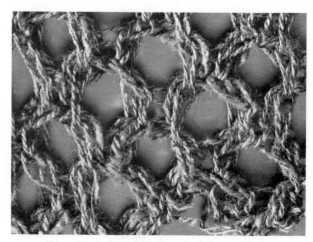

Fig. 26-9 Lacelike Raschel dress fabric.

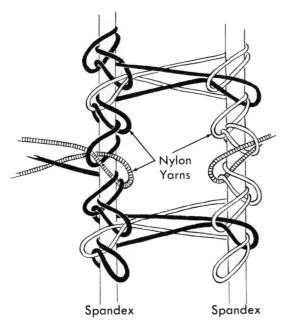

Fig. 26-10 Raschel power-net stitch.

Nylon Yarns

Spandex   Spandex

Minor Warp Knits

Simplex. The simplex machine, which is similar to the tricot machine, uses spring-beard needles, two needle bars, and two guide bars. It produces a two-faced fabric somewhat like circular double knits. End uses are gloves (traditional), swimwear, and dresses.

One company, Blue Ridge Winkler Textiles of Bangor, Pennsylvania, produces most of the simplex knits. Glove fabrics are given a suede finish

by passing them two or three times over revolving sandpaper-covered rollers. The number of times the fabric is passed through the machine is determined by the degree of sueding desired. Dyeing follows.

Milanese. The Milanese machine is especially constructed to produce superior warp-knit fabrics. The machine can use both kinds of needles. It is equivalent to a 2-bar tricot fabric and is made from two sets of warp yarns with one needle bar and one guide bar but the lapping movements are arranged so each warp thread moves *across the full width* of the fabric, one set knitting from right to left and the other from left to right. This results in a diagonal formation (Figure 26-11), which shows up on the back of the cloth. The face has a very fine rib. The fabric is runproof and is used for gloves and lingerie.

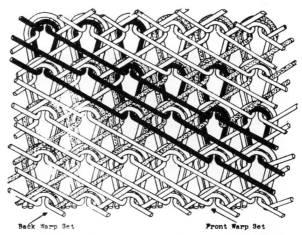

Back Warp Set   Front Warp Set

Fig. 26-11 Milanese. (*Courtesy of* Knitting Times, *official publication of Knitted Outerwear Association.*)

Knitting Variants: Knit-weave and knit-sew

Knit-Weave Techniques

A new concept[1] in fabric formation is that of combining knitting and weaving by

1. Weft insertion using a modified warp knitting machine
2. Warp insertion using a modified weft knitting machine
3. Warp and weft insertion (true knit-weave)

Weft Insertion

Weft insertion is done by a *warp* knitting machine with a weft-laying attachment. Several models have been developed. The simplest at-

[1]Peter Lennox-Kerr, "Fabric Forming," *Textile Industries,* **135**:135 (September 1971).

tachment carries a single filling yarn to and fro across the warp knitter, and this yarn is then fed steadily into the needle zone of the machine. A firm selvage is formed on each side.

More complex attachments supply a sheet of filling yarns to a conveyor that travels to and fro across the machine. Figure 27–1 shows the Weft-Loc machine, which carries as many as 24 filling yarns in 6-inch bands. The yarns are then fed into the stitching area of the machine. A cutting device trims filling yarn "tails" from the selvages and a vacuum removes the tailings.

Weft-insertion fabrics offer the best properties of both woven and knitted cloth: namely, strength, comfort, cover without bulk, and weight. They are lighter in weight than double knits but have more covering power. They have increased crosswise stability of weaves but retain the comfort of knits. The fabric in Figure 27–2, which was made on a Weftamatic modified tricot machine, resembles a tricot jersey. It has a 20-

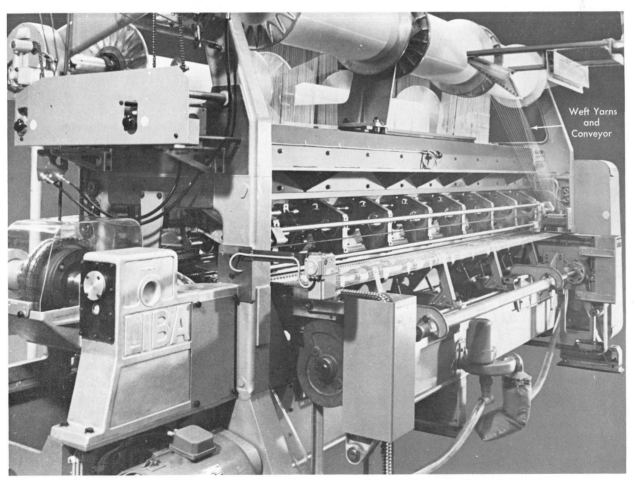

Weft Yarns and Conveyor

Fig. 27–1 Weft-Loc machine. (*Courtesy of Crompton & Knowles Corporation.*)

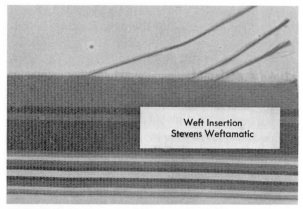

Fig. 27-2 Weftamatic fabric. The raveled yarns are the polyester filling that are inserted in the warp knit stitches.

denier nylon knitting yarn and a 150-denier polyester insertion yarn. The polyester is of several colors, making a horizontal stripe. Warp knits usually have vertical stripes unless printed because by nature the fabric contains only vertical yarns.

Warp Insertion

The insertion of warp yarn into a circular knit structure gives the fabric the vertical stability of woven cloth while retaining the horizontal stretch of knit fabric (Figure 27–3). The cloth is basically a single jersey.

Figure 27–4 shows the circular weft knitting

Fig. 27-4 Warp-insertion machine (*Courtesy of* Textile Industries.)

machine modified by the addition of five warp beams, such as are used on a weaving loom. (Three warp beams can be seen in the center of the picture.) Notice that the warp yarns are carried up to the top of the knitting machine and then down to the knitting needle bar along with the knitting yarns, which come from the spools at the upper part of the machine. The warp yarns interlace with alternate rows of courses. The yarns are *not* laid-in or lain-in and floated. They are actually woven in.

Warp-and-Weft Insertion (*True Knit-Weave*)

Machines that perform warp-and-weft insertion are an interesting aspect of fabric-forming technology but they are still in the trial stage and have yet to prove themselves. A modified circular weft knitting machine that inserts both warp and filling yarns (Figure 27–5) into a single jersey knitted construction was developed in England.[2] A warp shedding device controls the warp yarns

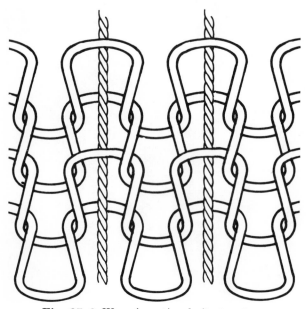

Fig. 27-3 Warp-insertion knit structure.

[2]"Knit-Weave Machines for Improved Fabric Structure," *Textile Industries,* **134**:170 (April 1970).

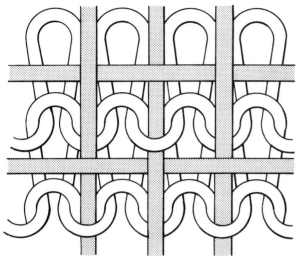

Fig. 27-5 Warp-and-weft-insertion structure.

and a rapier guide inserts the filling yarns. The machine produces fabrics with good recovery from stress—particularly in the filling direction—at speeds comparable to single jersey production.

The Co-We-Nit machine by Carl Mayer is an adaptation of the Raschel warp knitting machine.[3] It inserts both warp and filling into the

[3] Peter Lennox-Kerr, "Fabric Forming," *Textile Industries,* **135:**135 (September 1971).

knit structure. The fabrics tend to be coarse but can be very fine. Fabrics have rows of chains, as in the standard Raschel, with four warp ends between the pillars and weft inserted in a zigzag pattern (Figure 27-6). The advantage of this structure is that lower grade yarns can be used.

Knit-Sew Techniques

The term *knit-sew* (or *stitch-through*) applies to methods that create fabrics by passing a threaded needle from one side of a structure (yarns or fiber web) to the other side, causing interconnected loops to be formed that sufficiently stabilize the structure so it can be called a fabric. It is *knit* because interlocking loops are formed and *sew* because the loops hold the structure together with a chain stitch similar to that made by a child's sewing machine. Knit-sew has had limited use in the United States. The approach taken in this country was wrong. Fabrics were not presented on their own merits but as a means of outproducing looms and knitting machines.

The three groups of knit-sew machines are Malimo, Arachne, and Kraftamatic. All are

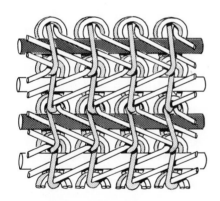

Left, two-guide bar fabric with weft insertion; right, typical structure of a Co-We-Nit fabric.

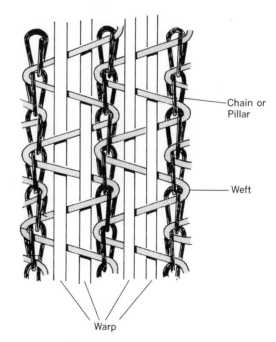

Fig. 27-6 Co-We-Nit. (*Courtesy of* Knitting Times, *official publication of Knitted Outerwear Association.*)

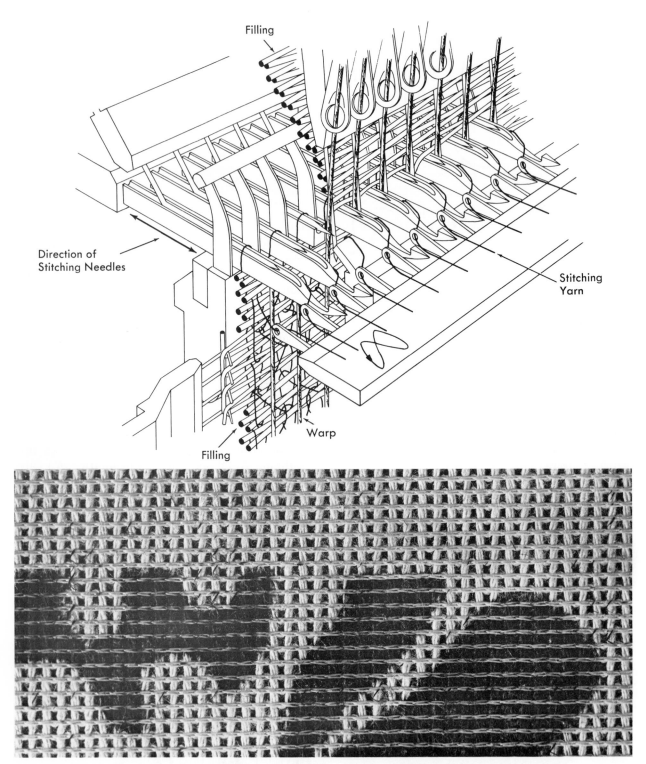

Fig. 27-7 (*Top*) Malimo textile machine. (*Bottom*) Malimo knit-sew fabric.

high-speed machines. The structures to be stitched may be

1. A set of warp yarns resting at right angles on a set of filling yarns and held together by a stitch that most closely resembles a tricot knitting stitch (Malimo)

2. A fibrous bat
a. Stitched by a yarn (Arachne, Maliwatt)

b. Stitched by using the fibers themselves
(Arabeva, Malifleece, Voltex)

3. A substrate base fabric for pile insertion
(Kraftamatic, Malipool, Araloop)

Malimo

Malimo was developed in East Germany in about
1950 by Hendrick Mauersburger, who got the idea
from watching his wife sewing back and forth to
mend a tablecloth. Malimo combines some of the
characteristics of knitting and weaving. The fabric is described in terms of gauge—needles per 1
inch of the needle bar. It is made with three sets
of yarns.

- One set of *warp* yarns is fed from a warp beam
  (Figure 27–7).
- One set of *filling* yarns is threaded into a carrier
  that moves horizontally back and forth across
  the machine while moving forward. The carrier
  fastens the filling yarns to hooks at the sides.
  All filling yarns are, therefore, at an angle with
  the warp rather than perpendicular to them.
- One set of *sewing* yarns is fed from a beam
  through compound needles that sew between
  the warp and across the filling. A guide can
  move the needles sideways so that the yarn is
  wrapped around the warp.

The stitch is called a *tricot stitch* and is nonraveling. A single chain stitch can also be used.
Control of design is limited to the yarns—color,
size, and kind. The construction is better for
heavier and napped-type fabrics.

Two companies—Indian Head and Burlington—were the first producers in the United
States, but Burlington discontinued its operation
in 1970. Draperies and tablecloths are the principal end uses.

Arachne

Arachne is essentially a nonwoven, bulky, lightweight fabric that consists of a fibrous web
stitched through by a binder yarn carried by a
knitting needle (Figure 27–8). The technique was
developed in Czechoslovakia and that country is
still the largest producer. Fabric patterns can be
controlled somewhat as they are in knitting. A
broad range of fibers can be used. The fibers are
carded and then fed, as a sheet or web, into the

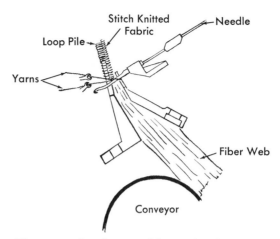

Fig. 27-8 Arachne machine makes loop pile.

Arachne machine, where the web is cross-laid and
then fed to the needle zone. The end uses are
babywear, outerwear and sportswear, thermal
underwear, blankets, and hospital supplies.

There are three machine adaptations:

- *Araloop* produces a loop pile.
- *Arabeva*—the needle grasps a group of fibers on
  one side of the web, pulls them through into a
  loop on the other side, and locks them into a
  previously formed loop. No yarns are used. The
  fibers must be longer than 1.25 inches.
- *Araknit*—a warp-knit rib fabric is knit and simultaneously stitched to a web. Thermodomo
  is the trade name of thermal underwear produced by the Polylock Corporation. It has a
  cotton rib stitched with nylon thread to a polyurethane web.

Fig. 27-9 Kraftamatic machine makes loops on both
sides.

Kraftamatic

Kraftamatic is a way of forming a double-sided pile fabric with locked-in loops (Figure 27-9). The machine was developed in England. It takes up the space of 6 looms but has an output equal to 120 looms.

The technique is a cross between tufting and warp knitting: a sewing machine above and a knitting machine below. The difference between Kraftamatic and tufting is that the loops of Kraftamatic are locked firmly in the backing.

Kraftamatic fabrics can be cut in any direction, have unusual strength, and there is no seam slippage, raveling, or fraying. End uses are diapers, blankets, carpets, and cloth for terry towels.

Pile Fabrics

28

Pile fabrics are three-dimensional fabrics that have yarns or fibers forming a dense cover of the ground fabric. Pile fabrics can be both functional and beautiful:

- A high pile is used to give warmth as either the shell or the liner of coats and jackets and as the liner of gloves and boots.
- High-count fabrics give durability and beauty in carpets, upholstery, and bedspreads.
- Low-twist yarns give absorbency in towels and washcloths.
- Unique uses for pile fabrics are stuffed toys, wigs, paint rollers, buffing and polishing cloths, and decubicare pads for bed-ridden patients.

Interesting effects can be achieved by combinations of

- Cut and uncut pile (Figure 28–1)
- Pile of various heights
- High- and low-twist yarns
- Areas of pile on a flat surface
- Curling and crushing or forcing pile into a position other than upright.

In pile fabrics the pile wears out first, but it is still necessary to have a durable base structure in order to have a satisfactory pile. Tight weave increases the resistance of a looped pile to snagging and of a cut pile to shedding and pulling out. A dense pile will stand erect, resist crushing, and give better cover. Care must be taken in cleaning

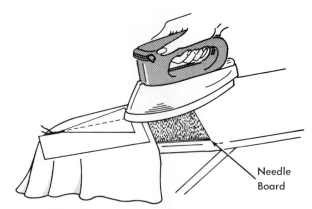

Fig. 28-2 Pressing velvet on "needle" board.

and pressing to keep the pile erect. Cut pile usually looks better if dry-cleaned, but some pile fabrics, such as pinwale corduroy, can be washed if the laundry procedures are suited to the fiber content. All pile fabrics are softer and less wrinkled if tumble dried or line dried on a breezy day. Pressing should be done with a minimum of pressure—or none at all. Flattening of the pile causes the fabric to appear lighter in color. For fabrics such as velvet and velveteen, if pressing is done at home, a "needle" board should be used (Figure 28-2).

Many pile fabrics are pressed during finishing so that the pile slants in one direction, giving an *up and down* (Figure 28–3). Garments cut with the pile *directed up* wear better, give a richer color, and prevent garments from "working up" under a coat or jacket. However, it is more important that the pile be directed the same way in all pieces of a garment. Otherwise, light will be reflected differently and the garment will appear to be made of two colors. Direction of the pile can be determined by running the hand over the fabric.

The chart Comparison of Pile Fabrics gives the methods of making pile fabrics.

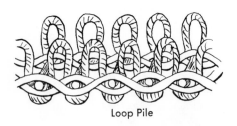

Loop Pile

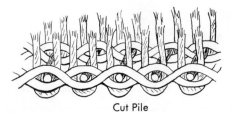

Cut Pile

Fig. 28-1 Cut pile and loop pile: woven fabric.

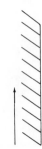

Fig. 28-3 Pile should be directed up.

Method	Types and Kinds	Fabrics—End Uses	Identification
Weaving	1. Filling floats cut and brushed-up 2. Made as double cloth and cut apart 3. Over wires 4. Slack tension	1. Velveteen, corduroy 2. Velvet, velour, fake fur 3. Frieze, Wilton and Velvet carpets 4. Terry cloth, friezé	Ravel adjacent sides Filling pile around warp Warp pile around filling
Knitting	Filling knit: laid-in yarn Sliver knit Warp knit: laid-in yarn	Velour, terry, fake fur Islon, Velcro	Stretchy— Rows of knit stitches on wrong side
Tufting	Low twist yarns punched into substrate	Rugs and carpets Robes, bedspreads Upholstery Fake furs	Rows of stitches (like machine stitches) on wrong side
Flocking	Fibers anchored to substrate	Blankets, jackets Designs on outerwear Runners for car windows	Fiber surface rather stiff
Chenille yarns	Pile-type yarns made by weaving Chenille yarns woven or knitted into fabric	Upholstery Outerwear fabric Rugs	Ravel adjacent yarns and examine novelty yarn

Woven Pile Fabrics

Woven pile fabrics are three-dimensional structures made by weaving an extra set of warp or filling yarns into the ground yarns to make loops or cut ends on the surface (Figure 28–1). The pile is usually ½ inch or less in height. Woven pile is less pliable than knitted or tufted pile and sometimes, when the fabric is folded, the rows of tufts permit the back to show or "grin through."

Filling Pile Fabrics

The pile in filling pile fabrics is not made in the weaving stage but by cutting floats on the surface after weaving (Figure 28-4). Two sets of filling yarns and one set of warp are used. The extra filling yarns float across the ground yarns in weaving. In *corduroy* the floats are arranged in

lengthwise rows; in *velveteen* they are scattered over the base fabric.

Cutting is done by a special machine consisting of guides that lift the individual floating yarns from the ground fabric and of revolving knives that cut the floats (Figure 28–5). A gray-goods corduroy with some of the floats cut is shown in Figure 28–6. When wide-wale corduroy is cut, the guides and knives can be set to cut all the floats in one operation. For pinwale corduroy and velveteen, alternate rows are cut and the cloth must be run through the machine twice. The little cutting knives are dulled very quickly by nylon yarn, and this has presented one of the technical difficulties

Fig. 28-4 Filling pile. Cross section of weave in corduroy.

	Wales per Inch	Ounces per Yard	Characteristics
Pinwale	16–19	5±	Shallow pile, flexible
Feather wale	18–21	7±	Shallow pile, flexible
Midwale	11	10±	Men's and women's outerwear
Wide wale	2–9	12±	Car coats, etc.; toughest corduroy made

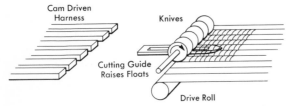

Fig. 28-5 Knives for cutting floats to make corduroy.

in the development of a nylon corduroy. Polyester/cotton corduroy became available in 1976.

After cutting, the surface is brushed crosswise and lengthwise to open and raise the pile and to intermesh the cut yarns from separate floats. It is then singed and waxed. The final pressing lays the pile at a slight angle in one direction, thus giving the up and down to the pile. The back of both velveteen and corduroy is given a slight nap. In *no-wale* corduroy, evidence of wales is nearly eliminated by napping and shearing.

Fig. 28-6 Corduroy gray goods showing some of the floats cut.

Both velveteen and corduroy are made with long staple combed, mercerized cotton for the pile. In good-quality fabrics, long-staple cotton is used for the ground as well. The ground may be made with plain or twill yarn interlacing patterns. With the twill pattern it is possible to have a higher count and, therefore, a denser pile. *Corduroy* can be recognized by lengthwise wales. It is warm, durable, washable, and, if tumble-dried, needs no ironing. *Velveteen* has more body and less drapability than velvet. The pile is not over $\frac{1}{8}$ inch high.

Warp Pile Fabrics

Warp pile fabrics are made with two sets of warp yarns and one set of filling. The extra set of warp makes the pile. Several methods are used.

Double-Cloth Method. Two fabrics are woven, one above the other, with the extra set of yarns interlacing with both fabrics. There are two sheds, one above the other, and two shuttles are thrown with each pick. The fabrics are cut apart while still on the loom by a traveling knife that passes back and forth across the breast beam. With this method of weaving, the depth of the pile is determined by the space between the two fabrics (Figure 28–7).

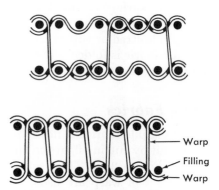

Fig. 28-7 Warp pile: double-cloth method. (*Above*) W-interlacing. (*Below*) V-interlacing.

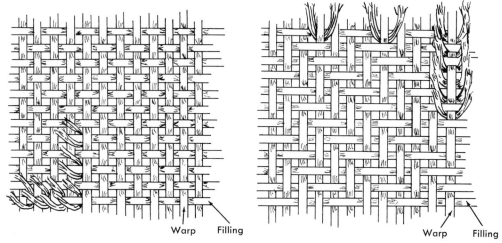

Fig. 28-8 Comparison of filling pile and warp pile. (*Left*) Velvet: warp pile yarn is around ground filling. (*Right*) Velveteen: filling pile yarn is around ground warp.

Velvet was originally made of silk and was a compact, heavy fabric. Today velvet is made of rayon, nylon, or silk filaments with a pile $\frac{1}{16}$ inch high or shorter. (See the Glossary for types.) Velvet is not wound on bolts as are other fabrics but is attached to hooks at the top and bottom of a special bolt so that there are no folds and creases in the fabric.

Velvet and velveteen, the hard-to-tell-apart fabrics, can often be distinguished by fiber content, since velvet is usually made with filaments and velveteen with staple. To tell warp directions in these fabrics, ravel adjacent sides. In velvet the tufts will be interlaced with a filling yarn (Figure 28-8). Another way to tell warp direction is to bend the fabric. In velveteen the pile "breaks" into lengthwise rows, since the filling tufts are around the warp threads. In velvet the pile breaks in crosswise rows, since the warp tufts are around the ground filling yarns. This technique works best with medium- to poor-quality fabrics. To distinguish cotton velvet from velveteen, pull the fabric to determine the filling direction which will have more stretch and then ravel adjacent sides.

Panné velvet is an elegant fabric that has had the pile pressed *flat,* by heavy pressure, in one direction to give high luster. There was a revival of interest in panné velvet in 1968 for sports and casual wear. It was not particularly suited to this use, because it is definitely not an easy-care fabric. If the pile is disturbed or brushed in the other direction, the smooth, lustrous look is destroyed. Panné velvet is made in Europe.

Crushed velvet is made by manually twisting the wet cloth.

Velour is a cotton fabric used primarily for upholstery and draperies. It has a much deeper pile than velveteen and is heavier in weight. (Velour can also be made by knitting.)

Plush may be cotton, wool, or rayon. It has a deeper pile than velour or velvet, usually longer than $\frac{1}{4}$ inch.

Furlike fabrics may be finished by curling, sheering, sculpturing, or printing to resemble different kinds of real fur. (Most furlike fabrics are now made by knitting, see Figure 28-15.)

Over-Wire Method. A single cloth is woven with wires placed across the width of the loom over the

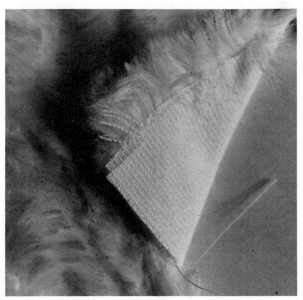

Fig. 28-9 Woven furlike fabric.

Fig. 28-10 Friezé is woven over wires.

ground warp and under the pile warp. Each wire has a knife edge, which cuts all the yarns looped over it as it is withdrawn. Uncut pile can be made over wires without knives or over waste picks of filling yarns. The wires are removed before the cloth is off the loom, and the waste picks are removed after the fabric is off the loom. Friezé and mohair-pile plush are made in this way. Most woven carpets are made over wires.

Friezé, an uncut pile fabric, is an upholstery fabric usually made of mohair, nylon, or cotton with a cotton back. Durability of friezé depends on the closeness of the weave (Figure 28-10).

Slack-Tension Pile Method. The pile in terry cloth is formed by a special weaving arrangement in which three picks are put through and beaten up with one motion of the reed. After the second pick in a set is inserted, there is a let-off motion that causes the threads on the warp-pile beam to slacken, while the threads on the ground-pile beam are held at tension. The third pick is inserted, and the reed moves forward all the way and all three picks are beaten up firmly into the fell of the cloth (Figure 28-11). These picks move along the ground warp and push the pile warp yarns into loops. The loops can be on one side only or on both sides. The height of the loops is determined by the distance the first two picks are left back from the fell of the cloth.

The Ruti terry loop machine can weave fabric 107 inches wide—multiple towels side by side.[1] Terry cloth is highly absorbent cotton fabric used for bath towels, beach robes, and sportswear. Each loop acts as a tiny sponge. When the loops are sheared and the surface is brushed to loosen

[1]T. Hargreaves, "Modern Terry Weaving Machines," Part I, *Textile Industries*, **134**:45 (June 1970); Part II, *Textile Industries*, **135**:83, (February 1971).

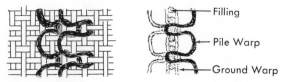

Fig. 28-11 Warp pile: slack-tension method for terry cloth.

and intermesh the fibers of adjacent yarns, the surface becomes more compact and less porous and, therefore, less absorbent than the loop-pile terry. Polyester/cotton terry has blended ground yarns and cotton pile, the pile yarns for absorbency and the polyester ground yarns for strength and durability—especially in selvages.

There is no up and down in terry cloth unless the cloth is printed. Some friezés are made by the terry-cloth method. *Shagbark gingham,* which has spaced rows of loops, is also made this way.

Chenille-Yarn Pile Fabrics

Chenille yarn[2] is made by cutting a specially woven ladderlike fabric into warpwise strips (Figure 28-12 and 28-13). The cut ends of the softly

[2]Chenille yarn is produced only in Spain. "Novelty Yarns," *Textile Industries,* **134**:123 (August 1970).

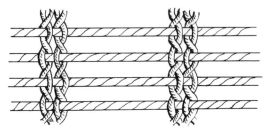

Fig. 28-12 Fabric from which chenille yarn is cut.

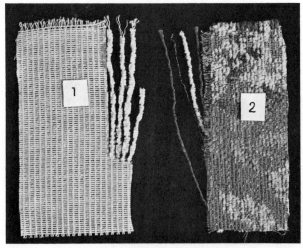

Fig. 28-13 (1) Chenille yarn is made by cutting a specially woven fabric into strips. (2) Fabric made from chenille yarn.

twisted yarns loosen and form a pilelike fringe. This fringed yarn may be woven to make a fabric with pile on one side or on both sides. If the pile is on one side only, the yarn must be folded before it is woven. The yarn is sometimes referred to as a "caterpillar" yarn. Chenille-type yarns can be made by flocking. "Jontille" chenille-type yarns are novelty yarns made by twisting. As the effect yarn is wound around a core yarn and secured by a binder yarn, it is cut at the same time. Chenille yarns are not widely used except in drapery and upholstery fabrics.

Knitted Pile Fabrics

Pile-knit jerseys are made on a modified circular jersey machine. The fabrics look like woven pile but are more pliable and stretchy. The pile surface may consist of (1) cut or uncut loops of yarn

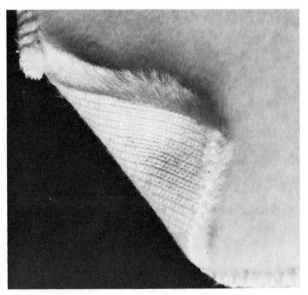

Fig. 28-15 Sliver-knit—furlike fabric.

or (2) fibers (see the following discussion of sliver knits). *Knitted terry cloth* is a loop pile used for beachwear, robes, and babies' towels and washcloths. It is softer and more absorbent than woven terry but does not hold its shape as well. *Velour* is a cut-pile fashion fabric used in men's wear, in women's pant suits, and in robes. Velour is knit with loops that are cut evenly. Then the yarn twist is uncurled to give better coverage and the fabric is dyed, tentered, and steamed. The fabric is 60 inches wide and about $17\frac{1}{2}$ ounces/ yard.

Sliver pile knits are made on a special weft-knit, circular, sliver knitting machine and are called furlike, high-pile, or deep-pile fabrics. They have been available since 1955. Examine Figure 28–14 and notice that yarns are used for the ground; the *sliver*[3] furnishes the fibers for the pile. Fibers from the sliver are picked up by the knitting needles—along with the ground yarns—and are locked into place as the stitch is formed. A denser pile can be obtained with sliver than with yarn because the amount of face fiber is not limited by yarn size or by the distance between yarns (Figure 28–15).

The steps used in finishing furlike fabrics are

• *Heat setting,* which shrinks the ground fabric and expands the diameter of the individual face fibers.

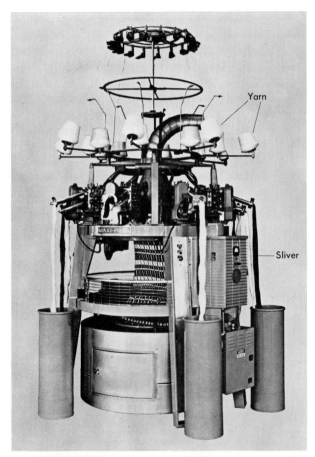

Fig. 28-14 Sliver-knitting machine. (*Courtesy of North American Rockwell.*)

[3]Sliver is an untwisted rope of fiber and is the product of either carding, drawing, or combing (page 129).

- *Tigaring,* a brushing operation that removes surplus fiber from the face of the fabric.
- *Electrifying,* also known as *polishing,* is a brushing operation originally designed to take the crimp out of wool fiber for mouton coats. The fibers are combed first in one direction and then in the other by grooved heated cylinders that rotate at high speed. This may be repeated several times to develop the required finish. The process gives high luster.

The furlike knits are usually made from acrylic, modacrylic, polyester, and olefin fibers or of blends or combinations of these fibers. Dynel modacrylic was originally used for the ground yarns of the pile because its high shrinkage could be used to advantage to make a much more compact pile. Cotton and olefin are now used to reduce the cost.

The surface pile can be made with guard hairs to resemble mink, for example (Figure 13-4); printed to resemble pony, ocelot, or leopard; or printed in other designs for fun furs. Fibers are usually solution-dyed because piece dyeing distorts the pile very badly. Prints are made by screen printing. (The fibers used in these fabrics are usually those that are hard to dye.)

Furlike fabrics are used for the shells (the outer surface) and for liners (the inner surface) of coats and jackets. The difference is mainly one of weight, the shells being heavier than the liners. In actual use the dividing line is less distinct because shell fabrics are used as liners in expensive garments and as shells in low-priced garments. Furlike fabrics are much lighter in weight, are much more pliable, and have better comfort characteristics than real fur. They require no special storage and can be successfully dry-cleaned by using a cold tumble dryer and combing the pile rather than steam pressing it.

Tufted Pile Fabrics

Tufting is a process of making pile fabrics by punching extra yarns into an already woven fabric. The ground fabric ranges from thin cotton sheeting to heavy burlap, and the pile yarns can be of any fiber content. Textured filament nylon yarns gave great impetus to the tufting industry.

Tufting developed in the southeastern United States as a handcraft. It is said that the early settlers used candle wicks and carefully worked them into bedspreads to create interesting textures and designs, and the making of candlewick bedspreads grew into a cottage industry. Hooked rugs were also made by hand in the same way. In the 1930s machinery was developed to convert the hand technique to mass production. Cotton rugs, bedspreads, and robes were produced in many patterns and colors at low cost.

Tufting is done by a series of needles, each carrying a yarn from a series of spools held in a creel (Figures 28-16 and 28-17). The backing fabric is held in a horizontal position, the needles all come down at once and go through the fabric at a predetermined distance, much as a sewing machine needle goes through cloth. Under each needle is a hook that moves forward to hold the loop as the needle is retracted. For cut-loop pile, a knife is attached to the hook and it moves forward as the needles are retracted to cut the loop. The fabric moves forward at a predetermined rate, and the needles move downward again to form another row of tufts.

The yarns must be opened and the fibers teased from the yarn. The tufts are held in place by the "blooming" (untwisting) of the yarn, by shrinkage of the ground fabric in finishing, and frequently by using a coating on the back. In sliver knits the fibers from the sliver are already loose on the surface and a denser pile can be

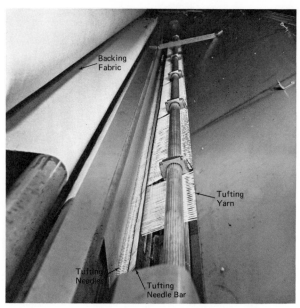

Fig. 28-16 Needle area of tufting machine.

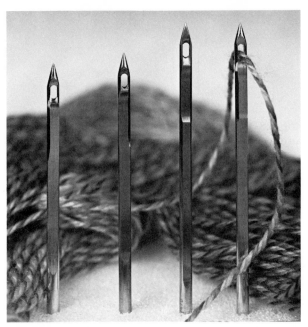

Fig. 28-17 Tufting needles and yarn.

obtained because the amount of face fiber is not limited by yarn size or distance between the yarns as it is in tufting and weaving.

Tufting is a less costly method of making pile fabrics because it is an extremely fast process and involves less labor and time to create new designs. *Tufted apparel fabrics* are made on $\frac{5}{64}$-gauge machines. This gauge is the distance in inches between the tufting needles. Normal tufting specifications on this gauge call for 10 to 11 stitches per inch and a pile height of $\frac{1}{8}$ inch. Tufted fabrics with a woven base are usually $\frac{1}{2}$ inch or less in pile height.

Furlike tufted fabrics are used for shells or liners of coats and jackets (Figure 28-19).

Carpeting of room width size was first made by tufting in 1950; by 1970, 95 per cent of broadloom carpeting was made by tufting. A tufting machine can produce approximately 645 square yards of carpeting per hour compared to an Axminster loom, which can weave about 14 square yards per

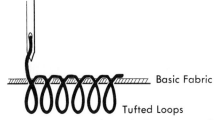

Fig. 28-18 How tufting stitches are made.

Fig. 28-19 Tufted fabric. Notice machine-like stitches on wrong side.

hour. Variations in texture can be made by loops of different heights. Cut and uncut tufts can be combined. Tweed textures are made by the use of different-colored plys in the tufting yarns. New techniques of dyeing have been developed to produce colored patterns or figures in which the color penetrates the tufts completely. In carpeting, a latex coating is put on the back to help hold the tufts in place (Figure 28-20).

Tufted bed-size blankets can be made in two minutes. In 1960, Barwich Mills, Inc. started pilot-plant operations to make tufted blankets. This end use combines pile construction with napped finish. It has the advantage over traditional blanket fabric of maintaining a strong, firm ground fabric, since the fibers are teased from the pile yarns to create the nap. Also, the thickness of the blanket is determined by the height of the pile rather than by the thickness of the yarn. Tufted blankets have not been successful in the United States but are being produced in Europe.

Tufted upholstery fabric is made in both cut and uncut pile.

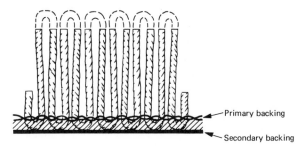

Fig. 28-20 Tufted Carpet. Tufts punched through primary backing. Secondary backing is bonded to primary backing to lock in pile.

Flocked Pile Fabrics: A Finish

Flock are very short fibers attached to the surface of a fabric by an adhesive to make a pilelike design or fabric.[4] Flocking was used as a technique for wall decoration in the fourteenth century. Short silk fibers were applied to freshly painted walls by a bellows. The technique was revived in the 1970s. Flocked walls give excellent noise reduction—they are three times quieter than concrete block.[5] Flock can be applied to many base materials: cloth, foam, wood, metal, and concrete. Flock can be applied to an adhesive film that can then be laminated to a base fabric.

Cotton and rayon flocks have been used for dress and curtain fabrics since 1920. Interest in flocking was intensified in the 1960s with the development of new, improved adhesives[6] that will withstand repeated washings or dry cleanings. The new emulsions are not stiff and thick as were the early adhesives; they have good flexibility, durability, drape, and hand. They are also colorless and free of undesirable odor. Flocking may become an important competitor of tufting as a way of making pile fabrics.

Rayon fibers are inexpensive and easy to cut, and are thus used in large quantities. Rayon can be made fire-retardant. Nylon has excellent abrasion resistance and durability. Acrylics, polyesters, and olefins can also be used. Fibers for flocking must be straight, not crimped. As the fiber length is increased, the denier also must be increased so that the fiber will stand up straight in the fabric. Fibers that are cut square at the ends will anchor more firmly in the adhesive (Figure 28-21). Adhesives were for many years the "bottleneck" to satisfactory flocking. Most of the problems have been overcome. Over half of the adhesives used are aqueous-based acrylic resins.

Flocked products are used in all areas of textiles. The largest use is in household items, the second largest use is children's clothing, and women's clothes rank third. The potential for flocked fabrics is great. T. W. Qualman says:

[4]"Flocking Techniques Defy Traditional Textile Methods," *Modern Textiles Magazine,* **49**:22 (June 1968).
[5]F. H. Foster, "Flockers Are on the Move Again," *Textile World,* **120**:94 (June 1970).
[6]R. C. Smucker, "Adhesives in Flocking: The Acrylates," *Modern Textiles Magazine,* **49**:25 (June 1968).

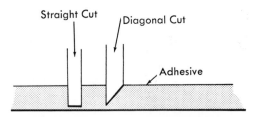

Fig. 28-21 Flock with square-cut ends anchors more firmly.

We can impart a pleasing flannel surface to a rubber bed sheet, make burlap with a hand like the most luxurious suede, or transform a whole boat deck into one continuous, soft, cool, sure-footed carpet. We impart beauty and styling to foundation garments for the ladies and at the same time engineer the adhesive and design areas to add control where desired.

Chenille-type yarns have been made by flocking. Fleece and furlike fabrics utilizing two pile heights and guard hair can be made.

One of the interesting new products is the Vellux blanket, a revolutionary product made by West-Point Pepperell. The blanket is made of soft nylon fibers electronically bonded to two layers of polyurethane foam that are permanently sealed to nylon scrim (Figure 28-22). The blanket is so light in weight that users are hardly aware of it. It is "super" warm, and can withstand over 50 washings and dryings with no ill effect. The price is competitive with other types of blankets. Some producers have predicted that this blanket may make conventional blankets obsolete.

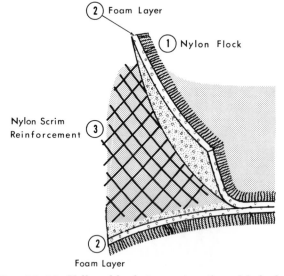

Fig. 28-22 Vellux blanket construction. Made by flocking.

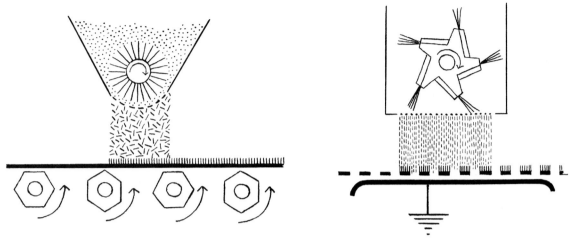

Fig. 28-23 Flocking process. (*Left*) Mechanical flocking. (*Right*) Electrostatic flocking. (*Courtesy of the Monsanto Textiles Company.*)

1. Flock is sifted onto the adhesive coated fabric. Vibration of beater bars causes those fibers that do not fall flat against the adhesive to stand erect, and, once erect, the fibers penetrate fully into the adhesive. The erect fibers help the free fibers to align themselves and to work down to the adhesive.
2. Most units consist of 6 to 20 beater bars and one or more sifting hoppers and run as high as 10 or more yards per minute.
3. Simpler in design, usually less expensive, and most widely used in the United States.

1. Flock passes through an electrostatic field that orients the fibers. In coating irregular surfaces, the lines of force are always perpendicular to the substrate, so this method is best for three-dimensional surfaces.
2. Most units operate at speeds of 3 to 5 yards per minute.
3. Can "up-flock" as well, so both sides of a fabric can be flocked.
4. Requires generators, proper insulation, gives better end-on-end fiber orientation, and higher densities are possible.

Some of the major end uses of flocking are

- Velvets for furniture
- Brocaded velvets for evening wear
- Draperies, bedspreads, blankets
- Flocked designs on dress fabrics
- Flocked carpets
- Flocked wall coverings for esthetics and noise reduction
- Automotive fabrics
- Toys, books, shoes, hats
- Industrial uses such as conveyor belts and air filters
- Flocked lawns—in the future.

The two basic methods of applying the flock fibers are mechanical and electrostatic. In both processes the flock is placed in an erect position, and after flocking, the fabric is sent to an oven to dry the adhesive. A comparison of the two methods is given in Figure 28–23. Overall flocking or space flocking can be done by either method. The newest development utilizes a rotating screen to deposit the flock.

Comparisons of Look-alike Fabrics

Pile fabrics, no matter how they are made, are called by woven fabric names. A recognition of the construction process may help to evaluate a fabric, at the point of sale, in terms of expected performance, realistic cost, and care required.

In all woven and tufted fabrics, yarns make the pile surface and they must be untwisted by a finishing process to obtain a fiber surface. Both of these techniques also make fabrics with uncut loops. Knitted pile fabrics have the pile surface made from yarns or fibers. Flocked fabrics have the pile surface made directly from fibers.

Napped fabrics (see page 268) often are confused with pile fabrics.

Furlike Fabrics—Used for Shells, Liners, Decubicare Pads, and Accent Rugs

	Woven warp pile	Sliver knit	Tufted
Fibers used	Cotton ground; wool, acrylic, rayon, polyester pile	Cotton, olefin, or mod-acrylic ground. Acrylic, modacrylic pile	Cheesecloth or soft filled sheeting substrate, acrylic, mod-acrylic pile
Cost	Most expensive	Variable	Least expensive
Characteristics	Pile firmly held in place: tendency to "grin-through" in low-count fabrics	Most widely used Dense underfibers and guard hairs possible, like real fur. Denser surface possible	Mostly used for sheepskin-type goods. Blooming of yarns and shrinkage of ground holds tufts in place

Carpets—Residential, Commercial, and Automotive

	Woven warp pile	Filling knit Raschel knit	Chenille yarns	Tufted	Flocked
Types and kinds	Wilton Axminster Velvet	Laid-in yarn	Usually woven to order	Most widely used. All kinds of textures. Tufts held in by double back	Not very durable. Limited pile height.
Cost	Most expensive	Raschel knits expensive	Expensive	Inexpensive	Low cost

Velour

	Woven warp pile	Filling knit—jersey	Warp knit
Fiber content	Cotton	Cotton, polyester	Nylon/Arnel
Characteristics	Heavy fabric, durable	Medium weight, soft, drapable	Medium to heavy weight
End uses	Upholstery, draperies	Robes, shirts	Robes

Velvet

	Woven warp pile	Tufted	Flocked
Fibers	Filament yarns, cotton	Nylon	Nylon
Characteristics	Filament—dressy, pile flattens. Cotton or nylon—durable. Rich looking—heavy weight fabric	Pile not held in as firmly as woven, less expensive	Does not flatten. Least expensive. Since process is done by finishing no way to tell if flock is permanent
End uses	Filament—apparel. Cotton, nylon—upholstery	Upholstery	Upholstery, draperies, bedspreads

Terry Cloth

	Slack-tension weave	Filling knit—jersey
Characteristics	Usually cotton. Holds its shape	All fibers. Soft, stretchy. Cotton does not hold its shape well. Very pliable
End uses	Towels, washcloths, robes	Baby towels and washcloths. Baby sleepers, adult sportswear, socks

Figured Fabrics
and Piqué

29

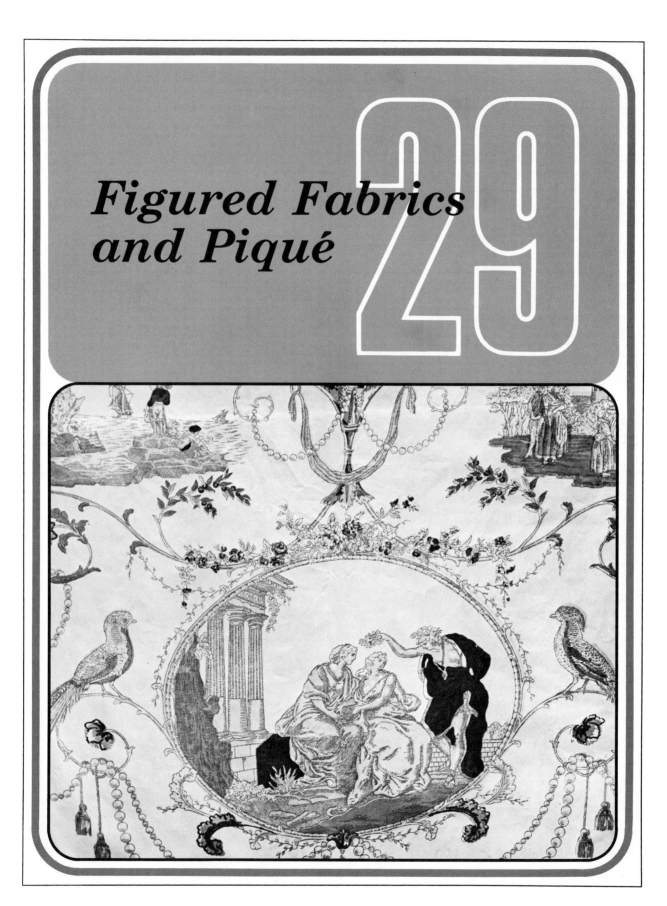

225

Figured fabrics may be structural designs or applied designs. *Structural designs* are woven or knitted in the fabric. *Applied designs* are finishes put on an already woven or knitted fabric. Stripes, checks, and plaids woven in or printed on are not considered in this chapter.

The techniques used to obtain figured fabrics vary in complexity and influence the cost of fabric. Some techniques result in permanent designs, whereas others are less permanent. Recognition of the technique used should be helpful in selecting the appropriate fabric. It may help in naming a fabric correctly although in today's market fabric names are not very precise.

A comparison of structural and applied designs are listed in the following chart.

Comparison of Structural and Applied Designs

Structural Designs	Applied Designs
Usually more expensive because decisions must be made farther in advance of market	Usually less expensive
Permanent design	Permanent or temporary
Figures are always on grain (circular knit Jacquards are the exception)	Figures may be off-grain
Kinds and types	
Woven—Jacquard, dobby, extra yarns, swivel dots, lappet designs	Color prints Flocked Embroidered Burnt out Embossed
Knitted—Jacquard single knits, Jacquard double knits Lace	
Typical Fabrics	
Damask, brocade, tapestry, shirting madras, dotted swiss, matelassé	Flock dotted swiss, embroidered linen, batiste

Structural Designs

Woven Figures

Woven figures are made by changing the interlacing pattern in the design from that of the background. The interlacing pattern is controlled by the warp threads in the harnesses. In a 3-harness loom there are 3 possible arrangements of the warp yarns; in a 4-harness loom there are as many as 12 different arrangements. As the number of harnesses increases the number of possible different interlacings also increases. But there is a limit to the number of harnesses that can be used efficiently. Consider the number of interlacings needed to make a figure: if the figure is $\frac{1}{4}$ inch in length, there will need to be 20 different interlacings in an 80-square cloth; if the figure is $\frac{1}{2}$ inch long on a nylon satin background (320×140), there would need to be 70 different interlacings. To make woven figures by mass production, therefore, special looms or special attachments to the loom are necessary.

Jacquard Weaves. Large-figured designs, which require more than 25 different arrangements of the warp yarns to complete one repeat design, are woven on the Jacquard loom (Figure 29–1). Each warp is controlled independently by punched cards that are laced together in a continuous strip. As the cards move over the loom, all the warp yarns are raised by rods attached to them. When the rods hit the cards, some will go through the holes and thus raise the warp yarns; others will remain down. In this manner the shed is

Fig. 29-1 Jacquard loom for weaving large-figured fabrics. (*Courtesy Crompton & Knowles Corporation.*)

Fig. 29-2 Woven-tapestry picture.

Fig. 29-4 Brocade.

formed for the passage of the filling yarn. Figure 29-2 shows a picture woven with fine silk yarns on a Jacquard loom. Notice that there is no repeat of the pattern from top to bottom or from side to side. The repeat would be another picture. Figure 29-3 was made by a textile engineering student as a class exercise. It has a repeat both crosswise and lengthwise.

Fabrics made on a Jacquard loom are damask, brocade, and tapestry. *Damask* has satin floats on a satin background, the floats in the design being in the opposite direction from those in the background. It is made from all kinds of fibers and in many different weights for apparel and home furnishings. Quality and durability are dependent on high count. Low-count damask is not durable because the long floats rough up, snag, and shift during use. *Brocade* has satin floats on a plain, ribbed, or satin background (Figure 29-4). Bro-

Fig. 29-3 Special problem exercise (by textile student) on threading a Jacquard loom.

cade with a satin ground differs from damask in that the floats in the design are more varied in length and are often of several colors. Originally, *tapestry* was an intricate handwoven picture, usually a wall hanging that took years to weave. The Jacquard tapestry is mass produced for upholstery, handbags, and the like. It is a complicated structure consisting of two or more sets of warp and two or more sets of filling interlaced so that the face warp is never woven into the back and the back filling does not show on the face. Upholstery tapestry is durable if warp and filling yarns are comparable. Very often, however, fine yarns are combined with coarse yarns, and when these wear off, they release the floats as long loose strings. Fabrics that have figures made by floating yarns on a background that is typical for certain fabric are called by the background name; for example, figured gingham, figured denim, figured crepe, and the like.

Wilton rugs are figured pile fabrics made on a Jacquard loom. These rugs, once considered imitations of Oriental rugs, are so expensive to weave that the tufting industry has found a way to create similar figures by printing techniques.

Dobby Weaves. Small-figured designs, which require less than 25 different yarn arrangements to complete one repeat of the design, are made on a loom with a dobby attachment—usually referred to as a dobby loom (Figure 29-5).

The weave pattern consists of a plastic tape with punched holes (Figure 29-6). These tapes resemble, somewhat, the rolls for a player piano. The holes control the raising and lowering of the

Fig. 29-5 Loom with a dobby attachment.

warp yarns. Many of the designs made on the dobby loom are small geometric figures.

Bird's-eye has a small diamond-shaped filling-float design with a dot in the center that resem-

Fig. 29-6 Plastic punched tape that controls warp shedding. (*Courtesy Crompton & Knowles Corporation.*)

bles the eye of a bird. This design was originally used in costly white silk fabric for ecclesiastical vestments. At one time it was widely used for towels and diapers. *Huck* or *huck-a-back* has a pebbly surface made by filling floats. It was used primarily in face towels.

Shirting madras has small satin float designs on a ribbed or plain ground. See the Glossary for descriptions of other fabrics called madras.

Extra Yarn Weaves. When yarns of different colors or different sizes than the background are wanted for a figure, extra yarns are woven. The figure portion has warp or filling floats. When not used in the figure the extra yarns float across the back of the fabric and are usually cut off during finishing. In handwoven fabrics the warp yarns can be manipulated by hand and the extra yarns can be laid in where they are wanted by using small shuttles. But in power looms, an attachment that can be operated automatically must be used.

Extra warp yarns are wound on a separate

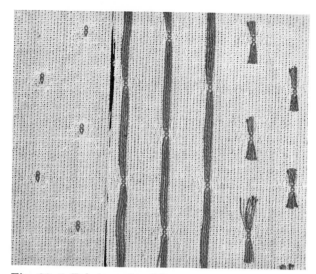

Fig. 29-7 Fabric made with extra warp yarns. (*Left*) Face side of fabric. (*Right*) Wrong side, before and after clipping.

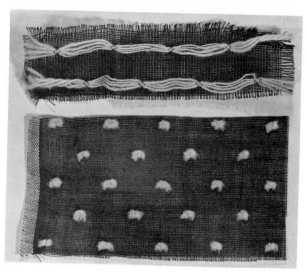

Fig. 29-8 Dotted swiss, extra filling yarns: before and after clipping.

beam and threaded into separate heddles. The extra yarns interlace with the regular filling yarns to form a design and float above the fabric until needed for the repeat. The floats are then clipped close to the design or clipped long enough to give an eyelash effect. Figure 29-7 shows a fabric before and after clipping.

Extra filling yarns are inserted in several ways, and many of the fabrics have small dot designs called dotted swiss. *Dotted swiss* is a name used rather loosely to refer to clipped dot, "tied" dot, or paste dot designs on sheer fabrics.

Clipped dot designs are made with low-twist filling yarns inserted by separate shuttles. The shedding is done so that the extra yarns interlace

with some warp and float across the back of others. Clipped spots are woven on a box loom that has a wire along the edge to hold the extra yarns so that they need not be woven in the selvage. Figure 29-8 shows a clipped dotted swiss before and after clipping.

True dotted swiss or swivel dots are made on a loom that has an attachment holding tiny shuttles. The fabric is woven face down to keep the shuttles and extra yarns above the ground fabric. Each shuttle carrying the extra yarn goes four times around the warp yarns in the ground fabric and then the yarn is carried along the surface to the next spot. The yarn is sheared off between the spots (Figure 29-9).

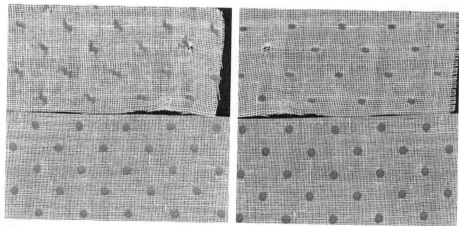

Fig. 29-9 Dotted swiss showing right and wrong sides of swivel dot and paste dot. Swivel dot is at the top. Wrong sides are shown at left.

Knitted Figures

In filling knits, figures are made by using a combination of stitches—knit, purl, tuck, miss, and transfer—or by using different colored yarns in the same stitch as in the background. A Jacquard mechanism is used to position the needles. Figure 29–10 shows a punch card that can be attached to a plain jersey flat bed needle frame to knit the fabric shown. Yarns, when not used in the figures, float across the back of the fabric or are knitted on the back as horizontal stripes or in a scrambled colored area called *bird's-eye*. Intarsia designs do not have floating yarns on the back (see page 191).

Fabrics are usually called Jacquard single

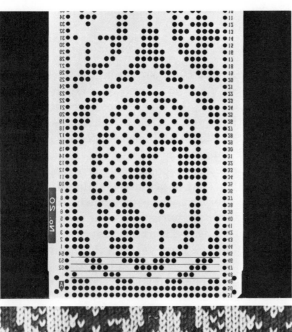

Fig. 29-10 Punched card and figured knit.

knits or Jacquard double knits. Jacquard knits may present problems in cutting since they are made on a circular machine and the yarns (and figures) spiral rather than being perfectly straight. Printed tricots are more common than structural designs.

Raschel knits, except for lace, do not have figures; the design is usually a zigzag of novelty yarns (see page 204).

Applied Designs

Applied figures, with the exception of embroidery, are much cheaper to produce than structural figures. Effects not possible with weaving or knitting are also made. Color prints are discussed in Chapter 38, flocked figures are discussed on page 222, burnt-out figures are discussed on page 267, and embossed figures are discussed on page 266.

Embroidery

Embroidery is a hand or machine technique. It is the art of decorating a fabric with a needle and thread.

The machine embroidery operation is similar to making fancy stitches on a sewing machine with zigzag stitches of various lengths very close together. The Schiffli embroidery machine is a frame 10 to 15 yards long (Figure 29–11) with 684 or 1,026 needles, respectively.

The designer makes a careful sketch of the embroidery pattern, which is enlarged six times and is used as a guide for punching holes in a roll of thin, flexible cardboard. The perforated roll guides the placement of each stitch in the automated machine. Some embroidered fabrics are shown in Figures 29–12 and 29–13. Embroidering can be done on any kind of fabric.

Embroidered figures are very durable, often outlasting the ground fabric. It is expensive compared to the same fabric unembroidered. Like other applied designs the figure may or may not be on grain.

Eyelet is a widely used embroidery fabric. Small round holes are cut in the fabric, and stitching is done completely around the hole. The closeness and amount of stitching, as well as the quality of the background fabric, vary tremendously.

Fig. 29-11 Schiffli embroidery machine.

Fig. 29-13 (*Right*) Embroidered linen. (*Left*) Printed to look like embroidery.

Eyelet fabrics are a perennial favorite. In 1978 a lower cost fabric which looks like eyelet came on the market. The technique used to make this fabric is called expanded foam. A colored foam substance is printed on the fabrics. The substance expands during processing to give a three dimensional effect. Initially the pattern simulated hand embroidery stitches such as the cross stitch. The effect seems to be durable.

Fig. 29-12 Embroidery used in purse. (*Courtesy of Lesco Lona.*)

Piqué

The word *piqué* comes from the French word meaning "quilted"; the raised effect in these fabrics is similar to that in quilts.

Piqué weave produces a fabric with ridges, called wales or cords, that are held up by floats on the back. The wales vary in width. *Wide-wale piqué* (0.25 inch) is woven with 20 or more warp yarns in the face of the wale and then two warps in between. *Pinwale piqué* (0.05 inch) is a six-warp wale with two consecutive filling yarns floating across the back of the odd-numbered wales and then woven in the face of the even-numbered wales. The next two consecutive picks alternate with the first two by floating across the back of the even-numbered wales. Figure 29–14 shows a six-warp pinwale piqué. Figure 29–15 shows the right and wrong side of a piqué fabric.

Stuffer yarns are laid under the ridges in the better-quality fabrics to emphasize the roundness or quilted effect, and their presence or absence is one way of determining quality. The stuffer yarns are not woven in the main part of the fabric and may be easily removed when analyzing a swatch of fabric. Piqué fabrics, depending on the complexity of the design, are woven on either a dobby or Jacquard loom.

Fabric Descriptions. Cords or wales usually run in the *lengthwise* direction, with the exception of bird's-eye and bull's-eye piqués, in which the cords run crosswise. Cord fabrics have a definite right and wrong side. The fabric tears more easily in

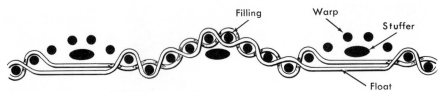

Filling   Warp   Stuffer   Float

Fig. 29-14 Six-warp pinwale piqué.

the lengthwise direction. If there are stuffer yarns, it is especially difficult to tear the fabric crosswise. In wear, the floats on the wrong side usually wear out first.

Piqué fabrics are more resistant to wrinkling and have more body than flat fabrics, and for these reasons they have less need to be given a resin finish for wash-and-wear. Piqué fabrics should be ironed on the wrong side because the beauty of the fabric is in the roundness of the cord and pressing on the right side will flatten it.

Fabrics in this group are called piqué, with the exception of a wide-wale fabric called Bedford cord. Cord weave may be combined with other

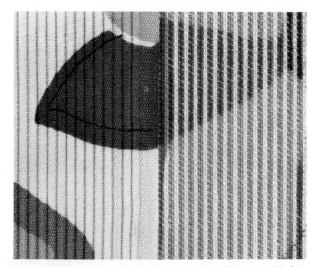

Fig. 29-15 Piqué. (*Left*) Right side of fabric. (*Right*) Reverse side of fabric. Note stuffer yarns.

weaves to produce such fabrics as seersucker piqué, crepe piqué, and novelty piqué.

Bedford cord is a heavy fabric with warp cords. It is used for slacks, trousers, uniforms, and upholstery. It is made with carded cotton yarns, woolen or worsted yarns, rayon or acetate, or combinations. The wales are wide and stuffer yarns are usually present.

Piqué is lighter in weight than Bedford cord and has a narrower wale. The better-quality fabrics are made with long-staple, combed, mercerized yarns and have one stuffer yarn. The carded yarn piqués are made without the stuffer and are sometimes printed.

Bird's-eye piqué has a tiny "eye-shaped" design formed by the wavy arrangements of the cords and by the use of stuffer yarns. *Bull's-eye piqué* is made like bird's-eye but has a much larger design. Both these fabrics have crosswise rather than lengthwise cords. They are used for collars and cuffs, hats, and dresses.

Fabrics Called Piqué but not Piqué Weave. A honeycomb weave fabric with a wafflelike design is often incorrectly called waffle piqué. A skipped-dent (see page 153), sheer, plain-weave fabric is incorrectly called dimity piqué. Plain-weave cotton fabric, embossed to look like piqué or bird's-eye piqué, was widely used in the 1960s for collars and cuffs on children's dresses.

Swiss piqué and French piqué are two stitches used to make a polyester double knit. They are called piqué double knits and look a bit like bird's-eye.

Double Cloth and Multicomponent Fabrics

Double cloth and multicomponent fabrics tend to be heavier and have more body than single cloths. Double cloth is a woven fabric made from three or more sets of yarns, and double knit is made from two or more yarns. Multicomponent fabrics are made from previously constructed fabric combined with a foam, a fiber batt, or another fabric.

Double Cloth

Three types of woven double cloth are

1. True double cloth—coat fabrics: melton, kersey, beaver, saxony, whitney, montagnac.

2. Double cloth—dress and suit fabrics: matelassé, brocatelle.

3. Double-faced—blanket cloth, double satin ribbon, Sunbac, silence cloth.

True Double Cloth

True double cloth is made with five sets of yarns: two fabrics woven one above the other on the same loom with the fifth yarn (warp) interlacing with both cloths (Figure 30–1). True double cloth can be separated by pulling out the yarns holding the two cloths together. It can be used in reversible garments such as capes and skirts. Edges can be "self-finished" by separating the two cloths for about $\frac{3}{4}$ inch at the cut edges and folding both cut edges toward each other and into the center. Slip stitching or top stitching completes the edge.

Fig. 30-1 True double cloth made with five sets of yarns.

Fig. 30-2 Double cloth. (*Lower portion*) Right side of cloth. (*Upper portion*) Reverse side of cloth.

Seam allowances can be concealed between the two cloths in a similar manner.

True double cloth is expensive to make but it is more pliable than the same weight fabric using two sets of heavy yarns.

Double Cloth

Double cloth is made with four sets of yarns woven separately on the same loom except that the warp and filling of one cloth change positions with the warp and filling of the other cloth (crisscross), locking the two cloths at intervals as required by the design. In between the crisscross points, the two cloths are completely separate (Figure 30–2).

Double-Faced

Double-faced fabrics are made with three sets of yarns: two warp and one filling or two sets of

Fig. 30-3 Double-faced blanket. One set of warp and two sets of filling.

filling and one set of warp. Blankets, satin ribbon, interlinings, and suitings are often made using this process (Figure 30–3).

Double Knit

Two yarns are knitted together as one in plain, rib, or purl knits or two yarns are knitted separately in some areas and together in others (Figure 30–4). Double knits are discussed in detail on page 190.

Fig. 30–5 Pinsonic Thermal Joining machine quilts seven times as fast as conventional quilting machines. Quilted layers are welded together by heat from ultrasonic vibrations. (*Courtesy of Branson Sonic Power Company.*)

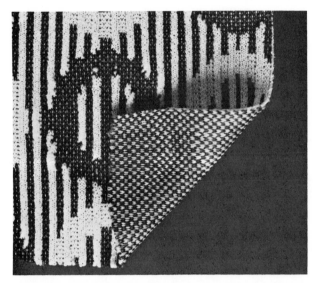

Fig. 30–4(a) Polyester double knit. Notice bird's-eye effect on wrong side.

Fig. 30–4(b) Polyester double knit. Knitted separately in some areas.

Multicomponent Fabrics

Quilted Fabrics

Quilted fabrics are multicomponent fabrics consisting of one fabric above and one below a layer of fiberfill, wadding, or batting. The three components are held together by machine stitching with thread or by stitchless sewing in which the layers are fused by heat or adhesives or they may consist of two layers of fabric. Figure 30–5 shows a Pinsonic Thermal Joining machine that "sews" by heat-sealing thermoplastic materials by ultrasonic vibrations. Figure 30–6 shows Pinsonic fabric.

Most quilted fabric is made by stitching with thread. Twistless nylon monofilament thread is often used because of its strength and abrasion resistance and because it is transparent and picks up the colors of the fabric. Quilting is usually done in squares, or in straight or wavy lines. In upholstery and expensive quilts and comforters or bedspreads, the stitching is done outlining printed figures. This is a hand process (machine quilting by hand) and thus makes the fabric more costly. A cost comparison of thread and ultrasonic quilting machines in 1973 was

Quilting Machine	Ultrasonic
1 yard per minute @ $6.16	10 yards per minute @ $1.44
Production cost 10¢ per yard	Production cost 3¢ per yard

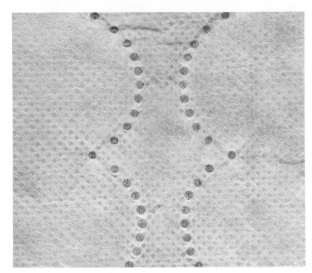

Fig. 30-6 Mattress pad. Two layers of nonwoven fabric, fiberfill batt joined by Pinsonic Thermal Joining Machine.

Any fabric can be used for the shell or covering. A fashion fabric is always used on one side. If the article is reversible or needs to be durable or beautiful on both sides, two fashion fabrics are used. If the fabric is to be lined or used as a chair covering or bedspread, the under layer is often white or black cheesecloth or a nonwoven fabric.

The wadding or batting may be foam, cotton, down, or fiberfill of acetate or polyester. Fiberfill (see page 112) is a modified fiber type with crimp designed to help maintain fluffiness and air space. The polyester fiberfill is more expensive than acetate but it is more washable than the others.

The disadvantage of quilting is that threads break when one sits in the garment or on the bed,

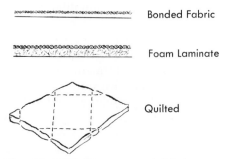

Bonded Fabric

Foam Laminate

Quilted

Fig. 30-7 Multicomponent fabric.

or from abrasion. Broken threads are unsightly and with cotton, wool, down or acetate fiberfill, the loose fiber is no longer held in place. Beauty of fabric is important for all end uses. For ski jackets and snowsuits, a closely woven water- and wind-repellent fabric is desirable; for comforters, resistance to slipping off the bed is important; for upholstery, durability and resistance to soil are important. Figure 30-7 shows machine-quilted fabric as well as bonded and laminated fabrics.

Bonded Fabrics

Bonded or laminated fabrics consist of two fabrics made to adhere together by an adhesive or a flame-foam process, shown in Figure 30-8. The terms *bonded* and *laminated* are used somewhat interchangeably.

The first bonded fabric (1958) was an inexpensive wool flannel bonded to acetate jersey with an adhesive. In the early stages, bonding was a way to deplete inventories of tender or lightweight fabrics. Some converters were marginal operators

Fig. 30-8 Bonded herringbone fabric and label for coin-bonded fabrics.

The FLA quality mark.

Fig. 30-9 Quality symbol of Fabric Laminators Association.

who were not interested in quality. A bonder could buy two hot rolls discarded by finishers and be in business. The fabric could be stretched as it went through the rollers. Consequently, many problems were associated with these bonded fabrics. The layers separated (delaminated) or shrank unevenly. There were problems with colors. All these things led to the establishment of quality controls set up by the Tricot Institute, the Fabric Laminators Association, and the Foam Fashion Institute. A quality-control symbol was adopted (Figure 30-9), which serves as a guarantee that the fabric has met standards for care, shrinkage, stiffening, and delamination. The consumer must rely on trade names[1] and examination of fabric and/or garments. The National Institute of Dry Cleaning has recommended a test to determine the durability of the laminate. The fabric is soaked for 10 minutes in perchloroethylene. If the face and back do not separate, the fabric should withstand normal dry cleaning.

The clingier, drapier fashions of the 1970s led to a decline in the use of bonded fabrics, and bonded fabrics have suffered from the competition of double knits.

Some advantages and limitations are given in the chart.

Backing. Knits are usually used as the backing fabric. Knit will give with the stresses applied to the face fabric. Acetate tricot, the least expensive, is most often used. Other fabrics used are triacetate and nylon. Loosely woven scrims of cotton are sometimes used. The color of the backing can be a decorative feature in bonded laces.

Two methods of bonding are used (Figure 30-10):

[1] Some trade names are Coin, Celabond, and Certifab.

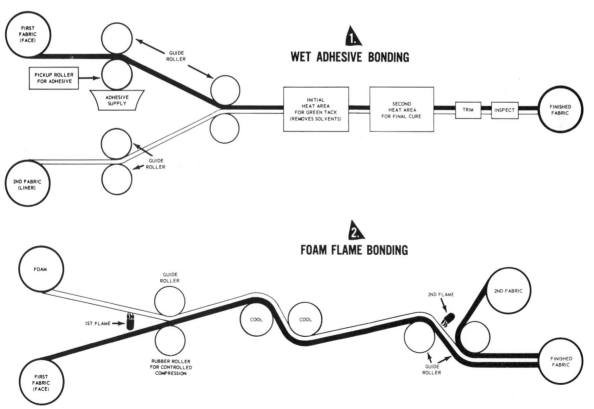

Fig. 30-10 Two basic methods for producing bonded textiles. (*Courtesy of* American Fabrics.)

1. Wet-adhesive method:
Aqueous acrylic adhesive
Solvent urethane adhesive.

2. Flame-foam method.

In the *wet-adhesive method,* the adhesive is applied to the underside of the face fabric, and the liner fabric is joined by being passed through rollers. It is heated twice, once to drive out solvents and to give a preliminary cure, and a second time to effect a permanent bond.

In the *foam-flame process,* polyurethane foam acts as the adhesive. Foam laminates consist of a layer of foam covered by another fabric or between two fabrics. The foam is made tacky first on one side and then on the other by passing the foam under a gas flame. The final thickness of the foam is about 15/1,000 of an inch. This method gives more body but reduces the drapability of the fabric.

Another foam process generates the foam at the time it is to be applied, flowing it onto the cloth, and curing on the cloth. Foam laminates were first visualized as thermal garments for outdoor workers because they are light in weight but warm. Foams were quilted to lining fabrics for a lining, interlining combination. In 1958 they were introduced in inexpensive fabrics primarily as a way to use up undesired fabric (yardage that did not sell). The first fabric to sell in volume was a dress-weight jersey laminated to foam and made up in spring coats. This was so successful that coats were made for all-purpose uses.

Foam laminates today are made using all kinds and qualities of fabric with many different thicknesses of foam.

Bonded or Laminated Fabrics

Advantages	Limitations
Less costly fabrics are upgraded.	Top-quality fabrics are not bonded.
Self-lining gives comfort.	Backing does not prevent bagging so a lining may be needed.
Stabilized if good quality.	Uneven shrinkage* possible.
Reduces time in sewing.	May be bonded "off-grain."
Interfacings may be eliminated.	May delaminate.*
Underlinings, stay-stitching, and seam finishing are not needed.	Hems, darts, and facings are stiff and boardy.
	Do not hold sharp creases.
*These are the two major problems.	

Lace, Leno Weave, and Narrow Fabrics

Lace

Lace is the third basic method of making fabric from yarns. Weaving has interlaced yarns, knitting has interlooped yarns, and lace has intermeshed yarns—yarns twisted around each other.

Lace has open spaces between and around solid areas of cloth. *Lace* is handmade or machine-made on special lace machines, or on Raschel knitting machines. Lacelike fabrics are made by weaving or knitting, and imitation lace fabrics are made by finishing fabrics in lacy patterns by printing or flocking (Figure 31-1).

The term *lace* probably comes from the strings that were used to fasten garments together—before buttons and buttonholes, hooks and eyes, or zippers. The solid areas or design portions of lace are held together by narrow twisted or buttonholed yarns called *brides*. These tie points are like the lace or strings holding edges together—thus the name of an open work fabric—lace.

Lace was very important in men's and women's fashion during the sixteenth, seventeenth, eighteenth, and nineteenth centuries and all countries in Europe developed lace industries. The names given to lace often originated from the town in which the laces were made. For example, the best quality needlepoint lace was made in Venice in the sixteenth century—hence the name Venetian lace. Alençon and Valenciennes are towns in France, which are also names of lace.

Hand-Made Lace

Hand-made lace has always been as it is today—a prestige textile. Some people use old lace on garments or as decorative wall hangings. With the interest in crafts today, many of the old lace-making techniques are being used to make less delicate lace. For example, macramé, crochet, tatting, and hairpin laces are made as wall hangings, belts, bags, shawls, afgans, bedspreads, and tablecloths.

Lace is classified according to the way it is made and its appearance. Handmade laces are needlepoint, pillow or bobbin, crochet, and darned.

Needlepoint Lace. *Needlepoint lace* is made by drawing a pattern on paper, laying down threads over the pattern, and, with a needle and thread, making buttonhole or blanket stitches over the threads. The network of fine threads making the ground is called *reseau* or *brides*. The solid part of the pattern, which may be made with buttonhole stitches or interlaced as a woven area, is called *toile*. Needlepoint laces are Alençon, which has a hexagonal mesh, Rosepoint, and Venetian Point, which have an irregular mesh. Needlepoint laces have birds, flowers, and vases as the design (Figure 31-2).

Bobbin Lace. *Bobbin lace* is made on a pillow. The pattern is drawn on paper and pins are inserted at various points. The threads, which are on many bobbins, are twisted and plaited around the pins to form the mesh and the design (Figure 31-3). Bobbin laces are Cluny, Duchesse, Honiton, Maltese, Mechlin, Torchon or Begger's, Valenciennes, Chantilly, and Bruges. Cluny is a course, strong lace. Duchess has a fine net ground with raised patterns. Maltese has the Maltese cross in the pattern. Mechlin has a small hexagonal mesh and very fine threads. Torchon is a rugged lace with very simple patterns. Valenciennes has a diamond-shaped mesh. Chantilly has a double ground with filling of flowers, baskets, or vases.

Crocheted Lace. *Crocheted lace* is a combination of loops but differs from knitting in that the loops are thrown off and finished, whereas in knitting the entire series of loops is held on needles while new loops are made. Crocheted laces are Irish lace and Syrian lace. Crocheting is done with a crochet hook.

Darned Lace. Darned lace has a chain stitch outlining the design on a mesh background. The mesh is square in Filet and rectangular in Antique.

Machine-Made Lace

In England in 1802 Robert Brown perfected a machine that made nets on which lace motifs could be worked by hand. In 1808, John Heathcoat made the first true lace machine by developing brass bobbins to make bobbinet. In 1813, John Leavers developed a machine that made patterns and background simultaneously. A card system, based on the Jacquard loom, made it possible to

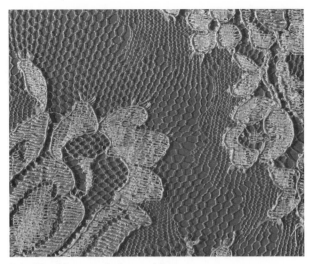

(a) Machine-made lace. Alençon.

(b) Raschel lace.

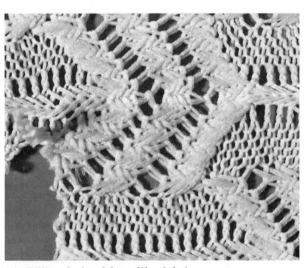

(c) Filling knitted lace like fabric.

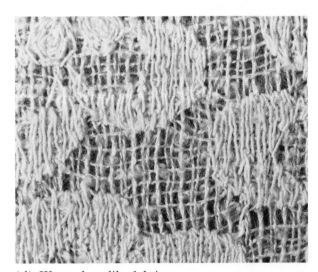

(d) Woven lace like fabric.

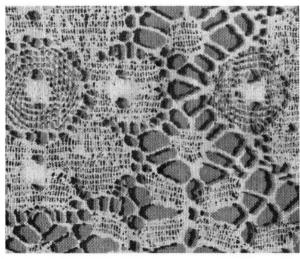

(e) Imitation lace.

Fig. 31–1 Lace and lace like fabrics. (a) Re-embroidered lace made on Leavers lace machine. (b) Lace fabric made on Raschel warp knitting machine. (c) Lace like fabric made on Purl weft knitting machine. (d) Woven lace like fabric. (e) Imitation lace. Cotton percale printed to look like lace.

Fig. 31-2 Needlepoint lace. (*Left*) Handmade (*Right*) Machine-made.

Fig. 31-3 Bobbin Lace. (*Left*) Handmade lace. (*Right*) Machine-made lace.

produce intricate designs with the Leavers machine (Figure 31–4).

Leavers. The Leavers machine, a machine of tremendous size and weight, consists of warp yarns placed in the machine and oscillating bobbins that are set in frames called *carriages*. The carriages move back and forth with the bobbins swinging around the warp to form a pattern. These little brass bobbins, holding 60–300 yards of yarn, are thin enough to swing between adjacent warp yarns and twist themselves around one warp before moving to another yarn (Figures 31–5 and 31–6). The Leavers machine has approximately 20 brass bobbins for each inch width of the machine. A machine 200 inches wide would have 4,000 brass bobbins side by side.

Laces made on the Leavers machine are fairly expensive depending on the quality of yarns used and the intricacy of the design. On some of the dress fabrics a yarn or cord outlines the design.

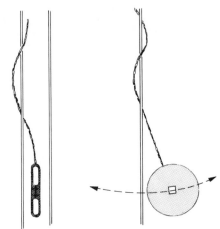

Fig. 31-5 Brass bobbins. Reproduced from "Textiles," 1973, Vol. 2, No. 1, a periodical of the Shirley Institute, Manchester M20 8RX, U.K.

Fig. 31-4 Leavers lace machine.

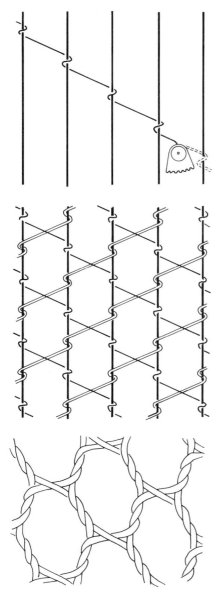

Fig. 31-6 Brass bobbins, carrying thread, twist around warp yarns. Reproduced from "Textiles" 1973, Vol. 2, No. 1, a periodical of the Shirley Institute, Manchester M20 8RX, U.K.

These are called *Cordonnet* or *re-embroidered* lace (Figure 31–1a).

Raschel. Raschel knitting machines (see page 203) are used to make patterned laces that look like those made on a Leavers machine. They can be made at much higher speeds and thus are less expensive to produce. Filament yarns of nylon, polyester, or acetate are commonly used. Raschel machines are also used to make crocheted fabric (Figure 31-7). In these machines, needles are set in the machine horizontally instead of vertically.

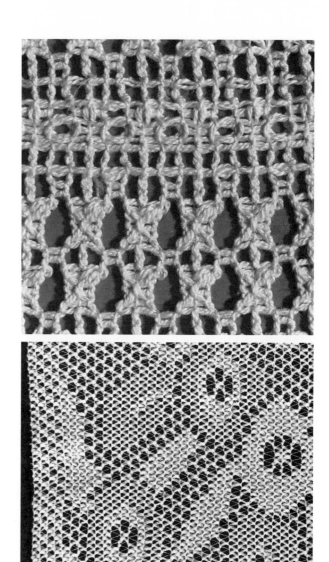

Fig. 31-7 (Upper) Raschel crochet. (Lower) Raschel lace.

Quality. Quality in laces is determined by: (1) fineness of yarns, (2) number of yarns per square inch or closeness of background net, and (3) intricacy of the design.

Care of Lace. Since lace has open spaces it is likely to snag and tear easily. Fragile laces should be washed by hand squeezing suds through the fabric rather than rubbing. Some laces can be put into a cloth bag or pillowcase and machine washed.

Leno Weave

Leno is a weave in which the warp yarns do not lie parallel to each other but one yarn of each pair is *crossed* over the other before the filling yarn is inserted, as shown in Figure 31-8.

Leno is made with a *doup attachment,* which may be used with a plain or a dobby loom. The attachment consists of a thin hairpinlike needle supported by two heddles. One yarn of each pair is threaded through an eye at the upper end of the needle, and the other yarn is drawn between the two heddles. Both yarns are drawn through the same dent in the reed. During weaving, when one of the two heddles is raised, the doup warp yarn that is threaded through the doup needle is drawn across to the left. When the other heddle is raised, the same doup warp yarn is drawn across to the right.

By glancing at a leno fabric, one might think that the yarns were twisted fully around each other, but this is not true. Careful examination shows that they are *crossed* and that one yarn of the pair is always above the other. The fabrics made with leno weave are lacelike in character. The word *leno* comes from the French word *linon,* which means "flax." At one time this weave was called *gauze* weave, meaning fine peculiar weave originating in Gaza, Asia. Today the word *gauze* refers to a low-count plain weave used for ban-

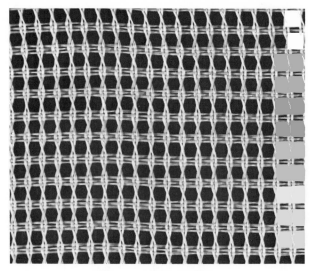

Fig. 31-9 Marquisette.

dages, and a wrinkled looking fashion fabric. Leno refers to the lacelike weave.

Fabrics made by leno weave include *marquisette* (Figure 31-9), mosquito netting, and bags for laundry, fruit, and vegetables. Polyester marquisettes are widely used for glass curtains. Casement draperies are frequently made with leno weave and novelty yarns. Thermal blankets are sometimes made of leno weave. All these fabrics are characterized by sheerness or open spaces between the yarns. The crossed-yarn arrangement gives greater firmness and strength than plain weave fabrics of the same low thread count and also gives resistance to slippage of yarns. Care is determined by the fiber content.

Narrow Fabrics

Narrow fabrics include ribbons of all sorts, elastic tapes, zipper tapes, Venetian blind tapes, Couturier's labels, Velcro tapes, pipings, carpet edge tapes, safety belts, and harnesses, and braids (Figure 31-10).

Braids. *Braids* are narrow fabrics in which yarns are interlaced lengthwise and diagonally (see Figure 21-4). They are very pliable, curve around edges nicely, and are used primarily for trims.

Woven Fabrics. Narrow fabric looms weave many fabrics side by side. Each fabric has its own

Fig. 31-8 Leno weave.

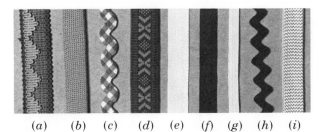

(a) (b) (c) (d) (e) (f) (g) (h) (i)

Fig. 31–10 Narrow fabrics. (a) Raschel knit. (b) Flat filling knit. (c) Circular knit. (d) Woven fancy. (e) Twill tape. (f) Woven ribbon. (g) Woven elastic. (h) Woven rick-rack. (i) Braid.

shuttle, or rapier, but shares all other loom mechanisms. Plain, twill, satin, pile, and Jacquard are the kinds of weaves made.

Bias tape is similar in appearance to braid and has much the same characteristics, but it is made from a plain weave fabric by cutting strips on the bias and then folding in the edges.

Knitted Fabrics. *Knitted fabrics* are made on a few needles on a multiknit machine.

Both woven and knitted thermoplastic fiber narrow fabrics are made on regular machines in wide widths and slit with hot knives to seal the edges. These are much cheaper to produce and are satisfactory if the heat-sealing is properly done. Christmas ribbon of rayon or acetate is often made this way, and even though the heat-sealing may not be satisfactory, the throwaway ribbon is.

Fiber to Fabric Textiles: Nonwovens, felt, batting, needled

32

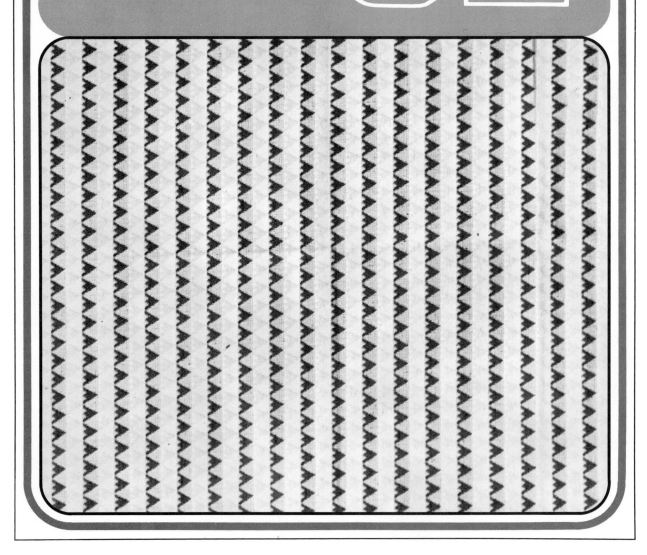

Nonwoven Fabrics

The first nonwoven—Tapa cloth—dates back to biblical times and was made from the fibrous inner bark of the fig tree. It was used chiefly for clothing. The fig tree is a native of Turkey. The bark was used by primitive people in many areas where the fig tree grows, the Pacific Islands, Central America, and elsewhere. The cloth was made by soaking the inner bark to loosen the fibers, beating them with a mallet, smoothing them out into a paperlike sheet, and decorating them with block prints (Figure 32-1). The finest cloth was made by the Hawaiians.

Nonwovens are sheet or web structures made by bonding fibers, yarns, or filaments by mechanical, thermal, chemical, and/or solvent means. The textile industry excludes wool felts, other heavyweight felts, carpets, blankets, and conventional paper products. The term *nonwoven,* therefore, applies to specific types of fabric and *not* to all structures other than weaving; in fact, nonwoven *does not* apply to all fiber-to-fabric structures.

Nonwovens were introduced in the mid-1950s in the United States as a substitute for crinoline (see Glossary), which was widely used as interfacing in full skirts. Since that time the value of nonwovens consumed in the United States has increased from $125 million in 1968 to $550 million in 1974, and is expected to increase to $1.5

billion in 1980. Reasons for the increased usage of nonwovens are

1. Changes in life-styles of families.

2. Increased cost of reconditioning traditional textiles—especially the labor cost.

3. Scarcity and fluctuating cost of low-cost fibers (cotton, rayon, jute).

4. Production and promotion of some man-made fibers.

5. Easier cutting and sewing with nonwovens especially with unskilled labor.

6. Better-looking apparel especially after laundering.

Production processes

The steps in making nonwovens are

1. Selecting the fibers.

2. Laying the fibers to make a web.

3. Laying webs to make a fleece.

4. Bonding the web or fleece together to make a fabric.

Fibers. Any fiber can be used to make nonwovens. The inherent characteristics of the fibers are reflected in the fabric. Filaments and strong fibers are used where strength and durability are important; rayon and cotton are used for absorbency; thermoplastics are used for spun-bonded webs. Nonabsorbency and wicking are important in some end uses. Rayon is the major fiber used in disposables. Polyester and olefin are the fibers most commonly used in durable fabrics.

Web Formation. Webs are made in the following ways

1. Dry laid.

2. Wet laid.

3. Spunbonded.

4. Spunlaced.

Dry-laid nonwovens are made by carding or air laying. Webs delivered from the carding machine have fibers oriented lengthwise. Webs can be cross-laid by folding the carded web so that one layer is oriented lengthwise and the next layer is oriented crosswise to give added strength and

Fig. 32-1 Tapa cloth from Samoa.

Fig. 32-2 Spunbonded filament: Reemay.

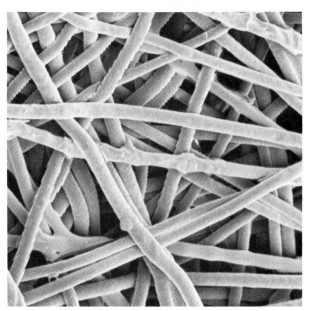

Fig. 32-3 Mirafi 140 fabric. (*Courtesy of Celanese Fibers Marketing Co.*)

pliability. Cross-laid webs do not have grain and can be cut more economically. Air-laid or random webs are made by special machines that disperse the fibers by air and lay them down with a vacuum. This web is much like the cross-laid web but has more random distribution.

Wet-laid nonwovens are made from a slurry of short (paper-process length) and textile length fibers and water. The water is extracted leaving a fiber web. The advantage of these webs is their exceptional uniformity. They comprise 15 per cent of the nonwoven fabric market.

Spunbonded webs are made directly from spinnerets. The continuous filaments are laid down in a random fashion on a fast-moving belt, and, in their semimelted state, they fuse together at their cross points. They may be further bonded by heat and pressure. Spunbonded nonwovens have high tensile and tear strength, and low bulk (Figure 32-2).

Spunlaced webs are similar to spunbonded webs except that jets of water are forced through the web separating the filaments into a wovenlike structure to produce a looser bonded fabric. They have more elasticity and flexibility than spunbonded fabrics. End uses of spunlaced fabrics are in draperies and bedspreads. Spunbonded and spunlaced fabrics comprise 25 per cent of the market for nonwovens.

Bonding. Webs become fabrics by

1. Needling, a mechanical process.

2. Using a chemical substance or adhesive.

3. Using heat.

Needle-punched nonwovens are dry-laid webs that have been run through a needle bed to interlock them mechanically (see page 251). Needled nonwovens are used as interlinings in ski jackets where they are less bulky than fiberfill batts, in blankets, for primary or secondary carpet backings, and for indoor-outdoor carpeting.

Chemicals or adhesives are used with dry-laid or wet-laid webs. Acrylic emulsions are usually used.

Heat and pressure are used to bond thermoplastic fiber webs. Figure 32-3 shows Mirafi 140 fabric composed of a random mixture of two different continuous filament fibers that are heat-bonded. The fibers are polypropylene (olefin) homopolymer and biconstituent polypropylene core nylon sheath filaments. Mirafi 140 is an industrial fabric used for roadbed and area stabilization.

Composite Nonwovens

Composite nonwovens are multicomponent fabrics consisting of various layers of nonwovens made by different processes: wet- and dry-laid nonwovens, needled and spunbonded, and nonwoven fabrics with nylon scrim between them and so on (Figure 32-4).

Fig. 32-4 Composite nonwoven.

Fusible Nonwovens

Fusible nonwovens give body and shape to outerwear and are widely used in tailored garments. They also are used as interfacing in shirts, blouses, and dresses, and as interlining in outerwear (Figure 32-5).

A fusible is a fabric that has been coated with a heat-sealable adhesive that is thermoplastic but inactive at room temperature. It also may be a thin, spiderlike web of thermoplastic filaments (Figure 32-6). The fusible fabric is applied to a face fabric and bonded to it by heat and pressure. Figure 32-7 shows a fusible web used in skirt hem to eliminate thread hemming.

The adhesives used are polyethylene, hydrolyzed ethylene vinyl acetate, plasticized polyvinyl chloride, and polyamides. Adhesives were first applied to the woven or nonwoven substrate as continuous coatings that resulted in very stiff end products or as discontinuous coatings in which powdered adhesives were spread over the fabric surface to give a softer hand. Today, the adhesive is usually printed on the substrate in a precisely

Fig. 32-5 (a & b) Fusible interfacings.

Fig. 32-6 Fusible interfacing. Tape under web to show sheerness of web.

Fig. 32-7 Wonder-Under (Pellon) spun-bonded nonwoven fabric used in hem of a skirt.

positioned manner to give the desired hand to the end product.

The advantages of fusibles in apparel are

1. They eliminate certain areas of stitching such as zigzag stitches used in coat and suit lapels.

2. They require less skilled labor in garment production.

3. They increase productivity.

4. They improve the appearance of garments at the point of sale and over time.

End Uses

Nonwovens are used for disposable goods, such as diapers and wipes, durable goods that are incorporated into other products or used alone for draperies, mattress pads, and possibly some apparel (see the following chart).

Durable	Type	Share of Market	Disposable	Type	Share of Market
Bedding and coated fabrics, mattress ticking, backing for quilting, dust cloth for box springs	Spunbonded	8%	Diapers, underpads, sanitary napkins/ tampons	Dry-laid	20%
			Surgical packs and accessories	Dry-laid	7%
Carpet backing	Needled	12%	Wipes and towels	Dry-laid	10%
Filters		7%			
Interfacings	Dry or wet-laid	11%			
Interlinings	Needled				
Others—draperies, upholstered furniture, backings, facings, dustcovers, automotive, shoe parts		25%			

Reference: 1975 International Directory of the Nonwoven Fabrics Industry IDEA 74 Conference Papers. International Nonwovens and Disposables Association

Felt

Felt refers to fabrics made from wool, whereas nonwoven applies to fabrics made from other fibers.

True felt is a mat or web of wool or part-wool fibers held together by the interlocking of the scales of the wool fibers. Felting is one of the oldest methods of making fabrics. Primitive peoples made felt by washing wool fleece, spreading it out while still wet, and beating it until it had

matted and shrunk together in fabriclike form. Figure 32–8 shows a Numdah felt rug. These rugs are still made in India. In the modern factory, layers of fiber webs are built up until the desired thickness is attained and then heat, soap, and vibration are used to mat the fibers together and to shrink or full the cloth. Finishing processes for felt resemble those for woven fabrics.

Felts do not have grain; they are rather stiff and less pliable than other structures; they do not ravel; they are not as strong as other fabrics; they vary in quality depending on the quality of the wool fiber used.

Felt has many industrial and some clothing uses. It is used industrially for padding, sound-proofing, insulation, filtering, polishing, and wicking. In the past, felt was used under practically all machinery to absorb sound. Foams, being much cheaper, have replaced felt in this end use. Felt is not used for fitted clothing because it lacks the flexibility and elasticity of fabrics made from yarns. Felt has wide use in such products as hats, house slippers, clothing decorations, and pennants. Because felt does not fray, it needs no seam finish. Colored felt letters or decorations on white sport sweaters or other garments often fade in washing and should be removed or the garments should be sent to a professional dry cleaner.

Fig. 32–8 Numdah felt rug.

Comparison of Properties of Commonly Used Battings

Fiber	Density	Resiliency	Resistance to Shifting	Care
Down (costly)	Lightweight	Excellent	Poor	Dry-cleanable
Acetate (low cost)	1.30	Fair	Poor	Washable, dries more quickly than cotton
Polyester (medium cost)	1.30–1.38	Good	Good—can be spot-welded	Washable, quick drying
Cotton (low cost)	1.52	Poor	Poor	Washable but slow drying

Batting, Wadding, and Fiberfill

Batting, wadding and fiberfill are not fabrics, but they are important components in apparel for snowsuits, ski jackets, quilted robes, and jackets, and in household textiles for quilts, comforters, paddings for furniture, and in mattresses and mattress pads.

Batting is made from new fiber, *wadding* is made from waste fiber, and *fiberfill* is the name given to a man-made staple made especially for these end uses. Carded fibers are laid down to form the desired thickness and are often covered with a sheet of nonwoven fabric.

The importance of *density* is that, for a unit volume, the fabric will be heavy or light. Today, people want lightweight fabrics, especially for outer garments. *Resiliency* is important because fabrics that maintain their loft incorporate more air space. When fibers stay crushed, the fabric becomes thinner and more compact. *Resistance to shifting* is important in maintaining uniformity of thickness in the fabric. For instance, down comforters need to be shaken often because the filling tends to shift to the outer edges. The thermoplastic fiber batts can be run through a needle-punch machine in which hot needles melt parts of the fibers that they touch, causing them to fuse together to form a more stable batt. The thicker the batt, the warmer is the fabric regardless of fiber content. In apparel there is a limit to the thickness, however, because too much bulk restricts movement, a limiting factor in styling.

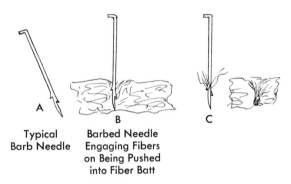

A Typical Barb Needle

B Barbed Needle Engaging Fibers on Being Pushed into Fiber Batt

C

Action of Cooperating Pair of Barbed Needles

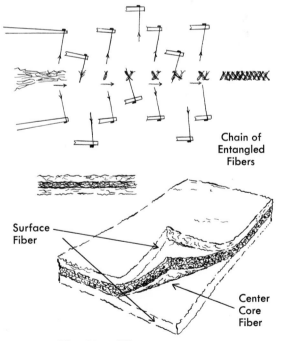

Chain of Entangled Fibers

Surface Fiber

Center Core Fiber

Fig. 32-9 Fiberwoven process.

Needle Punching

Needle punching consists of passing a properly prepared web over a needle loom as many times as is necessary to produce the desired strength and texture. A needle loom is a board with barbed needles protruding 2 or 3 inches from the base (Figure 32–9). As the needles push up and down through the web, the barbs catch a few fibers causing them to interlock mechanically. The construction process is relatively inexpensive.

Attractive blankets and carpeting have been made by needle punching. In the Fiberwoven blanket, 100 per cent Acrilan fiber or blends of Acrilan fiber and other fibers have been used. Fiber denier and fiber type may be varied. Blankets may be lofty or compact.

Indoor/outdoor needle-punched carpeting made of olefin fibers is used extensively for patios, porches, pools, and putting greens. The fiber is impervious to moisture. Locktuft, a needled nonwoven made of Marvess olefin, is a carpet backing designed especially for use with tufted carpets.

Needled fabrics can be made of a web consisting of two layers, each with a different color. By pulling colored fibers from the lower layer to the top surface, geometric designs can be made. If the fibers are pulled above the surface, a pile fabric will result. The army has developed a ballistics protective vest for combat use from needle-punched fabrics. Needle-punched fabrics are finished by pressing, steaming, calendering, dyeing, and embossing. Solution-dyed fibers are often used.

The Arachne and Maliwatt systems of knit-sew can be used without stitching threads to make nonwovens. In these processes, a closed needle penetrates the web, opens, grabs some fibers, and draws them back as a yarnlike structure that is then chain-stitched through the web.

Film, Foam, Leather, and Fur

33

Film, foam, leather, and fur usually are not classified as fabrics but they are used for apparel and home furnishings and can have a fabriclike hand and drape. Many films are given a leatherlike grain and are widely used where the more expensive leathers were formerly used. Since leather suede is such an attractive, desirable, and expensive material, many fabrics are finished to resemble it. Fur, like leather, is a natural product, highly prized for its beauty and durability and widely imitated in various fabric constructions.

Films and Film Coatings

Films are made directly from solution to fabric by melt-extrusion or by casting the solution onto a hot drum. The solutions are similar to the spinning solutions for fibers.

Apparel and household textile films are made from vinyl or polyurethane solutions. They are similar in appearance but vary in the care required. Vinyl films become stiff in dry-cleaning solvents. They are washable but not dry cleanable. Urethane films are both washable and dry cleanable. Urethane films remain soft in cold weather whereas vinyl films stiffen.

There are several kinds of films. *Plain* films are firm, dense, and uniform. *Expanded* films are spongier, softer, and plumper as a result of a blowing agent that incorporates tiny air cells into the compound. They are not as strong or as resistant to abrasion as plain films. *Supported* films have a woven, knitted, or nonwoven backing. Supported films are more durable, easier to sew, and less likely to crack and split.

Plastic films and coated fabrics are better than any other material for waterproof items. They can be made to look like most any other textile by printing or embossing or flocking. They can vary in thickness from very thin transparent film to heavy leatherette. They have the advantage of being uniform in appearance and quality, and they can be obtained by the yard or meter in wide widths so that they are much cheaper and easier to cut into apparel items than leather.

End Uses for Films and Film-Coated Fabrics

Air-supported roofings	Shower curtains
Draperies	Tablecloths
Hospital bed coverings	Umbrellas
Hose containers for fuel and water	Upholstery
Inflatable flood gates for water control	Waterproof apparel such as raincoats, boots, and mittens
Leatherlike coats, jackets	

Solution	Fiber	Film	End Uses for Film
Acetate	Acetate	Acetate	Photographic film; projection film
Polyamide	Nylon	Nylon	Cooking Magic Bags*
Polyester	Polyester	Mylar*	Packaging; metallic yarns
Polypropylene	Olefin		
Polyethylene		Polyethylene	Packaging, garment bags, squeeze bottles
Polyurethane	Spandex	Polyurethane	Leather-like fabrics
Polyvinyl chloride	Vinal	Vinyl	Packaging, garment bags, leather like fabrics for apparel and upholstery, seed tapes, water-soluble bags.
Vinylidene chloride	Saran	Saran Wrap*	Packaging
Viscose (regenerated cellulose)	Rayon	Cellophane	Glitter weaving yarns—mostly in hand-woven textiles

*Trade names

Foam

Foams are made by incorporating air into an elasticlike substance. Rubber and polyurethane are the most commonly used foams. The outstanding characteristics of foams are their bulk and sponginess. They are used as carpet backings and underlays, padding for furniture, pillow forms, and foam laminated to fabric for apparel and household textiles (Figure 33-1). Shredded foam is used as stuffing for accent pillows and stuffed toys.

Polyurethane foam can be obtained in a wide range of physical properties from very stiff to rubbery. The size of the cells can be controlled. Foams will yellow on exposure to sunlight, but this does not cause a chemical change in the urethane foam nor does it affect its usefulness and durability. It does, however, cause rubber to disintegrate. Polyurethane is prepared by the reaction of diisocyanate with a compound containing two or more hydroxyl groups in the presence of a suitable catalyst. Chemicals and foaming agents are mixed together thoroughly. After the foam is formed, it is cut into blocks 200 to 300 yards long, and strips of the desired thickness are cut from these blocks.

Leather

Leather is a product manufactured from the skins and hides of animals, reptiles, fish, and birds. It is an organic substance derived from living animals and, therefore, varies greatly in uniformity. The hides from different animals differ in size, thickness, and in grain. Grain is the marking that results from the skin formation and varies not only from animal to animal but also within one hide. Other factors influence the surface of hides. Animals scratch themselves, run into barbed wire fences, and get into fights causing scars that cannot be erased; brand marks or skin diseases mar the hides. Animals are raised primarily for meat or fiber, not for their hides or skins. Leather is made from a relatively unimportant by-product. Of 100 hides it is estimated that less than 5 per cent are suitable for conversion into smooth top-grain cowhide in aniline finish, 20 per cent are

Fig. 33-1 Nylon taffeta laminated to polyurethane foam.

suitable for smooth leathers with a pigment finish, and the remaining 75 per cent must be embossed, buffed, snuffed, or corrected.

Dried skins and hides are stiff, boardy, nonpliable, and subject to decay. Tanning is the process in which skins and hides are treated with a tanning agent to make them pliable and water resistant. Vegetable tanning, the most expensive process, is done with an extract leeched out from the bark of various trees. Chrome tanning (bichromate of soda, sulfuric acid, and glucose) is used to make soft pliable leather. Oil tanning is used to make chamois. Alum tanning is used for white leather.

Skins go through many processes to become leather: they are salted; cleaned to remove the hair and epidermis; tanned; bleached; stuffed; colored or dyed; staked; and finished by glazing, boarding, buffing, snuffing, or embossing depending on the desired end use. These many processes explain why leather is an expensive product.

Leather is a nonseparable fiber product. As shown in Figure 33-2, the fibers are very dense on the skin side and less dense on the flesh side. Thick hides are often split to make them more pliable and economical (Figure 33-3).

The first layer is called *top grain* and it has the typical animal grain. It takes the best finish and wears well. Splits have a looser, more porous structure and are cut across the fibers. They do not take as smooth finishes as top grain and tend to rough up during wear. Most split leathers are given an embossed finish. Although splits are not identified as such on labeled products, top grain is usually mentioned.

Fig. 33-2 Cross-sectional drawing of a strip of leather, showing variations in density of fiber.

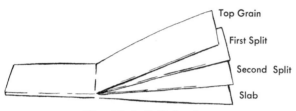

Top Grain

First Split

Second Split

Slab

Fig. 33-3 Split leather.

Leather is a durable product with a pleasant odor. It varies greatly in quality—not only from skin to skin but within one skin. Like wool fibers, leather from the backs and sides of the animal is

better whereas that from the belly and legs tends to be thin and stretchy or very coarse. Leather picks up oils and grease readily. It requires special care in cleaning since it is stiffened by solvents.

Reconstituted leathers have been made by grinding up leather, mixing with urethane, and forming into sheets. This "leather" product is uniform in thickness and quality and is not limited in length and width.

Suede. Suede is a popular leather for coats, jackets, dresses, and trims. The soft, dull surface is made by napping (running the skin under a coarse emery board) on the flesh side to pull out the fibers. Suede is a very durable product but requires special care.

Suedelike fabrics are made in various ways. (See the following chart).

Furs

Furs are considered luxury items by the United States government. Consumers usually purchase furs because of their beautiful appearance rather than for their warmth, durability, or ease of care. It is important to know about the kinds of fur, how fur garments are made, and how to care for them in order to make wise selections and to maintain their beauty.

Suedelike Fabrics

Construction Technique	Characteristics	Trade Name
Composite fabric—polyester fibers and polyurethane mixed, cast on drum, napped	Washable, dry cleanable Looks like leather	Ultrasuede
Composite fabric	Easy care Looks like natural leather	Belleseime
Woven cotton/polyester substrate with surface coating of polyurethane Substrate with polyurethane on both sides	Dry cleanable Washable	Cav Suede
100 per cent polyester pile fabric with suedelike finish	Dry cleanable Washable	Coltra
Flocked cotton	Least expensive. Flock may wear off at edges of garment	Butter-suede
100 per cent polyester warp knit-napped	Washable, dry cleanable	Super-suede

Furs are natural products and, therefore, vary in quality. Good quality fur has a very dense pile and if it has guard hairs they are long and very lustrous. The fur is usually soft and fluffy. The quality depends on the age and health of the animal and the season of the year in which it is killed. Fur trapping has long been an important industry in all parts of the world. Fur farming, started in 1880, has been a boon to the fur industry because better pelts are produced as a result of scientific breeding, careful feeding and handling of the animals, and slaughtering them when the fur is in prime condition. Silver fox, chinchilla, mink, Persian lamb, and nutria are the animals raised on ranches and by crossbreeding and inbreeding new and different colored furs have been produced.

The cost of fur garments depends on fashion to a large extent, to the supply and demand of fashionable furs, and to the work involved in producing the garment. Chinchilla, mink, sable, platina fox, and ermine have always been very expensive. Leopard has entered this class in the last few years because of fashion and the scarcity of the animals. For many years, leopards have been killed indiscriminately and curbs have had to be placed on this practice to keep them from becoming extinct.

Furs go through many processes before they are sold. Dressing of fur is comparable to tanning of leather and the purpose is the same—to keep the skins from putrifying and to make them soft and pliable. The processes of dressing must be more carefully done than with leather so that the fur will not be damaged. After tanning, pelts are combed, brushed, and beaten. The final process is drumming in sawdust to clean and polish the hair and to absorb oil from the leather and fur. The sawdust is removed.

Many furs are dyed. Originally furs were dyed to make less expensive furs look like the expensive ones and this is still done. Muskrat is dyed to resemble seal, rabbit is stenciled to look like leopard or ocelot, and so on. But today furs are dyed to improve their natural color as well as to give them unnatural colors—red or green, for example. Tip dyeing is brushing the tips of the fur and guard hairs with dye. Furs also are dip dyed in which the entire skin is dipped in dye. Some furs are bleached and some are bleached and then dyed.

Skins are gathered together from all over the world and sold at public auction. The four largest markets for fur are St. Louis, New York, London, and Montreal.

Furs require care to keep them beautiful. They should not be stored in damp places or in hot humid places and never in plastic bags. Between seasons, if possible, garments should be sent to a furrier for cold storage where the furs are kept in special vaults in which the temperature and humidity are controlled. To restore luster and to clean the garment it is usually best to send it to a furrier once a year. Furs should never be dry-cleaned.

Furs should be protected from abrasion. Avoid sitting on them; hang on a wide, well-constructed hanger and allow plenty of space between garments; shake rather than brush. Driving in furs is very hard on them. Much of automobile upholstery, which is made of plastic or from synthetic fibers, breaks off the fur in the shoulder and seat area of the garment.

The Fur Products Labeling Act, which became effective on August 9, 1952, requires that the true English-language name of the animal must be used, and if the fur is dyed, this must be stated. In addition, the country of origin must be indicated. This law protects the consumer from buying furs sold under names resembling expensive furs. For example, prior to the enactment of this law, rabbit was sold as lapin, chinchilette, ermaline, northern seal, coney, marmink, Australian seal, Belgian beaver, and Baltic leopard. Hudson seal was muskrat plucked and dyed to look like seal. The law does not provide for quality designations; poor quality mink is still mink. Fur dealers sometimes deplore this law because the consumer may misinterpret it. The consumer may not realize that the price represents the quality of the fur and the quality of construction of the garment.

Finishes: General or routine

A *finish* is defined as anything that is done to fiber, yarn, or fabric either before or after weaving or knitting to change the *appearance* (what you see), the *hand* (what you feel), and the *performance* (what the fabric does). All fabric finishing adds to the cost of the fabric.

Finishing may be done in the mill where the fabric is constructed or it may be done in a separate establishment by a highly specialized group called *converters*. Converters operate in two ways: they perform a service for a mill by finishing goods to order, in which case they are paid for their services and never own the fabric; or they buy the fabric from a mill, finish it according to their own needs, and sell it to the cutting trade or as yard goods under their own trade name.

A *permanent finish* lasts the life of the garment. *Durable* refers to a finish that lasts longer than a temporary finish but not for the life of the garment. A *temporary* finish lasts until the garment is washed or dry-cleaned. A *renewable* finish can be applied by the homemaker with no special equipment, or it may be applied by the dry cleaner. Two important durable finishes, which have been used for over 60 years, are *mercerization* and *tin weighting* of silk. The uses of mercerization have increased whereas weighting of silk has almost ceased.

Some finishes such as color or embossing are easy to recognize because they are visible. Other finishes, such as durable press, are nonvisible but may have an important effect on fabric performance. The consumer needs to recognize visible finishes and to recognize the *need* for nonvisible finishes. He needs to know how good the finish is in terms of serviceability.

Gray goods (grey, greige, or loom state) are fabrics, regardless of color, which have been woven on a loom and have received no wet- or dry-finishing operations. Some gray-goods fabrics have names, such as print cloth and soft-filled sheeting, which are used only for the gray goods. Other gray-goods names, such as lawn, broadcloth, and sateen, are also used as names for the finished cloth.

Converted or finished goods have received wet- or dry-finishing treatments such as bleaching, dyeing, or embossing. Some converted goods retain the gray-goods name. Others, such as madras gingham, are named for the place of origin; and still others, such as silence cloth, are named for the end use. Figure 35–1 (page 265) depicts some of the fabrics that can be converted from a single gray goods.

Mill-finished fabrics can be sold and used without converting, although they may be sized or Sanforized before they are sold.

General or Routine Fabric Finishes

Cleaning. All gray goods must be cleaned and made ready for the acceptance of the finish. Gray goods contain a warp sizing, which makes the fabric stiff and interferes with the absorption of liquids. The fabric must be desized before further finishing can be done. Also, fabrics are often soiled during weaving and must be cleaned for that reason. Warp sizing, dirt, and oil spots have always been removed by a washing process—*degumming* of silk, *kier boiling* of cotton, and *scouring* of wool.

Large amounts of water are used by the finishing industry and most of this water has been discharged as waste into rivers and streams. With the rising cost of water and the cost of pollution-control installations, there has been a trend toward processing in solvent media—dry-cleaning-type materials.

Bleaching. Most bleaches are oxidizing agents. The actual bleaching is done by *active oxygen*. A few bleaches are reducing agents. These are used to strip color from dyed fabrics. Bleaches may be either acid or alkaline in nature. They are usually unstable, especially in the presence of moisture. Bleaches that are old or have been improperly stored will lose their oxidizing power.

Any bleach will cause some damage, and since damage occurs more rapidly at higher temperatures and concentrations, these factors should be carefully controlled.

The same bleach is not suitable to all kinds of fibers. Because fibers vary in their chemical reaction, bleaches must be chosen with regard to their fiber content. The anklets in Figure 34–1 had been all white, but when bleached with a chlorine bleach, the wool-ribbed cuff section became discolored while the cotton feet remained white.

The consumer uses bleaches to remove stains. Any off-white "tattle-tale" gray caused by the soil and soap curds from wash water should be removed by reconditioning treatments rather than by a bleach. Better still, wash often, and use correct washing procedures from the start. Reconditioning is done by soaking the article in a solution made with a nonprecipitating water softener and then washing it in hot, sudsy, *softened* water. This must be repeated several times.

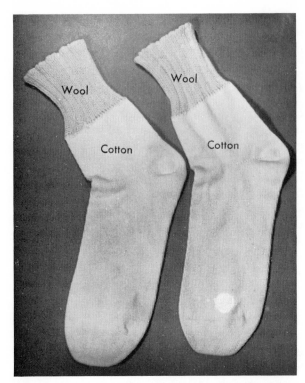

Fig. 34-1 Cotton and wool socks after bleaching. Chlorine bleach caused wool to yellow and stiffen.

Oxygen bleaches may be used on fabric to remove stains without damage to the original color of the fabric. Garments that have a resin finish should not be bleached with chlorine since yellowing will result.

The *finisher* uses bleaches to clean and whiten gray goods. The natural fibers are an off-white color because of the impurities they contain. Since these impurities are easily removed from cotton, most cotton gray goods are bleached without damage. The bleaching step is often omitted with wool because it has good affinity for dyes and other finishes even if not bleached.

Liquid chlorine bleaches were, for many years, the common household bleaches. They are efficient bactericidal agents and as such can be used for sterilizing fabrics. They are cheap and efficient bleaches for cotton and rayon. The bleaching is done by the hypochlorous acid liberated during the bleaching process. This *tenders* cellulose fibers, and the bleach must be thoroughly rinsed out or an antichlor (sodium thiosulfate) should be used. Chlorine bleaches other than sodium chlorite are of no value on the protein and thermoplastic fibers and if used will cause yellowing. The weekly wash also contains many fabrics with crease-recovery and embossed finishes, which should *not* be bleached with chlorine.

Powdered oxygen bleaches also called *all-fabric* bleaches may be used safely on all fibers and colored fabrics. Their bleaching effect is much milder than chlorine bleaches.

Peroxide bleaches are common factory bleaches for cellulose and protein fibers and fabrics. *Hydrogen peroxide* is an oxidizing bleach. A 3 per cent solution is relatively stable at room temperature and is safe to use. Peroxide will bleach best at a temperature of 180 to 200°F in an alkaline solution. These bleaching conditions make it possible to do peroxide bleaching of cellulose gray goods as the final step in the kier boil.

In the *peroxide cold bleach* procedure the fabric is soaked overnight or for a period of 8 hours. This procedure is often used on cotton knit goods and wool to preserve a soft hand. Peroxide is good for removing light scorch stains.

Sodium perborate is a powder bleach that becomes hydrogen peroxide when it combines with water. It is a safe bleach for home use with all kinds of fibers. Satisfactory results have also been obtained with the thermoplastic fibers by use of the cold bleach process. Powder bleaches are recommended for regular use in the wash water to maintain the original whiteness of the fabric rather than as a whitener for discolored fabrics.

Acid bleaches, such as oxalic acid and potassium permanganate, have limited use. Citric acid and lemon juice are also acid bleaches that are good rust spot removers.

Reducing bleaches such as white Rit will whiten nylon and strip color from some dyed fabrics.

Optical brighteners are also used to whiten off-white fabrics. They are fluorescent white compounds, not bleaches. The fluorescent white compounds are absorbed into the fiber and emit a bluish fluorescence that covers up yellowish tinges. At the mill optical brighteners give best results when used in combination with the bleach rather than as a substitute for it. For home use, they work most effectively if the detergent solutions and laundry are agitated for several minutes before the chlorine bleach is added. These new fluorescent whites are often incorporated in soaps and detergents as "whiter than new" ingredients. They also are added to the spinning solution of some man-made fibers to optically brighten them.

Carbonizing. Carbonizing, which is the treatment of wool yarns or fabrics with sulfuric acid, destroys vegetable matter in the fabric and more level dyeing can be obtained. Carbonizing is also done on reused and reprocessed wool to remove any cellulose that may have been used in the original fabric. Carbonizing gives better texture to all-wool fabrics.

Mercerization. Mercerization is the action of an alkali (caustic soda) on a fabric. Mercerizing was a revolutionary development discovered in 1853 by John Mercer, a calico printer. He noticed that his cotton filter cloth shrank, and became stronger, more lustrous, and more absorbent after filtering the caustic soda used in the dye process. Little use was made of mercerization at that time because the shrinkage caused a 20 to 25 per cent yardage loss, and the increased durability caused mill men to fear that less fabric would be used. In 1897, Lowe discovered that if the fabric were held under tension, it did not shrink but became very lustrous and silklike.

Mercerization is used on cotton and linen for many different reasons. It increases the luster and softness, gives greater strength, and improves the affinity for dyes and water-borne finishes. Plissé effects can be achieved in cotton fabrics. "Mercerized cotton" on a label is associated with luster. Cotton is mercerized for luster in both yarn and fabric form.

Yarn mercerization is a continuous process in which the yarn under tension passes from a warp beam through a series of boxes with guide rolls and squeeze rolls, through a boil-out wash, and a final wash (Figure 34-2).

Fabric mercerization is done on a frame that contains mangles for saturating the cloth, a

Fig. 34-2 Mercerization of warp yarn. (*Courtesy of Coats & Clark Inc.*)

tenter frame for tensioning the fabric both crosswise and lengthwise while wet, and boxes for washing, neutralizing with dilute sulfuric acid, scouring, and rinsing. Turn to page 40 for a discussion of the changes that occur in the cotton fiber.

Greater absorbency results from mercerization because the caustic soda causes a rearrangement of the molecules, thus making the hydroxyl groups available to absorb more water and water-borne substances. Thus, dyes can enter the fiber more readily, and when they can be fixed inside the fiber, they are more fast. (Caustic soda is also used in vat dyeing to keep the vat dye soluble until it penetrates the fiber.) Mercerized cotton and linen take resin finishes better for the same reason.

Increased strength is an important value from mercerization. Mercerized cotton fibers are stronger because in the swollen fiber, the molecules are more nearly parallel to the fiber axis. When stress is applied, the attraction, which is an end-to-end molecular attraction, is harder to rupture than in the more spiral fibril arrangement.

Slack mercerization consists of dipping 100 per cent cotton cloth in a 23 per cent caustic solution, allowing it to react for $1\frac{1}{2}$ minutes, and then washing and drying. The cloth shrinks and the yarn crimp is increased. The straightening of the crimp when stress is applied gives the stretch. One-way or two-way stretch can be obtained by variations in the mercerization conditions. *Stretch* is achieved in cotton by *slack mercerization*. It gives comfort in fabrics. Stretch diapers are the major end use.

Ammoniating finishes. Ammoniating finishes are used on cotton and rayon yarns and fabrics. Yarns or fabrics are treated with a weak ammonium solution at $-33°C$ and are then passed through hot water, stretched, and dried in hot air. The finish is similar to mercerization but is less expensive and less polluting. It gives more strength to cotton yarns and fabrics, increases luster, gives better affinity for dyes, and improves the hand of fabrics. Duralized and Sanforset are trade names.

Singeing. Singeing is the burning of free projecting fiber ends from the surface of the cloth. These protruding ends cause roughness, dullness, pilling, and interfere with finishing. Singeing is the first finishing operation for all smooth-finished cotton fabrics and for clear-finished wool fabrics. Fabrics containing heat-sensitive fibers such as polyester/cotton blends are often singed after dyeing because the little melted balls on the ends of the fibers may cause unevenness in the color. Singeing is one of the best remedies for the problem of pilling.

Shearing. Shearing is a finishing process done by a machine similar to a lawn mower. Gray-goods fabrics are sheared to remove loose fiber or yarn ends, knots, and the like. Napped and pile fabrics are sheared to control the length of the pile or nap surface and to create a design or a smooth surface. *Sculptured* effects are made by flattening portions of the pile with an engraved roller and then shearing off the areas that are still erect. Steaming the fabric raises the flattened portions.

Brushing. Brushing follows shearing to clean the surface of clear-face fabrics. When combined with steaming, it will lay nap or pile in one direction and fix it in that position thus giving the up-and-down direction of pile and nap fabrics.

Fulling. Fulling is done on wool fabrics to improve the appearance and hand. Fabrics are fulled by moisture, heat, and friction—a very mild felting process.

Crabbing. Crabbing is a wool finishing process used to set wool fabrics. Fabrics are immersed in hot water, then in cold water, and passed between rollers.

Decatizing. Decatizing produces a smooth, wrinkle-free finish and lofty hand on woolen and worsted fabrics and on blends of wool and man-made fibers. The process is comparable to steam ironing. A high degree of luster can be developed by the decating process because of the smoothness of the surface. The dry cloth is wound under tension on a perforated cylinder. Steam is forced through the fabric. The moisture and heat cause the wool to become plastic and tensions relax and wrinkles are removed. The yarns become set in the shape of the weave and are fixed in this position by the cooling off, which is done with cold air. For a more permanent set, dry decating is done in a pressure boiler. Wet decating often precedes napping or other face finishes to remove wrinkles that have been acquired in scouring. Wet decating as a final finish gives a more permanent set to the yarns than does dry decating.

Beetling. Beetling is a finish that is used on linen and a few fabrics resembling linen. As the cloth revolves slowly over a huge wooden drum, it is pounded with wooden block hammers. This pounding may continue for a period of 30 to 60 hours. It flattens the yarns and makes the weave appear less open than it really is. The increased surface area gives more luster, greater absorbency, and smoothness to the fabric.

Calendering. Calendering is a mechanical finishing operation performed by a "stack" of rollers through which the cloth passes. There are several types: the simple calender, the friction calender, the moiré calender, the Schreiner calender, and the embossing calender. Each produces a different finish. See p. 265.

Most calender machines have three rollers. (Others have two, five, or seven.) Hard metal rollers alternate with softer, cloth-wrapped rollers or with solid paper rollers. Two metal rollers never run against each other.

The *simple calender* corresponds to the household ironer and gives a smooth, ironed finish to the fabric. The cloth is slightly damp before it enters the calender. The metal roll is heated. The cloth travels through the calender at the surface speed of the rollers so the rollers simply exert pressure to smooth out the wrinkles and give a slight sheen (Figure 34–3).

Tentering. Tentering, one of the final finishing operations, performs the double process of straightening and drying fabrics. If the fabric is

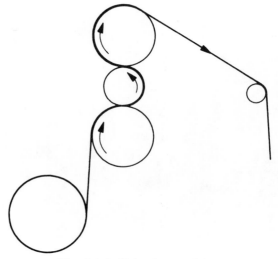

Fig. 34-3 Calender machine.

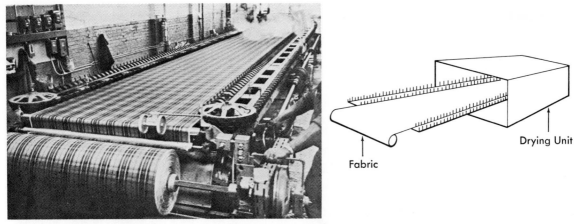

Fig. 34-4 Tenter Frames: (*Left*) Clip tenter. (*Right*) Drawing of pin tenter frame.

started into the tenter frame in a crooked position, it will be dried in an "off-grain" shape. Weft-straighteners are discussed on page 160.

Tenter machines are similar to a curtain stretcher in principle. They are of two types: the pin tenter and the clip tenter (Figure 34-4). The mechanism on the two sides moves around like a caterpillar tractor wheel, holding the fabric by a series of pins. More tension can be exerted by the clip tenter, but it may also damage some fabrics, in which case the pin tenter is used. The marks of the pins or the clips are often evident along the selvage.

Loop Drying. Fabrics with a soft finish, towels, and stretchy fabrics such as knits are not dried on the tenter frame but are dried on a loop dryer, where the drying can be done without tension. Many rayon fabrics are dried on loop dryers.

Inspecting. Fabrics are inspected by pulling or running them over an inverted frame in good light. Broken threads are clipped off, snagged threads are worked back into the cloth, and defects are marked so that adjustments can be made when fabrics are sold. The fabric is then wound on bolts or cylinders ready for shipment.

Finishes: Aesthetic or beauty

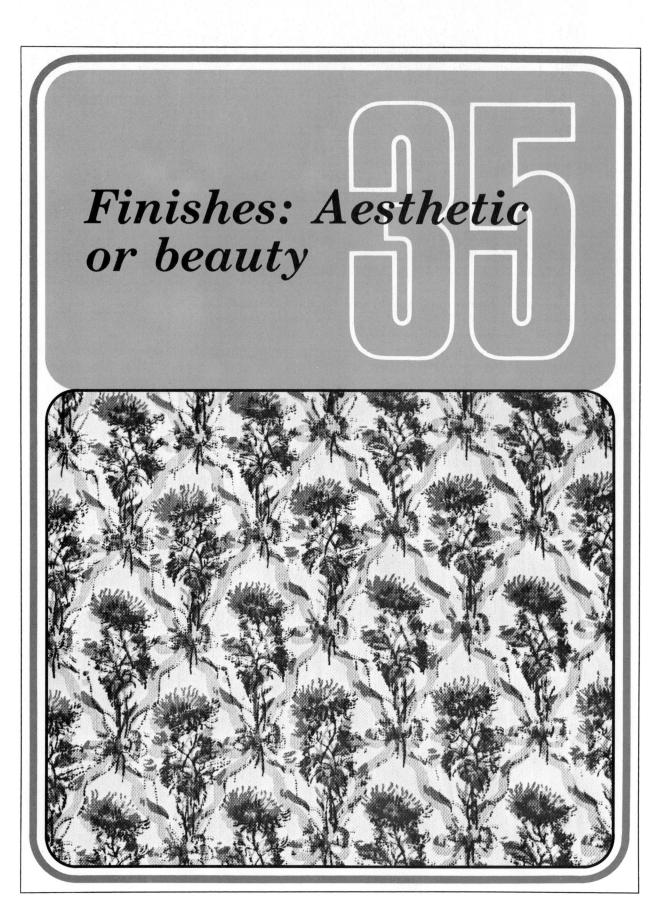

Finishes that change the appearance and/or hand of fabrics often create a new or particular fabric; for example, eyelet embroidery, flannel, and organdy are made by special finishes. Figure 35–1 shows several fabrics that were converted from cotton print cloth. Percale is roller printed, chintz is waxed and friction calendered, plissé is printed with caustic soda, and the embossed cotton was run through an embossing calender. This same fabric could be flocked, embroidered, or given a surface coating.

Special Purpose Calendering

Friction Calender. The *friction calender* is used to give a highly glazed surface to the cloth. If the fabric is first saturated with starch and waxes, the finish is only temporary; but if resin finishes are used, the glaze will be durable. The cloth is first passed through the finishing solution and then dried to a certain degree of dryness. It is then threaded into the calender. The speed of the metal roller is greater than the speed of the cloth, and the roller polishes the surface just as the sliding motion of the hand iron polishes the fabric. If the metal roll is hot, a higher glaze is obtained. Ciré is a taffeta or satin fabric friction calendered to give a high gloss or "wet" look.

Moiré Calender. The *moiré calender* has been used for more than 200 years to produce a "watermarked" design on ribbed silk and wool fabrics. Permanent designs can be made on thermoplastic fibers.

True moiré is applied to ribbed fabrics such as taffeta and faille. The rib is essential in producing the pattern, since the rolls of the calender are smooth. True moiré is made by placing two layers of ribbed fabric, one on top of the other, so that the ribs of the top layer are slightly "off-grain" in relation to the under layer. The two layers are stitched or held together along the selvage and

(a) *Print cloth*   (b) *Percale*   (c) *Chintz*

(d) *Plissé*   (e) *Embossed cotton*

Fig. 35–1 Fabrics converted from print cloth (a) Gray goods. (b) Roller printed. (c) Waxed and friction calendered. (d) Printed with caustic soda. (e) Run under embossing calender.

are then fed into the smooth, heated, metal roll calender. Pressure of 8 to 10 tons causes the rib pattern of the top layer to be pressed into the bottom layer and vice versa. Flattened areas in the ribs reflect more light and create a contrast to unflattened areas. This procedure can be modified to produce patterned moiré designs other than the watermarked one.

Schreiner Calender. The *Schreiner calender* (Figure 35–2) has a metal roller engraved with 200 to 300 fine diagonal lines that are visible only under a hand lens. (The lines should not be confused with yarn twist.) Until the advent of resins and thermoplastic fibers, this finish was temporary and was removed by the first washing. The primary purpose of this finish is to produce a *deep-seated luster,* rather than a shine, by breaking up reflectance of light rays. It also *flattens* the yarns to reduce the openness between them and give *smoothness* and *cover.* It can upgrade a sleazy material. This finish was originally used with cotton sateen and table damask to make them more lustrous and more salable. It was later used on polished resinated cottons and sateens as a durable finish. In 1957 it was first used to produce the *Satinette* finish on nylon and polyester tricot jersey.

Embossing Calender. The *embossing calender* produces either flat or raised designs on the fabric. Embossing became a much more important finish after the heat-sensitive fibers were developed because it was possible to produce a durable, washable, embossed pattern. Nylon, acrylics, acetate, polyesters, and fabrics made of nylon and metallic yarns are used. If the fabrics are made of solution-dyed fibers, they can be embossed di-

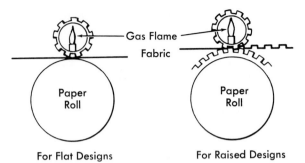

For Flat Designs   For Raised Designs

Fig. 35–3 Embossing process.

rectly off the loom and are then ready for sale. Embossed satins are used in high-style garments and can be sold for a much higher price than the unembossed fabric.

The embossing calender consists of two rolls, one of which is a hollow engraved metal roll heated from the inside by a gas flame. The other is a solid paper roll exactly twice the size of the engraved roll (Figure 35–3).

The process differs for the production of flat and raised designs.

1. Flat designs are the simplest to produce. A copper roll, engraved in deep-relief (Figure 35–4) revolves against a smooth paper roll. The hot engraved areas of the roll produce a glazed pattern on the fabric. Embossed brocades are an example of this type of design.

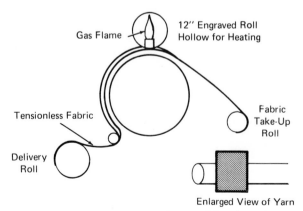

Fig. 35–2 Schreiner calender machine for tricot.

Fig. 35–4 Embossing rolls. (*Courtesy of Consolidated Engravers Corp.*)

2. Raised or relief designs require a more complicated routine. The paper roll is soaked in water and then revolved against the steel engraved roll (without fabric) until the pattern of engraving is pressed into the paper roll. The temperature is adjusted to suit the fabric, which is then passed between the rolls.

Pleating. Pleating is really a variation of embossing. It is an ancient art that dates back to the Egyptians, who used hot stones to make the pleats. Colonial women in the United States used heavy pleating irons to press in fancy pleats and fluting. Today, pleating methods are highly specialized operations done by either the paper-pattern technique or by the machine process.

The *paper pattern method* is a hand process and is, therefore, more costly, but it produces a wider variety of pleated designs. Garments in partly completed condition, such as hemmed skirt panels, are placed in a pleated paper pattern mold. The fabric is placed in the paper mold by hand and another pattern mold is placed on top so that the fabric is pleated between the two pleating papers. The whole thing is rolled into a cone shape, sealed, and put in a large curing oven for heat setting.

The *machine pleating method* is less expensive. The machine has two heated rolls. The fabric is inserted between the rolls as high-precision blades put the pleats in place. A paper backing is used under the pleated fabric and the pleats are held in place by paper tape. After leaving the heated roll machine, the pleats are *set* in an aging unit.

Acid Finishes

Parchmentized. Transparent (or parchment) effects in cotton cloth are produced by treatment with strong sulfuric acid. One of the oldest finishes is a Swiss or organdy finish produced by the Heberlein process. Since acid damages cotton, the process must be very carefully controlled, and "split-second" (5 to 6 seconds) timing is necessary to prevent *tendering* or weakening of the fabric. These effects are possible: all-over parchmentization, localized parchmentization, and plissé effect on either of the first two.

Since all-over parchmentizing is for the purpose of producing a transparent effect, a sheer fabric of combed lawn is used. The goods are singed, desized, bleached, and mercerized. Mer-

Fig. 35-5 Localized parchmentizing—acid finish—gives transparent background.

cerization is such an important part of the process that the fabric is mercerized again after the acid treatment in order to improve the transparency. The fabric is then dyed or printed with colors that will resist acid damage. The cloth is immersed in the acid solution and partial solution of the surface of the cellulose takes place. Upon drying, this surface rehardens as a cellulose film and gives permanent crispness and transparency. After the acid treatment the cloth is neutralized in weak alkali, washed, and then calendered to give more gloss to the surface. This all-over treatment produces *organdy* fabric.

In localized parchmentizing, if the design is a small figure with a large transparent area, an acid-resist substance is printed on the figures and the fabric is run through the acid bath. The acid-resistant areas retain their original opacity and contrast sharply with the transparent background (Figure 35–5). If a small transparent design is desired, the acid is printed on and then quickly washed off.

The three-dimensional plissé effect is achieved by printing caustic soda on the parchmentized fabric. The untreated areas pucker as the caustic soda causes the printed areas to shrink. The plissé effect can also be made on fabric with local parchmentization.

Burnt-out. *Burnt-out or etched effects* are produced by printing certain chemicals on a fabric made of fibers from different fiber groups: rayon and silk, for example. One fiber will be "eaten" away, leaving sheer areas. Figure 35–6 shows an

Fig. 35-6 Burnt-out design. Etched effect achieved by acid destroying rayon pile to leave a transparent background.

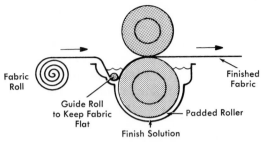

Fig. 35-7 Padding machine.

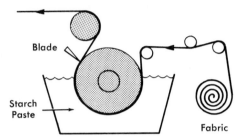

Fig. 35-8 Backfilling machine.

etched rayon/silk velvet. The rayon has been eaten away by acid.

Puckered Surfaces. *Puckered surfaces* are created by partial solution of the surface of a nylon or polyester fabric. Plissé, sculptured, and "damasque" effects are made by printing a chemical on the fabric to partially dissolve it. Shrinking occurs as it dries, thus creating a puckered surface.

Plissé.—See Chapter 24.

Flocking.—See Chapter 28.

Embroidered.—See Chapter 29.

Sizings and Coatings

Starching at the mill is similar to starching at home except that the starch mixture contains waxes, oils, glycerine, and similar compounds, which act as softeners. For added weight, talc, clay, and chalk are used. *Gelatin* is used on rayons because it is a clear substance that does not detract from the natural luster of the fibers but enhances it. *Surface coatings* of rubber latex, acrylic latex, resins, and urethane are used to increase abrasion resistance, serve as a binder, give luster, or provide waterproofing.

Additive finishes are applied to give texture (body, stiffness, softness), luster, embossed designs, and abrasion resistance to the fabric. They are held on the surface mechanically and their permanence depends on the efficiency of the finish and the type of finish itself.

The *pad machine,* often called the "workhorse" of the textile industry, is used to apply dyes, chemicals, and additive finishes. It will apply them in either liquid or paste form, on one or both sides (Figure 35–7).

Padding is done by passing the fabric through the finishing solution, under a guide roll, and between two padding rolls. The rolls are metal or rubber, depending on the finish to be applied. The rolls exert tons of pressure on the fabric to squeeze the finish into the fiber or fabric to assure good penetration. Excess liquid is squeezed off. The fabric then travels into the steaming or washing and drying machine.

The *backfilling machine* is a variation of the pad machine. It applies the finish to one side only, usually to the wrong side of the fabric (Figure 35–8).

Napping

Nap consists of a layer of fiber ends, on the surface of the cloth, that are *raised from the ground weave* by a mechanical brushing action. Thus, napped fabrics are literally "made" by a finishing process. Figure 35–9 shows a fabric before and after napping.

Napping was originally a hand operation in

Before Napping   After Napping

Fig. 35-9 Fabric before and after napping.

which the napper tied together several teasels (dried thistlelike vegetable burs, shown in Figure 35-10) and swept them with a plucking motion across the surface of the cloth to raise fibers from the ground weave. The teasels had a gentle action and the barbs would break off before causing any damage to the cloth. The raised fibers formed a nap that completely changed the appearance and texture.

Teasels are still used in the machine finishing of fine wool fabrics such as duvetyn. For machine processing (gigging) they are mounted on rollers, and as the barbs wear off or break off, the worn

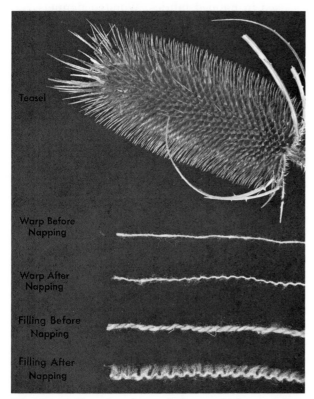

Teasel

Warp Before Napping

Warp After Napping

Filling Before Napping

Filling After Napping

Fig. 35-10 Teasel and yarn before and after napping.

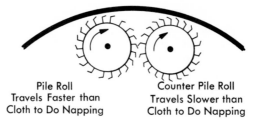

Pile Roll   Counter Pile Roll
Travels Faster than   Travels Slower than
Cloth to Do Napping   Cloth to Do Napping

Fig. 35-11 Napping rolls.

teasels are replaced by new ones. The fabric may be either wet or dry.

Most napping is now done by rollers covered by a heavy fabric in which bent wires are embedded (Figure 35-11). Napping machines may be single action or double action. Fewer rollers are used in the single-action machine. They are all alike and travel at the same speed. They are called *pile rolls,* and the bent ends of the wires point in the direction in which the cloth travels but the rollers are all mounted on a large drum or cylinder that rotates in the same direction as the cloth. The pile rolls must travel faster than the cloth in order to do any napping.

In the double-action napping machine every other roll is a *counter-pile roll.* This roll has wires that point in the direction opposite to those of the pile roll. The counter-pile roll must travel slower than the cloth in order to produce a nap. When the speed of the rolls is reversed (pile rolls at slower speed and counter-pile rolls at faster speed), a "tucking" action occurs. Tucking pushes the raised fibers back into the cloth and makes a smooth surface. Reasons for napping include the following:

1. *Warmth.* A napped surface and the soft twist of the filling yarns increase the dead air space. Still air is one of the best insulators.

2. *Softness.* This characteristic is especially important in baby clothes.

3. *Beauty.* Napping adds much to fabric attractiveness.

4. *Water and stain repellence.* Fiber ends on the surface cut down on the rapidity with which the fabric gets wet.

Quality, Characteristics, and Care. The amount of nap does not indicate the quality of the fabric. The amount may vary from the slight fuzz of Viyella flannel to the very thick nap of imitation fur. Short compact nap on a fabric with firm yarns and a closely woven ground will give the best wear. Stick a pin in the nap and lift the fabric. A good durable nap will hold the weight of the fabric. Hold the fabric up to the light and examine it. Press the nap aside and examine the ground weave. A napped surface may be used to cover defects or a sleazy construction. Rub the fabric between the fingers and then shake it to see if short fibers drop out. Thick nap may contain flock (very short wool fibers). Rub the surface of the nap to see if it is loose and will rub up in little balls (pilling). Notice the extreme pilling in the sweater in Figure 35–12.

Some napped fabrics have an up and down. To test this, brush the surface of the fabric. Brushing aginst the nap roughs it up and causes it to look darker because more light is absorbed. This is the "up" direction of the fabric. When the nap is smoothed down, the reflection of light from the surface gives a lighter shade of color. Napped fabrics should be made with the nap "down" so that garments will be easier to brush. However, the direction of the nap is not as important as the fact that the same direction of nap is used in all parts of a garment.

Low-count fabrics usually have low-twist yarns; when strain is applied, the fibers slip past one another and do not return to their original position. Thus, garments tend to "bag" in the seat and elbow areas. Tightly twisted yarns are more resistant to bagging. It is best to line low-count napped fabrics or to make the garment with gored or flared skirts.

Wear on the edges of sleeves, collars, buttonholes, and so forth causes an unsightly contrast to unworn areas. Very little can be done to it except that a vigorous brushing will give a fuzzier appearance. *Price is no indication of resistance to wear,* since the more expensive wool fibers are

Fig. 35-12 Pilling on a wool sweater.

finer and less resistant to abrasion. Wear will flatten the nap, but if nap is still present on the fabric it can be raised by brushing or steaming. Loosely napped fabrics will shed short fibers on other garments or surfaces. They also shed lint in the wash water so should be washed separately or after other articles are washed. Napped fabrics are fluffier if dried on a breezy day or dried in a dryer.

Construction. Napped fabrics must be made from especially constructed gray goods in which the filling yarns are made of *low-twist* staple (not filament) fibers. Turn back to page 138 and reread the information about yarn twist. The difference in yarn structure makes it easy to identify the lengthwise and crosswise grain of the fabric. Figure 35–10 shows the warp and filling yarns from a camel's-hair coat fabric, before and after napping.

Fabrics can be napped on either or both sides. The nap may have an upright position or it may be "laid down" or "brushed." When a heavy nap is raised on the surface, the yarns are sometimes weakened. Wool fabrics are fulled or shrunk to bring the yarns closer together and increase fabric strength.

Yarns of either long- or short-staple fibers may be used in napped fabrics. Worsted flannels, for example, are made of long-staple wool. The short-staple yarns used in woolen flannels have more fiber ends per inch and thus can have a heavier nap. In blankets, which are heavily napped for maximum fluffiness, a fine cotton (core) ply is sometimes used in the yarn to give strength.

Napped Fabrics. Napped fabrics can be made of any staple fiber. They are most frequently made of cotton, rayon, wool, or the acrylic fibers. Pilling and attraction of lint due to electrostatic properties are problems with the nylons and polyesters. Napping is less expensive than pile weave as a way of producing a three-dimensional fabric.

Napped fabrics may be plain weave, twill weave, or knit. More filling yarn is exposed on the surface in a $\frac{2}{2}$ twill or a filling-faced twill; therefore, a heavier nap can be raised on twill fabrics. The knit construction in napped fabrics is often used for articles for the baby. Some brands of coats are always made of napped knit fabrics.

The name *flannel* is almost synonymous with the word *napped*. When the name is used alone it implies wool fiber content. If the fabric is made of fiber other than wool, a descriptive adjective is used with the word *flannel*—for example, *cotton flannel.*

Flannel is an all-wool napped fabric made in dress, suit, or coat weights. It may be made with either worsted or woolen yarns. They may be yarn-dyed. *Worsted flannels* are important in men's suits and coats and are used to a lesser extent in women's suits and coats. They are firmly woven and have a very short nap. They wear well, are easy to press, and hold a press well. *Woolen flannels* are fuzzier, less firmly woven fabrics. Many have been given a shrinkage control treatment which alters the scale structure of the fiber. Because napping causes some weakening of the fabric, 15 to 20 per cent nylon or polyester is blended with the wool to improve the strength.

Fleece is a coat-weight fabric with long brushed nap or a short clipped nap. Quality is very difficult to determine.

Cotton flannels flatten under pressure and give less insulating value than wool because cotton fibers are less resilient. The fibers are also shorter, thus there is more shedding of lint from cotton flannels. The direction of nap (up and down) is relatively unimportant in these fabrics because their chief uses are robes, nightwear, baby clothes, and sweat shirts. Polyester/cotton blends are often used. *Flannelette* is a plain-weave fabric that is converted from a gray-goods fabric called soft-filled sheeting. It is napped on one side only, has a short nap, and has a printed design, unless it is white. The nap will form small pills and is subject to abrasion. *Suede* and *duvetyn* are also converted from the same gray goods but are sheared close to the ground to make a smooth, flat surface. Of the two, duvetyn is lighter in weight. *Outing flannel* is a yarn-dyed fabric (or white) that is similar in fabric weight and length of nap to flannelette but is napped on both sides.

As the warp yarns in both flannelette and outing flannel are standard weaving yarns, it is easy to identify the grain of the fabric. Napped knitted fabrics are often given pile fabric names such as velvet or velour.

Finishes: Special purpose

Special purpose finishes usually do not alter the appearance of fabrics but they improve their performance. They help solve some of the problems that consumers have had with textile products.

Stabilization:
Shrinkage Control

A fabric is stabilized when it retains its original size and shape during use and care. Unstable fabrics shrink or stretch. Of these, shrinkage is the more serious problem. *Shrinkage* is the reduction in size of a fabric or garment.

The shrinkage problem with cotton began when spinning, weaving, and finishing were mechanized. Fabrics are under tension on the loom, and in wet finishing, fabrics are pulled through machines in long continuous pieces and finally set under excessive warpwise tension that leaves the fabric with high residual shrinkage. This shrinkage will take place when tensions are released by laundering or steam pressing.

Shrinkage is used to advantage in the manufacture of some fabrics. For example, *fulling* of wool cloth closes up the weave and makes a firmer fabric, and shrinkage of the high-twist yarns in crepes creates the surface crinkle. Shrinkage is a disadvantage to the consumer when it changes the length or size of a garment. Shrinkage of 5 per cent in a size 15 shirt can shorten the sleeve length $\frac{3}{4}$ inch and reduce the chest size by 2 or 3 inches. A washable garment should not shrink more than 2 per cent. Before the 1930s, washable cotton garments were often purchased one size too large and then shrunk down to fit. Then the compressive shrinkage-control process was invented and garments bearing the label Sanforized could be purchased in the correct size with the assurance that they would not shrink more than 1 per cent (unless tumble-dried).

Before Redmanizing   After Redmanizing

Fig. 36-1 Knit stitches stretched and relaxed.

There are two types of shrinkage: *relaxation* (or fabric) shrinkage, which occurs in the first wash, and *progressive* (or fiber) shrinkage, which occurs during subsequent washes. Mechanical control methods or heat are used to eliminate relaxation shrinkage, and chemical control methods are used to prevent progress shrinkage.

1. *Cotton, linen, and high-wet-modulus rayon:*
Exhibit relaxation shrinkage
No progressive shrinkage

2. *Regular rayon:*
Exhibits high relaxation shrinkage
Moderate progressive shrinkage

3. *Wool:*
Exhibits moderate relaxation shrinkage
High progressive shrinkage

4. *Other man-made fibers:*
Exhibit relaxation shrinkage
No progressive shrinkage

Relaxation Shrinkage and Methods of Control

Knit Fabrics. Knit fabrics shrink because the loops are elongated 10 to 35 per cent lengthwise in knitting and in wet finishing (Figure 36–1). During home laundering the stitches will reorient themselves to their normal shape, and the garment will become shorter and wider. Length is a critical dimension in knit apparel because width shrinkage is restorable when the clothing is worn.

The first guaranteed shrinkage-control treatment for cotton knits—Shrink-No-Mor (1971)—guarantees that the fabric will not shrink more than 1 per cent in length when it is washed and tumble dried. Control is achieved by a combination mechanical and resin process applied after dyeing. Products are home-sewing yardage, shirts, women's wear, and sportswear.

Pak-nit is a trademark of Compax Corporation, which guarantees less than 1 per cent shrinkage in knits. The process consists of running the fabric through rollers, but overfeeding the fabric between sets of rollers that results in lengthwise shrinkage. *Sanfor-Knit* was developed for 100 per cent cotton or cotton/polyester blends. The increased use of polyester in cottonlike knits permits the fabric to be heat-set for stabilizing.

Woven Fabrics. All woven fabrics shrink when the strains of weaving, warp-yarn sizing, and wet

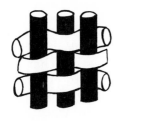 

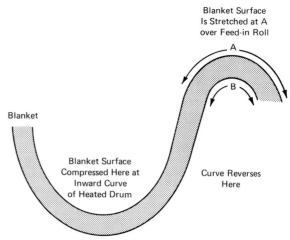

Fig. 36-2 (*Left*) Position of the warp on the loom. (*Right*) After the fabric relaxes when it becomes wet.

finishing are released when the fabric gets wet in laundering. The warp yarns are stretched out straight while they are on the loom, and the filling is inserted in a straight line. The filling takes on crimp as it is beaten back into the cloth, but the warp stays straight (Figure 36-2). When the fabric is thoroughly wet and allowed to relax, the yarns readjust themselves and the warp yarns move to a crimped position also (Figure 36-2). This crimp shortens the fabric in the warp direction. With the exception of crepe fabrics, less change occurs in the filling direction.

Compressive shrinkage processes are used on woven fabrics of cotton, linen, and high-wet-modulus rayon. Regular rayons will not hold a compressive shrinkage treatment because of the high swelling and wet elongation of the rayon fibers.

Sanforize and Rigmel are trade names for compressive shrinkage processes used on woven cloth. The trade name Sanforized Plus may be used on wash-and-wear and durable-press garments that meet specified standards of shrinkage control, wrinkle resistance, smoothness after washing, tensile strength, and tear strength. The principles involved in compressive shrinkage can be demonstrated by placing a piece of fabric over the clenched fist, then placing a rubber band over the cloth. When the fist is opened and the band is released, the cloth will be squeezed or compressed.

In the factory process, a woolen felt blanket is the medium that shrinks the cloth. A thick blanket will shrink the cloth more than a thin one. The blanket, with the moist cloth adhering to its surface, is passed around a feed-in roll. In this curved position the outer surface stretches and the inner surface contracts. The blanket then reverses its direction around a heated drum. The outer curve becomes the shorter inner surface and the fabric adhering to it is compressed. The fabric, which is now against the drum, is dried and set with a smooth finish. The number of yarns per

Fig. 36-3 How reversal of curve can cause change in size to compress fabric.

square inch will increase, and the cloth will actually be improved after compressing (Figures 36-3 and 36-4).

Research has shown that faulty laundering will cause compressively shrunk fabrics to shrink as much as 6 per cent. Tumble drying may also compress the yarns beyond their normal shrinkage.

London Shrunk is a 200-year-old relaxation finish for wool fabrics, which removes strains caused by spinning, weaving, and finishing. Originally fabric was laid out in the fields of the city of London and the dew soothed away the stresses

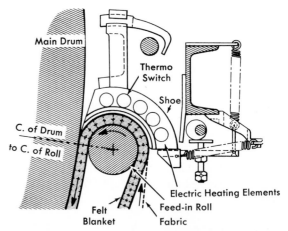

Fig. 36-4 Enlarged cross-sectional diagram of the point in the compressive-shrinkage process where length shrinkage is obtained. The electrically heated shoe holds the fabric firmly on the outside of the blanket so that when the blanket collapses in straightening out, the fabric is shrunk accordingly. (*Courtesy of Sanforized Division of Cluett, Peabody & Co., Inc.*)

and improved the hand of the fabric. Although techniques have been modernized, there is still much hand labor involved. A wet blanket, wool or cotton, is placed on a long platform, a layer of cloth is then spread on it, and alternate layers of blankets and cloth are built up. Sufficient weight is placed on top to force the moisture from the blankets into the wool. The cloth is left in the pile for about 12 hours. The cloth is then dried in natural room air by hanging it over sticks. When dry, the cloth is subjected to hydraulic pressing by building up layers of cloth and specially made press boards with a preheated metal plate inserted at intervals. A preheated metal plate is also placed on the top and bottom. This setup of cloth, boards, and plates is kept under 3,000 pounds of pressure for 10 to 12 hours. London shrinking is done for men's wear fine worsteds—not for woolens or women's wear.

Today the right to use the label "Genuine London Process" or something similar is licensed by the Parrot group of companies, Clothworkers of London, Leeds, and Huddersfield, to garment makers all over the world. A label from a suit is shown in Figure 36–5. The permanent-set finish Si-Ro-set, which produces washable, wrinkle-free wool fabrics, is now applied to some fabrics during London-shrunk processing.

A similar method for home use is that of rolling wool cloth in a wet sheet, allowing it to stand for 6 hours, and then placing it flat on a table or floor to dry. If it is straightened while wet, pressing may be unnecessary. This is the best means for straightening wool that has been tentered or decated "off-grain." It should not be used on wool crepe. Fabrics that have a napped surface, such as wool broadcloth or some wool flannels, may be changed in appearance. Wool fabrics should always be tested for shrinkage prior to cutting. A simple method of testing is to draw a right angle on the ironing board, place the warp edge along one side and the filling edge along the other side, and hold the steam iron over the fabric. If either edge draws away from the pencil line, the fabric will shrink during steam pressing and it should be shrunk.

Progressive Shrinkage and Methods of Control

Thermoplastic Fibers. Thermoplastic fibers are stabilized by heatsetting, a process in which fabrics are heated at temperatures at or above the glass transition temperature (Tg) and then cooled. The Tg temperature is the point at which the amorphous regions of the fiber melt. It is lower than the melting point of the fiber and differs for various fibers. If properly heat-set, fabrics will exhibit no progressive shrinkage and relaxation shrinkage will also be controlled (Figure 36–5).

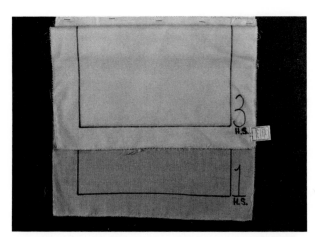
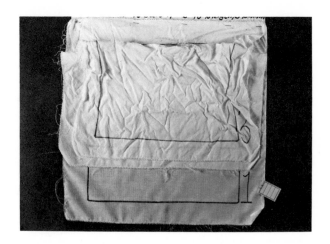

Fig. 36–5 Comparison of thermoplastic fiber fabrics. (*Left*) heat set. (*Right*) not heat set. Note wrinkling and shrinkage.

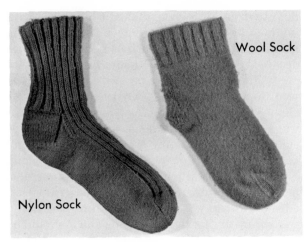

Wool Sock

Nylon Sock

Fig. 36-6 These socks were the same size when purchased. (*Left*) nylon. (*Right*) wool.

Wool Fibers. Washable wool is important in clothing, in skin-contact clothing, and in blends with washable fibers. If wool fabrics are to improve their position in the competitive market with fabrics made from woollike fibers that have easy-care characteristics, they must be finished to keep their original size and surface texture with home-cleaning methods. It might be assumed that people who can afford professional care will not be interested in washing wools. Another assumption might be that washable wools (those given a felting shrinkage-control treatment) are the poor- to medium-quality wools. Whether or not these assumptions are true, felting shrinkage is important today, as evidenced by the fact that 250 patents for feltproofing wool were issued prior to 1957 and more have been issued since (see page 25). Figure 36-6 shows shrinkage of a wool sock.

To prevent felting shrinkage, the finish must alter the scale structure by "smoothing off" the free edges and thus reduce the differential friction effect that prevents wool fibers from returning to their original position in the cloth. The effectiveness of felting shrinkage treatments depends on the kind and amount of finish used, and on the yarn and fabric construction. Worsteds need less finish than woolens. Low-count fabrics and low-twist yarns need more finish to give good washability. Treated wool fabrics are usually considered machine washable, but care should be taken to use warm, not hot, water and a short agitation period. Hand washing is preferable, since soil is easy to remove from the fiber and the hand-washing process ensures lower temperature and less agitation. Machine washing may cause more

loosening of fibers, which results in a fuzzy or slightly pilled surface.

Two methods are used to smooth off the free edges of the scales: halogenation treatments and surface coatings.

Halogenation treatments are the most widely used—primarily chlorine. They are low in cost, can be applied to large batches of small items such as wool socks, do not require padding or curing equipment, and are fairly effective. The processes are quite delicate and, if not carefully done, are likely to damage the fibers. The scales are more resistant to damage than the interior of the fiber and should not be completely removed or there will be considerable reduction in wearing properties, loss of weight, and change in hand. The fabric will feel harsh and rough. To maintain the strength of the fabric, 18 per cent nylon fiber is blended with the wool before weaving. *Superwash* is the trade name for a process combining chlorination and resin to make wool knits machine washable and dryer dryable. Shrinkage is less than 3 per cent in length and 1 per cent in width, and goods retain their loft and resiliency.

Surface coatings of a polyamide-type solution are applied to mask the scales. This is a very thin, microscopic film on the outside of the fiber. In addition to controlling shrinkage, the coating tends to minimize pilling and fuzzing (one of the greatest problems in wash-and-wear wools), gives the fabrics better wash-and-wear properties, and increases resistance to abrasion. This process, which carries the trade name *Wurlan,* was developed at the Department of Agriculture Laboratory in Albany, California.

Rayon Fibers. The shrinkage of regular rayon varies with the handling of the fabric when wet. While it is wet the fabric can be stretched, and it is difficult to keep from overstretching it during processing. If it is dried in this stretched condition, the fabric will have high potential shrinkage and shrink when wet again and dried without tension because the moisture in the fabric adds enough weight to stretch it.

Shrinkage-control treatments for rayon reduce the swelling property of the fiber and make it resistant to distortion. Resins are impregnated inside the fiber to form cross-links that prevent swelling and keep the fiber from stretching. The resin also fills up spaces in the amorphous areas of the fiber, making it less absorbent. The non-nitrogenous resins (the aldehydes) are superior to the other resins because they do not weaken the fabric and are nonchlorine retentive and have excellent wash fastness. Treated rayons are machine washable, but the wash cycle should be short. High wet modulus rayon is also resintreated, mainly for durable press purposes, since its shrinkage can be controlled by the relaxation shrinkage-control method of Sanforization.

Shape-Retentive Finishes

Before 1940 creases were pressed in and wrinkles were pressed or ironed out after garments were washed or dry cleaned. Most people sent silks and wools to the dry cleaner and washed cottons and linens at home. Cottons were starched to prevent mussing. Significant changes have taken place in clothing care. Today, most people want to wash everything in the automatic washer, dry everything in the dryer, and wear the garments with no other care required. With thermoplastic fibers and special shape-retentive finishes wash, dry, and wear is possible. It took nearly 20 years to change the care requirements for textiles.

Wrinkle Resistant. The first step was the development of *wrinkle-resistant* finishes for spun rayon. Resin finishes were first used in England in 1920 and in the United States in 1940 for this purpose. The resin finishes were found to be equally good on cotton and linen fabrics.

Wrinkles, caused by crushing fabrics during wear and washing, are usually undesirable; creases and pleats made by pressing are desirable style features. Fibers that have strong molecular bonds (good molecular memory) resist wrinkling and creasing, whereas those with weak bonds wrinkle and crease readily.

Theory of Wrinkle Recovery. Fiber recovery is dependent on cross-links that hold adjacent molecular chains together and pull them back into position after the fiber is bent, thus preventing the formation of a wrinkle.

The cellulose fibers do not have natural cross links. Molecular chains are held together by hydrogen bonds that operate like the attraction of a magnet for a nail. The hydrogen bonds of cellulose break with the stress of bending and new bonds form to hold the fiber in this bent position, thus forming a wrinkle. Resin cross links will prevent this and give the fiber good wrinkle recovery (Figure 36–7).

Urea formaldehyde was the first resin used to prevent wrinkles; other resins and improved resin combinations were developed later. Although fabrics treated with these resins were smooth and flat and wrinkle resistant, they had poor abrasion resistance and lessened tear strength and often developed a fishy odor.

Wash-and-Wear. *Wash-and-wear finishes* were the next development. More resin was used to produce fabrics for drip-dry garments; about 7 per cent resin compared with 3 per cent for wrinkle resistance. Garments made of these fabrics could be washed and rinsed but removed from the washer before the spin cycle. They could be hung on wooden or plastic hangers, buttoned or zipped, straightened out, and allowed to drip dry. Touch-up pressing might be needed if there were puckers at the seams or in the zipper area.

Durable Press. Durable press is a descriptive term applied to garments that retain their shape and their pressed appearance even after many washings, wearings, and tumble dryings. The terms *durable press* and *permanent press* are

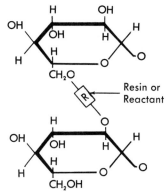

Fig. 36–7(b) Resin crosslink.

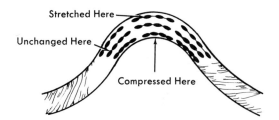

Fig. 36–7(a) Effect on internal structure when fiber is bent.

used interchangeably, but *durable* is preferred as being a more realistic description.

The concept of *permanent shape for garments*—durable press—was introduced in the early 1960s when Koratron's "Oven-Baked" pants for men were marketed with tremendous and instantaneous success, even though the higher resin content (10 per cent) needed for durable press caused the pants to split at the creases and cuff edges after two or three washings. Men's shirts were the second durable-press item made. It was said that each garment had a certain drama. For example, in slacks the focal point is the crease; if it is a good sharp crease, some puckering or wrinkling does not dissatisfy the consumer. In shirts the focal point is the collar; if it is smooth and crisp a slight lack of smoothness of the body fabric may not be objectionable. This may account for the immediate acceptance of the durable-press concept.

The Precured Process

1. Saturate the fabric with the resin cross-linking solution and dry.

2. Cure in a curing oven (cross-links form between molecular chains).

3. Cut and sew garment. Press with iron. (All yard goods for home sewing are made this way).

4. Some trade names:
Disciplined cotton (Bates), Regulated cotton (Penney's), and Belfast (Deering-Millikin).
If Sanforized, the fabrics are labeled Sanforized Plus.

The Postcured Process

1. Saturate the cloth with a resin cross-linking solution and dry.

2. Cut and sew garment and press shape with hot-head press.

3. *Cure* by putting pressed garment into a curing oven at 300° to 400° F.

4. Curing gives shape to the cotton component. The polyester component (or any other thermoplastic fiber) was *set* by the hot-head pressing. Some trade names:
Koratron (Korot of California), Dan-Press (Dan

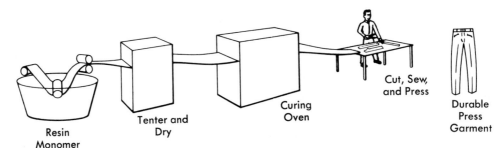

Fig. 36-8 Precured process.

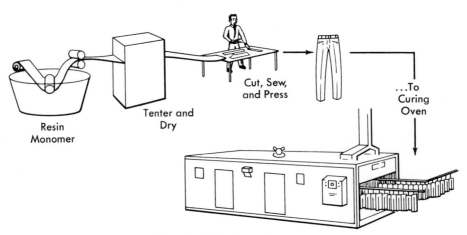

Fig. 36-9 Postcured process.

River Mills), Reeve-set (Reeves Bros.), Super crease (J. P. Stevens), Coneprest (Cone Mills).

The two processes, *precured* and *postcured,* for durable press garments and fabrics are outlined on the opposite page. The major difference in these two processes is the stage at which cutting, sewing and pressing take place (Figs. 36–8 and 36–9).

Problems associated with resin finishes—other than reduced tensile strength and abrasion resistance—are listed.

1. Fabric stiffness and poor hand.

2. Chlorine absorption, which causes yellowing and loss of strength.

3. Offensive odors—fishy or formaldehyde smell.

4. Color problems: "frosting" or loss of color on abraded edges; migration of color from the polyester fibers to the cotton component as a result of the high curing temperature.

5. Soiling—especially the affinity of resins for oily soils. Soil-release finishes now help with this (see page 281).

6. Static pilling.

7. Garment construction problems—seam puckering, pressing-in or removing creases when altering garments.

Many of these problems have been solved or minimized.

By using blends of polyester/cotton instead of 100 per cent cotton less resin is needed. The high strength and abrasion resistance of polyester makes these fabrics much more durable. Special pressing equipment has been developed for use on precured fabrics. Pretreatment of cotton with liquid ammonia or mercerizing cotton under tension adds strength to fabrics so they are not weakened as much from the finish. Polymer sizing on the yarns before curing gives the fabric greater abrasion resistance.

Coneprest, by Cone Mills, is a process in which precured fabrics are made into garments. Where creases are desired, the garment is sprayed with a substance that temporarily inactivates the wrinkle-resistant finish. The garments are then pressed under pressure to recure the finish.

Ameriset, developed by American Laundry

Machinery Industries, is a finish in which untreated fabrics are cut, sewed, and pressed and the garments are placed in a gas chamber where formaldehyde and sulfur dioxide vapor enters the fabric causing cross-links in the cellulose fibers.

Durable-Press Wool. Wool has good resiliency when it is dry but it does not have durable press characteristics when it is wet. Durable-press wool is achieved with resin treatments, but this must be accompanied by a treatment with shrink-resist resins in order to control wool's tendency to excessive shrinkage. Several procedures are used, but the one described here is typical.

1. Flat fabric is treated with 1 to 2 per cent of the durable-press resin and steamed (semidecated) for 3 to 5 minutes.

2. The garment is made up, sprayed with more durable-press resin, and pressed on a Hoffman press. This gives the permanent-crease effect.

3. Shrink-resist resin is mixed with a dry-cleaning solvent and the garment is dry-cleaned. The resin is then allowed to cure in the garment for 3 to 7 days before the garment can be laundered.

Quality Standards and Care. Quality-control standards had not been developed during the wash-and-wear era and there was wide variation, dependent on the economic objectives of the individual converter. Wash-and-wear and durable press have been one of the major profit areas of the textile industry, and there were those who were interested in quick profits rather than quality. To avoid this problem the industry worked on the development of standards for durable press, and quality has been much more dependable. Registered trade names have been adopted by many producers. These trade names are an indication to the consumer that the product has met certain performance tests. The consumer can also check the fabric for objectionable odor or excessive stiffness—both of these indicate poor processing. If the fabric is a blend, there should be an adequate amount of the polyester or other thermoplastic fiber for the garment to meet performance standards.

Some suggestions for care:

• Wash frequently and do not allow soil to build up. Resins have a special affinity for oil and grease which should be removed quickly before they can penetrate.

- Pretreat stains, collars, and cuffs. Use a dry-cleaning solvent on the grease spots.
- Keep wash loads small. Crowding makes wrinkles.
- Heat sets wrinkles so avoid heat as much as possible in the laundering process. Avoid wringing and squeezing. Use an automatic dryer if possible but remove clothes promptly.

Other Finishes

Water-Repellent Finishes. Waterproof fabrics are compared with water-repellent fabrics in the following chart.

A water-repellent fabric is resistant to wetting, but if the water comes with enough force, it will penetrate the fabric.

The Federal Trade Commission has suggested the use of the terms *durable* and *renewable* in describing water-repellent fabrics.

Water repellency is dependent on surface tension and fabric penetrability and is achieved by (1) finish and (2) cloth construction.

Finishes that can be applied to fabric to make it repellent are wax emulsions, metallic soaps, and surface-active agents. They are applied to fabrics such as tackle twill, poplin, and rayon and cotton sateen, all of which have a very high warp count and are made with fine yarns.

Wax emulsions and metallic soaps coat the yarns but do not fill the interstices between the yarns. These finishes are not permanent but tend to come out when the fabric is washed or dry-cleaned. They can be renewed.

Surface-active agents have molecules with one end that is water-repellent and one end that will react with the hydroxyl (OH) groups of cellulose. After they are applied, heat is used to seal the finish to the fabric. This finish is permanent to washing and dry cleaning.

Cloth can be water-repellent without a finish. Cloth bags are used for carrying water when crossing the desert.

It is more difficult to select a water-repellent coat than a waterproof coat because the finish is not obvious and one must depend on the label for information. However, the consumer can recognize some guides for buying. *The cloth construction is far more important than the finish.* The closer the weave, the greater is the resistance to water penetration. The kind of finish used is important in selection because it influences the cost of upkeep. The use of two layers of fabric across the shoulders gives increased protection, but the inner layer must also have a water-repellent finish, or it will act as a blotter and cause more water to penetrate. Care is important in water-repellent fabrics. The greater the soil on the coat, the less water repellent it is.

Water-repellent finishes render fabrics spot and stain resistant. Some of the finishes are resistant to waterborne stains, some to oil-borne stains, and some to both. Durable water-repellent finishes often hold greasy stains more tenaciously than untreated fabrics. Unisec, Scotchgard, and Zepel are trade names for finishes that give resistance to both oily and waterborne stains. Hydro-Pruf and Syl-mer are silicone finishes that resist waterborne stains.

Soil-and stain-repellent finishes are fluorocarbons applied by a pad-dry-cure process. They are effective against water and oil-borne stains and

Waterproof Fabrics	Water-Repellent Fabrics
Fabrics are plastic films or low-count fabrics with a film coating.	High-count fabrics with a finish that coats the yarn but does not fill up the interstices of the fabric.
Characteristics	
No water can penetrate.	Heavy rain will penetrate.
Most plastic fabrics stiffen in cold weather.	Fabric is pliable, and is no different from untreated fabric.
Cheaper to produce.	Fabric can "breathe," is comfortable for raincoats.
Permanent.	Durable or renewable finish.

are durable. Zepel, Scotchgard, and Fybrite are trade names.

Soil-Release Finishes. The term *soil release* refers to the property of a fabric that permits oil-borne stains to be readily removed in the home washer. Redeposition is the property that permits a fabric to pick up soil—from wash water—that was previously released into the wash water.

A large quantity of the washable material on the market now has a soil-release finish that definitely improves the fabric performance in *resisting* soil, *releasing* soil, and retaining fabric whiteness by *resisting redeposition* of soil from the wash water. The big problem is that these finishes do not last the life of the garment. Some are durable enough to last through 20 to 30 washings. Lack of permanence results from the fact that the finish is applied to the surface.

Soil-release finishes were developed for use on durable-press garments because of their tendency to pick up and *hold* oily stains and spots. The resin content of durable press is much higher than that of the older wash-and-wear, so the problem of soiling is much more acute. The tendency to pick up oil (oil affinity) means that oil is absorbed into the resin or the fiber.

Most durable-press garments are blends of polyester/cotton. Untreated cotton is hydrophilic, and hydrophilic surfaces give the best soil release performance, so cotton releases soil when it is laundered. The resin finish, however, is hydrophobic and does not release the oily soil. Polyester is hydrophobic (oleophilic) and has an affinity for oil. It must be spot-treated to remove oily soil from contact areas of a garment such as the collar. When the polyester is coated with resin as it is in durable press, its oil affinity is increased. Finer fibers soil more readily than coarse fibers, and soil can penetrate low-twist yarns more easily than high-twist yarns.

Oily soil does not come out of resinated cottons or polyester in washing, so they must be dry-cleaned or spot-cleaned with a dry-cleaning solution. Soil-release finishes make the surface less attractive to oil and more easily wetted—more hydrophilic. Many finishing materials fall into two general classes; they are mechanically or chemically bonded to the surface. Some of the new finishes are said, by producers, to be permanent.

Standardized test methods are being developed. The varied nature of staining materials has made it difficult to produce a soil-release finish that will be effective for all of them. Some are waterborne and some are oil-borne; some, for example, mustard and lipstick, contain dyes; others, such as motor oil, may contain metals abraded from the engine.

Some trade names for soil-release finishes are Fybrite, Visa, Zelcon, and Zip Clean. Fantessa is a new finish by J. P. Stevens.

Absorbent Finishes. *Absorbent finishes* are used on towels, diapers, underwear, and sportswear. They are applied as surface coatings for fibers and yarns. On nylon a solution of nylon 8 is used; on polyesters the finish changes the molecular structure of the fiber surface so that moisture is broken up into smaller particles that wick more readily; on cellulosics the finish makes them absorb more moisture. Fiber modifications and different fabric structures are more effective than finishes. Fantessa, Visa, and Zelcon are trade names.

Anti-Static Finishes. *Anti-static* finishes are important in both the production and utilization of fabrics. Static charges that develop on fabrics cause them to cling to machinery in the factory, cling to people, attract dust and lint, and produce sparks and shocks.

Control of static buildup on natural fiber fabrics was done by increasing humidity and using lubricants but these controls were not adequate with the thermoplastic fibers.

Finishes were developed to (1) improve the surface conductivity so that excess electrons move to the atmosphere, (2) attract water molecules, or (3) neutralize electrical charges on the fibers. Many finishes combine all three effects. Finishes are usually not durable. They are cationic surface agents based on quaternary ammonium compounds. Washing aids, such as Downy, Sta-Puf, Nu-Soft, and Negastat, help to control static.

Incorporating antistatic substances into the fibers gives the best static control. Most man-made fibers are produced in antistatic form especially for rugs and carpets, lingerie, and uniforms (see page 110).

Abrasion-Resistant Finishes. *Abrasion-resistant* finishes are used on pocket linings and sometimes on other lining fabrics. Thermoplastic resins seem to fix fibers more firmly into the yarns so they do not break off as readily. Blending nylon or polyester with cotton or rayon gives better resistance to abrasion than using finishes.

Antislip Finishes. *Antislip finishes* are used on low-thread count, smooth-surfaced fabrics. Fabrics are treated with resins, stretched, and dried under tension causing the yarns to be somewhat bonded together at their interlacing points.

Moth Control. It has been estimated that $100 million is lost annually from damage of textiles by moths and carpet beetles. Most of this damage occurs where storehouses store raw wool, manufacturers store fabrics, and stores carry over suits and coats from one season to another. Moth damage is an equally serious problem for consumers.

Both moths and carpet beetles attack not only 100 per cent wool but also blends of wool and other fibers. Although they can digest only the wool, moths and carpet beetles also eat through the other fibers. The damage is done by the larvae and not the adult moth. Clothes moths are about $\frac{1}{4}$-inch long; they are not the large moths that we may occasionally see about the house. Larvae shun bright sunlight and do their work in the dark. For this reason it is necessary to clean often under sofas, under sofa cushions, in creases of chairs and garments, and in dark closets. Larvae are supposed to be killed by direct sunlight, so it is a good practice to hang garments in the sun occasionally.

Means of controlling moth damage are as follows:

1. Cold storage.
2. Odors that repel. Paradichlorobenzene and naphthalene (moth balls) used during storage.

3. Stomach poisons. Fluorides and silicofluorides are finishes for dry-cleanable wool.
4. Contact poisons. DDT is very effective but requires frequent application.
5. Chemicals added to the dye bath permanently change the fiber, making it unpalatable to the larvae.

Mold and Mildew Control. Molds and mildew will grow on and damage both cellulose and protein textiles. They will grow on, but not damage, the thermoplastic fibers. Losses are estimated in the millions of dollars.

Prevention is the best solution to the problem in apparel since cures are often impossible. To prevent mold or mildew, keep textiles clean and dry. Soiled clothes should be kept dry and washed as soon as possible. Sunning and airing should be done frequently during periods of high humidity. An electric light can be used in dark, humid storage places. Dehumidifiers in homes are very helpful.

If mildew occurs, wash the article immediately. Mild stains can be removed by bleaching.

Antiseptic Finishes. *Antiseptic finishes* are used to inhibit the growth of bacteria and other odor-causing germs and to prevent decay and damage from perspiration. These finishes are important in skin-contact clothing, shoe linings, and especially hospital linens. The chemicals used are surface reactants, mostly quaternary ammonia compounds. Zirconium peroxides can be formed on the surface of cotton fabrics to give antibacterial properties. Those substances can be added to the spinning solution of rayon and acetate fibers. Most diaper-service establishments add the finish during each laundering. Eversan and Sanitized are two trade names.

Flammability and Flame-Retardant Finishes

37

Children and old people are the most frequent victims of fire because they are unable to protect themselves. Each year a large number of fatalities, as well as nonfatal injuries, result from fires associated with flammable fabrics. Financial loss from such fires is estimated in the millions of dollars. Five common causes of these fires are smoking in bed, starting fires with flammable liquids, playing with matches and lighters (by children), burning trash, and being caught in a burning house. Smoke inhalation is as great a danger as burns and is regarded as the major cause of death in fires.

Construction of a fabric or garment determines the degree to which oxygen is made available to the fibers. Cloth constructions that burn quickly are sheer or light weight fabrics and napped, pile, or tufted surfaces. Some items of apparel made from these constructions ignite quickly, burn with great intensity, and are difficult to extinguish. "Torch" sweaters, fringed cowboy chaps, and chenille berets are examples of some apparel items that have been the cause of tragic accidents. When the chenille berets were tested in the laboratory, test strips taken from the berets would begin to burn while the flame was several inches away, indicating that it would be extremely dangerous to wear the beret while lighting a cigarette. Some style features of wearing apparel also present a fire hazard. Long full sleeves, flared skirts, ruffles, frills, and flowing robes are examples.

Flammable Fabrics Act

Congress enacted the first national law dealing with flammable fabrics in 1953 after an incident in Washington, D.C., in which several Boy Scouts burned to death when the fringe on their suits caught fire. The Flammable Fabrics Act prohibited the marketing of dangerously flammable material, including all wearing apparel, regardless of their fiber content or construction. The act covered items that were imported or that were in interstate commerce. One purpose of the law was to develop standards and tests to separate the dangerously flammable fabrics from the normally combustible ones.

The act was amended in 1967 to cover a broader range of apparel and interior furnishings with the responsibilities for its implementation divided among the secretary of Commerce, the secretary of Health, Education, and Welfare, and

Fig. 37-1 Flame-retardant children's flannel pajamas.

the Federal Trade Commission. In 1972, the Consumer Product Safety Act was passed and the Consumer Product Safety Commission (CPSC), which has broad jurisdiction over consumer safety, was established. The responsibilities and functions, as stipulated in the Flammable Fabrics Act, were transferred to the CPSC. Federal standards were established under the direction of the Department of Commerce and later under the CPSC as shown in the following chart. These standards and/or test methods may be modified in the future depending on further research and evaluation.

Notices of findings that flammability standards may be needed have been issued for children's wearing apparel, upholstered furniture, and blankets. It takes considerable time to develop a standard. First, facts must be collected to indicate a need. A notice is published in the Federal Register that there is a need for a standard. Interested persons are requested to respond. Test methods are developed and published in a second notice. A final notice, which includes details of the standard and test method, is published with the effective date of compliance. One year is usually allowed so that merchandise that does not meet the standard can be sold or otherwise disposed of, and new merchandise can be altered (if necessary) to meet the standard.

Some cities and states have established standards for textile items. Various sectors of industry have adopted voluntary standards for such items as tents, blankets, and career clothing for people who work near fires. It has been estimated that in

Federal Standards Implementing the Flammable Fabrics Act

Effective Date	Item	Requirements	Test Method
1954	Flammability of clothing Title 16 CRF 1610 (formerly CS 191–53)	Articles of wearing apparel except interlining fabrics, certain hats, gloves, footwear.	A 2 × 6″ fabric placed in a holder at a 45° angle exposed to flame for 1 second will not ignite and spread flame up the length of the sample in less than 3.5 seconds for smooth fabrics or 4.0 seconds for napped.
1954	Flammability of vinyl plastic film Title 16 CRF 1611 (formerly CS 192–53)	Vinyl plastic film for wearing apparel.	A piece of film, placed in a holder at an angle of 45° will not burn at a rate exceeding 1.2 inches per second.
1971	Large carpets and rugs Title CFR 1630 (formerly DOC FF1–70)	Carpets that have one dimension greater than 6 feet and a surface area greater than 24 sq. ft. Excludes vinyl tile, asphalt tile, and linoleum. All items must meet standard.	"Pill" test. 9″ × 9″ specimens exposed to methenamine tablet placed in center of each specimen does not char more than 3″ in any direction.
1971	Small carpets and rugs Title 16 CFR 1631 (formerly DOC FF2–70)	Carpets that have no dimension greater than 6 feet and a surface area no greater than 24 sq. ft. May be sold if they do not meet standard if labeled: Flammable. (Fails U.S. Department of Commerce Standard FF 2–70)	Same as for large carpets and rugs.
1973	Mattresses (and mattress pads) Title 16 CFR 1632 (DOC FF4–72)	Ticking filled with a resilient material intended for sleeping upon, including mattress pads. Excludes pillows, box springs, sleeping bags, and upholstered furniture. All items must meet standard.	"Cigarette" test. A minimum of 9 cigarettes allowed to burn on smooth top, edge, and quilted locations of bare mattress. Char length must not be more than 2″ in any direction from any cigarette. Tests are also conducted with 9 cigarettes placed between two sheets on the mattress surfaces.

Federal Standards Implementing the Flammable Fabrics Act *(Cont.)*

Effective Date	Item	Requirements	Test Method
1972	Childrens' sleepwear, Sizes 0–6X Title 16 CFR 1615 (DOC FF3–71)	Any product of wearing apparel up to and including size 6X such as nightgowns, pajamas, or other items intended to be worn for sleeping. Excludes diapers and underwear. Items must meet requirements as produced and after 50 washings and dryings. All items must meet standard.	"Vertical Forced Ignition" Test. Each of five 3.5″ × 10″ specimens is suspended vertically in holders in a cabinet and exposed to a gas flame along the bottom edge for 3 seconds. Specimens cannot have average char length of more than 7 inches.
1975	Childrens' sleepwear Sizes 7–14 Title 16 CFR 1632 (DOC FF5–74)	Same as preceding. All items must meet standard.	Same as preceding.

the future half of all apparel items will be flame resistant. However, the issue of flame-resistant fabrics has created so many problems and there are so many conflicting results from research that the future is hard to predict. Progress on an upholstery standard has been delayed; a standard for general apparel has been delayed and may never be set.

Flame-Resistant Fibers and Flame-Retardant Finishes

Flame resistant does not mean flameproof. Flame resistant means slow to burn and/or self-extinguishing. *Flame retardant* refers to finishes that are applied to fabrics to make them flame resistant.

Fabrics may be made flame resistant in three ways:

1. Use inherently flame-resistant fibers.

2. Use fiber variants that have been made flame resistant by adding flame retardants to the spinning solution.

3. Apply flame-retardant finishes to the fabrics.

The burning characteristics of fibers are given in the chart on page 16. Fibers that are inherently flame-resistant are aramid, modacrylics,

novoloid, saran, and vinal/vinyon matrix fibers. Fibers in which flame-retardant chemicals have been added to the spinning solution are some acetates, nylons, polyesters, and rayons. See chart on page 111.

Flame-retardant finishes are used on cotton, rayon, nylon, and polyester fabrics. Flame-retardant finishes must be durable (withstand 50 washings), nontoxic, and noncarcinogenic. They should not change the hand and texture of fabrics or have unpleasant odors. Most finishes are not visible and they add to the cost of the garment, so the consumer is asked to pay for something that he cannot see. According to existing theories, flame-retardant compounds either cut off the supply of oxygen to the fabric by forming a coating or by producing a noncombustible gas, or they chemically alter the fiber so that it forms a nonvolatile charred residue rather than the usual flammable tarry products.

Flame-retardant finishes are less expensive than flame-resistant fibers or fiber variants. Knitting or weaving gray-goods that can be given a topical flame-retardant finish or not, depending on its end use, is a more economical procedure for fabric producers than weaving or knitting fabrics for children's sleepwear, for example. In the early 1970s, satisfactory flame-retardant finishes were prepared with variable characteristics of hand and strength loss. One of the most efficient was

Some Durable Flame-Retardant Finishes

Fiber/Fabric	Trade Name	Chemical Composition	Designed to Meet Federal Standard*
Cotton	Fireaway 2	Chloride containing phosphonium condensate	DOC FF 3-71 DOC FF 5-74
Cotton Rayon	Fyrol® 76	Vinyl phosphate oligomer	DOC FF 5-74
Polyester	Apex Flameproof	Halogenated organic compound	DOC FF 5-74
Nylon	Apex Celluset	Thiourea resin	DOC FF 5-74
Acetate Triacetate Polyester	Pyrolux 593	Organo phosphates	DOC FF 3-71
Synthetics Wool	Pyron 5115	Aryl bromophosphate	DOC FF 3-71 DOC FF 5-73
All fibers	Caliban F/R P-44	Decabromo diphenyl ether + antimony trioxide	DOC FF 5-73
Cotton Rayon	Glo-Tard TN	Buffered inorganic salt	DOC FF 4-72
Nylon	Nytro-gard FR	Nitrogenous resin	DOC FF 4-72
Wool	ORCO Flame	Organic halogen-	DOC FF 1-70
Wool/nylon	Retardant	phosphorous	DOC FF 2-70

Flame Retardants Buyer's Guide, American Dyestuff Reporter, 67:1, January 1978.
*See federal standards implementing the flammable fabrics act chart for new standard title.

Tris (2,3 dibromopropyl phosphate). Tris was thought to be carcinogenic (according to the CPSC) and in 1977 all sleepwear garments treated with Tris were removed from the market. Other flame-retardant finishes were satisfactory (or had not been tested) and still others have been prepared. In the following chart a few of the many flame retardant finishes that meet federal standards are listed.

Not all of the flame-retardant finishes have been tested. Some of them as well as chemicals used for other finishes may prove to be unsafe. Other substances will, no doubt, be found to be satisfactory.

Problems

Cost and care are the greatest problems for the consumer. The high cost of research and development of fibers and finishes, testing of fabrics and garments, and liability insurance result in a higher cost of apparel and household items. Because the items look no different, the consumer often thinks the item is overpriced. Because of government standards the consumer has no choice; for example, people who do not smoke in bed must pay a higher price for mattresss since only those mattresses that pass flammability standards can be sold in interstate commerce.

Most of the topical finishes require special care in laundering to preserve the flame resistancy of the garments. Labels on garments are very good and should be followed. Most labels indicate the following care: use phosphate detergents, do not bleach, do not use soap, do not use hot water. In cities where phosphates are banned, soft water and heavy-duty liquid detergents should be used.

For the producer the problems are much greater. The Flammable Fabrics Act is protective legislation. The producer must not only meet government standards for fabrics and garments but must protect himself from damage suits resulting from disfiguring burns or death caused by burn damage.

Using flame-retardant fibers would seem to be the best solution to making flame-resistant articles. Flame resistance is only one of the many properties of fibers needed for good fabrics. The nonburning fibers, glass, modacrylic, and vinyon, are lacking in many desirable properties; aramids and novoloids are too expensive for general use at the present time. The modified fibers, rayon, acetate, polyester, and nylon, may be questionable in the future depending on the additive used, or they may not be available in the desired denier or fiber length. Topical finishes for nylon and polyester fabrics have been satisfactory and more widely used than modified fibers.

Protective fibers and finishes do not sell merchandise. Color, texture, and fashion features are more important to most consumers so the producer must provide these features in flame-resistant items.

Dyeing and Printing

Coloring processes used for textiles are fiber, yarn, or fabric finishes depending on the stage at which the dyes or pigments are applied. Dyeing and printing of fabrics are usually done after routine finishing but prior to other finishes. Solution and fiber dyeing are done prior to spinning. Yarn dyeing and yarn printing are done before weaving or knitting.

Color is often the primary consideration when purchasing clothing and household textiles. When the color fades or streaks, items are discarded before they are worn out. (Denim is an exception—consumers like faded denim). Permanence of color depends on the kind of dye used and the method and the stage of its application. One cannot tell by looking at a fabric the kind of dye that has been used or how fast the color will be. It is very important, therefore, to look for labels that guarantee fastness of color and suggest fabric care. One can identify the stage at which color is applied and in many cases determine if there is good dye penetration.

Color has always been important in textiles. Until 1856 natural dyes and pigments were used as coloring agents. These dyes and pigments were obtained from plants, insects, and minerals. When Perkin, a young chemist, discovered mauve, the first synthetic dye, a whole new industry came into being. Europe became the foremost center for synthetic dyes and it was not until World War I, when our trade with Germany was cut off, that a dye industry was developed in the United States. Since that time, many dyes and pigments have been developed, so that today there are hundreds of colors from which to choose.

Pigments are insoluble color particles that are held on the surface of a fabric by a binding agent. Their application is quick, simple, and economical. Any color can be used on any fiber, since the pigments are held on mechanically. Stiffening of the fabrics, crocking, and fading are some of the problems encountered. Pigments are also mixed with the spinning solution for man-made fibers. *Fluorescent colors* are pigments that glow when exposed to ultraviolet light. They have been increasingly useful in safety clothing and furnishings.

Dye must be in small particles that can be thoroughly dissolved in water or some other carrier in order to penetrate the fiber. Undissolved particles stay on the outside and the colors then have poor fastness to crocking and bleeding.

A *dye process* is the environment created for the introduction of dye by hot water, steam, or dry heat. Accelerants and regulators are used to regulate penetration of the dye. A knowledge of fiber-dye affinity, methods of dyeing, and equipment will give the consumer a better understanding of color behavior.

The stage at which color is applied *has little to do with fastness* but has a great deal to do with *dye penetration* and is governed by fabric design. In order for a fabric to be colored, the dye must penetrate the fiber and either combine chemically with it or be locked inside the fiber. Fibers that dye easily are those that are absorbent and that have dye sites in their molecules, which will react with the dye molecules. The dye reacts with the surface molecules first. Moisture and/or heat swell the fibers, causing the molecule chains to move farther apart so that more reactive groups are exposed to react with the dye. During drying, the chains move back together, trapping the dye in the fiber.

The dyeing of the wool with acid dyes is a good example of dyeing fibers that are both absorbent and have many dye sites.

Nylon resembles wool in dyeing properties except that it has fewer dye sites—1 amino group for every 30 in wool. The thermoplastic fibers are difficult to dye because their absorbency is low. Many of the acrylic fibers have anionic dye sites that react with cationic dye stuffs.

Cellulosic fibers are absorbent because of the many hydroxyl groups, but most dyes do not combine chemically with them. With direct dyes, the dye particles move into the amorphous areas of the fibers and form large aggregations that are too large to move back out of the fiber. The addition of salt gives better dye absorption. Other dyes are developed on or in the fibers. Fiber-reactive dyes were introduced in 1956 and are the first dyes that actually combine with the hydroxyl groups of cellulose.

Most of the man-made fibers are modified to accept different classes of dyes. This makes it possible to achive different color effects or a good solid color in blends of unlike fibers by piece dyeing.

No one dye is fast to everything, and *the dyes within a group are not equally fast.* A complete range of shades is not available in each of the dye groups. The dyer chooses a dye suited to the fiber content and the end use of the fabric. He must apply the color so that it penetrates and is held in the fiber. Occasionally the garment manufacturer or the consumer selects fabrics for uses that are different than the fabric manufacturer intended. For example, an apparel fabric used for draperies may not be fast to sunlight. The consumer should know what to expect from the textile and report to the retailer if fabrics do not give satisfactory performance.

Dyes are classified by chemical composition or method of application. The following chart lists the major dyes, along with some of their characteristics and end uses.

Textiles may be dyed during the fiber, yarn, or fabric stage depending on the color effects desired and perhaps on the quality or end use of the fabric. Better dye penetration is achieved with fiber dyeing than with yarn dyeing, and with yarn dyeing than with piece dyeing.

Classification of Dyes

Dyes	End Uses	Characteristics
Cationic (basic) Used with mordant on fibers other than silk and wool. Complete color range	Used primarily on acrylics. Direct prints on acetate. Discharge prints on cotton. Used on modified polyester and nylon	Fast colors on acrylics. On natural fibers—poor fastness to light, washing, perspiration. Tends to bleed and crock
Acid (anionic) Complete color range	Wool, silk, nylon, modified rayon	Bright colors. Vary in fastness to light. Poor fastness to washing
Azoic (naphthol and rapidogens) Complete color range Moderate cost	Cotton primarily	Good to excellent light fastness and washing. Bright shades
Developed Dyes developed in the fiber. Complete color range. Duller colors than acid or basic	Cellulose fibers primarily Discharge prints	Good to excellent light fastness. Fair wash fastness
Disperse Dye particles disperse in water and dissolve in fibers. Good color range	Developed for acetate but used on all fibers except silk and wool	Fair to excellent light and wash fastness Blues and violets on acetate fume fade
Mordant (chrome) Fair color range Duller than acid dyes	Primarily used on wool	Good to excellent light and wash fastness. Dull colors
Reactive Combines chemically with fiber. Produces brightest shades	Primarily used on cotton	Good light and wash fastness. Sensitive to chlorine bleach
Sulfur Insoluble in water Complete color range except for red. Dull colors	Primarily for cotton. Heavy work clothes Most widely used black dye	Poor to excellent light and wash fastness Sensitive to chlorine bleach. Stored goods become tender
Vat Insoluble in water Incomplete color range	Primarily for cotton work clothes, sportswear, prints, drapery fabrics	Good to excellent light and wash fastness

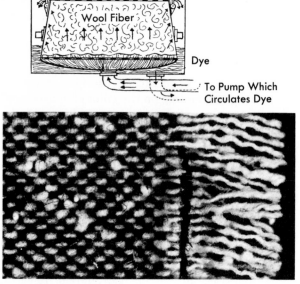

Fig. 38-1 Stock or fiber dye: process and tweed fabric example (cross dyeing).

Fiber Dyeing

In this process the fiber is *dyed before yarn spinning.*

1. *Solution (spun or dope) dyeing* consists of adding colored pigments or dyes to the spinning solution; thus each fiber is colored as it is spun.

2. *Stock or fiber dye* is used when mottled or heather effects are desired. Dye is added to loose fibers before yarn spinning. Good dye penetration is obtained but the process is fairly expensive (Figure 38-1).

3. *Top dyeing* gives results similar to stock dye and is more commonly used. Tops, the loose ropes of wool from the combing machine, are wound into balls, placed on perforated spindles, and enclosed in a tank. The dye is pumped back and forth through the wool. Continuous processes on loose fiber and wool tops are also used using a pad-steam technique.

Yarn Dyeing

Yarns are dyed in skeins or packages. Rayon is usually dyed in the cakes in which it is laid after spinning. Yarn dyeing is less costly than fiber dyeing but more costly than piece dyeing and printing. Yarn-dyed designs are more limited and larger inventories are involved (Figure 38-2).

Fig. 38-2 Yarn dye.

Piece Dyeing

Piece dyeing usually produces solid-color fabrics. It generally costs less to dye fabric than to dye loose fiber or yarns. One other advantage is that decisions on color can be delayed so that fashion trends can be followed more closely.

Cross dyeing is piece dyeing of fabrics (Figure 38-3) made of fibers from different generic groups

Fig. 38-3 Cross-dyed fabric. White is acetate, dark is rayon.

such as protein and cellulose, or by combining acid-dyeable and basic-dyeable fibers of the same generic group.

Union dyeing is piece dyeing of fabrics made of fibers from different groups, but, unlike cross dyeing, the finished fabric is a solid color. Dyes of the same hue, but of composition suited to the fibers to be dyed, are mixed together in the same dye bath. Piece dyeing is done with various kinds of equipment.

Methods

The method chosen for piece dyeing depends on fiber content, weight of the fabric, dyestuff, and degree of penetration required in the finished product. Time is money in mass production so that processes in which the goods travel quickly through a machine are used whenever possible. Dyeing and afterwashing require a great deal of pure water, and the waste water is a cause of stream pollution. For this reason, dyers and finishers are always searching for new methods.

Jig Dyeing. *Jig dyeing* consists of a stationary dye bath with two rolls above the bath. The cloth is carried around the rolls in open width and is rolled back and forth through the dye bath once every 20 minutes or so and is on rollers the remaining time. There are some problems of level dyeing. Acetate, rayon, and nylon are usually jig dyed (Figure 38-4).

Pad Dyeing. *Pad dyeing* is a method in which the fabric is run through the dye bath in open width and then between squeeze rollers that force the dye into the fabric. Notice in Figure 38-5 that the pad box holds only a very small amount of dye liquor, making this an economical method of

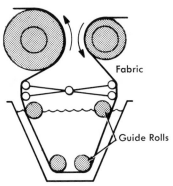
Fig. 38-4 Jig dyeing.

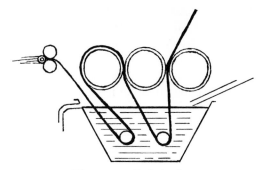
Fig. 38-5 Pad dyeing.

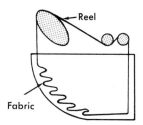
Fig. 38-6 Winch dyeing.

piece dyeing. The cloth runs through the machine at a rapid rate, 30 to 300 yards a minute. Pad-steam processes are the most widely used.

Winch, Reel, or Beck Dyeing. *Winch, reel, or beck dyeing* is the oldest type of piece dyeing (Figure 38-6). The fabric, in a loose rope sewed together at the ends, is lifted in and out of the dye bath by a reel. The fabric is kept immersed in the dye bath except for the few yards around the reel. Penetration of dye is obtained by continued immersion in slack condition rather than by pressure on the wet goods under tension. This method is used on lightweight fabrics that cannot withstand the tension of the other methods, and on heavy goods, especially woolens. Reels are of various shapes—oval, round, octagonal.

Continuous Machines. *Continuous machines* called *ranges* are used for large lots of goods. They consist of compartments for wetting-out, dyeing, aftertreatments, washing, and rinsing.

Printing

Color designs are produced on fabrics by printing with dyes in paste form or by positioning dyes on the fabric from specially designed machines.

Printed fabrics usually have clear-cut edges in the design portion on the right side and the color seldom penetrates completely to the wrong side of the fabric. Yarns raveled from printed fabrics will have color unevenly positioned on them.

Printed designs are done by various processes, as listed on the following chart.

Direct	Discharge	Resist	Others
Block	Discharge	Batik	Electrostatic
Direct roller		Tie and Dye	Microjet
Heat transfer			Polychromatic
Screen			TAK
Warp			Differential

Direct Printing

Block Printing. *Block printing* is a hand process and the oldest technique for decorating textiles. It is seldom done commercially because it is costly and slow. A design is carved on a block. The block is dipped in a shallow pan of dye and stamped on the fabric (Figure 38–7). Slight irregularities in color register or positioning are clues to block prints but these can be duplicated in roller printing made to resemble them.

Direct Roller Printing. *Direct roller printing* was developed in 1785, about the time all textile operations were becoming mechanized. Figure 38–8 shows the essential parts of the printing machine. A cast-iron cylinder (1 in Figure 38–8) is the roller around which the cloth is drawn as it is printed. The copper printing roller (2 in Figure 38–8) is etched with the design. There are as many different rollers as there are colors in the

Fig. 38-7 Carved wooden block and design made from it.

fabric. In the diagram, three engraved rollers are used. Furnisher rollers are covered with hard rubber or brushes made of nylon, or hard-rubber bristles. They revolve in a small color trough, pick up the color, and deposit it on the copper rollers. A doctor blade scrapes off excess color so that only the engraved portions of the copper roller are filled with dye when it comes in contact with the cloth. The cloth to be printed, a rubberized blanket, and a back gray cloth pass between the cylinder and the engraved rollers. The blanket gives a good surface for sharp printing; the gray goods protects the blanket and absorbs excess dye.

Rayon and knitted fabrics are usually lightly coated with a gum sizing on the back to keep them from stretching or swelling as they go through the printing machine. After printing, the cloth is dried, steamed, or treated to set the dye.

Duplex printing is roller printing that prints on both sides of the fabric with the same or different patterns.

Heat Transfer Printing. *Heat transfer printing* is a process in which designs are transferred to fabric from specially printed paper by heat and pressure. The paper is printed by gravure, flexograph, offset, or converted rotary screen processes. The fabric or garment is placed on a plastic frame and padded with a special solution. The paper is placed over the fabric and is then covered with a silicone-rubber sheet. The sandwich is then subjected to high pressure at a temperature of 200°C for a few seconds during which the print vaporizes and migrates from the paper to the fabric.

The advantages of heat transfer printing are better penetration and clarity of design, lower production costs, and elimination of pollution problems. Transfer printing can be done on circular knits, without splitting them first, and on garments.

Print papers using disperse dyes were developed for polyester fiber fabrics and have been

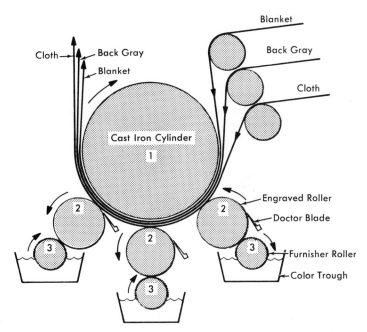

Fig. 38-8 Direct roller printing.

successful on high polyester/cotton blends and on nylon. For cotton fabrics and 50/50 blends of cotton/polyester the fabric is treated with a resin that has an affinity for disperse dyes. Print papers with acid dyes for nylon, silk, and wool and with cationic dyes for acrylics are available.

Screen Printing. *Flat screen printing* is done commercially for small yardages, 50 to 5,000 yards, and is used extensively for designs larger than the circumference of the rolls used for roller printing.

The design is applied to the screen so that all but the figure is covered by a resist material. One screen is used for each color. The color is forced through the screen by a squeegee.

In the hand process, the fabric to be printed is placed on a long table. Two people position the screen on the fabric, apply the color, move the screen to a new position, and repeat the process until all the fabric is printed.

In the automatic screen process, the fabric to be printed is placed on a conveyer belt. A series of flat screens are positioned above and are lowered automatically. Color is applied automatically, and the fabric is moved automatically and fed continuously into ovens to be dried.

Rotary screen printing is done with cylindrical metal screens that operate in much the same way as the flat screens except that the operation is continuous rather than started and stopped as the screens are raised and lowered in the flat

Fig. 38-9 Rotary screen printing.

process (Figure 38-9). The rotary screens are cheaper than the copper rollers used in roller printing.

Warp Printing. *Warp printing* is done on the warp yarns prior to weaving. This technique gives an interesting, rather hazy pattern, softer than other prints. To identify, ravel adjacent sides. Color in the form of the design will be on the warp yarns. Filling yarns are white or solid color. Imitations have splotchy color on both warp and filling yarns. Warp printing is usually done on taffeta, satin ribbons, or cotton fabric, and on upholstery or drapery fabric (Figure 38-10).

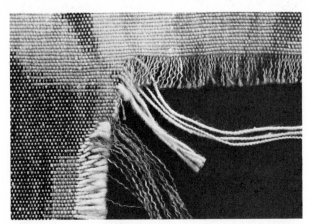

Discharge Printing

Discharge prints are piece-dyed fabrics in which the design is made by removing color.

Discharge printing is usually done on dark backgrounds. The fabric is first piece-dyed in any of the usual methods. A discharge paste, which contains chemicals to remove the color, is then printed on the fabric. Dyes that are not harmed by the discharging materials can be mixed with printing solution if color is desired in the discharge areas. The fabric is then steamed to develop the design, either as a white or colored area. Better dye penetration is obtained with piece dyeing than with printing, and it is hard to get good dark colors except by piece dyeing.

Discharge prints can be detected by looking at the wrong side of the fabric. In the design area the color is often not completely removed and one can see evidences of the background colors, especially around the edges of the design. Background colors must be colors that can be removed by strong alkali. Discharge prints are usually satisfactory (Figure 38-11).

Resist Printing

Resist prints are piece-dyed fabrics in which color is prevented from entering the fabric.

Batik. *Batik* is a hand process in which hot wax is poured on a fabric in the form of a design. When the wax is set, the fabric is piece-dyed. The wax prevents penetration of color into the wax-covered portions. Colors are built up by piece dyeing light colors first, covering portions, and redyeing until the design is complete. The wax is later removed by a solvent.

Tie and Dye. *Tie and dye* is a hand process in which yarn or fabric is wrapped in certain areas with fine thread or string. The yarn or fabric is then piece-dyed and the string is removed, leaving undyed areas (Figures 38-12 and 38-13). *Ikat* is a hand process in which warp (and filling) yarns are tied and dyed and then woven (Figure 38-14).

Other Printing Methods

Differential printing. Differential printing is a printing technique using screen printing on carpets tufted with yarns that have different dye affinities.

Fig. 38-11 Discharge print versus direct print.

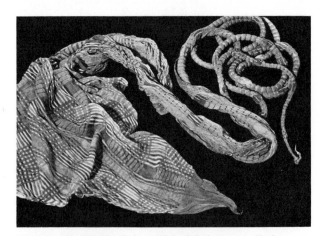

Fig. 38-12 Tie and dye. This fabric was rolled up on the bias, tied, and piece-dyed. A second dyeing was done with fabric rolled up on the opposite bias.

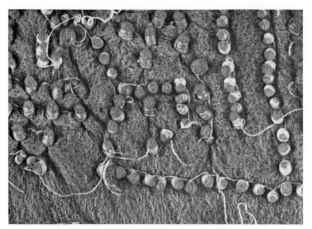

Fig. 38-13 Tie and dye showing thread used to make the design.

Electrostatic Printing.
Electrostatic printing is similar to electrostatic flocking. A screen that has the design on it is covered with powdered dye mixed with a carrier that has dielectric properties. The screen is about $\frac{1}{2}$ inch above the fabric and when passed through an electric field the dye-resin is pulled onto the material where it is fixed by heat.

Polychromatic Printing.
Polychromatic printing is an economical process for use with thick fabrics. Designs are multicolored stripes, abstract splashes, or tie-and-dye effects. Several colors are applied in one operation from jets set in bars. The fabrics move over an inclined plane, and dye comes out of jets onto the fabric. The cloth then

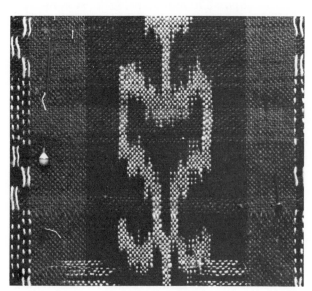

Fig. 38-14 Ikat.

goes through heavy rollers that press the dye completely through the fabric.

TAK.
TAK are the initials of a German rug manufacturer and a machinery supplier who invented a machine to print carpets. The machine can be used for other hard-to-print fabrics such as terry cloth, velvet, and upholstery fabrics. Dye is dropped on the fabric from individual channels fed by a trough. A special mechanism deposits drops of dye in a desired design. The fabric is then run through a padder to force the color into the cloth.

Microjet Injection.
Millitron is a computer-controlled microjet system developed by the Milliken Company. It is used on carpets and upholstery to produce Jacquardlike designs. The machine consists of a series of horizontal bars containing the dye, which is fed through small dye jets (10 per inch in a carpet machine, 16 per inch in an upholstery machine). The prepared cloth passes under the bars, and by the use of an electronically controlled tape, dye is deposited in the proper place from the jets on the bars. Dye penetrates to the backing and patterns can be easily changed.

Color Problems

Good color fastness is expected in fabrics but it is not always achieved. When one considers all the variables connected with dyeing and printing and the hostile environment in which fabrics are used, one can appreciate how good most of our colored fabrics are.

The factors that influence color fastness are

1. Chemical nature of fibers.
2. Chemical nature of dyes and pigments.
3. Penetration of dyes into the cloth.
4. Fixing the dyes or pigments on or in the fabrics.

The coloring agents must resist washing, dry cleaning, bleaching, spot, and stain removal with all of the variables of time, temperature, and substances used. They must be resistant to light, perspiration, abrasion, fumes, and other factors.

If the color is not fast in the fabric as purchased, it is not possible to make it fast. Salt and vinegar are used as exhausting agents for household dyes, but there is no available research to

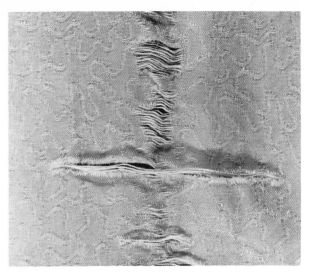

Fig. 38-15 Cotton and rayon drapery fabric. After dry cleaning, yellowish streaks were obvious; after washing, splits occurred.

Fig. 38-16 Tendering of cotton draperies caused by sulfur dye, atmospheric moisture, and heat.

support the theory that they will "set" color. Color loss occurs through bleeding, crocking, and migration or through chemical changes in the dye. *Bleeding* is color loss in water. *Crocking* is color loss from rubbing or abrasion. *Migration* is shifting of color to the surrounding area or to an adjacent surface. *Atmospheric gases* (fume fading), *perspiration,* and sunlight may cause fading as a result of a chemical change in the dye.

Tendering. Certain vat and sulfur dyes will tender or destroy cotton cloth. Green, red, blue, and yellow *vat dyes* and black, yellow, and orange *sulfur dyes* are the chief offenders. Manufacturers know which dyes cause the trouble and can correct it by thoroughly oxidizing the dyestuff within the fiber. Damage is increased by moisture and sunlight. The problem is sometimes critical in draperies. Damage may not be evident until the draperies are cleaned and then slits or holes occur (Figure 38-15). In Figure 38-16 the orange and black figures have completely disintegrated. Sunlight, smog, and acidic atmospheric gases, as well as dyes, will cause fabric damage.

Wear may remove the surface color of heavy fabrics (Figure 38-17). Movement of yarns in bending causes undyed fibers to work out to the surface. Color streaks may result from uneven removal of sizing before the dye is applied because the portions of the fabric that did not come in contact with the dye were not even dyed. Some resin-treated fabrics show this sort of color change because the dye either was applied with the resin and did not penetrate sufficiently, or the fabric was dyed after being resin-treated, in which case there were not enough places for the dye to be anchored. The best way to check the dye penetration in heavy fabrics is to examine the fabric. In yard goods, ravel off a yarn to see if it is the same color throughout. In ready-to-wear, look at the edge of seams. In heavy prints, look at the reverse side. The more color on the wrong side, the better the dye penetration is.

Printed fabrics are often printed "off-grain." Off-grain prints create problems because the fabric cannot be both straight with the print and cut "on-grain." If cut "off-grain," the fabric tends to assume its normal position when washed, causing twisted seams and uneven hemlines. If cut "on-grain," the print will not be straight and will be unpleasing aesthetically. In an allover design, this is not important, but in large checks and plaids or designs with crosswise lines, matching at seam lines is impossible and slanting lines across the

Fig. 38-17 Denim jeans: loss of surface color.

fabric are seldom desirable. The reason for off-grain prints is that the fabric is started into the machine crooked or the mechanism for moving the fabric does not work properly. It is a problem that can easily be corrected at the mill. If consumers would refuse to buy off-grain prints and let retailers know why they are not buying them, better prints would be on the market (see page 159).

A *"frosting" effect* often results from abrasion in polyester/cotton durable press garments that have been dyed with two different, but color-matched, dyes (union dyed). During wear, the cotton wears off and becomes lighter in color, while the unabraded polyester keeps its color.

The fastness of the dye often determines the method of care that should be used. The consumer must depend on the label, but some knowledge of color problems that occur in use and care will enable him to make more intelligent choices.

Selection and Care of Textile Products

39

Facts about fibers, yarn types, fabric constructions, and finishes are useful because they guide consumer decisions in purchases of fabrics, ready-to-wear apparel, and home-furnishing fabrics. Selection of textile products is a personal decision based on fashion, life style, income, sex, and age. It is influenced by aesthetic, psychological, sociological, and economic factors. The decision to buy a product may be rational or it may be impulsive. This chapter summarizes textile information that can help the consumer in making rational decisions.

Selection of Textile Products

As a consumer starts shopping for a textile product he must think through the pertinent factors. Who will be using the item? How will it be used? Where will it be used? When will it be used? How long will it need to last? Which of the following factors are most important if the item is to be usable, or serviceable, in the specified end use: durability, comfort, care, appearance, fashion, fit, quality of construction, or price? Which factors are least important? What is the ranking of the other factors?

With the end use in mind and a realization of the factors that are important for serviceability of the item, the consumer may follow these steps in making the decision:

1. Determine a price range or price ceiling for the goods that will be examined.

2. Find items with an acceptable fit or of the appropriate size.

3. Evaluate color, fashion, appearance, and quality of construction.

4. Evalute the serviceability of the textile components of the item.

5. Decide to buy a specific item or decide to do more shopping.

The satisfaction that the consumer receives from the textile material will depend on his values as well as the performance of the product. The performance and care of the textile depend on the fibers, yarns, fabric construction, and finishes. Remember that the manufacturer has already made decisions about what combinations he feels would be serviceable for that item. The consumer's job is to further personalize the decision and choose the item that will be most appropriate for his own use.

Influence of Fibers on Textile Performance

The Textile Fiber Products Identification Act requires that the generic name of fibers be given for most garments, yard goods, and household textiles. A major portion of this text has been devoted to describing the characteristics of each fiber. The expected performance of major fibers is summarized in Table 39–1. The table does not include fiber blends. In blends the good fiber properties are lessened a bit and the poor properties are minimized. The degree of change depends on the quantity of fiber used. In purchasing curtains and draperies, remember that sunlight resistance is important. Review Table on p. 13 for that information.

Influence of Yarns on Textile Performance

The type of yarn that is in a fabric can be observed. Comparisons among the types of yarns given in Table 39–2 can then be made. Remember that these generalizations hold true when considering fabrics of the same fiber content and similar fabric construction. Fiber properties, of course, will influence the actual performance of fabrics.

Influence of Fabric Construction on Textile Performance

Fabrics may have similar appearance even though they are constructed differently. Frequently woven and knit fabrics have the same look. Structural design fabrics can often be duplicated in appearance by applied design fabrics. Pile and napped fabrics may look similar. Being able to correctly determine how a fabric is constructed can provide important information about fabric performance. Commonly found woven and knit fabrics perform well. Generally, twill weave fabrics are strongest because of their high warp thread count. Balanced and 2:1 unbalanced plain

Table 39-1 Performance of Fibers That Are Often Used in Clothing and Household Textiles

| Fiber | Durability | | Comfort | | Appearance | |
	Abrasion Resistance	Tenacity	Absorbency	Thermal Retention	Resiliency	Pilling Resistance
Acetate	Low	Low	Medium	Medium	Medium	High
Acrylic	Medium	Medium	Low	High	Medium	Medium
Cotton	Medium	Medium	High	Low	Low, Med. if DP	High
Flax	Medium	Medium	High	Low	Low, Med. if DP	High
Glass	Low	High	Low	High	High	Low
Modacrylic	Medium	Medium	Low	High	Medium	Medium
Nylon	High	High	Low	Medium	High	Low
Olefin	High	High	Low	Medium	High	Low
Polyester	High	High	Low	Medium	High	Low
Rayon	Low	Low	High	Low	Low	High
Rayon HWM	Medium	Medium	High	Low	Low, Med. if DP	High
Silk	Medium	Medium	High	Medium	Medium	High
Triacetate	Low	Low	Medium	Medium	Medium	High
Wool	Medium	Low	High	High	High	High

Table 39-2 Performance of Yarns in Fabrics

Yarn Type	Durability	Comfort	Appearance	Care
Spun Yarns	Weaker than filament yarns Ply yarns stronger than simple yarns Fabrics tend to resist raveling and running	Warmer More absorbent	Fabrics are cottonlike or woollike in appearance Fabrics lint and pill	Yarns do not snag readily Soil readily
Filament yarns	Stronger than spun yarns Fabrics ravel and run readily	Cooler Least absorbent	Fabrics are smooth and lustrous Fabrics do not lint or pill readily	Yarns may snag Resist soiling
Textured filament yarns	Stronger than spun yarns Fabrics ravel and run less than those made with filament yarns, but more than those made with spun yarns	Warmer than filament yarns More absorbent than filament yarns Stretch more than other yarns	Fabrics are less lustrous; more similar to those made of spun yarns Fabrics do not lint, but may pill	Yarns likely to snag Soil more readily than filament yarns
Novelty yarns	Weaker than filament yarns Most resist raveling	Warmer More absorbent if part is spun	Interesting texture Greater novelty effects show wear sooner than smaller novelty effects Fabrics lint and pill	Yarns likely to snag Soil readily

weave fabrics are strong and abrasion resistant. Unless satin weave fabrics have a very high thread count, they will not be as strong as other woven fabrics. Because of the long floats, these fabrics may snag and be less abrasion resistant than the others.

Fabrics with fewer interlacings ravel more than fabrics with more interlacings. When comparing similar fabrics, ones with a higher thread count are better quality fabrics.

The effect of routine fabric finishes and fabric finishes applied for beauty can often be judged by comparing the appearance of several similar fabrics. Frequently information about functional

Table 39-3 Influence of Fabric Construction on Fabric Performance

	Woven Fabrics	Knitted Fabrics
Durability	High count Many interlacings per square inch Balanced Short floats Medium to heavy weight	High gauge. Warp knits do not run
Comfort	Absorbency—Uncut pile Low count Thermal retention—Pile fabrics. Very high count for wind and water repellency	Absorbency—Low gauge Pile knits Thermal retention—All knits tend to be warmer than woven fabrics of same weight and fiber content in still air. Knits are less wind repellent than woven fabrics Stretch—Can be form fitting without binding— allows free body movement
Appearance Retention	Resiliency—Low count. Heavy weight pile fabrics. Figured fabrics show wrinkles less	Resiliency—Excellent. Bagging is common in low gauge knits

When comparing knitted and woven fabrics, knits are generally stretchier, more likely to shrink, and less likely to wrinkle. They do not ravel the way woven fabrics do, but filling knits do run, especially when made of filament yarns. Information about durability, comfort, and appearance retention of woven and knitted fabrics is summarized in Table 39-3.

Other fabric structures are used less frequently and may have limitations on the ways they are used. These have been discussed in earlier chapters.

finishes will be found on labels. Durable-press finishes, shrinkage-control finishes, and soil-resistant finishes are often identified. The presence or absence of such detailed information may influence whether the consumer buys that particular article or not. Information about dyeing or printing textile materials is found infrequently on labels. Vat dyes may be identified in cellulosic fabrics intended for draperies since most of these have good fading resistance. Some fabrics may be labeled color fast. It is difficult to predict color performance of fabrics, although some generalizations can be made. Better performance can be anticipated from fabrics with

1. A more thorough color penetration.
2. Woven-in color designs rather than printed on designs.
3. On-grain rather than off-grain prints.

It is necessary to use many facts when predicting textile performance but the mind works very quickly. Stored facts and experience in buying should help one make rational choices.

Care of Textile Products

Care labeling is required for nearly all ready-to-wear and yard goods, including many home furnishing fabrics. The labels should be attached to garments, and should be available where fabrics are sold although frequently the consumer must ask for the label.

The care that is required for a fabric or garment depends on the fiber, yarn, fabric construction, and finishes that are part of the textile product. The construction of the item and the component parts such as thread and linings must also be considered. Occasionally a consumer will decide against buying a textile because he dislikes the care that it requires. Some consumers are careful and conscientious in the way they maintain an item, other consumers are not. Manufacturers should simulate home laundry conditions as they test fabrics in an effort to determine the appropriate care method.

The care labels that are commonly available with yard goods are listed in Table 39–4. Table 39–5 lists terms that are often found on care labels of garments. The table clarifies the meaning of the terms used on the labels.

During 1976 and 1977, The Federal Trade Commission conducted hearings about care labeling. Their findings and proposed revision of the regulation clarify a number of points that had confused consumers. The FTC intends to extend coverage of the rule to include suede and leather garments as well as knitting yarns. Upholstered furniture and carpets also will be covered by the regulations; spot care and maintenance instructions will be available for consumers.

Basic fiber properties largely determine the

Table 39–4 Fabric Care Labels

For Piece Goods	
△ 1	Machine wash, warm
△ 2	Machine wash, warm Line dry
△ 3	Machine wash, warm Tumble dry, remove promptly
△ 4	Machine wash, warm, delicate cycle Tumble dry, low Use cool iron
△ 5	Machine wash, warm Do not dry clean
△ 6	Hand wash separately Use cool iron
△ 7	Dry clean only
△ 8	Dry clean, pile fabric method only
△ 9	Wipe with damp cloth only
△ A	Home launder only, machine wash, warm; tumble dry to retain flame retardant properties. Use phosphate detergent or nonphosphate heavy-duty liquid detergent; do not use soap, chlorine bleach, or nonphosphate powder detergents.

care required of textile products. Appropriate care for textile products based on fiber content is listed in Table 39–6. The consumer who is knowledgeable about textiles will understand the properties of the fibers and will be able to examine and evaluate the effect of yarn, fabric construction, and finishes on the care of the textile product. He will be in a better position to interpret incomplete care labels or to provide appropriate care when labels are missing than the consumer who lacks this knowledge.

Knowledge about laundry and dry-cleaning procedures is also essential in properly caring for textiles. Many suggestions about laundering have been given at appropriate places throughout the

Table 39-5 Consumer Care Guide for Apparel

	When Label Reads:	It Means:
Machine Washable	Machine wash	Wash, bleach, dry and press by any customary method including commercial laundering and dry cleaning
	Home launder only	Same as above but do not use commercial laundering
	No chlorine bleach	Do not use chlorine bleach. Oxygen bleaches may be used
	No bleach	Do not use any type of bleach
	Cold wash Cold rinse	Use cold water from tap or cold washing machine setting
	Warm wash Warm rinse	Use warm water or warm washing machine setting
	Hot wash	Use hot water or hot washing machine setting
	No spin	Remove wash load before final machine spin cycle
	Delicate cycle Gentle cycle	Use appropriate machine setting; otherwise wash by hand
	Durable press cycle Permanent press cycle	Use appropriate machine setting; otherwise use warm wash, cold rinse, and short spin cycle
	Wash separately	Wash alone or with like colors
Non-Machine Washing	Hand wash	Launder only by hand in luke warm (hand comfortable) water. May be bleached. May be dry cleaned
	Hand wash only	Same as above, but do not dry clean
	Hand wash separately	Hand wash alone or with like colors
	No bleach	Do not use bleach
	Damp wipe	Surface clean with damp cloth or sponge
Home Drying	Tumble dry	Dry in tumble dryer at specified setting—high, medium, low or no heat
	Tumble dry Remove promptly	Same as above, but in absence of cool-down cycle remove at once when tumbling stops
	Drip dry	Hang wet and allow to dry with hand shaping only
	Line dry	Hang damp and allow to dry
	No wring No twist	Hang dry, drip dry or dry flat only. Handle to prevent wrinkles and distortion
	Dry flat	Lay garment on flat surface
	Block to dry	Maintain original size and shape while drying
Ironing or Pressing	Cool iron	Set iron at lowest setting
	Warm iron	Set iron at medium setting
	Hot iron	Set iron at hot setting
	Do not iron	Do not iron or press with heat
	Steam iron	Iron or press with steam
	Iron damp	Dampen garment before ironing
Miscellaneous	Dry clean only	Garment should be dry cleaned only, including self-service
	Professionally dry clean only	Do not use self-service dry cleaning
	No dry clean	Use recommended care instructions. No dry cleaning materials to be used

This care guide was produced by the Consumer Affairs Committee, American Apparel Manufacturers Association and is based on the Voluntary Guide of the Textile Industry Advisory Committee for Consumer Interests. *The American Apparel Manufacturers Association, Inc.*

text. The consumer must seek additional information as new products become available. Read the information on the labels and use correct textile information and good judgment in following the instructions.

Responsible manufacturers and retailers can work together to provide serviceable textiles. Responsible consumers can evaluate the product before purchase and properly care for it after purchase for maximum satisfaction.

Table 39-6 Suggested Care of Textile Products by Fiber Group

Fiber Group	Cleaning Method	Water Temperature	Safe to use Chlorine Bleach	Dryer Temperature	Iron Temperature	Special Storage Considerations
Acetate	Dry clean*	Warm (100–110°F)	Yes	Low	Very low	Avoid contact with nail polish remover
Acrylic	Launder	Warm	Yes	Warm	Medium	—
Cotton	Launder	Hot (120–140°F)	Yes	Hot	High	Store dry to prevent mildew
Polyester/Cotton DP	Launder	Hot	Yes	Warm	Medium	—
Flax	Launder	Hot	Yes	Hot	High	For longest wear, do not press in sharp creases
Glass	Hand wash only	Hot	Yes	Line dry	Do not iron	Prevent fiber breakage by storing as flat as possible
Modacrylic	Launder	Warm	Yes	Low	Very low	—
Nylon	Launder	Hot	Yes	Warm	Low	—
Olefin	Launder	Warm	Yes	Warm	Very low	—
Polyester	Launder	Hot	Yes	Warm	Low	—
Rayon	Launder	Hot	Yes	Hot	High	Store dry to prevent mildew
Rayon HWM	Launder	Hot	Yes	Hot	High	Store dry to prevent mildew
Silk	Dry clean*	Warm	No	Warm	Medium	—
Spandex	Launder	Warm	No	Warm	Very low	—
Triacetate	Launder	Warm	Yes	Warm	Medium	—
Wool	Dry clean*	Warm	No	Warm	Medium, with steam	Protect from moths, do not store in plastic bags

* Or hand wash, avoiding excessive agitation and stretching

Fabric Glossary

Alpaca is a flat, dull fabric with the appearance of wool. It contains two-ply yarns, one ply a crepe viscose and the other ply a larger, regular twist acetate (grenai yarns). Crepiness is obtained from the viscose ply and body is obtained from the acetate ply. (Alpaca is also a speciality hair fiber used to make pile-weave coating fabric.)

Antique satin is a drapery fabric. Satin weave, satin floats on wrong side. Dull, often slub yarns on right side. Acetate and rayon.

Balbriggan is a plain knit fabric used for lingerie.

Balloon cloth is a fine yarn cotton fabric in balanced plain weave. It is used for dresses, blouses, coverings for balloon gas cells, airplane coverings, and typewriter ribbons.

Barathea is a ribbed fabric with a broken-surface effect because of weave. It has filament yarn in the warp and filament or staple in the filling. It may be silk, rayon, or acetate.

Batiste wool, is a smooth, balanced fabric that is white or light in color. It is not as sheer as wool voile, but is very lightweight for a wool fabric.

Bolivia is a silky, long pile (cut to give a ridged-effect) fabric. Ridges are vertical or diagonal. Usually wool.

Broadcloth is a lustrous woolen fabric that is highly napped and then pressed flat. The weave is not visible. Broadcloth has an up and down, and will reflect light differently if all pieces of a pattern are not cut going in the same direction.

Brocatelle is a slipcover or upholstery fabric. Jacquard design, usually raised.

Buckram is similar to crinoline except that it has a stiffer finish. Often two layers of crinoline are glued together to make a very heavy and stiff fabric. It is converted from cheesecloth gray goods.

Bunting is a loosely woven cotton or wool fabric used for flags and banners.

Burlap is a coarse, heavy plain weave fabric made of jute. It is used primarily as carpet backing and furniture webbing, but can also be used for decorative textiles.

Butcher rayon is a crashlike fabric that is made in various weights. Many names are given to this fabric. In heavier weights it looks like linen suiting. Butcher rayon may be an acetate and rayon blend or it may be 100 per cent rayon. It is often given a crease-resistant finish. A Federal Trade Commission ruling prohibits the use of the word *linen* in this type of fabric.

Cambric is a fine, firm, plain weave balanced fabric finished with starch and has a slight luster on one side. It is difficult to distinguish from percale, nainsook, or longcloth.

309

Canvas is a heavy, firm, rather stiff fabric made of cotton or linen and is used for awnings, slipcovers, shoes, and the like.

Hair canvas is a woven interfacing material in various weights. Coarse goat hair combined with wool, cotton, or rayon is used in the filling direction. Armo and Hymo are trade names.

Casement cloth is any open weave fabric used for glass curtains.

Cavalry twill is a smooth-surfaced twill with a pronounced double twill line.

Challis (pronounced "shal'i) is a lightweight, plain weave balanced fabric with a soft finish. Originally of wool, it is now made of any staple fiber or blend of fibers. Cotton challis has a slight nap to achieve softness. Challis has been used for lingerie, blouses, and dresses and is usually printed.

Cheesecloth has a very soft texture and may be natural color, bleached, or dyed. It is used for interlinings, flag buntings, and sign cloths. Cheesecloth of very low count is used for covering tobacco plants that must be grown in the shade, and is called *tobacco cloth*.

Cheviot is a medium- to heavyweight fabric in plain, twill, or herringbone weave. Rough, shaggy surface texture. Originally made of wool from sheep raised in Cheviot hills of England.

China silk is a soft, sheer, plain weave fabric used for sheath linings and scarves.

Chinchilla is a heavy, twill-weave wool coating that has a napped surface that is rolled into little balls. It is one of the most durable coating fabrics.

Chino is a steep twill, cottonlike, bottom weight fabric.

Covert was first made in England, where there was a demand for a fabric that would not catch on brambles or branches during fox hunts. To make this tightly woven fabric, a two-ply yarn, one cotton and one wool, was used. Because the cotton and wool did not take the same dye, the fabric had a mottled appearance.

Cotton covert is always mottled and it may be made with ply yarns, one ply white and the other colored, or it may be fiber dyed white and a color. It is a $\frac{2}{1}$ twill of the same weight as denim and is used primarily for work pants, overalls, and service coats.

Rayon covert looks like wool covert. It is made with a blend of rayon and acetate in dress weight.

Wool covert is made from woolen or worsted yarns. It may be mottled or solid color and may be suit or coat weight. It may be napped slightly or have a clear finish. The mottled effect is obtained by using two different colored plys or by blending different colored fibers.

Crepe refers to any fabric made with crepe yarns (true crepe) or with a puckered surface (crepe effects).

Canton crepe is a filling crepe made with coarse yarns of alternate S- and Z-twist (2S and 2Z); (4S and 4Z); (6S and 6Z). It has a low count and is rough looking. There is much crosswise stretch in the fabric. It is used for dresses and suit dresses. Dry cleaning is preferable.

Chiffon is a smooth, plain weave, balanced fabric. It is a soft, filmy fabric with fine yarns.

Crepe-backed satin is a satin weave with crepe filing yarns.

Crepe de chine was originally a washable silk crepe woven in the gum. Now it refers to a lightweight flat crepe.

Crepe romaine, triple sheer and semisheer, is a heavier fabric than georgette and not as transparent. It is a 2×1 basket weave.

Crepon and bark crepe are heavy crepes with a rough appearance. Bark crepe has the appearance of tree bark. Crepon has wavy lines in the warp direction caused by high-twist filling yarns. Dry cleaning is preferable.

Georgette has a duller texture than chiffon, with a texture similar to voile.

Crinoline is a cheesecloth that has been stiffened with sizes, glue, or resins. It is usually black or white and is seldom colorfast. Some have a nonwoven material pressed on the back to make them more comfortable to wear.

Dimity is a Greek word that means "double thread." Dimity cord has warpwise cords made by weaving two or more yarns as one and separating them by areas of plain weave. Dimity is sheer with a crisp finish.

Barred dimity has cords in both warp and filling.

Doeskin is a very fine napped fabric finished to look like soft leather.

Duvetyn is similar to suede, but is lighter in weight and is more drapable. It has a soft, velvetlike surface made by napping, shearing, and brushing.

Flannel refers to any napped fabric.

Cotton flannel is a twill weave cotton fabric napped on one side. It has a long nap. It is used for work mittens and pocket linings.

Tarnish resistant flannel is a solid-color cotton fabric that is impregnated with chemicals to absorb sulfur fumes. It is used for silverware cases and chest linings.

Viyella flannel is part wool, part cotton flannel similar to outing flannel, but with a twill weave. The cotton content makes it more washable than an all-wool flannel. It is used for shirts and baby clothes. The fabric is imported from England.

Foulard is a printed lightweight twill weave fabric of silk, cotton, rayon, or wool. Silk surah is a similar fabric.

Gauze is a low count plain-weave balanced fabric used for bandages and fashion fabrics.

Theatrical gauze is made from linen fiber, which has more body and luster than cotton. It may be yarn-dyed or plain color. Its chief use is for curtains.

Gingham is a yarn-dyed, plain-weave fabric that varies in weight from tissue to suiting. It may be balanced or ribbed. Usually it is made of cotton, but silk, rayon, and blends are called ginghams.

Shagbark gingham has slack tension loops scattered over the surface.

Habutai is a soft, lightweight silk fabric.

Herringbone fabrics have warp stripes made by changing the direction of the twill line. The chevron like stripes may be of equal prominence, or one may be prominent and the other subdued. These fabrics are made in all weights, of all fiber contents, and in many types of interlacings.

Homespun is a coarse, balanced, plain-weave fabric with a handwoven look. It is used for coats, suits, and dresses.

Honan was originally of Chinese silk. Now made of silk or man-made fibers. Slub yarns in both warp and filling.

Hopsacking is a suiting-weight fabric made with a basket weave.

Interfacing is a woven or nonwoven fabric used to give body to a garment. Any fabric may be used. Choice depends upon weight of fabric and proper cleaning method. Specially prepared interfacings are

Nonwoven: Pellon, Keybak, Textryl, Pelonite, Remay

Woven: Hair canvas, Armo, Hymo, Wigan, Lamicel

Jaspé cloth is a plain-weave suiting-weight cloth made with multicolored warp yarns and plain filling yarns. It is used for slipcovers and draperies.

Kasha is a type of flannel that has black and colored fibers in the filling yarns.

Kersey is a very heavy, thick, boardy wool coating fabric that has been fulled and felted.

Lamé is a fabric containing metallic yarns.

Linen[1] is the only fabric that can be called by the fiber name. Linen usually means a plain-weave, suiting-weight fabric.

Crebasi linen refers to a dress-weight, plain-weave linen fabric.

Handkerchief linen is similar in luster and count to batiste, and it wrinkles badly. Linen yarns are more uneven than cotton yarns. This helps in identifying the fabric. Cotton and rayon yarns are sometimes made to resemble linen yarns by being purposely spun with irregularities.

Lining refers to any fabric used on the back of a shell.

Metal coated or reflective linings are lining fabrics that have a finish of metallic particles sprayed on the inner side. Aluminum is used because it is economical and lightweight, but any metal that flakes could be used. The metal can be applied to any type of fiber.

Sheath lining is a medium-weight, plain-weave, balanced fabric that resembles China silk.

Longcloth is a plain-weave, balanced white cotton fabric used for handkerchiefs, lingerie, and blouses.

Melton is similar to kersey, but is heavier in weight.

Monk's cloth is one of the oldest homespun-type fabrics. Others are called friar's cloth, bishop's cloth, druid's cloth, or mission cloth. They are heavy, coarse fabrics in a 2×2 or 4×4 basket weave, and are usually brownish white or oatmeal.

Mousseline de soie is French for "silk muslin." It is a plain-weave, balanced sheer fabric with a crisp finish.

---

[1] *Linen* and *flax* are terms that are used interchangeably.

Nainsook is a soft-finished and sometimes mercerized, plain-weave, balanced cotton fabric. It may be white, pastel-colored, or printed. Nainsook is similar to batiste, but it is less transparent. It is used for lingerie, handkerchiefs, interfacings, and infant's wear.

Ninon is a plain-weave, sheer fabric made of acetate or polyester filaments and used for glass curtains. Warp yarns appear to be in pairs.

Nun's veiling is a sheer, plain-weave fabric of wool or man-made fibers.

Organza is a filament organdy.

Osnaburg is a coarse, suiting-weight cotton fabric characterized by uneven yarns that have bits of cellulosic waste. It is used for slipcovers, draperies, and sportswear.

Ottoman is a ribbed fabric with alternate large and small ribs made by adjacent filling yarns of different sizes.

Pajama check is similar to dimity in construction but it is made with carded yarns and is not as sheer. It has a soft finish and grouped yarns in both directions.

Peau de soie is French for "skin of silk." It is a very smooth semidull satin construction that has satin floats on both sides of the fabric. It is a fairly heavy fabric made in silk, acetate, or in mixtures.

Piqué (see page 231).
Dimity piqué is neither like piqué nor like dimity. It has the sheerness of dimity, but not the double thread. It has the appearance of a piqué cord, but is not a cord weave. Dimity piqué is made with combed, cotton yarns and spaces are left at regular intervals between the warp threads (skipped dents).
Embossed piqué is a plain-weave, balanced fabric that is treated with a resin, and then embossed in a piqué stripe. The resin finish is cured to make it durable.
Novelty piqué is any fabric that has a combination of piqué weave with another weave. Often the piqué stripe does not go the entire length of the fabric.
Picolay (trade name) is an embossed fabric that resembles bird's-eye piqué. Proper care must be given if the design is to last satisfactorily.
Seersucker piqué is made with slack tension weaving in which the tight stripe is a piqué weave.

Wales and crinkle stripes are in the warp directions. Like all piqué, and unlike seersucker, the fabrics have a right and wrong side.
Waffle cloth is sometimes incorrectly called waffle piqué. Waffle cloth has a honeycomb or waffle design that is woven in. A dobby loom is used. It looks the same on the right and wrong sides. Waffle cloth is made in the same weight as pinwale piqué with carded or combed cotton, and is made in a heavier drapery fabric that has large waffle squares. Baby blankets with wool yarns are sometimes made with this weave.

Pongee is a wild-silk, plain-weave fabric. It is also the name of a ribbed fabric comparable to broadcloth in weight that is made with acetate filament warp and cotton filling yarns.

Scrim—strong open fabric similar to voile but of lower construction. There are two types: a heavy-ply yarn used for buckram and bunting, the other a lightweight higher-count curtain scrim.

Sailcloth is a suiting-weight cotton fabric in a 2×1 basket weave often called canvas or duck.

Sharkskin is a woolen or worsted $\frac{2}{2}$ twill made with yarns of two different colors and having a smooth, flat appearance. The twill line, unlike most of the wool twill fabrics, goes up to the left. Acetate or Arnel sharkskin is a plain weave, solid-color fabric, but it has the smooth, flat appearance of the wool fabric. It is used primarily for women's summer suits.

Suede is a plain-weave or twill-weave fabric that is napped and then sheared to resemble leather. Suedes for jackets and ski wear are often napped on both sides. Any suitable fiber can be used.

Taffeta refers to any plain weave, balanced, or ribbed fabric made with filament yarns.
Faille taffeta has a crosswise rib made by using many more warp yarns than filling yarns. All ribbed taffetas have crispness.
Paper taffeta is a very lightweight, stiff, transparent fabric.
Pigment taffeta is woven with delustered rayon filaments with little or no twist, into a plain weave, balanced fabric. It is not crisp.

Tarlatan is a low-count, plain weave, cotton cheesecloth with a starched finish.

Ticking is made in plain, twill, satin, or figure weave. Fabrics are used for mattress covers, slipcovers, and upholstery. A lighter-weight fabric is used for sportswear.

Tricotine is a clear-finish twill-weave fabric in cotton, wool, or man-made fibers. It has a double twill line.

Velvet comes from the Latin *vellus* meaning "a fleece" or "tufted hair." It is not known where or when it originated, but it was made the official fabric for both the court and the church during the Middle Ages. In France, blue velvet was reserved exclusively for the King's family. As people attained wealth and power, the use of velvet became more widespread.

Brocade velvet has a pile of different heights cut to form a design.

Chiffon velvet is a soft light weight fabric made with a rayon pile and a silk back. *Faconné velvet* is patterned by burnt out designs.

Embossed velvet has certain areas pressed flat.

Lyons velvet is a closely woven fabric with a deep pile that sometimes has a cotton pile and a silk back. It is used for coat collars, suits and coats, and for millinery.

Nacré velvet is a changeable fabric with the back of one color and the pile of another.

Panne velvet has the pile pressed flat and is a smooth, lustrous fabric.

Venetian is a smooth, strong, lustrous, warp-faced satin weave fabric used for slipcovers and upholstery.

Wool plaids and checks are often made with a $\frac{2}{2}$ twill weave. They may be made with woolen or worsted yarns; they may be napped or smooth; they are always yarn dye. They are named according to the arrangement of the colored yarns; for example, shepherd's check, hound's-tooth check, Glen plaid.

Zibilene is a heavy coating fabric with a long, shaggy nap laid in one direction. The fabrics sometimes have crosswise ridges caused by a longer nap in those areas.

Index